❖

A LIBRARY OF PROTESTANT THOUGHT

❖

A LIBRARY OF PROTESTANT THOUGHT

✣ ✣ ✣

HORACE
BUSHNELL

Edited by

H. SHELTON SMITH

New York

OXFORD UNIVERSITY PRESS

1965

PRINTED IN THE UNITED STATES OF AMERICA

In Loving Memory of

EFFIE BOWDEN BUTT

1903–1964

❖

A Library of Protestant Thought

A LIBRARY OF PROTESTANT THOUGHT is a collection of writings intended to illumine and interpret the history of the Christian faith in its Protestant expression. It is as variegated in its literary forms and theological positions as is the movement it mirrors. Tracts, letters, sermons, monographs, and other types of literature comprising the heritage of Protestant thought find a place in this series. Works that were originally composed in English, whether in Great Britain or in the New World, and works that were originally written in other languages, many of them not previously translated into English, are included. But it is neither necessary nor desirable that every segment of Protestant theology, piety, and ethics receive equal space. The trite theology, the conventional piety, and the platitudinous ethics always bulk larger in any tradition, also in the Protestantism of the past four centuries, than does the creative output of the religious spirit. The latter is our primary interest in this Library. While we have not felt obligated to grant them equal attention, we have included works that are typical of the more commonplace literature of the Protestant tradition. On the other hand, some works which logically belong in this series have not been included because they are readily available elsewhere.

In keeping with the fundamental purpose of this Library, the voices of Protestantism are allowed to speak for themselves, with only as much introduction, commentary, and exposition as will in fact allow them to do so. Wherever feasible, documents are reproduced in their entirety. A few representative selections have been preferred to more numerous but shorter passages, for the Library tries to depict the structure of thought rather than the genetic development of a man or a movement. Nevertheless, the variety of Protestant forms precludes a uniform treatment throughout. Our aim has been to be representative rather than exhaustive and to employ the best available tools of critical historical scholarship. Despite its ambitious scope, A Library of Protestant Thought is not an encyclopedia of Protestantism. It is a series of volumes from which not only clergymen and theologians, but students of philosophy, history, literature, political science and other disciplines can gain a more balanced view of how the Protestant mind has thought and spoken since the Reformation.

The Board is grateful to the Hazen Foundation for an initial grant enabling it to begin its work; to the Sealantic Fund, Inc. for a grant making possible Board meetings, consultations, and editorial assistance in the preparation of specific volumes; and to the Oxford University Press for undertaking the publication of the Library.

THE EDITORIAL BOARD

Preface

Horace Bushnell, like Jonathan Edwards, is once again being rediscovered. In the early part of this century he was celebrated chiefly for his prophetic writing in the field of Christian nurture. Recently, however, his more distinctively theological works have become the center of attention. This renewed interest in Bushnell's theology has no doubt been stimulated to some extent by the general theological awakening, but it is above all a tribute to the wealth of his religious insights. With the exception of Edwards, Bushnell was probably the most creative Protestant theologian that America produced before the twentieth century.

The twelve selections here reprinted from Bushnell's works fall logically into two parts: (1) theological method, and (2) theological reconstruction. Since Bushnell attached primary importance to method in theological inquiry, three of the selections deal with this aspect of his thought. The nine selections in Part II embrace all the major themes on which Bushnell wrote. Except for the reduction of excessive punctuation and the regularization of the spelling and capitalization, the selections follow the text in the first editions of Bushnell's publications.

This volume owes much to others. I am especially indebted to a great teacher, Dean Emeritus Luther A. Weigle of Yale University Divinity School, who first opened my eyes to the remarkable mind and spirit of Horace Bushnell. The members of my Advisory Committee—Professors Robert T. Handy of Union Theological Seminary, Thomas A. Schafer of McCormick Theological Seminary, and Clarence L. F. Gohdes of Duke University—read the entire manuscript and made valuable suggestions for its improvement. During a sabbatical year in Durham, Professor Gordon Harland of Drew University read all of Bushnell's major writings and greatly enriched my understanding of Bushnell's theological thought. My dear friend and colleague, Professor Stuart C. Henry, examined the manuscript with characteristic care and helped me to improve it at many points. The general librarians at Yale and Harvard lightened my labor by supplying photographic copies of their Bushnell manuscripts. Professor Raymond P. Morris, librarian of Yale University Divinity School, generously allowed me unrestricted use of the excellent Bushnell collection in that School. Miss Corrine Nordquest, head of the Congregational Library (Boston), was unfailingly prompt in supplying relevant materials. Dr. James F. English, minister emeritus of the Connecticut Conference of Congregational Christian Churches, and Mr. Carl H. Holdridge, business manager of the Conference, kindly gave me access to the valuable holdings of Congregational House (Hartford), including the manuscript minutes of Hartford Central Association, the Association of Fairfield West, and the General Association of Connecticut. I shall always remember a delightful three-hour visit in the charming home of Mrs. Austin Cheney of Manchester, Connecticut, who showed me some important books that belonged to Bushnell's library. Mr. Horace Bushnell Learned of Hartford arranged helpful contacts in that city, and he allowed me to go through a parcel of manuscript papers and letters. Through the kindness of Mr. William H. Mortensen, director of Bushnell Memorial Hall (Hartford), I had the privilege of consulting an almost complete set of the first editions of Bushnell's books and pamphlets. Professor Donn Michael Farris, librarian of Duke University Divinity School, and his associate, Miss Harriet Leonard, reference librarian, always went the second mile in providing expert assistance. Mr. Emerson Ford, head of Duke Interlibrary Loan Service, was never too busy to secure a book that was requested. Once again Professor Doralyn J. Hickey of the School of Library Science, University of North Carolina (Chapel Hill), assisted me in many ways, including the preparation of the index. Hearty thanks are due Miss Amy Clampitt, special editor of A Library of Protestant Thought, for regularizing the spelling and capitalization in the Bushnell texts. Mrs. Jacob Kaplan typed an almost flawless manuscript for the press.

H. SHELTON SMITH

Dogwood Road
Durham, North Carolina
September 1965

Table of Contents

HORACE BUSHNELL

Introduction

IT WAS THE DESTINY of Horace Bushnell (1802–76) to shape the pattern of his religious thought in an era of intra-Protestant controversy. Throughout the first half of the nineteenth century it was a rare year in which New Englanders did not engage in theological debate. Three of their controversies were especially influential in setting the stage for the distinctive role of Bushnell.

The first of these conflicts centered in Massachusetts, where Congregationalists had been gradually polarizing into liberal and conservative factions long before Bushnell was born. Already by 1805 a decisive battle had been waged over the control of Harvard College, with victory going to the liberals. Having lost that battle, the conservatives founded Andover Theological Seminary (1808) in which to educate their future ministers. For many years thereafter Harvard and Andover engaged in heated dialogue. The final outcome is well known: a new denomination launched under the banner of Unitarianism.

The second controversy arose in Bushnell's own native state of Connecticut in the late 1820's, revolving around the liberal Calvinist of Yale Divinity School, Nathaniel W. Taylor (1786–1858), and the conservative Calvinist, Bennet Tyler (1783–1858).[1]

A strong factor in provoking the outburst was Taylor's *Concio ad Clerum* of 1828, championing a new interpretation of native depravity. Believing that Taylor's views were undermining evangelical religion, Tyler and other conservatives militantly opposed Taylorism. In 1833 they organized a Pastoral Union and founded Connecticut Theological Institute (now Hartford Seminary Foundation) through which to disseminate their doctrines. Since the Taylor-Tyler controversy reached its peak while Bushnell was at Yale Divinity School (1831–33), he must have been often briefed on the questions at issue. Although Congregationalism in Connecticut escaped actual schism, it remained deeply divided in spirit for many years.

1. The two partisan groups were often styled new-school and old-school men, or simply Taylorites and Tylerites.

3

The third conflict shook the Unitarian household in the 1830's and 1840's. A more progressive party, led by Ralph Waldo Emerson (1803–82) and Theodore Parker (1810–60), assailed the older Unitarians as only halfway liberal. Emerson's "Divinity School Address" (1838) and Parker's "The Transient and Permanent in Christianity" (1841) rejected basic elements of Unitarian faith. These new pioneers, nicknamed transcendentalists, were strenuously resisted by old-line Unitarians such as Andrews Norton, who branded Emerson's Address as "the latest form of infidelity."

I

Involved in these three controversies were important theological questions with which Bushnell had to grapple. Significantly, the four issues to which he devoted his major theological writings were all raised in William E. Channing's Baltimore sermon of 1819, published under the title of "Unitarian Christianity." [2] These questions had been debated long before 1819; yet Channing articulated them so forcefully that they became the foci of New England dialogue over the next generation. It is therefore appropriate to take his historic discourse as the starting point in sketching Bushnell's theological background.

First of all, Channing condemned the doctrine of the trinity. Opposition to trinitarianism had been growing in New England ever since the period of Jonathan Mayhew (1720–66) and Charles Chauncy (1705–87), both of whom were definitely anti-trinitarian.[3] The trend became strong in Boston, where the oldest Anglican church in New England, King's Chapel, purged its liturgy of trinitarian elements as early as 1785. Two years later the Chapel ordained James Freeman (1759–1835) as its minister, a step which cut its cords with Anglicanism and freed it to become the first Unitarian church in America. Many Boston ministers were moving in the same direction. Indeed, eight of that city's nine Congregational pastors were at least mildly anti-trinitarian when the new century dawned. Many of their clerical brethren in the neighboring towns and villages were likeminded. The Baltimore sermon was therefore the culmination of a long theological development.

Channing put the Unitarian view of God succinctly, saying: "We be-

---

2. *Works of William E. Channing, D.D.*, 11th ed. (6 vols., Boston, 1849), III, 59–103.
3. Conrad Wright, *The Beginnings of Unitarianism in America* (Boston, 1955), Chap. 9.

lieve in the doctrine of God's UNITY, or that there is one God, and one only." [4] He admitted that his orthodox brethren professed the doctrine of one God, but he charged that they were in effect tritheists, since they held that the three persons in the Godhead "love each other, converse with each other, and delight in each other's society." Prevailing trinitarianism was therefore "irrational and unscriptural."

This criticism of orthodoxy speedily aroused Moses Stuart (1780–1852) of Andover Seminary, the foremost biblical scholar in America.[5] He argued that Channing had misrepresented the view of New England Calvinists. Their real view was twofold: (1) that "God is ONE; numerically one, in essence and attributes"; (2) that "the Son, (and so the Holy Spirit,) does in some respect *truly* and *really*, not merely nominally and logically, differ from the Father." [6] Did that meet Channing's objection? It did, explained Stuart, since the second part of the statement did not employ the word "person" in a literal sense. "We profess to use it [person]," said Stuart, "merely to designate our belief of a real distinction in the Godhead; and NOT to describe independent, conscious beings, possessing *separate* and *equal essences*, and *perfections*." [7] What, then, did the word "distinction" mean? Stuart frankly acknowledged that he could not give a positive explanation. He had, he said, contended for a distinction merely because it was required by a correct exegesis of the Bible.[8]

Stuart deplored efforts to define the interior nature of the Godhead. This was, he thought, a mistake of the Nicene Fathers, as when they introduced the speculative words "eternal generation," words which involved "a palpable contradiction of language." [9] He also expressed regret that the word "person" should have been employed to explain the distinctions in the Godhead. It had led to "much unnecessary dispute and difficulty." Here he doubtless had in mind such men as Nathanael Emmons (1745–1840). Emmons often spoke of "a trinity in Unity," but by the term trinity he meant "three distinct persons, or agents," each being "able to understand, to will, and to act of himself," and the whole comprising

---

4. *Works*, III, 69.

5. *Letters to the Rev. Wm. E. Channing, Containing Remarks on His Sermon Recently Preached and Published at Baltimore* (Andover, 1819).

6. *Ibid.*, 19.   7. *Ibid.*, 22.   8. *Ibid.*, 24, 36.

9. *Ibid.*, 31. Some three years later Stuart published a pamphlet against Samuel Miller of Princeton Theological Seminary in which he elaborated this same position. See *Letters on the Eternal Generation of the Son of God, Addressed to the Rev. Samuel Miller, D.D.* (Andover, 1822), 89–125, 157–59.

an eternal society.[10] Certainly this view of the trinity gave aid and comfort to the Unitarians.

Channing declined to answer Stuart, but Andrews Norton (1786–1853) of Harvard published a caustic pamphlet against him. The "proper modern doctrine of the trinity," he remarked, holds "that there are three persons in the Divinity, who equally possess all divine attributes." From that premise he reached a foregone conclusion: "The doctrine of the trinity . . . affirms that there are three Gods." [11] Having thus aligned modern trinitarians with tritheists, Norton branded them as irrational and unbiblical. The latter charge he somewhat softened by conceding that possibly a few texts could bear a trinitarian interpretation, but nonetheless he insisted that the Unitarian exegesis was "the true one." [12] Whence came the doctrine of the trinity? Norton had a neat answer: it derived from Platonism and was "introduced into our religion by the early fathers." [13]

Stuart published no reply to Norton, but the question under debate interested him so much that during the next few years he carefully restudied the history of Christian thought on the trinity, giving special attention to the ante-Nicene period. This fact is authenticated by his *Letters* (1822) to Samuel Miller of Princeton Seminary [14] and by his publication in 1835 of an English translation of Schleiermacher's essay on the early history of trinitarian theory.[15] Stuart's commentary on the essay is important in two respects. First, it shows that he had become deeply disturbed by the tendency of some of his orthodox brethren to overstress the threeness of God in their protest against Unitarianism. Deploring "the license" with which they were describing the persons of the Godhead, he warned:

> When authors speak of their eternal and mutual society and converse
> together; of their taking counsel together and deliberating, just as

10. *The Works of Nathanael Emmons, D.D.*, edited with a memoir by Jacob Ide (7 vols., Boston, 1842), IV, 106–7, 115.

11. *A Statement of Reasons for Not Believing the Doctrines of Trinitarians Respecting the Nature of God, and the Person of Christ, Occasioned by Professor Stuart's Letters to Mr. Channing* (Boston, 1819), 4.

12. *Ibid.*, 38; see also *ibid.*, 46.   13. *Ibid.*, 35.

14. *Letters on the Eternal Generation of the Son of God, Addressed to the Rev. Samuel Miller, D.D.* (Andover, 1822).

15. Friedrich Schleiermacher, "On the Discrepancy Between the Sabellian and Athanasian Method of Representing the Doctrine of the Trinity," translated with notes, by Moses Stuart, *Biblical Repository and Quarterly Observer*, V (April 1835), 265–353; VI (July 1835), 1–116. For the original essay, see Schleiermacher, "Über den Gegensatz zwischen der Sabellianischen und der Athanasianischen Vorstellung von der Trinität," *Theologische Zeitschrift*, III (Berlin, 1822), 295–408.

if an effort were necessary in order to harmonize them, or to bring them to one and the same conclusion, or to be of one and the same mind, or in order to cast light upon what it may be proper for them to do; when they tell us of one person entering into covenant with another simply as divine, and before the foundation of the world; of one divine person commanding, and another simply as divine obeying; all this and much more of the same nature, so long as it is indulged in, will continue to bring upon Trinitarians the reproach of Polytheism.[16]

Second, the commentary indicates that he was impressed with Schleiermacher's interpretation of Sabellius's doctrine of the trinity. The German theologian, he believed, was himself a Sabellian. Stuart then indicated in the following passage his own position in relation to that of Schleiermacher:

Dr. S. makes the personality of the Trinity to consist in the hypostatic developments of the Godhead as Creator and Legislator, as Redeemer and Sanctifier; and thus makes the doctrine of the Trinity to depend on the manifestations of God in respect to the great work of redemption. That God, as Father, Son, and Spirit, has thus manifested himself; and that this is the great and peculiar manifestation of the Trinity, and unspeakably the most glorious one, I have no doubt. So far as he goes in this direction, I can cheerfully accompany him. But I am not willing to stop where he does, nor to conclude that a distinction like that of Father and Son and Spirit in the Godhead has commenced altogether in time, and has no foundation in the *Monás* of the divine being.[17]

From this account, it is evident that Stuart predicated an original or uncreated distinction in the Godhead. Yet again he admitted that he could not define that distinction. "If you ask how this modification or property or distinction can be described, as it originally existed in the Godhead, my answer is, that we have no data by which we can make out a distinction." [18] Actually, Stuart almost agreed with Schleiermacher when he remarked "that the full development of Trinity was not made and could not be made, until the time of the Saviour's incarnation." [19] The same was true, when he declared that the names Father, Son, and Spirit could not be applied to God "in their full and appropriate sense" prior to the incarnation.[20]

Stuart held that one's doctrine of the trinity was reflected in the meaning assigned to the names Father, Son, and Spirit. Thus if one should view

---

16. *Biblical Repository*, VI (July 1835), 99.   17. *Ibid.*, 94.
18. *Ibid.*, 96.   19. *Ibid.*, 107.   20. *Ibid.*, 108.

them as the names of the simple and original nature of God, he could be
placed in the Nicene camp. On the other hand, if one regarded them as
names merely of the manifestation of God in various modes, then he
could be put in the Sabellian camp.[21] Stuart himself endeavored to stand
between the two camps. He wrote: "Both parties have gone to the extreme. From eternity there existed the distinction in the Godhead, which
was developed in the economy of redemption. The names of the persons
in the Trinity I view as including and recognizing this fact. But the names
themselves have also an express reference to the parts which the Godhead
has actually sustained, and sustains, in the work of redemption. Their *full*
significancy is and can be never given, without a reference to *this*." [22]
Stuart found it hard to distinguish his position from that of the other two
parties. As a matter of fact, in his reaction against tritheism, he veered
extremely close to Schleiermacher.

Bushnell knew this essay thoroughly, and valued it highly.[23] He had
good reason to praise it, for many of his own criticisms of New England
trinitarianism were anticipated in Stuart's acute commentary. Furthermore, his own theory of the trinity probably owed more to Schleiermacher and Stuart than he was inclined to acknowledge.

Bushnell's theological teacher at Yale Divinity School, Nathaniel W.
Taylor, evidently viewed the Unitarian controversy with deep concern.
For although his lectures were not published until after his death,[24] they
still bore the marks of that controversy. He could not accept Stuart's theory because it seemed to deny a real tri-personality in God. Nor, on the
other hand, could he agree with Emmons.[25] Like most current New England Calvinists, he also opposed the Nicene Council on the ground that its
doctrine of the "eternal generation of the Son" contradicted the idea of
God as eternal, self-existent, and immutable.[26] None of these views of the
trinity, he maintained, took into account the peculiar nature of biblical
language, and so they applied the term person to God in an unauthorized
sense. According to him, it was biblically invalid to hold that "God is one

21. *Ibid.,* 110.   22. *Ibid.,* 112.   23. *God in Christ* (Hartford, 1849), 111–12.
24. *Essays, Lectures, etc., upon Select Topics in Revealed Theology,* Noah Porter
et al., eds. (New York, 1859). In the introduction to this volume, Porter remarked
that Taylor revised his lectures on the trinity after the Unitarian controversy. Taylor's
unpublished (and perhaps earlier) lectures are recorded in student notes which were
transcribed by R. C. Learned and his brothers in 1838–40 under the title of "Notes."
These MS. "Notes" are in two volumes, the first of which is on "Mental Philosophy,
Ethics, etc.," and the second is on "Revealed Theology." For Taylor's views on the
trinity, see "Notes," II, 1–27 (MS. in Yale Divinity School Library).
25. Taylor, *Revealed Theology,* 121–26.   26. *Ibid.,* 119–21.

being in three persons" unless one understood the peculiar signification of the language involved. Thus he urged that the words "being" and "person" must not be employed in the normal sense, since the mode of God's subsistence was unlike that of a human person. The word "being" must be so extended in meaning as to denote not merely "one substance with one phenomenal nature," but also to signify "the fact, in some sense, of three persons in one being." With these restrictions, one may properly regard the "tri-personality of the being" of God as a doctrine of the Bible.[27] The term "person" must also be employed with equal care. When applied to the Godhead, "person" also must be understood restrictively; and yet, not so restrictively as to deny God's phenomenal action in three distinct personal forms.[28] Having thus qualified the two crucial terms, Taylor defined what he regarded as the biblical doctrine of the trinity as follows: "God is one being in such a modified and extended sense of the language, as to include three persons in such a modified and restricted sense of the terms, that he is qualified, in a corresponding restricted sense, for three distinct personal forms of phenomenal action." [29]

That definition is an exhibition of Taylor's supreme determination to defend the doctrine of the trinity against both Unitarians and tritheists. But even if it was technically correct, it had little chance of being understood or of changing the mind of a Unitarian. As Bushnell saw, a new approach to the question of the trinity was imperative.

The second question raised by Channing related to christology. Having rejected the doctrine of the trinity, he necessarily concluded that Jesus was a being inferior to God.[30] Still, although he spoke of the human birth, bodily form, and mortal suffering of Jesus, he nowhere in the sermon expressly put him on the same level with a purely human creature. Nor did he ever do so in his later writings. George Park Fisher is justified in saying that Channing's Jesus was "a pre-existent rational creature, an angel or spirit of some sort, who had entered into a human body. He was not even a man except so far as his corporeal part is concerned, but a creature from some upper sphere." [31] But instead of clarifying his idea of that strange creature, who was strictly neither God nor man, Channing attacked the two-nature christology of New England Calvinism. "According to this doctrine," said he, "Jesus . . . consists of two souls, two minds; the one divine, the other human; the one weak, the other almighty;

27. *Ibid.*, 13.   28. *Ibid.*, 14–16.   29. *Ibid.*, 54.   30. *Works*, III, 78–80, 82.
31. "Channing as a Philosopher and Theologian," *Discussions in History and Theology* (New York, 1880), 272.

the one ignorant, the other omniscient. Now we maintain, that this is to make Christ two beings." [32] Channing argued that this view of Jesus outraged reason and violated the Scripture. He also contended that it in effect invalidated the New England doctrine of atonement. For while that doctrine emphasized the importance of Christ's suffering, it confined that suffering to his human nature. How then could merely human suffering make an infinite atonement for sin? The Unitarians, said Channing, ascribed Jesus' suffering to his whole nature. "This, we believe, renders his sufferings, and his patience and love in bearing them, incomparably more impressive and affecting than the system we oppose." [33]

Replying to Channing, Moses Stuart frankly admitted that the early church made a mistake when it decided to employ the words "two natures" to describe the person of Jesus. "They certainly serve, in most cases, merely to keep up the form of words without definite ideas." [34] Yet it is a fact, he observed, that the Bible represents Jesus at one time "as the Creator of the Universe; and at another, as a man of sorrows, and of imperfect knowledge." Thus it was "impossible to reconcile these two things, without the supposition of two natures." Since, then, the two-nature scheme represented a necessary deduction from the Bible, it was irrelevant to appeal to reason for a solution to the problem. For reason could say nothing either for or against the doctrine.[35] But Stuart himself at once began to speculate with respect to the interior composition of Christ. He professed his ignorance of the way in which the two natures were united in Christ. "If you ask me how such a union can be effected between natures so infinitely diverse as the divine and the human; I answer (as in the case of the distinction in the Godhead), I do not know *how* this is done." Nevertheless, in the very same paragraph he declared that the union "neither destroyed, nor essentially changed either the divine or human nature." Going even further, he said that Christ's two natures were so sharply separated that he could, as the occasion demanded, act and think either as human or as divine. Finally, he asserted: "One person, *in the sense in which each of us is one,* Christ could not be." [36] Manifestly Stuart not only appealed to reason, but he indulged in just the sort of speculation which Bushnell would later condemn as fruitless and confusing.

With apparent relief, Stuart found a weak spot in Channing's own pe-

32. *Works*, III, 76.   33. *Ibid.*, 82.
34. *Letters to the Rev. Wm. E. Channing*, 49.   35. *Ibid.*, 46.   36. *Ibid.*, 45-46.

culiar theory. "Will you refuse your assent to the proposition, that Christ participated in the divine nature, because you cannot see *how* such a union of different natures could take place; and yet believe in *a human body united to a soul not human?* To what order or class of beings, then, does this new *compound*, and strangely mixed person belong?" [37] Channing never answered Stuart.

Continuing the debate on Channing's behalf, Andrews Norton argued that orthodox christology was even more absurd than the traditional notion of the trinity. "The very term *double nature*," he complained, "seems to us to imply an absurdity. The nature of a being is ALL that which constitutes it what it is; and when one speaks of a double nature, it appears to us to be the same sort of language, as if he were to speak of a double individuality." [38] Besides, the double-nature theory was "nowhere *directly*" taught in the Bible. Consequently, churchmen who had endeavored to make the Bible prove that absurd theory had actually "turned the Scriptures . . . into a book of riddles." [39]

Leonard Woods (1774–1854) of Andover and Henry Ware (1764–1845) of Harvard soon entered the controversy, but what they had to say concerning the person of Christ amounted to little more than warming over the charges and countercharges already advanced by their predecessors. Woods contended that Christ's sufferings "belong to him, *as* one person," even though he had two distinct natures. However, he virtually undermined that claim by saying: "The suffering of Christ was therefore of as high importance or value, in making an atonement, as if it . . . in reality had been, in the most proper sense, the suffering of the Divinity. So that whatever may be the conceptions of Arians or Socinians, as *we* view the subject, the fact that Christ endured suffering in his human nature, and not directly in his divine, occasions no difficulty as to the preciousness, which we ascribe to his atonement." [40] The "as if" was an admission that Jesus did not really suffer in his divine nature, but only in his human.

Ware saw the weakness in Woods's argument and bluntly reminded him that the root of his confusion stemmed from his two-nature doctrine, the effect of which was to make Jesus "two distinct minds, two distinct

37. *Ibid.*, 127–28.
38. *A Statement of Reasons for Not Believing the Doctrines of Trinitarians*, 14.
39. *Ibid.*, 14–16.
40. *Letters to Unitarians Occasioned by the Sermon of the Reverend William E. Channing* (Andover, 1820), 104.

intelligent beings, with each its separate consciousness, knowledge, capacity, and will." On those terms, Jesus "cannot be other than two distinct persons." [41]

By now the argument had reached a stalemate, for the disputants on both sides were merely repeating themselves. On the whole, however, the Unitarians had scored at least a partial victory; for although their own christology was confused, they had effectively exposed the artificial scheme of their opponents. New England Calvinists had blundered into a serious christological predicament, from which the mere reiteration of old formulae would not deliver them. Bushnell clearly recognized this fact and urged his brethren to suppress their fruitless speculations with respect to Christ's interior composition and to accept him as God's medium of self-expression to the world.

Having rejected the orthodox view of the trinity and of the person of Christ, Channing then turned to the question of native depravity. This was no new issue to New Englanders; indeed, it had been vigorously debated during the previous century by Jonathan Edwards (1703–58) [42] and Charles Chauncy (1705–87),[43] not to speak of many lesser figures.[44] Recently, however, that question had lost much of its interest. Channing's Baltimore discourse thrust it again into public debate. The following passage expresses the essence of his contention:

> This [Calvinist] system indeed takes various shapes, but in all it casts dishonor on the Creator. According to its old and genuine form, it teaches, that God brings us into life wholly depraved, so that under the innocent features of our childhood is hidden a nature averse to all good and propense to all evil, a nature which exposes us to God's displeasure and wrath, even before we have acquired power to understand our duties, or to reflect upon our actions. According to a more modern exposition, it teaches, that we came from the hands of our Maker with such a constitution, and are placed under such influences and circumstances, as to render certain and infallible the total depravity of every human being, from the first moment of his moral agency; and it also teaches, that the offence of the child, who brings into life this ceaseless tendency to unmingled

41. *Letters Addressed to Trinitarians and Calvinists, Occasioned by Dr. Woods' Letters to Unitarians* (Cambridge, 1820), 99–100.

42. *The Great Christian Doctrine of Original Sin Defended* (Boston, 1758).

43. *Five Dissertations on the Scripture Doctrine of the Fall; and its Consequences* (London, 1785).

44. H. Shelton Smith, *Changing Conceptions of Original Sin: A Study in American Theology Since 1750* (New York, 1955), Chaps. 2–3; Conrad Wright, *The Beginnings of Unitarianism in America* (Boston, 1955), Chap. 3.

crime, exposes him to the sentence of everlasting damnation. Now, according to the plainest principles of morality, we maintain, that a natural constitution of the mind, unfailingly disposing it to evil and to evil alone, would absolve it from guilt; and that to give existence under this condition would argue unspeakable cruelty; and that to punish the sin of this unhappily constituted child with endless ruin, would be a wrong unparalleled by the most merciless despotism.[45]

Concentrated in that statement are issues which aroused the popular mind. Only a few churchmen could explain the metaphysical subtleties connected with the trinity and the two-nature view of Christ, but every parish minister could explain the radical nature of Channing's attack upon the orthodox doctrine of native depravity. Hence this question became the storm center of the controversy.[46] It is important to grasp the main thrust of Channing's argument. In sum, he argued that the Calvinist doctrine of native depravity denied in effect the benevolent character of God, since "it teaches, that God brings us into life wholly depraved" and with a nature "which exposes us to God's displeasure and wrath, even before we have acquired power to understand our duties, or to reflect upon our actions." In the eighteenth century, John Taylor (1694–1761) of Norwich had put forth this same argument, and his followers in New England had repeated it with good effect.[47] Channing renewed it with explosive consequences.

Leonard Woods of Andover replied on behalf of orthodoxy. He reaffirmed the doctrine of native depravity, but he had difficulty in showing wherein it was consistent with the benevolence of God. Amazingly he held that God could be benevolent and yet perform acts which a human father would never stoop to do. Thus after citing some biblical examples, he asked: "What human father, possessing even a common degree of paternal kindness and compassion, would ever treat his children, as God treated his rational offspring, when he destroyed the world by a deluge, or Sodom by fire, or when he caused the earth to open and swallow up the company of Korah?"[48] This line of argument revealed Woods's utter moral confusion. After a few more bumbling remarks, he tried to extricate himself by contending that he was not required to prove the consistency between one doctrine and another, but only to show that any

45. *Works*, III, 85–86.
46. Fisher, "Channing as a Philosopher and Theologian," *Discussions in History and Theology*, 269.
47. Smith, *Changing Conceptions of Original Sin*, Chaps. 2–3.
48. *Letters to Unitarians*, 21–22.

given doctrine was taught in the Bible.[49] Accordingly he expounded a series of familiar texts from which he concluded that New England Calvinists were soundly biblical in teaching *"that men are by nature destitute of holiness; . . . or, in other words, that they are from the first inclined to evil, and that, while unrenewed, their moral affections and actions are wholly wrong."* [50]

Henry Ware rejoined sharply, charging that his opponent had dodged the question of the consistency between total depravity and divine benevolence. However, far more significant than Ware's criticism of Woods's views was his own theory of original human nature. He wrote: "Man is by nature . . . innocent and pure; free from all moral corruption, as well as destitute of all positive holiness; . . . He is by nature no more inclined or disposed to vice than to virtue, and is equally capable, in the ordinary use of his faculties, and with the common assistance afforded him, of either." [51] Ware firmly insisted that this optimistic view of man fully harmonized with both human experience and the Scripture.

Woods and Ware exchanged two more pamphlets apiece, but neither added much to his substantive position. After frequent prodding by Ware, Woods finally made a half-hearted attempt to harmonize native depravity and divine benevolence, but he left his argument at loose ends. "The native depravity of man is plainly consistent with the divine benevolence," he explained, "if it is, on the whole, consistent with the greatest good of the intelligent system." [52] He was obligated to sustain his position by showing wherein total depravity had in fact contributed to "the greatest good of the intelligent system." This, however, he failed to do.

Nathaniel Taylor of Yale had watched the lame performance of Woods with anxiety. He is reported as saying, "Dr. Ware had the better of the argument." [53] Unquestionably he spoke the truth. Taylor attacked Andrews Norton in order to get into the controversy. In the fall of 1820 Norton had published an article in the *Christian Disciple,* echoing Channing's criticism of Calvinism. Calvinism is a "system of blasphemy," he wrote, because it "teaches that he [God] has formed men, so that they are by nature wholly inclined to moral evil," and yet punishes them for the very nature which he himself gave them.[54] In a pungent article, Tay-

---

49. *Ibid.,* 29–30, 59.   50. *Ibid.,* 31.
51. *Letters Addressed to Trinitarians and Calvinists,* 20–21.
52. *A Reply to Ware's Letters to Trinitarians and Calvinists* (Andover, 1821), 80.
53. Bennet Tyler, *Letters on the Origin and Progress of the New Haven Theology* (New York, 1837), 6.
54. "Thoughts on True and False Religion," *Christian Disciple,* new series, II (1820), 340.

lor characterized Norton's essay as a "distorted caricature" of Calvinism, and he demanded that the accuser either prove his slanderous charge from reputable Calvinist sources or retract it.[55] Feeling certain that he could sustain his position, Norton supplied a bill of particulars, based on the writings of esteemed Calvinists, including Jonathan Edwards. "I now affirm it to be the doctrine of Calvinism," he triumphantly wrote, "that *God* creates men with a sinful nature." [56]

That startling allegation elicited from Taylor one of his most penetrating theological essays.[57] He perceived at once wherein Norton had unwittingly opened himself to attack. His first move was to indicate the sense in which his opponent had evidently employed the term "nature." By that term Norton meant, he said, "not a state of voluntary moral action, but the original *structure and constitution* of our being." Native depravity "must therefore be a PHYSICAL PROPERTY of which God is the efficient cause." [58] Now if Calvinists were found to hold that depravity was actually a physical property or substance in human nature, they would certainly be guilty of denying human freedom and of making God the author of sin in his creatures. But had reputable Calvinists in fact advocated any such idea? "The doctrine ascribed to Calvinists by Professor N.," replied Taylor, "is not maintained by Calvinists *as a class*, and therefore is not properly *Calvinism*." [59]

Yet underline those three crucial words, "as a class." For Taylor knew that some of his fellow Calvinists had indeed maintained a theory of depravity which logically made God the efficient cause of man's corrupt nature. That was true, for example, of Nathanael Emmons (1745–1840).[60] Hence Taylor had to exclude men of Emmons's view in order to parry Norton's thrust. Calvinists as a class, he therefore asserted, agree that *"mankind come into the world in such a state, that without the interposition of divine grace, all as soon as they become moral agents, sin in every accountable act."* [61]

A potential hornet's nest lay in that indefinite phrase, "in such a state." For therein Taylor hid five different theories whereby Calvinists were currently explaining why all men, from the beginning of their moral agency, would certainly sin.[62] Actually, then, Calvinists were in agree-

55. "Review of Erskine's Evidence, and Norton on True and False Religion," *Christian Spectator*, IV (1822), 301, 303.
56. *Views of Calvinism* (Cambridge, 1822), 31.
57. "Review of Norton's Views of Calvinism," *Christian Spectator*, V (1823), 196–224.
58. *Ibid.*, 197.   59. *Ibid.*, 216.   60. *Works*, IV, 456, 492–93, 508.
61. "Review of Norton's Views of Calvinism," *Christian Spectator*, V, 217.
62. *Ibid.*, 217, 219.

ment in their theory of native depravity on only one point: that all men, on becoming moral agents, would certainly sin in every responsible act. As to *why* all men would thus sin, they split into five parties. Taylor played down the differences in order to present a united Calvinist front against the Unitarians. However, some conservative Calvinists were already becoming alarmed at Taylor's views, believing that he agreed substantially with Henry Ware's theory of original nature. Their concern was deepened by the fact that his Yale colleagues, Chauncey Goodrich (1790–1860) [63] and Eleazar T. Fitch (1791–1871),[64] were in agreement with him. Yet instead of seeking to reassure his conservative brethren, Taylor became even more outspoken in condemning those doctrines of native depravity which were tending to confirm the Unitarian criticisms of orthodoxy.

Of decisive impact on the growing intra-Calvinist controversy was Taylor's *Concio ad Clerum* of 1828, preached at Yale before the Congregational ministers of Connecticut.[65] He advanced no ideas in the *Concio* which he had not already expressed in the debate with Norton, but he articulated them with consummate skill. Two purposes dominated the address. The first was to define depravity. "*It is man's own act,*" said he, "*consisting in a free choice of some object rather than God, as his chief good.*" [66] That statement is distinctive in two respects. First, Taylor defined moral depravity in terms of action, not in terms of any property or propensity in human nature. Second, he specified that the particular action involved in moral depravity must be freely chosen. Taylor's design was to undercut the contention of the Unitarians that the Calvinist doctrine of native depravity made God the author of sin and denied human freedom.

The second purpose of the *Concio* was to define the meaning of the words "depraved by nature." According to Taylor, those words did not signify that man's original nature was inherently sinful or corrupt; nor did they denote that man's nature constituted the physical or efficient cause of his sinning. The only thing they really signified was that man's

63. *Autobiography, Correspondence, etc., of Lyman Beecher,* Charles Beecher, ed. (2 vols., New York, 1865), I, 469–71; Tyler, *Letters on the Origin and Progress of the New Haven Theology,* 7–10.

64. *Two Discourses on the Nature of Sin* (New Haven, 1826); *Inquiry into the Nature of Sin* (New Haven, 1827).

65. *Concio ad Clerum. A Sermon Delivered in the Chapel of Yale College, September 10, 1828* (New Haven, 1828).

66. *Ibid.,* 8.

nature constituted "the occasion, or reason" of his sinning. Thus Taylor defined "depraved by nature" by saying, *"Such is their [men's] nature, that they will sin and only sin in all the appropriate circumstances of their being."* [67] Evidently Taylor himself had no clear idea as to how human nature determined that all men would certainly sin. In any case, the elusive words, "such is their nature," convey no definite idea of what he meant. Nevertheless, he insisted that "the very birth of a human being is an event which involves the certainty of entire moral depravity." [68]

Whatever may have been the effect of the *Concio* on the Unitarians, it raised an uproar among the more conservative New England Calvinists. [69] The most vigorous critics were in Connecticut, where Joseph Harvey and Bennet Tyler bitterly assailed Taylorism. They charged that the Taylorites had scuttled the historic doctrine of native depravity as taught by Edwards. On the other hand, Taylor and his friends argued that the Tylerites were propagating a theory of native depravity which denied human freedom and made God the author of man's sinful nature.

The prolonged debates on native depravity which emerged from Channing's discourse of 1819 created no little tension in the churches, but at the same time they served to prepare the ground for the constructive contribution of Bushnell. In particular, they revealed the wide diversity of opinion with respect to theories of human nature. Henry Ware's theory of the essential goodness of man stood out in sharp contrast to Bennet Tyler's doctrine of total depravity. Taylor's theory fell somewhere between the two. Bushnell developed his own conception of human nature in light of the strength and weakness of these conflicting theories. Characteristically, he found both truth and error in all of them, but the whole truth in none of them. Thus the way was prepared for the application of what he called the "comprehensive method."

The fourth basic question raised by Channing concerned the nature of Christ's redemptive mission. In his opinion, the orthodox view of Christ's work was fundamentally defective. Before considering his criticism, it is necessary to indicate an important development in the Calvinist conception of the atonement.

Until the latter part of the eighteenth century, New England Congregationalists remained committed to a view of Christ's work which was set

67. *Ibid.*, 13.   68. *Ibid.*, 23.
69. Sidney E. Mead, *Nathaniel William Taylor, 1786–1858: A Connecticut Liberal* (Chicago, 1942), Chap. 13; Smith, *Changing Conceptions of Original Sin*, 110–25.

forth in the Shorter Catechism of the Westminster Assembly. According to that Catechism, Christ, by paying the full debt which sinners owed to God and by appeasing the divine wrath, opened the way for the salvation of the elect. On the whole, Jonathan Edwards accepted this penal-satisfaction doctrine of Christ's work; but there are certain remarks in his published writings which anticipated elements of what came to be known as the "governmental" or "Edwardean" theory of the atonement.[70] In discussing the atonement, he often referred to God as "governor" or "Rector";[71] he emphasized the majesty and honor of God's "moral government" and the necessity of punishing offenders against God's law;[72] he occasionally remarked that it "did not become" the Moral Governor to permit sin to occur without "giving some public manifestation and tokens of his infinite abhorrence of it";[73] and he now and then observed that Christ suffered the "equivalent" of the penalty with which God threatened sinners.[74] These emphases are characteristic of the theory of the atonement as developed by Edwards's successors. Thus the elder Edwards may be considered a forerunner of it.

This new accent became stronger in Joseph Bellamy's *True Religion Delineated* (1750), for which Edwards wrote a commendatory preface. Bellamy's pupil, Jonathan Edwards, Jr. (1745–1801), has the distinction of being the first New Englander to systematize the theory.[75] In 1785 he published *Three Sermons on the Necessity of the Atonement*, in which he integrated the several ideas into a coherent scheme.[76] Thus began a pattern of thought whose ultimate roots are usually traced to Hugo Grotius.[77] Since this theory was developed chiefly by the successors of the

70. See especially "Miscellaneous Remarks on Important Doctrines," *Works of President Edwards*, Sereno Dwight, ed. (10 vols., New York, 1829-30), Vol. VII, Chaps. 1 and 6. See also Edwards A. Park, "The Rise of the Edwardean Theory of the Atonement: An Introductory Essay," in Park, ed., *The Atonement: Discourses and Treatises by Edwards, Smalley, Maxcy, Emmons, Griffin, Burge, and Weeks* (Boston, 1859), xi–xxxix.

71. *Works*, VII, 512-14, 533, 535.   72. *Ibid.*, 360–74, 509-16.

73. *Ibid.*, 508.   74. *Ibid.*, 521, 526-27, 534.

75. For a concise account of developments in New England which culminated in the Edwardean conception of the atonement, see Joseph Haroutunian, *Piety Versus Moralism: The Passing of the New England Theology* (New York, 1932), Chap. 7. See also Frank H. Foster, *A Genetic History of the New England Theology* (Chicago, 1907), Chap. 8.

76. "Three Sermons on the Necessity of the Atonement, and the Consistency Between That and Free Grace in Forgiveness," in Edwards A. Park, ed., *The Atonement*, 3–42.

77. Hugo Grotius, *A Defence of the Catholic Faith Concerning the Satisfaction of Christ, Against Faustus Socinus*, translated with notes and an historical introduction,

elder Edwards, it has been appropriately characterized by Edwards A. Park as the "Edwardean theory of the atonement." Park further remarked that it was Calvinistic in substance and Edwardean in form.[78] By the dawn of the nineteenth century, the Edwardean theory was more acceptable to New England Calvinist theologians than was that of the Shorter Catechism. Caleb Burge's *An Essay on the Scripture Doctrine of the Atonement* (1822) may be cited as evidence of this fact. Emphatically Edwardean, it bore the written commendation of four prominent Congregational thinkers, among them Nathanael Emmons and Asa Burton. Although Bushnell was critical of it in some respects, he acknowledged that it was "more deserving than any modern treatise" he had seen.[79]

Since Burge's *Essay* came out in the midst of the Unitarian controversy, it will be helpful to outline its basic ideas on the atonement. Those ideas may be summarized in five propositions. (1) The atonement was necessary, not to appease God's wrath nor to increase his love, but to enable him, in a manner consistent with his honor and law, to pardon sinners.[80] (2) Jesus did not pay the literal debt of sinners; he only satisfied the demands of general justice.[81] (3) Jesus' pains alone constituted the atonement; his obedience "formed no part" of it.[82] (4) The pains of Jesus were not literally the same as the pains of the damned, but constituted only their equivalent.[83] (5) The atonement opened the door to all mankind; but even so, God is not obliged to save any one. The obstacle is unbelief, and God in his elective grace may or may not remove that obstacle.[84]

It was this Edwardean theory, as well as that of the Shorter Catechism, which Channing opposed. First of all, he outlined the Unitarian conception of the work of Christ, saying: "We believe that he [Christ] was sent by the Father to effect a moral, or spiritual deliverance of mankind; that is, to rescue men from sin and its consequences, and to bring them to a state of everlasting purity and happiness." [85] Jesus accomplished this mis-

---

by Frank H. Foster (Andover, 1889). Copies of the *Defence* were in the libraries of Harvard and Yale as early as 1723 and 1733 respectively. *Ibid.*, xliv, xlvi.

78. *The Atonement*, ix.

79. *The Vicarious Sacrifice, Grounded in Principles of Universal Obligation* (New York, 1866), 392.

80. *An Essay on the Scripture Doctrine of the Atonement* (Hartford, 1822), 33–36, 39–53.

81. *Ibid.*, 151–58, 161–65.   82. *Ibid.*, 94, 116, 120–21, 241–48.   83. *Ibid.*, 248.

84. *Ibid.*, 250–55. Burge strongly implied that God's glory would actually be more fully manifested if some men were left in perpetual unbelief. See *ibid.*, 264–65.

85. *Works*, III, 88.

sion, he said, by a variety of methods, including his teaching, moral example, death, and resurrection. Channing's main purpose, however, was to
point out the errors in the orthodox view of Christ's work. First, he condemned the idea that the death of Christ produces a change in the mind
of God toward the sinner. "No error seems to us more pernicious." [86]
Second, he repudiated the notion that sin against God could not be forgiven unless a substitute with the dignity of God actually suffered the
equivalent of that sin. "We ask for one text, in which we are told, that
God took human nature that he might make an infinite satisfaction to his
own justice; for one text, which tells us, that human guilt requires an infinite substitute; that Christ's sufferings owe their efficacy to their being
borne by an infinite being; or that his divine nature gives infinite value to
the sufferings of the human." [87] Third, Channing charged that the Calvinist scheme implied that Christ's highest mission was to rescue men
from punishment, not to build them up in Christian character. But,
"Why pluck the sinner from hell, if a hell be left to burn in his breast?" [88]

In his reply to Channing, Leonard Woods spent most of his time showing wherein the Edwardean theory of the atonement had been misrepresented in the Baltimore sermon.[89] For example, that discourse had
"*shaped and colored*" the orthodox system when it declared "that God
took human nature that he might make an infinite satisfaction to his own
justice." According to Woods, the false coloring arose from the fact that
Channing had failed to presuppose important distinctions within the
Godhead. "It is an essential part of our faith," he observed, "that there is
a real distinction between the Father and the Son, and that the distinction
is of such a nature, that they are two, . . . as *really* as Moses and Aaron,
though not in the same sense, nor in any sense inconsistent with their
being one. In consequence of this distinction, we consider it perfectly
proper to say, that the Father sends the Son to die for sinners, and accepts
the sacrifice he makes." [90] Woods agreed with Channing, "that God, as
God, cannot be a sufferer, or bear a penalty. And hence we infer the
necessity of the incarnation." [91] But granting the incarnation, did Christ
really suffer in his divine nature? After various circumlocutions, Woods
finally answered that question in the negative. Yet he argued that Christ's
atoning work was in no way lowered in value because of that fact.[92] He
also argued that the Edwardeans were as committed as Channing to the
idea that Christ's death did not render God more merciful or more loving.

86. Channing, *Works*, 90.   87. *Ibid.*, 91.   88. *Ibid.*, 92.
89. *Letters to Unitarians*, 83–106.   90. *Ibid.*, 84.   91. *Ibid.*, 85.   92. *Ibid.*, 104.

They uniformly held that the atonement originated in the love of God.[93] Nevertheless, he conceded that some Calvinists had occasionally used language which exposed them to Channing's charge. In this connection he endeavored to show wherein the Edwardean theory of the atonement avoided such pitfalls. We need not rehearse his argument, for it followed the general pattern developed in Burge's *Essay*.

Henry Ware reacted briskly to Woods. He exposed the confusion which Woods revealed when he employed the analogy of Moses and Aaron to explain the distinctions within the Godhead. "It belongs to him, who asserts this," said Ware, "to state intelligibly, what is the nature and import of the distinction here intended; to explain in what sense *two*, and what sense *one*. . . . He uses words without meaning, and merely casts a mist, where he is bound to shed light." [94] The chief significance of Ware's reply lay in his own interpretation of Christ's redemptive mission. Like Channing, he held that Christ's work had its effect solely upon man. He denied that Christ's sufferings either were a substitute for ours or could directly deliver us from punishment. Those sufferings, he explained, "are the ground of our forgiveness, only as they operate to bring us to that state of holiness, and conformity to the will of God, which has the promise of forgiveness, and qualifies us for it." [95]

Over the next decade or more, neither the Unitarians nor their opponents had anything new to say with respect to Christ's atoning work; both groups merely repeated their old arguments. On the Calvinist side, this fact is evident in the lectures of Nathaniel Taylor, the leading New England theologian of his generation.[96] To the question, how did Christ make an atonement? Taylor replied: *"By making a manifestation of the justice of God equal to that which would have been made by the actual infliction of the penalty of the law on transgressors."* [97] In explicating the various aspects of that thesis, Taylor expressed views which harmonized with the Edwardean theory, such as: (1) the atonement consisted exclusively of Christ's sufferings and death, and his active obedience constituted no part of it; (2) Christ did not pay the exact penalty threatened against sinners, but only an equivalent penalty; and (3) the atonement was sufficient for all men, but God designed to save only a part of mankind. At one point, however, he shifted somewhat from the prevailing view. He would neither affirm nor deny that Christ's divine nature

---

93. *Ibid.*, 86.   94. *Letters Addressed to Trinitarians and Calvinists*, 83.
95. *Ibid.*, 92–93; *cf. ibid.*, 96–97.   96. See Taylor, "Notes," II, 172–200.
97. *Ibid.*, 179.

suffered, and he maintained that the Bible itself was silent on the question.[98] Even so — if we may trust the student-recorded "Notes" — he went far enough in the direction of Patripassianism to say: "I don't believe that it can be proved *a priori* that it [the divine nature] could not suffer." [99] That statement would have impressed Bushnell, who insisted that Christ's suffering was not confined to his human nature.

This general survey is only a sketch, but it indicates that the New England Protestant mind was sharply divided on four basic questions: (1) the trinity, (2) the person of Christ, (3) native depravity, and (4) the atonement. The most fundamental cleavage was between the Unitarians and the Congregationalists; but within each of those two bodies there were serious differences on some questions.

II

Precisely how much the various controversies may have affected Bushnell's search for a stable pattern of religious belief cannot, of course, be determined; still, it is reasonable to assume that they were a considerable factor, especially after he entered Yale, where he came in contact with the wider currents of thought. Not until 1821, when he was nineteen years of age, did he join the church, even though he had been reared in a Christian home. In his middle teens, according to Noah Porter of Yale, Bushnell "became somewhat skeptical in his religious views and joined an infidel club in a neighboring town — at the head of which was a hard-headed Deist of the type of [Thomas] Paine — whereupon his father interposed his authority and refused to assist him in a college education, and he remained for some time in his father's domestic cloth works." [100]

A fact not sufficiently appreciated is that Bushnell's Christian life did not come easily, nor did it evolve smoothly. In fact, as he himself observed, his spiritual life "required *many* turns of loss and recovery to ripen it." [101] His conversion experience of 1821 soon cooled; indeed, within less than a year he acknowledged that he had backslidden. In his freshman year at Yale — on March 7, 1824 — he was admitted to mem-

98. *Ibid.*, 183.   99. *Ibid.*

100. "Horace Bushnell," *New Englander*, XXXVI (1877), 153–54. Mary Bushnell Cheney, in her *Life and Letters of Horace Bushnell* (New York, 1880), 20–31, discounted the idea that Bushnell was inclined to infidelity in his youth. Porter, however, was not a person to peddle mere gossip; besides, his account does not seem out of character for a youngster who did not enter the church until his later adolescence and who, even after becoming a Christian, was often torn by doubt.

101. *Ibid.*, 21.

bership in the college church; [102] and yet, as Porter remarked, "the growing spirit of doubt took strong possession of his mind as he advanced in college life." [103] Two years after his graduation he returned to Yale as a tutor, but he still took no real interest in religion. In fact, he was known to college officials and students alike as a doubting Thomas. It so happened, however, that in 1831 Yale became the scene of a powerful revival, with the result that more than a hundred students joined the college church and other churches in New Haven.[104] At first Bushnell held aloof from the upheaval, but in the end he renewed his religious commitment. The decision led to a vocational turning point in his life; he abandoned plans to become a lawyer and entered Yale Divinity School the following fall to prepare for the Christian ministry.[105]

However satisfying the renewal of 1831 may have been, it did not purge his mind of doubt respecting many commonly believed Christian doctrines. Nor did his study at Yale Divinity School seem to give him substantial relief on this score. For when he assumed pastoral charge of the North Church (Hartford),[106] the essentials of his Christian faith were so meager that he wanted to leave the ministry and become a teacher of ethics. Referring to this situation twenty years later, he said:

> I had many and great difficulties on my hands, in respect to the gospel truths. . . . I was coming into religion on the side of reason or philosophy, and, of course had small conception of it as a faith and a supernatural gift to the race. . . . I confess with some mortification, so deep was I in the beggarly elements of the school, that I did not really expect to remain in the ministry long. I thought if I could sometime be called to a professorship of moral philosophy, it would be a more satisfactory and higher field of exertion.[107]

The "small mustard seed of Christian experience" which Bushnell took with him to the North Church must have grown considerably during the

102. Manuscript "Records of the Church of Christ in Yale College," II (1817–77), 24 (MS. in Yale University Library).

103. "Horace Bushnell," *New Englander*, XXXVI, 154.

104. Roland H. Bainton, *Yale and the Ministry* (New York, 1957), 86.

105. Many years later Bushnell preached a sermon at Yale on "The Dissolving of Doubts," in which he alluded to the experience of 1831. See *Sermons on Living Subjects*, centenary ed. (New York, 1910), 166–84.

106. Bushnell served the North Church (Congregational) at Hartford, Connecticut, from 1833 until 1859, when failing health forced him to retire from the active ministry. Although he preached occasionally thereafter, he devoted most of his time to writing.

107. *Twentieth Anniversary: A Commemorative Discourse, Delivered in the North Church, of Hartford, May 22, 1853* (Hartford, 1853), 8–9.

next few years, or he probably would have left the ministry. Even so, it was not until the year 1848 that he experienced the personal transformation which revealed to him the profundity of the Christian gospel. His wife later remarked that he approached this "central point" in his life "through mental struggles, trials, and practical endeavor"; but she did not indicate the nature of those struggles and trials except to say that "five years before, God had spoken personally to him in the death of his beloved little boy, drawing his thoughts and affections to the spiritual and unseen." [108] The episode of 1847 could have been one of those trials. In that year he published his first book, *Discourses on Christian Nurture*, in which he contested the traditional conception of regeneration, especially as related to children. With a few notable exceptions, the guardians of orthodoxy raised such a loud outcry against him that the publishers quickly suspended the sale of his book without even consulting him. Stung by this treatment, he answered the publishers and the reviewers in a caustic pamphlet. On second thought, however, he rebuked himself for having spoken so intemperately. Thus this controversy may have been a factor in prompting him to search for a deeper experience of God. But explain it as one may, the fact is that Bushnell felt discontented with his spiritual life and groped for new light. His wife watched his personal search expectantly, and when, on a February morning in 1848, she saw a new radiance in his face, she asked, "What have you seen?" Back came the joyful words — "The gospel." [109]

In response to this new vision of the gospel, Bushnell preached to his congregation an arresting sermon on "Christ the Form of the Soul," using as a text the words of Saint Paul, "until Christ be formed in you" (Gal. 4:19).[110] "Sin takes away the image or form of God," he declared, "and makes the soul a truly deformed creature." The only remedy for this deformity, he urged, is Christ, who brought into humanity "the form of a divine character." When the morally deformed creature embraces "the divine Word," he is radically transformed. Bushnell insisted that the transforming power comes from God, not man. "It moves from him and not from you. It is no vague struggle to ascend some height you cannot see, no wearisome, legal drill of duty and self-cultivating discipline. It is simply and only to have your being filled and occupied and transformed by Christ." [111]

108. Cheney, *Life and Letters of Horace Bushnell*, 191.   109. *Ibid.*, 192.

110. Bushnell, *The Spirit in Man*, centenary ed. (New York, 1910), 39–51. This is an abridged version of the sermon; the MS. of the original text has apparently been lost or destroyed.

111. *Ibid.*, 43.

The idea that Christ radically transforms the sinfully deformed creature became thereafter the keynote of Bushnell's preaching. Undoubtedly this idea was the result of the experience of 1848. In one of his frequent references to this pivotal event, he declared: "I seemed to pass a boundary. I had never been very legal in my Christian life, but I passed from those partial seeings, glimpses and doubts, into a clearer knowledge of God and into his inspirations, which I have never wholly lost. The change was into faith — a sense of the freeness of God and the ease of approach to him." [112]

In its spiritual consequences, Bushnell's illumination bears a striking resemblance to that of Jonathan Edwards, at the age of twenty. Edwards had been the subject of previous awakenings, but they had not originated in what he later called "true religious affections." At length, however, as he recorded in his "Personal Narrative," he was graciously visited with a "new sense of divine things" which was "exceedingly different" from that of his earlier awakenings. The "former delights never reached the heart; and did not arise from any sight of the divine excellency of the things of God; or any taste of the soul-satisfying and life-giving good there is in them." [113] Out of this "new sense" emerged a new Edwards, the father of the Great Awakening in New England. Likewise, Bushnell's earlier spiritual quickenings were secondary to the decisive renewal of 1848. The renewal in 1831 centered in a resolution of the will to follow "the principle of rectitude." [114] But the experience of 1848 involved the personal discovery of Christ as the vitalizing principle of the soul. As his wife testified, "The greatness of this change and its profound reality made him a new man, or rather the same man with a heavenly investiture." [115]

Another important outcome of the awakening of 1848 was new theological light. Alluding to this fact in his twentieth anniversary sermon, he said: "When it had just now pleased God to conduct me into a fuller experience of divine things, and to open my spiritual understanding, as never before, to the great mystery of godliness, I found that certain reserved questions, before dark and insoluble, were correspondingly cleared. The veil was lifted, and the difficulties vanished, never to return." [116] Significantly, the "reserved questions" on which new light had dawned were precisely those which the Congregationalists and Unitarians

112. Cheney, *Life and Letters of Horace Bushnell*, 192.
113. Sereno Dwight, "Life of President Edwards," *Works of President Edwards*, I, 62.
114. Cheney, *Life and Letters of Horace Bushnell*, 445.   115. *Ibid.*, 193.
116. *Twentieth Anniversary: A Commemorative Discourse*, 22.

had debated for a full generation without resolving their differences. Bushnell had deplored this acrimonious debate, and he felt hopeful that the fresh insight given him might lead toward an eventual reunion of the estranged communions. Thus he regarded it as providential that, even before he finished writing the sermon on "Christ the Form of the Soul," three major institutions, representing both sides of the controversy, invited him to address them: Harvard, Yale, and Andover. Accepting all three invitations, he discussed the work of Christ at Harvard in July, the incarnation and the trinity at Yale in August, and religious renewal at Andover in September. Each lecture reflected a vital aspect of the vision of 1848. The discourse at Andover Seminary was, essentially, an expansion of "Christ the Form of the Soul."

Since the present volume is concerned primarily with Bushnell as a theologian, it is relevant to point out that the illumination of 1848 determined the creative center of his theology. All his theological works are christocentric. Bushnell's ultimate center, to be sure, was God; but it was God as revealed in Jesus Christ. Thus he entitled the volume growing out of his discourses of 1848, *God in Christ* (1849), and the one written in its defense, *Christ in Theology* (1851). His *Nature and the Supernatural* (1858) revolves around Christ as the center and goal of history. He gave most attention to the atonement, and in its explication he wrote *The Vicarious Sacrifice* (1866) and *Forgiveness and Law* (1874). Nor is the christocentric principle less dominant in his three volumes of sermons: *Sermons for the New Life* (1858), *Christ and His Salvation* (1864), and *Sermons on Living Subjects* (1872). Practically the only complaint Bushnell's congregation made against him was that he preached Christ too much. In reply to this, he said: "I cannot think [this] is a fault to be repented of, for Christ is all and beside him there is no gospel to be preached or received." [117] Thus it cannot be too strongly emphasized that Christ was the magnetic center of the thought and ministry of Horace Bushnell.

III

Next in importance to recognizing the significance of Bushnell's christocentric principle is the necessity of understanding the nature of his theological method. Three factors are involved in that method: (1) his conception of religious knowledge; (2) his view of the nature and limitations of theological language; and (3) his theory of "Christian compre-

117. *Twentieth Anniversary: A Commemorative Discourse*, 30.

hensiveness." We shall consider them in that order, giving most attention to the first two.

Although Bushnell nowhere developed his theory of religious knowledge at length, he did, in various brief discussions, set forth a recognizable epistemology. Basically, his theory derived from two sources: (1) German romantic idealism as mediated primarily through Samuel Taylor Coleridge (1772–1834) and Victor Cousin (1792–1867), and (2) the Puritan tradition as revived in Jonathan Edwards's doctrine of the "new sense of divine things."

Coleridge influenced not only the transcendentalists, but also many orthodox churchmen, among them James Marsh, celebrated for his edition (1829) of Coleridge's *Aids to Reflection*.[118] By 1830 the Marsh edition of the *Aids* "became the textbook of a little circle" of Yale undergraduates, including Noah Porter, Lyman Atwater, and W. W. Andrews of the class of 1831.[119] "We learned from Coleridge," said Andrews, "what it is which distinguishes man, made in God's image, from the inferior animals, viz., the Reason by which we are capable of knowing Him and having [direct] communion with Him, in distinction from the Understanding, the faculty of adapting means to ends for the uses of the present life." [120] The discovery of Coleridge's doctrine of the intuitive knowledge of God liberated them from total dependence upon Locke's empirical epistemology. Thus as Andrews remarked, Coleridge wrought in them "a great intellectual and spiritual revolution."

Interestingly, Bushnell (of the class of 1827) got hold of a copy of the *Aids* before he left college. At first the book "seemed foggy," and he put it aside for "a long time" — precisely how long is not certain — but when he picked it up again it was "lucid and instructive." [121] As his theological thought reveals, the *Aids* proved instructive to him on many questions, but it was particularly helpful in showing him how it was possible to know God intuitively. Hence he began losing interest in Locke's empiricism and in Paley's natural theology. Before leaving Yale Divinity School, he wrote a paper sharply challenging Paley's argument for the ex-

118. Noah Porter, "Coleridge and His American Disciples," *Bibliotheca Sacra*, IV (1847), 117–71; Ronald V. Wells, *Three Christian Transcendentalists* (New York, 1943), Chap. 2.

119. W. W. Andrews, "Noah Porter, Student at Yale," *Noah Porter, A Memorial by Friends*, George S. Merriam, ed. (New York, 1893), 17.

120. *Ibid.*, 18. See "Aids to Reflection," *Complete Works of Samuel Taylor Coleridge*, William G. T. Shedd, ed. (7 vols., New York, 1868), I, 241–53, 264–65.

121. Cheney, *Life and Letters of Horace Bushnell*, 208.

istence of God from evidences of design in the world of nature.[122] In 1839, in a lecture given at Andover Theological Seminary, he repeated his criticism of Paley.[123] Thus it is evident that Coleridge's doctrine of religious intuition had taken root in Bushnell's mind.[124]

Victor Cousin's theory of "spontaneous reason" increased Bushnell's interest in intuitive perception. By the 1820's, Cousin had emerged in Paris as a zealous foe of Lockean philosophy, contending that it logically led to religious skepticism. Beginning as a disciple of Thomas Reid, he soon moved through Kant to Schelling and Hegel. The last two philosophers became his acknowledged "Masters." [125] But although accepting much of Schelling and Hegel, Cousin combined with them much also of Locke, thus becoming the expounder of a scheme of philosophy which he called "eclecticism." In his theory of knowledge, Cousin began on the psychological plane, as did Locke, but he contended that human cognition always contained within itself an ontological element, since the idea of the finite necessarily included the idea of the infinite as its corollary. "I cannot," said Cousin, "have the idea of the finite and imperfect, without having the idea of the perfect and infinite. These two ideas are logical correlatives." [126] Since, then, according to Cousin, "the infinite and perfect, is God himself," the idea of the finite necessarily carried with it also the idea of God. Hence atheism was logically excluded. As Cousin put it, "The simple fact, of the conception of God by the reason, the simple idea of God, . . . implies the certainty and necessity of the existence of God." [127]

On this background, we can appreciate the distinctive nature of Cousin's epistemology. He held what might be called a two-level view of reason. On the first level, reason is primitive, involuntary, non-reflective; on the second, it is voluntary, reflective. The first type of reason Cousin characterized as "primitive spontaneity," "spontaneous reason," "spontaneous intuition," or "intuitive reason." He contended that reflective

122. Manuscript entitled "There is a Moral Governor" (July 1832), 1–3.

123. Manuscript entitled "Revelation," 31–32.

124. For a more comprehensive demonstration of Coleridge's epistemological impact upon Bushnell's thought, see John E. Howell, "A Study of the Theological Method of Horace Bushnell and Its Application to His Cardinal Doctrines" (unpublished Ph.D. dissertation, Duke University, 1963), 143–52.

125. *Philosophical Miscellanies, Translated from the French of Cousin, Jouffroy, and B. Constant, with Introduction and Critical Notices,* by George Ripley (2 vols., Boston, 1838), I, 89.

126. *Elements of Psychology: Included in a Critical Examination of Locke's Essay on the Human Understanding, Translated, with an Introduction, Notes, and Additions,* by Caleb Sprague Henry (Hartford, 1834), 265.

127. *Ibid.,* 266–67.

reason absolutely depended upon the antecedent action of spontaneous reason. What, then, is the special role of spontaneous or intuitive reason? According to Cousin, "it gives us ourselves, the world, and God." But how does it do this? Spontaneous reason, he replied, perceives truth intuitively "at first sight," and "without asking or giving account of its doing so." [128]

The New England transcendentalists enthusiastically welcomed the doctrine of spontaneous intuition as offering an antidote to Lockean "sensualism," and as being more reliable than Paleyism in proving the existence of God. In their opinion, Cousin based his epistemology on firmer philosophical foundations than did Coleridge.[129] Cousin sprang into popularity in America as well as in France. "I may venture to say," wrote Ripley in 1838, "that there is no living philosopher who has a greater number of readers in this country." [130] In response to the demand for Cousin's writings, his *Introduction to the History of Philosophy* was published in Boston in 1832, and his *Elements of Psychology* was issued in Hartford in 1834. In view of the general acclaim of the Frenchman, it is probable that Bushnell read these works soon after their appearance. Since he was already a strong believer in the doctrine of intuition as taught by Coleridge, he was receptive to Cousin's idea of "spontaneous intuition." [131]

The second root of Bushnell's theory of religious knowledge is the Puritan tradition as revived in Jonathan Edwards's doctrine of "the new sense," or "the sense of the heart." As already indicated, when Edwards underwent the decisive spiritual renewal of 1721, there came into his soul "a new sense" of the glory and excellency of God. This new sense was so all-engaging to him that he scrutinized it from every possible angle. After pondering its meaning for some two years, he preached a remarkable sermon from 1 Corinthians 2:14: "But the natural man receiveth not the things of the Spirit of God. . . ." From that text he expounded the doctrine "that there is a spiritual understanding of divine things which all natural and unregenerate men are destitute of." [132] The natural man, he

128. *Introduction to the History of Philosophy*, trans. by Henning G. Linberg (Boston, 1832), 168.

129. George Ripley, "Introductory Notice," *Philosophical Miscellanies*, I, 41–42.

130. *Ibid.*, 29.

131. For a fuller account of Cousin's epistemological influence upon Bushnell's theory of religious knowledge, see John E. Howell, "A Study of the Theological Method of Horace Bushnell and Its Application to His Cardinal Doctrines," 152–58.

132. Manuscript Sermon on 1 Corinthians 2:14 (booklet 1), 4. (The MS. is a part of the collection of Edwards MSS. owned by Andover Newton Theological School. I am indebted to Thomas A. Schafer, Professor at McCormick Theological Sem-

urged, has only a "notional knowledge" of God. The natural man may know all the tenets of orthodoxy, but still his knowledge will be merely notional or speculative.[133] On the other hand, the regenerated man possesses "spiritual light" immediately imparted to him by the Spirit of God, whereby he intuitively perceives "the excellency of divine and spiritual things." There is something in his perception comprising an actual "taste" of spiritual realities. Consequently the divinely illuminated man not only sees the excellency of divine things, but he tastes them with an awareness of their sweetnsss that is entirely unknown to the natural man.[134]

About ten years later, in 1733, Edwards preached on the same theme. As published, the sermon is entitled *A Divine and Supernatural Light, Immediately Imparted to the Soul by the Spirit of God*,[135] and its aim is twofold: (1) to show that the regenerated man is the subject of a special kind of illumination of which the natural man is entirely ignorant; (2) to indicate that the new kind of spiritual light is immediately conveyed to the soul by the Spirit of God. Within this perspective he once again articulated his theory of religious cognition. "There is," said he, "a twofold understanding or knowledge of good of which God has made the mind capable. The first, that which is merely notional; . . . And the other is, that which consists in the sense of the heart; as when the heart is sensible of pleasure and delight in the presence of the idea of it. In the former is exercised merely the speculative faculty, or the understanding, in distinction from the will or disposition of the soul. In the latter, the will, or inclination, or heart, are mainly concerned." [136]

For Edwards, "the sense of the heart" constituted the wellspring of evangelical religion. He believed that the loss of this sense accounted for the spiritual sterility that was creeping upon Christianity in New England. Commenting on the situation in 1740, he declared: "We have been long in a strange stupor; the influences of the Spirit of God upon the heart have been but little felt, and the nature of them but little taught. . . . Our people do not so much need to have their heads stored, as to have their hearts touched." [137] This doctrine of the sense of the heart, which constituted Edwards's major contribution to the Great Awakening, was

---

inary, for supplying a transcription of it. The sermon is not dated; but Schafer, who has given extended study to the Edwards MSS., estimates that Edwards probably preached it in the latter half of 1723 or early in 1724.)

133. *Ibid.*, 5–8.   134. *Ibid.*, 14–19.

135. *Works of President Edwards*, VI, 171–88.   136. *Ibid.*, 176–77.

137. "Some Thoughts Concerning the Present Revival of Religion in New England," *Works of President Edwards*, IV, 101, 159.

misunderstood or discounted by the rationalists and corrupted by the "enthusiasts." Largely in order to distinguish his conception from that of both groups — the Chauncys and the Davenports — he published *A Treatise Concerning Religious Affections* (1746). Once again he affirmed the necessity of distinguishing between two types of knowledge. "There is a distinction to be made between a mere notional understanding, wherein the mind only beholds things in the exercise of a speculative faculty; and the sense of the heart, wherein the mind don't only speculate and behold, but relishes and feels." [138]

The idea of "the new sense" did not, of course, originate with Edwards; indeed, it formed an important element in the theology of the early English Puritans, especially Richard Sibbes (1577–1635) and John Owen (1616–83). [139] Both of these men emphasized the distinction between speculative knowledge and knowledge "with a taste." [140] The same distinction also was stressed by Thomas Shepard (1605–49), especially in the *Parable of the Ten Virgins* (1660), a work frequently quoted in the *Religious Affections*. Edwards was well acquainted with the Puritan theory of immediate illumination, and his own doctrine bears its stamp. This does not rule out the influence of Locke upon Edwards, for which Perry Miller has contended. [141] However, there is increasing evidence that insufficient weight has been given to the Puritan element in Edwards's religious epistemology. [142]

The doctrine of spiritual light did not cease with Edwards; his two intimate friends and pupils, Joseph Bellamy (1719–90) and Samuel Hopkins (1721–1803), regarded it as an indispensable element of evangelical religion. Thus it occupied an important place in Bellamy's *True Religion Delineated* (1750). [143] It appeared conspicuously also in his *An Essay on*

138. *The Works of Jonathan Edwards*, II: *Religious Affections*, John E. Smith, ed. (New Haven, 1959), 272. For Edwards's "Miscellany" No. 782, on the sense of the heart, see *The Philosophy of Jonathan Edwards from His Private Notebooks*, Harvey G. Townsend, ed. (Eugene, Oregon, 1955), 113–26; Perry Miller, "Jonathan Edwards on the Sense of the Heart," *Harvard Theological Review*, XLI (1948), 123–45.

139. Geoffrey F. Nuttall, *The Holy Spirit in Puritan Faith and Experience* (Oxford, 1946), Chap. 2.

140. *Ibid.*, 39.

141. "Jonathan Edwards on the Sense of the Heart," *Harvard Theological Review*, XLI (1948), 123–45; *Jonathan Edwards* (New York, 1956), 175–82.

142. John E. Smith, "Editor's Introduction," *The Works of Jonathan Edwards*, II: *Religious Affections*, 52–74; Douglas J. Elwood, *The Philosophical Theology of Jonathan Edwards* (New York, 1960), Chap. 6.

143. *Works of the Rev. Joseph Bellamy, D.D.* (2 vols., New York, 1811), I, 426–42.

the Nature and Glory of the Gospel of Jesus Christ (1762).[144] In both of
these works, Bellamy explained the doctrine of the new sense in terms
reminiscent of his teacher, and he quoted directly from the *Affections* in
support of it. One of Edwards's most influential followers was Samuel
Hopkins, the father of a version of Calvinism often characterized as
"Hopkinsianism." His two-volume *System of Doctrines*, first published in
1793, is one of New England's distinguished theological monuments. For
at least a full generation, it exerted great influence upon the mind of
American Congregationalism. Like Bellamy's writings, it contains an extended exposition of the Edwardean theory of divine illumination, with
documentation from the *Religious Affections*.[145]

Bushnell was well acquainted with Hopkins's *System;* in fact, he quoted
several passages from it in the defense of his own doctrine of Christian
nurture.[146] Nor was he less familiar with Bellamy's writings. Since, then,
the doctrine of divine light appeared in the books of both of these Edwardeans, Bushnell was probably formally acquainted with it before he
underwent the transforming illumination of 1848. But if so, he had, to use
Edwards's term, merely a "notional" knowledge of it. However, after
that decisive event, it became a glowing experiential knowledge with
him, the nature of which he described in "Christ the Form of the Soul."
Thus, much in the Andover address on "Dogma and Spirit" reflected this
new experimental consciousness, as when he said:

> The human soul under sin, or considered simply as unreligious, is
> necessarily dark, because it is divorced from God, by whose inbeing
> it was made to have its light. It cannot make light, by opinions got-
> ten up in itself. Revolving God's idea, systematizing external cog-
> nitions, derived from his works, investigating the historic evidence
> of Christ, his life, his doctrine — busied in all such ways, it is rather
> creating darkness than light, until it receives God, as an inner light,
> and knows him by that spiritual manifestation within, which Christ
> promised.[147]

Bushnell recurred to this theme again and again in his sermons, articles,
and books. More than once he defined his theory as "the doctrine of the
heart," or as the doctrine of "the new inner sense." In a manner reminiscent of Edwards, he located the root of the currently decaying piety in

144. *Ibid.*, II, 499–526.
145. *Works of Samuel Hopkins, D.D., with a Memoir of His Life and Character,*
by Edwards A. Park (3 vols., Boston, 1852), I, 399–421.
146. *An Argument for "Discourses on Christian Nurture"* (Hartford, 1847), 16–18.
147. *God in Christ* (Hartford, 1849), 303; see also *ibid.*, 327–36; *Christ in Theology,*
(Hartford, 1851), 334–44.

the growing tendency to substitute a notional, speculative knowledge of God for an immediate experience of God. This is the central contention, for example, of the concluding seventeen pages of *Christ in Theology*. "We have taken the great truths of religion out of the sphere of faith," he said, "and subjected them to the dominion or disposal of the natural judgment; substituting, in this manner, a dogmatic and professional Christianity, in place of the divine teaching or doctrine that is called SPIRIT and is to be realized only by faith and an immediately divine experience. . . . Our religion is fed therefore by the light of notions, and not to any extent by the immediate illumination of God in the soul." [148]

Bushnell elucidated his theory of religious knowledge most completely in a sermon entitled "The Immediate Knowledge of God," published in 1872.[149] He clearly differentiated two kinds of knowledge: "mediate" and "immediate." The first kind, he remarked, derives from a study of God's manifestations in nature, and from a study of religious truths or doctrines involving the use of language.[150] Far from disparaging such knowledge, he said: "It is much to know about God, about his operations, his works, his plans, his laws, his truth, his perfect attributes, his saving mercies. This kind of knowledge is presupposed in all faith, and constitutes the rational ground of faith, and so far is necessary even to salvation." [151] Thus Bushnell would have been no less critical of the "enthusiasts" than was Edwards. Yet he observed that "medial" knowledge "is alone a knowing about God, as from a distance." "The roads of the natural understanding are in a lower plane, you must rise, you must go up in truth and *know God — God himself —* by the inward discovery of his infinite spirit and person." [152] This kind of knowing "is knowing God within, even as we know ourselves." Bushnell dwelt upon the parallel between knowing ourselves and knowing God. Every one, he explained, has two kinds of knowledge of himself. "One is what you know mediately about yourself, through language, and one that which you have immediately as being conscious of yourself." The latter kind of knowing is so absolutely immediate "that there is no language in it, no thought, no act of judgment or opinion, you simply have a self-feeling that is intuitive and direct." [153] In like manner one may know God immediately, without the intervention of language or discursive reflection.

148. *Christ in Theology*, 335, 337.
149. *Sermons on Living Subjects*, centenary ed. (New York, 1910), 114–28. Bushnell indicated that he had preached this sermon at Yale, but he did not say when.
150. *Ibid.*, 114, 119.   151. *Ibid.*, 115; see also *ibid.*, 123, 127.
152. *Ibid.*, 127.   153. *Ibid.*, 119.

According to Bushnell, men were originally created to have this immediate knowledge of God, but their sin cut them off from it. Consequently
they will never know God "till he becomes centered in their soul again as
its life, and the crowning good and blessing of its eternity. And this is
fitly called being born of God, because it is the entering of God again
into his place — to be the beginning there of a new movement and life
derivative from him, and fed by the springs of his fullness in the
heart." [154] And this new birth is the direct work of the Spirit, not the result
of self-culture.

In summary, Bushnell's theory of religious knowledge derived from
two traditions: German Romanticism, and Puritanism as revitalized in
Edwards's doctrine of the divine light. His relation to the former tradition is generally emphasized, but his connection with the latter has been
entirely neglected. Yet it is the Puritan element in his doctrine of the immediate illumination of the Spirit which explains his profound consciousness of Christ as "the form of the soul" and which invests his sermons and
theological works with their dynamic evangelicalism. Until this neglected
Puritan epistemological strain is accorded its proper recognition, Bushnell's full theological significance will not be understood. Owing in part
to this neglect, he has been linked too closely with the romantic modes of
religious thought, including transcendentalism. It is true that Bushnell was
significantly influenced by the romantic movement, but it is equally true
that both his epistemology and the content of his gospel message are fundamentally rooted in the Puritan tradition.

We shall gain further light on Bushnell's theological method by an understanding of the nature and religious import of his theory of language.
While still at Yale Divinity School he composed a perceptive essay in
which, among other things, he sketched the initial elements of his linguistic theory. Three closely interrelated ideas emerged in that essay:
first, that language has its basis entirely in sensory phenomena; second,
that the sensible world is an indispensable medium of intellectual exchange between persons; and third, that the world of nature is itself a significant language.[155]

Over the years Bushnell continued to explore various aspects of linguistic theory, despite the demands of a growing parish. The results of his
reflection appeared in an address which he gave at Andover Seminary in
the fall of 1839 on the subject of "Revelation." Language, he explained,
"is two stories high, being first a language of sense or fact and next a lan-

154. *Ibid.*, 118-19.   155. "There is a Moral Governor," 2-6.

guage of thought or truth." [156] The language of thought becomes possible in virtue of the fact that God has constructed the outward world "so as to furnish a vast storehouse of types or images fitted to represent thoughts and be interpreted between man and man." In other words, the external world "is analogical to thought and truth, and constitutes in the whole a grand system of figure work spiritually significant." Thus, for example, nature's type of right is a straight line; of hope, an act of reaching forth.[157]

The language of sense, Bushnell observed, is comparatively simple; even animals can acquire it in some measure. But only beings of intelligence can employ the language of thought. The language of sense "is completed at its birth," but the language of thought "expands as thought expands and changes as the ever versatile mind of man works out new phases of thought." [158] Yet, although the language of thought is continually refining and enriching itself, "it seldom or never gets away from the ground force of its root or type and is therefore always to be used in criticism or interpretation as being still a figure of speech." [159]

One of Bushnell's aims in this address was to show that in language itself we have a revelation of God. Thus he urged that at the root of language there are types or forms which God implanted in nature to represent and express thought. These types point to cosmic intelligence or mind.

> I stand here then a thinking creature in a vast temple of being. The sky is over me, the earth is beneath and around me. I gaze on the floor and the walls and the shafted pillars of the temple and behold all overlaid with types of thought. Whose thought? If I am intelligent, so is the world. I live here — amazing thought — embosomed in the eternal intelligence of God. . . . He is revealed to me. I see him with a distinct gaze of simple inspection as I see any man through his bodily types of work and action. Here then in language we have a revelation of God which shows as in a mirror one vast and varied image of his intelligence.[160]

This mode of reasoning demonstrates that Bushnell's theory of language involved a daring metaphysical speculation. It is ironic that a man who himself speculated so boldly should have cautioned his brethren against theological speculation.

156. "Revelation," 13.

157. *Ibid.*, 16–17. Emerson, in his first book, *Nature* (1836), had already presented a similar theory of language. See *Ralph Waldo Emerson: Representative Selections, with Introduction*, by Frederic I. Carpenter (New York, 1934), 21–22.

158. "Revelation," 22–23.   159. *Ibid.*, 24.   160. *Ibid.*, 29–32.

Ten years later Bushnell published a definitive essay on the nature of language, the immediate design of which was to assist his readers in interpreting the three discourses in *God in Christ*.[161] That essay, included in the present volume, speaks for itself. It is pertinent to observe here, however, that it is indispensable to an understanding of Bushnell's approach to theological problems.

It has been said that Bushnell's theory of language "was a reflection of the natural play of his mind." [162] In so far as that judgment implies that he produced an entirely original theory, it must be questioned. For while Bushnell exhibited unusual creative ability, he also read widely on the subject of language and absorbed ideas from various writers, many of whom he named in the dissertation of 1849.[163] The person who probably exerted the most decisive influence upon Bushnell's theory of language was his teacher of Greek and Hebrew in Yale Divinity School, Josiah Willard Gibbs (1790–1861), the leading scholar in that school and a distinguished philologist. Gibbs followed closely developments in linguistic theory in Germany, the acknowledged wellspring of comparative philology.[164] In 1857, near the end of his life, he published the results of his research in a book entitled *Philological Studies*. In the preface he acknowledged that he had derived his philological insights "for the most part from distinguished German philologians, particularly from the writings of Dr. Karl Ferdinand Becker [1775–1849]." Some of the more basic sections in the volume indicate that Gibbs had already arrived at the gist of his linguistic theory by the middle 1830's.[165]

According to Gibbs, "semasiology" — the theory of the development of the meaning of words — is founded "on the analogy and correlation of the physical and intellectual worlds." Thus it holds that all mental terms have their basis in terms of sense. "Every word expressing an intellectual or moral idea originally expressed a physical one," explained Gibbs.[166]

---

161. "Preliminary Dissertation on the Nature of Language, as Related to Thought and Spirit," *God in Christ*, 9–97.

162. Theodore T. Munger, *Horace Bushnell, Preacher and Theologian* (Boston, 1899), 107.

163. See Donald A. Crosby, "Horace Bushnell's Theory of Language: A Historical and Philosophical Study" (unpublished Ph.D. dissertation, Columbia University, 1962), Chaps. 2–3, 5, and *passim*.

164. William D. Whitney, *The Life and Growth of Language* (New York, 1875), 318.

165. For further evidence, see Gibbs, "Historical and Critical View of Cases in the Indo-German Language," *Quarterly Christian Spectator*, IX (1837), 109–34.

166. *Philological Studies with English Illustrations* (New Haven, 1857), 18.

But how does the transference from the physical world to the intellectual take place? "Words which originally belonged to the world of sense, and denoted sensible objects, operations, and relations," replied Gibbs, "are transferred by a metaphor depending on a perceived analogy, to the world of intellect to express mental objects, operations, and relations." [167] For example, breath or wind gives rise to spirit; a straight line, to rectitude; a going over, to transgression. As Gibbs emphasized, metaphors in such instances are not to be confused with "rhetorical metaphors," which are designed for adornment. Unlike the latter, the former type of metaphor is indispensable to the conveyance of a particular truth or idea. Since the literal or physical sense is no longer present to the user of such terms of thought and spirit, "they may be called faded metaphors."

Bushnell's theory of language bears a striking resemblance to that of his Yale teacher. "All things out of sense," he wrote, "get their names in language through signs and objects in sense that have some mysterious correspondence or analogy, by which they are prepared beforehand to serve as signs or vehicles of the spiritual things to be expressed." [168] That is essentially what Gibbs had been teaching for many years. Thus it is manifest that Gibbs had an important part in shaping Bushnell's theory of language. On the other hand, Bushnell applied the theory to a theological issue which apparently never concerned Gibbs. That issue related to the limitation of theological language. Although Bushnell agreed with Gibbs that terms of sense become "fellow to" terms of spirit, he argued that theological terms never can represent truth as it is in itself. That is to say, all theological language necessarily falls short of complete objectivity. Bushnell based his conclusion on the observation that there is an element of "form" latent in all terms of thought. Since the form element cannot be entirely eliminated, terms of thought inevitably "impute *form* to that which is really out of form. They are related to the truth, only as form to spirit — earthen vessels in which the truth is borne, yet always offering their mere pottery as being the truth itself." [169] From this it follows that there can be no absolutely objective or scientific theology. This defect cannot be corrected merely by the refinement of language, for the constituent terms of every theological proposition retain elements of form. "Whoever attempts," said Bushnell, "to bring any truth out of form, into an exact, literal, abstractive language clear of form, begins in a delusion at the outset, and is very certain to be deeper in delusion at the end." [170]

167. *Ibid.*, 15.   168. *God in Christ*, 25–26.   169. *Ibid.*, 48.
170. *Christ in Theology*, 51.

Shall one, then, cease to concern oneself with theology? Bushnell expressly rejected that conclusion. In the first place, he recognized the indispensability of the theological task, even though he sharply criticized certain types of theological method. In the second place, he believed that theology could become a more adequate discipline. But how? This leads us to consider summarily a third element of Bushnell's theological method: the theory of "Christian comprehensiveness." In January of 1848 he published an extended analysis of this theory, including a discussion of its applicability to personal character, theology, and church polity.[171] Our concern here is not with the essay as a whole, but merely with that part of it in which the author indicated how theology or Christian doctrine could become a more adequate vehicle of Christian truth. Basic with Bushnell in this respect was the assumption that "language cannot convey any truth whole, or by literal embodiment. It can only show it on one side, and by figure. Hence a great many shadows, or figures, are necessary to represent every truth." [172] Yet the theologians and creed-makers, he maintained, have generally failed at this point. Each has framed this or that doctrine on the tacit supposition that his particular theory represented *the* truth rather than merely a fraction of it. The inevitable result has been contention over whose theory is right. In reality, none of the competing theories has been completely right; yet each theory has been standing for an element of truth which is necessary to completeness in the truth. If therefore the theologian is to transcend his present partial understanding of the Christian truth, he must engage in a twofold process: (1) he must join his fellow theologians in a serious effort to uncover and clarify the conflicting or "repugnant" forms of truth involved in religious controversy; (2) he must then burrow beneath the surface of those conflicts and never cease his efforts until he has found a way to combine the insights of all parties in a more comprehensive truth. "Let Calvinism," said Bushnell, "take in Arminianism, Arminianism Calvinism; let decrees take in contingency, contingency decrees; faith take in works, and works faith; the old take in the new, and the new the old — not doubting that we shall be as much wiser as we are more comprehensive, as much closer to unity as we have more of the truth." [173]

Bushnell's orthodox fellow churchmen generally regarded him as a theological enigma. A close inspection of the bitter controversy which burst forth upon the publication of *God in Christ* leaves the impression that he

171. "Christian Comprehensiveness," *New Englander*, VI (1848), 81–111.
172. *Ibid.*, 84.   173. *Ibid.*, 111.

was an enigma to his brethren largely because they either misunderstood or actually distorted the fundamental principles and presuppositions of his theological method. But those who mastered his distinctive method of theological inquiry usually experienced an exhilarating liberation from an increasingly scholastic orthodoxy.

PART ONE

❖

Foundations of Theological Method

DOGMA AND SPIRIT [1]

EDITOR'S INTRODUCTION

Along with many New Englanders, Bushnell lamented the "mournfully low state of religion." But what was the remedy? Many were praying for a revival of revivals, but Bushnell viewed that remedy as "quite too slight for our disease." From the outset of his ministry at the North Church he had opposed the "machinery system of revivals." In a twentieth-anniversary sermon (1853), he explained why he had opposed revivalism.

> Things had come to such a pitch in the churches, by the tensity of the revival system, that the permanent was sacrificed to the casual, the ordinary swallowed up and lost in the extraordinary, and Christian piety itself reduced to a kind of campaigning or stage-effect exercise. . . . It was even difficult for the pastor, saying nothing of conversions, to keep alive in Christians themselves any hope or expectation of holy living, as an abiding state, in the intervals of public movement and excitement left to his care; because everything was brought to the test of the revival state as a standard, and it could not be conceived how any one might be in the Spirit, and maintain a continuance of growth, in the calmer and more private methods of duty, patience, and fidelity on the level of the ordinary life.[2]

But if the return to conventional revivalism was no cure for the current spiritual malady, might not the cure lie in developing a better theology? Since New Englanders had debated theological questions ever since the opening of the century, many churchmen apparently thought so. Bushnell did not. Although himself an able theologian, and one who was des-

1. "A Discourse on Dogma and Spirit; or the True Reviving of Religion: Delivered Before the Porter Rhetorical Society, at Andover, September, 1848," *God in Christ* (Hartford, 1849), 279–317.

2. *Twentieth Anniversary: A Commemorative Discourse, Delivered in the North Church, of Hartford, May 22, 1853* (Hartford, 1853), 19–20. For a more extended discussion of the same subject, see Bushnell, "Spiritual Economy of Revivals of Religion," *Quarterly Christian Spectator*, X (1838), 131–48.

tined to spend exhausting labor on theological questions, he nonetheless saw little prospect that the true reviving of religion would result from the mere refinement and purification of Christian doctrine.

If, then, neither the revival of revivals nor the perfecting of theology would revitalize Christianity, what was the answer? The true answer, replied Bushnell, is "not to uproot opinions, not to stop the intellectual and scientific activity of the church, but simply to invert the relations of dogma and spirit, so as to subordinate everything in the nature of science and opinion to the spirit, and thus to elevate everything in the nature of science and opinion into the region of spirit and life." [3] In other words, both dogma and spirit are necessary, but the former must be the servant of the latter. This is merely to recognize the truth of the Bible, that it is the spirit alone which gives life. Hence Bushnell insisted "that a soul truly given up to Christ, filled with the spirit of Christ, is filled, in virtue of that fact, with a supernatural light; in other words, it is brought into such a close, interior union with the will and spirit of God that it is acted by God, filled with the consciousness of God and, by means of this pure inward experience, lighted up to know the meaning of things." [4] When the spirit thus immediately illuminates the souls of men, a genuine reviving of religion will once again take place in New England. This is the essence of the Andover address.

What did his fellow Congregationalists think of the address? Most of them were critical of it. In 1850 Edwards Amasa Park (1808–1900), of Andover Seminary, gave an address before the Congregational clergy of Massachusetts on "The Theology of the Intellect and That of the Feelings," in which he assessed the validity of Bushnell's main thesis.[5] Although he indicated some slight agreement with Bushnell, he rejected his main contention. "In all investigations for truth," said Park, "the intellect must be the authoritative power, employing the sensibilities as indices of right doctrine, but surveying and superintending them from its commanding position. It may be roughly compared to the pilot of a ship, who intelligently directs and turns the rudder, although himself and the entire vessel are also turned by it." [6] In effect, the intellect will first decide what is a true doctrine, and then the sensibilities will furnish the emotional steam to propagate it. As Bushnell demonstrated in an article published in 1869, the two men stood poles apart.[7]

3. *God in Christ*, 352.   4. *Christ in Theology* (Hartford, 1851), 336.
5. *Bibliotheca Sacra*, VII (1850), 533–69.   6. *Ibid.*, 545–46.
7. "Our Gospel a Gift to the Imagination," *Hours at Home*, X (December 1869), 166–67.

Enoch Pond (1791–1882), of Bangor Seminary, sharply denounced Bushnell's idea of immediate spiritual illumination, charging that it undermined faith in the inspiration of the Bible and encouraged "enthusiasm." He was astonished that Bushnell should have commended the mystics, when in fact mysticism and theology were "wholly incompatible." [8] Chauncey A. Goodrich (1790–1860), of Yale Divinity School, also professed to see real danger in his former pupil's theory of illumination, and he insinuated that in this respect Bushnell had aligned himself with Theodore Parker of Boston.[9]

These typical examples demonstrate how far the professed disciples of Jonathan Edwards had drifted from his doctrine of the divine light. Unquestionably Bushnell was on this score a more authentic representative of Edwards than were his critics.

❖   ❖   ❖   ❖

It is a hope, cherished by many of the most thoughtful and earnest Christians of our time, that God is preparing the introduction, at last, of some new religious era. Here and there, in distant places and opposing sects, in private individuals and public bodies of disciples, we note the appearance of a deep longing felt for some true renovation of the religious spirit. As yet, the feeling is indefinite, as probably it will be till its ideal, or the gift for which it sighs, begins to shape itself to view, under conditions of fact and actual manifestation. In some cases, expectation seems never to go beyond the reproduction of old scenes, familiarly known as revivals of religion, and the reviving of revivals is regarded as the only admissible, or highest possible hope to be entertained. But, more generally, there appears to be a different feeling. A degree of dissatisfaction is felt with benefits of a character so partial, so mixed with defect, and especially so little efficacious in producing the fruits of a deep and thoroughly established piety. Hence there is a secret hope, cherished by all such, that something may transpire of a different character and of far higher moment to the cause of God in the earth—something that will set us on a firmer ground of stability, produce a more acknowledged and visible Christian unity, and develop a more consistent, catholic, permanent, free, and living exhibition of the renovating power of Christ and his truth.

This is the subject which I now propose to discuss:—THE TRUE

8. Enoch Pond, *Review of Dr. Bushnell's "God in Christ"* (Bangor, 1849), 110.
9. *What Does Dr. Bushnell Mean?* (Hartford, 1849), 12–16.

REVIVING OF RELIGION. I meet you here as a body of Christian ministers and candidates for the ministry, proposing, not some theme of a merely occasional interest, but one that is dear above all others, I am persuaded, not to me only, but to the heart of God himself; therefore one which it is my pleasure to believe will be as much more welcome to you, as it is closer to Christian feeling and the practical reign of Christ in the earth.

I know not how to open the subject proposed, from a better point of view, than to begin where Christanity descends into the world — the point that is given us, for example, in —

> For the Life was manifested, and we have seen it, and bear witness, and show unto you that Eternal Life, which was with the Father, and was manifested unto us (1 Jn. 1:2).

Thus it was that Christianity fell into the world's bosom as a quickening power, as Life and Spirit from God. It came into a world dead in trespasses and sins to make it live again — this, also, by depositing in it and uniting to it, as a regenerative and organific power, the Life of God. At the time when it appeared, death and blindness had enveloped the national religion. A few souls, spiritually enlightened by God, lingered about the temple, waiting like Simeon and Anna the prophetess, for the Lord's appearing. In the desert wilds of the Jordan, and the caves of the south, there were also, possibly, a few pious eremites, similarly exercised in the things of the spirit. The religion of faith, that which infuses life, and brings a soul into the light and freedom of God, was, for the most part, a lost idea. The speculations of the Sadducees and the interpretations of the Pharisees had developed so much of human light, that the light of God in the soul was no longer wanted or thought of. Religion had been fairly interpreted away. Debates, traditions, opinions of doctors and rescripts of schools — in a word, such an immense mass had been accumulated of what an apostle calls *dogmas* (translated "ordinances") and also, "commandments and doctrines of men," that there was no longer any place for faith, and the light of faith in the world. The law was held as letter, and had thus no real power but to discourage and kill; for it was the manner of this Jewish theology and its masters or rabbis, to practice on words and syllables, trying what wondrous lights of opinion they could produce by their learned ingenuity, and studied thus, in the letter, and without spiritual illumination, or even a thought of it, Moses and the prophets had become so overlaid with school wisdom, and the rescripts of rabbis, that no true light of God was visible any longer. Spiritual life was extinct, and only a wearisome drill, under legal rites and fleshly burdens, remained.

Just here Christ makes his appearance, denouncing the Pharisees and their rabbis, that they open not, but rather shut the kingdom of heaven against men. Therefore he is obliged to separate himself from their doctrine and from all the learning of his day. It is so perverse, so fortified by numbers, by conceit and the respect of the nation, as to be even hopeless. Giving, therefore, the plain testimony of God against it — "In vain do they worship me, teaching for doctrines the commandments of men" — he turns to the uneducated, humble class of the people, and out of these he takes his apostles; simply because they are able, it would seem, to come into the knowledge of spiritual things, hindered by no learned preconceptions or commandments of men, and with minds ingenuously open to the spiritual teachings of God. The sublime doctrine of the kingdom, which is hid from the wise and prudent, and which no school wisdom, or wisdom of dogma, can ever apprehend, God will be able to reveal to these sons of obscurity, these ingenuous "babes" of Galilee. To them, therefore, he turns, making it his first object to attract their faith by his friendly ministries, and fix it on his person. He gives them to understand that he is such, and such the message he brings, that he can be truly apprehended only by faith — that, as the swine have no capacity to conceive the value of pearls, so the unbelieving of the world will never, out of their mere natural wisdom, receive and appreciate the Christian truth. He declares that he comes as the Life, comes to form a life-connection between the world and God; — "As the Father hath sent me, and I live by the Father, so he that eateth me, even he shall live by me. This is that bread that came down from heaven — he that eateth of this bread shall live forever." And then he goes on immediately, while his disciples are debating his words, to show that his doctrine is not for the flesh or for any mere speculative wisdom; that faith only can so far seize it or enter into it, as to produce it internally, and prove its heavenly verity; that it requires a congenial spirit co-existing or dawning in the soul with it, so that it may flow through the soul as spirit, nay, as God's own Spirit, and not be tried dialectically or scientifically, by mere natural cognitions and judgments — "It is the spirit that quickeneth, the flesh profiteth nothing; *the words that I speak unto you they are spirit and they are life.*"

This is the conception of Christianity, as held by Christ himself. And for this reason it was, as he well understood, that his disciples could get no sufficient apprehension of the Christian truth in his lifetime and while he was visibly present among them. Therefore it was expedient that he should go away from before their eyes, and a plan be adjusted for calling their simple faith into exercise. Accordingly, they were to wait at Jerusalem, after his departure, for the descent of the Spirit upon them, and he, taking the things of Christ and shewing them internally, that is, breathing an inspiration of Divine Life through their soul, to quicken them internally to a right apprehension of Christ and his work, would bring them into such a knowledge of the truth of Christ and the new scheme of salvation, that they would be ready to go forth and preach him to mankind.

They did as he commanded — the result is known. Suffice it to say that just there, Christianity is inaugurated as Life and Spirit in the world. There it bursts in as a gale of Life and a quickening power from God, and we see, in the preaching of Peter and in the whole scene which follows, that a new conception of Christ as the Prince of Life — his death and resurrection, his final exaltation and his present reigning power — is at this moment seized upon. Before Christianity had been dark to them, they knew not what to think of it; now it is light — they have it as spirit and life in their hearts. God, who commanded the light to shine out of darkness, hath shined in their hearts, to give the light of the knowledge of the glory of God, in the face of Jesus Christ.

Accordingly, the first age of the church, or of Christianity, which opens at this point, is to be distinguished as an age of life and intense spiritual vivacity. It is an age, not of dogmas or speculations, but of gifts, utterances, and mighty words, and, more than all, of inspiration, insight, freedom, and power. Looking back upon it as revealed in the New Testament, and in the first chapters of the subsequent history, this one thing appears, predominant above all others, that the church is alive — simple, inartificial, partially erratic, but always alive. He that was crucified and rose again, liveth visibly in them — not in their heads, but in their hearts. They have an unction of the Holy One that teaches and leads them. The preaching is testimony, publication, prophesying — not theology. The doctrine has no dialectic or scholastic distribution; it is free, out of the heart, a ministration of the Spirit. It is luminous by a divine light within; it streams through a character congenial to itself, taking its mold not from any discipline of theory or of rhetoric, but from a nature and working that God has visibly configured to himself. The effect is known to all. Incredible as it may seem, it is yet indisputable, a fact of history, that, within three centuries, the fire that is thus kindled, catches and spreads, till its light is seen and its sanctifying power is felt, throughout the Roman Empire.

Many speak of this event as a wonder. In one view it is. But something like it will always appear, when religion casts off the incrustations of dogma, and emerges into life. Christianity was, indeed, a new truth, but in nothing so new as in requiring faith of its disciples, insisting that they draw their light from God, and have it, not in their natural reason, but in and through a character that is itself newness of life. Considering the deadness of the religious element in his nation when our Lord came into it, and the utter imbecility of the rabbinic theories and ordinances, who could have imagined that a man crucified as a malefactor was to begin such a reviving of the religious spirit in the world that, within a few generations, he will have the imperial city of the earth under his power, princes and principalities owning his dominion and laying their gods at his feet? But it is done, and something like it will always be done, when men are brought close enough to God, to be separated from the law of their mere human opinions and judgments, and brought to receive their light from God as an inspiration, or internal realization of faith.

Observe, especially, as regards these first centuries of the faith, that it was a faith. They had no theology at all, in our modern sense of the term. Not even Paul, so much praised as the "dialectic" apostle, was anything of a system-maker, and I shall show you presently that if he had any theoretic system, the first and fundamental truth of it was, that spiritual things must be spiritually discerned. Accordingly, if we examine the history of these first ages, we find them speaking in the utmost simplicity of the Father, Son, and Holy Ghost, but having still, confessedly, no speculative theory or dogmatic scheme of trinity. The word, in fact, is not yet invented. When they speak of Christ, it is of Christ as the Life — Emanuel, Saviour, Redeemer, Son of Man and Son of God, crucified and risen, wisdom, righteousness, sanctification, and redemption. They had not begun, as yet, to busy themselves in setting forth the internal composition of Christ's person. They had no forensic theory of justification, made out in terms of the civil law, and defended by speculative and dialectic judgments — they only saw the law confirmed and sanctified by Christ's death, and a way thus opened to peace with God. They had no theory about regeneration, assigning the parts, determining the how much on one side and on the other, and settling the before and after, as between God's working and man's. They had the word of God in power, but not as yet in science — Christian dogmatics were yet to be invented. If you desire to see the form in which they summed up the Christian truth, you have it in what is called the Apostles' Creed. This beautiful compend was gradually prepared, or accumulated, in the age prior to theology; most of it, probably, in the time of the apostolic fathers. It is purely historic, a simple compendium of Christian fact, without a trace of what we sometimes call doctrine; that is, nothing is drawn out into speculative propositions, or propounded as a dogma, in terms of science.

Now begins a change. After Christianity as spirit and life, uttered in words of faith and sealed by the testimony of martyrs in every city, has taken possession of the world, it finds another class of rabbis, whom Christ never saw, viz., the rabbis of the Greek philosophy; and these begin to try their hand upon it. Some of the Christian teachers are disciples of the Greek learning, and the scientific instinct of the Greek schools begins to meditate the preparation of some new form, for the Christian truth, that shall finally establish its sway over the world of thought and learning. Thus begins theology. With it, of course, enters controversy, and controversy being wholly out of the Spirit and in the life of nature, whittles and splits the divine truth of the gospel, and shapes it into propositions dialectically nice and scientific, till, at last, the truth of Jesus vanishes, his triumphs are over, and his spirit even begins to die in the world.

The change that is to come is sufficiently indicated by a comparison of the Apostles' Creed and the Athanasian, or the Nicene. Passing from one to the other, we consciously descend from a realm of divine simplicity and life, into a subterranean region, where the smoke of human wisdom, hereafter to stifle the breath of religion, is just beginning to rise, and the feeble cant of dogmatism is trying its first rehearsal. In both, you hear the disciple saying, it is true, "I believe"; but in one, he believes the grand, living, life-giving history of Christ; in the other, he believes his own scientific wisdom concerning it — his mental cognitions, judgments, and theories. In one, the faith professed is truly a faith. In the other, it is only such faith as follows sight, or opinion, or scientific reason. The process of descent from the spirit into the flesh is easy, and goes on rapidly. That historical and vital Christianity, which Christ presented in his life, is replaced, ere long, by what some call a doctrinal; that is, by a Christianity made up of propositions and articles. The teachers think they are shedding great light upon the new religion, but we, looking back, perceive a dark age just there gathering in upon Christendom. Dogma has eclipsed the sun. Even the religion of Jesus itself begins to wear the look of a work of darkness. It is as if the discords of hell had broken loose. Councils are called against heretics, and against councils. Bishops levy arms one against another. Excommunications are dealt back and forth. Whole provinces are deluged with the blood of Christian persecution. Princes mingle in the confusion, as exterminators, or patronizers of one or another dogma. The freedom of the spirit and of faith is even ruled out of the church itself, and no disciple is allowed to have any light that comes of spiritual discernment, or even to think a thought which transcends the dogma of his time. Finally, as all bishops have exalted themselves above truth, the bishop of Rome exalts himself above the bishops, and assuming thus the headship of the church, the work, long ago begun, is complete — the church becomes a vast human fabric of forms, offices, institutions, and honors; a storehouse of subtleties and scholastic opinions, a den of base intrigues and mercenary crimes, as empty of charity and humanity as of Christian truth itself.

Here it is that Luther appears, bursting up through the incrustations of ages, to assert, once more, Faith, and the rights of faith — justification and salvation by faith in Jesus Christ. A great reformation and reviving of the religious spirit follows, which is felt throughout the Christian world, not excluding the Roman Catholic portions. Many supposed, and I believe still suppose, that Luther righted everything — that he even set the church back into her original position. Others have had a different impression, among whom I may instance our own immortal Robinson.[1] In the ever memorable address he gave to the Pilgrims on their departure to the new world, the prophet father of New England had grace given him to "bewail the condition of the reformed churches, in so soon having come to a period in religion," refusing to go beyond "the instruments of their reformation." "Luther and Calvin," he said, "were great and shining lights, in their times, yet they penetrated not into the whole counsel of God. I beseech you, be ready to receive whatever truth shall be made known to you from the written word of God." He was right in these convictions. Luther had made a good beginning, but only a beginning. He left so much undone that the church has not been able to hold the vitality he gave it; but, as if some element of fatal obstruction were still retained in its bosom, has been gradually sinking into such divisions and infirmities, such deadness to truth and faith and spirituality of life, that the truest friends of God, in every part of the Protestant world, burdened by a common sorrow, are sighing at this moment for some deeper renovation, some more thorough reviving of religion.

Luther left the church connected with the state, subject to the corrupt-

---

1. [ED.] John Robinson (1575–1625), English dissenter and Pilgrim pastor of the church at Leyden (Holland), from which a group came to America in 1620 and established Plymouth Colony, the first English settlement in New England.

ing influences of courts and of state patronage. Here we have advanced upon him already, and with every reason to rejoice in the results. But the greater and most fatal defect of Luther's reformation was that he left the reign of dogma or speculative theology untouched. He did not restore the ministration of the Spirit. Opinions were left to rule the church, with just as much of consequence as they had before. He delivered us from the pope and the councils, but that which made both pope and councils he saved, viz., the authority of human opinions and of mere speculative theology. The man of sin was removed, but the mystery of iniquity, out of which he was born, was kept. Opinions, speculations, scholastic and theologic formulas, were still regarded as the lights of religion. All judgments of men as apostate or unchristian continued, as before, to be determined by their opinions, not as Christ required, by their fruits or their character. Love, mercy, faith, a pure and holy life, was still left a subordinate thing — important, of course, but not the chief thing. Christianity remained in the hands of schools and doctors, and that was called the faith, here and there, which, here or there, was reasoned out as the veritable theologic dogma. Formulas still reigned over faith, as the pope had done before. The natural reason was the keeper of God's supernatural truth. Indeed, we may say that Aristotle was the doctor still of doctors, and that Christ was dispensed by the Peripatetic method. The unction of the Holy One was virtually subjected still to the scholastic sentences, and graduated under the predicaments.

In short, the second chapter of the first epistle to the Corinthians was really not restored, and has not been, in the true spirit of it, to this day. We managed, indeed, to say that the things that are freely given to us of God, in Jesus Christ, are spiritual, and can only be spiritually discerned; sometimes, also, that we speak not in the words man's wisdom teacheth, but which the Holy Ghost teacheth, comparing spiritual things with spiritual — we say this because we have it as one of our articles that what the scriptures affirm, must be held by us; but we do not really mean it in the apostolic sense. On the contrary, we judge as the schools judge, speak what the formulas tell us, and will not even tolerate the belief that God can ever lead a disciple to discern what is different from these. We do not really understand, as Paul here declares, that Christian truth can be *in* our soul only as it is *of* it, begotten there by the indwelling of Christ, and the private rehearsal of the Spirit. We suppose that learning and debate can master the Christian truths, and handle them as it can questions of grammar and archeology. We do not put our theology to school to faith, but our faith to school to theology. The head is to be made wise in formulas, and then the head is to take care of the heart. "Private *judg-ment*" is the word. The natural man receives the things of the Spirit of God, and he that is natural judgeth all things.

These things I affirm, not in a sense so literal as to imply that we are not Christians. Enough, doubtless, of divine truth leaks into our conceptions to save us, but not enough to feed the true apostolic devotion in our lives. We really have not, and cannot have, the ministration of the Spirit in its power. Four important and most deplorable consequences follow. (1) Endless divisions, subdivisions, schisms, denunciations, simply because we are living not in spiritual insight, not in our heart as united to Christ, but in our head; that is, in articles that are only opinions of the head. Not being in the ministration of the Spirit, which is unity, love, gentleness, and peace, and would thus melt us into a common circle, through a common brotherhood of character, we are in the ministration of opinion; that is, of formulas, schools, and doctors, who have many heads, and of course can make nothing but diversity and division. (2) We are unspiritual for the same reason. We do not expect to live momentarily under the immediate guidance of God. As we measure piety by formulas and opinions, and put religion itself under their keeping, so we expect most of the time to live in the life of nature. We only expect to relapse, or fall back a little into the dominion of the Spirit, on Sundays, and yet a little further when there is some special movement called a revival of religion. I desire not to be uncharitable, but it must be evident to all thoughtful observers that our modern piety, considering especially what works of beneficence we have on hand, is marvelously unspiritual. It has little depth or unction — no real intimacy with God; but an air of lightness and outsideness rather, as if it were wholly of ourselves, not a life of God in the soul. Even in the highest scenes we have of religious attention or excitement, there is a show of rawness and passion, as if we had more of ourselves in exercise than we know how to manage. Then, again, (3) this subjection to dogma is quite too visibly a subjection, not of ourselves only, but also of the Spirit in us. It is marvelous, that in the highest tides of spiritual exercise we know, our demonstrations are molded still so exactly by our formulas and those of our sect. Thus a Methodist revival will go on visibly in the method of Wesley; a Congregational under the Cambridge [2] or Saybrook platform.[3] In both, the Spirit

2. [ED.] The Cambridge Platform, or form of church government, was adopted in 1648 by a synod of the New England Congregational churches, meeting at Cambridge, Mass.

3. [ED.] The Saybrook Platform was adopted in 1708 by the Congregational churches of Connecticut.

will ere long give way, and Wesley and the platforms will be all that is left. These will be constant, the Spirit occasional; for to be in the Spirit is not our law, but to be in our school; and it will be this (not the Spirit) that will be accepted always to teach us the things that are freely given to us of God. Again, (4) note as another consequence of mischief the desolating sweep of skepticism, connected with the Protestant church, and moving in parallel lines with it. If religion is first of all a doctrine, a formula, something worked out by the school — then, of course, let the school work, and the doctors manufacture opinions as industriously as possible. Learning, logic, ingenuity, audacity, here is a field for all. Hence rationalism, filling the sky of Germany with darkness, and hiding the sun Luther once looked upon, so that it can scarcely be seen longer. And as the same causes have the same effects, so we are destined to experience the same shade of obscuration here, unless we can let go the reign of dogma and ascend into the life of the Spirit. Then we may dare, with Christ, to declare that our pearls are not for swine, and since we have them in our *heart*, reason can never rob us of the treasure. Natural reason is impotent against a Christianity that is spirit and life. But if the defenders of the gospel offer it first of all as a book of articles, it will not be strange if, when they have separated the Life, it is unable to live.

I bring you thus to the very point where we now are, and where Protestant Christendom is. And here I rejoice to find a great many of our truly Christian ministers and brethren questioning, sighing, praying for the reviving of revivals. Conscious of the mournfully low state of religion, the growth of worldliness, the want of godliness, the decay of ministerial force, and the afflicting signs of a delicate and earthly spirit in the ministry — afflicted by this, as every Christian heart properly should be, they lift their voices in the pulpit, on the platforms, and in the religious newspapers, calling upon us to arise and seek unto God for the renewing of those scenes of fervor and Christian power which they remember in former years. They see no hope, save in the restoration of those operations which have had effect heretofore. They reprove us for the delicate or fastidious spirit we manifest. They tell us, kindly, that God will not do things according to our tastes and fashions, that we must have protracted exercises, and not scruple to enlist evangelists, and set on foot those religious measures which the distinguished operators of former times found to be so effective.

I accept these remonstrances, with that respect which is due to the Christian anxieties in which they emanate, but they seem to propose a

remedy quite too slight for our disease. A mere reviving of revivals does
not reach our case, and I do not expect that they ever will be revived,
unless it be with such modifications of manner and spirit as to produce a
different class of manifestations, and fill a different place in the practical
dispensations of religion.

God never restores an old thing, or an old state. If he produces something that has resemblance to an old state, it will yet be different. If he
brings us up at last out of dogma, and sect, and mutual judgments of each
other, and worldly living, into the ministration of the Spirit, we shall not
be there as the apostles and first Christians were, but we shall carry up all
the wealth of our bitter exercise with us. We shall be men of the nineteenth century, not of the first — republicans, men of railroads and commerce, astronomers, chemists, geologists, and even rationalizers in the
highest degree; that is, men who have reason enough to discover the insufficiency of reason, the necessity of faith, and the certainty that a soul
must die into darkness when it is not in the life and light of God. Let us
not expect, then, that God will restore revivals just as we have seen them.
It is a dull patient that expects always to be cured by the same medicine.

And why is it that these revivals are so long discontinued? Have we not
some evidence, in this fact, that their force is spent? Has not such a conviction come upon us, in spite even of ourselves? Did we not see them go
down, by gradations, into lower forms of exercise, and show, both in the
means devised to carry them on, and also in their fruits, what we could
look upon only as signs of exhaustion?

Besides, they manifestly do not belong to a really ripe and true state of
Christian living, but rather to a lower state, which we ought even to hope
may, at last, be discontinued. They were throes, in one view, of disease;
just as God works a diseased body into health by intermittences of pain
or fever. If the church were to abide in the Spirit, as it certainly ought,
for the promise of the Comforter is that he shall abide with us, still I suppose there would be changing moods and varieties of exercise, though not
any such alternations as these — alternations between death and life, the
spirit and the flesh. I make no question that there will always be displayed in the church scenes of variety or diversified impulse, times of social movement and public exaltation, times of stillness and privacy, times
when the word preached will have its effect more in one direction or
more in another. We must not require that the demonstrations made in
religion shall even be unexceptionable; for when we come to that, and are
able to act without any symptom of disease, it will be proved that we no

longer want medication under any system of exercise. But have we no right to complain of these sharp alternations between vitality and utter deadness? Is it not plain that, under this kind of regimen, we are even instigating disease? Are not the fruits we realize too visibly diseased themselves, and is it not precisely this that we are now bewailing?

What, too, are we declaring by our very sighs, unless it be the fact that our revivals have brought us no such fruits of character, stability, and spirituality as we may reasonably desire and ought, for the honor of the gospel, to exhibit? Is it wrong to believe that even these sighs themselves are divinely instigated, and that rightly interpreted they are yearnings, produced in us, after some better gift which God is preparing to bestow? For what, possibly, has he allowed the long suspension which many are now deploring, but for this very purpose — to awaken in us higher thoughts and prepare us for a new Christian era? What, possibly, is he now offering, if only we are ready to receive it, but a grand inaugural of the Spirit throughout Christendom — an open day of life and love and spiritual brotherhood, in which our narrow confines of bigotry and prejudice shall be melted away, and all the members of Christ's body, holding visibly the Head, shall visibly own each other; shining in the light, revealing the spirit, co-operating in the works of Christ, and living for the common object of establishing his kingdom?

It is not for me to prophesy, nor do I pretend to publish the secrets of God. But I think I see, by signs which others may inspect as freely as I, that there is a gift waiting for the church, if only she had room to receive it. I can also see what most visibly we want. We want, as the great Robinson believed, "more light to break forth from God's holy word" — not from the formulas, or the catechisms, or the schools, or the doctors, but from God's holy word; and especially from those parts of the word which represent the Christian truth as spirit and life, attainable only as our heart and spirit are configured to it, and able to offer it that sympathy which is the first condition of understanding — attainable only by such as are in the Spirit themselves. This will bring a true reviving of religion — not sporadic manifestations of the Spirit here and there, now in one village or town, now in another; not *revivals*, possibly, in the plural, such as our friends and fathers stir us up to look for, apparently not observing that, in this plural word, they carry the implication that we are to look for successions here and there, in time as well as place, and, of course, that we set out with the expectation of resting ourselves by another relapse into deadness and sin when it is convenient. No, it will bring us what is

more and higher, an era of renovated faith, spreading from circle to circle
through the whole church of God on earth; the removal of divisions, the
smoothing away of asperities, the realization of love as a bond of perfect-
ness in all the saints. It will bring in such an era as many signs begin to
foretoken; for it comes to me publicly, as relating to bodies of Christian
ministers, and circles of believers in distant places, that they are longing
for some fuller manifestation of grace, and debating the possibility of another and holier order of Christian life. It comes to me also privately,
every few days, that ministers of God and Christian brethren, called to be
saints, having no concert but in God, are hungering and thirsting after
righteousness in a degree that is new to themselves, daring to hope and
believe that they may be filled, testifying joyfully that Christ is a more
complete Saviour, and the manifestation of God in the heart of faith, a
more intense reality than they had before conceived. Meantime, as we all
know, a feeling of fraternity is growing up silently, in distant parts of the
Christian world. Bigotry is tottering, rigidity growing flexible, and Christian hearts are yearning everywhere after a day of universal brotherhood
in Christ Jesus. These are the signs we have before us. It is in view of
these that we are to form our expectations; also, in part, that we are to
shape our plans and settle our Christian aims. Indeed, it is even a great
maxim of philosophy that when we see men wide asunder beginning to
take up the same thoughts and fall into the same sentiments, and that
without concert or communication, we are generally to believe that
something decisive, in that direction, is preparing; for it is the age that is
working in them, or the God rather, probably, of all ages; and accordingly, what engages so many at once is only the quickening in them of
that seed on whose stalk the future is to blossom.

Should we not, therefore, expect a gradual appearing of new life,
which years only can prepare? Shall we not even dare to spread our
Christian confidences by the measures of Providence, and in this manner
take up the hope that, when so many signs and yearnings meet in their
fulfillment, we may see a grand reviving of religion that shall be marked
by no village boundaries, no walls of sect or name, but shall penetrate,
vivify, and melt into brotherhood, at last, all who love our Lord Jesus
Christ on earth?

In this protracted statement I have set forth what I conceive to be our
position, both as related to the past and the future. If, as I have intimated,
results of so great consequence are hanging on the reduction or displace-

ment of dogma, it becomes my duty, in the next place, to verify that conviction. And in order to this, I must first of all endeavor to distinguish, as accurately as possible, the true idea of dogma.

The word *dogma* literally means an opinion, but it is almost uniformly understood to include something more, viz., an authoritative force. We see this element conspicuous in the word *dogmatize*, and it belongs historically to the word *dogma* itself. Thus it was anciently used to signify a decree, as when Caesar decreed the taxing. The epistle sent out to quiet the churches, by the council of the brethren at Jerusalem, was also called a dogma (Acts 16:4), where the term is used in a milder sense to denote a basis which had been agreed upon for the pacification of difficulties, and which it was hoped would be generally respected. Paul uses the word three times in his epistles, where it is translated "ordinances" — for example, when he speaks of "the law of commandments contained in ordinances" — the reference being, in this and the other cases, to that overgrowth of opinions, speculations, and religious rescripts, under which the doctrine of Moses had been hidden, and in sweeping which away Christ brought in, as we have seen already, a new era of religious freedom and power. When we speak of Christian dogmatics, or of dogmatic theology, we associate the same idea of authority in a little milder sense, understanding some scheme or system of religious opinion, propounded as a guide to others who are theologic pupils or Christian disciples. And when we come to the testing of Christian character, or to terms of fellowship, then it will be seen that our dogma, by whatever name we call it, is taken to be a fixed rule of authority to all who are concerned.

Two elements, then, as I conceive, enter into the notion of dogma: first an opinion, which is some decision of natural judgment, or some merely theologic conclusion; secondly the propounding or holding of that opinion as a rule to the opinions, the faith, or the Christian experience, whether of ourselves or of others.

It is also to be noted, in regard to the first-named element, the opinion that enters into dogma, that it holds a decided contrast with faith, heart, spirit, and life; which contrast also belongs, of course, to dogma.

An opinion is some result which is prepared out of the mere life of nature; some perception, cognition, or judgment that we produced out of our natural activity, as intelligent beings. But faith carries us above nature, into apprehensions that transcend the reach of mere natural judgments. Being that act in which a man passes off his own center, to rest himself practically in God, it unites the soul to him, and becomes, in that manner, an experience of him. In one view, faith is grounded in evidence; but it also creates evidence by the realizations it makes of spiritual things. Hence it is declared to be the evidence of things not seen, the substance or substantiator of things hoped for. It is in this way, more than by all opinions, that we are able to give reality to things invisible.

Opinion, too, is of the head; it is the knowledge gotten by thought and reflection. But there is also a knowledge of God and Christian truth which is of the heart; for a right sensibility is as truly perceptive as reason, and there are many truths, of the highest moment, that can never find us save as we offer a congenial sensibility to them. What is loftiest and most transcendent in the character of God, his purity, goodness, beauty, and gentleness, can never be sufficiently apprehended by mere intellect, or by any other power than a heart configured to these divine qualities. And the whole gospel of Christ is subject, in a great degree, to the same conditions. It requires a heart, a good, right-feeling heart, to receive so much of heart as God here opens to us. Indeed, the gospel is, in one view, a magnificent work of art, a manifestation of God which is to find the world, and move it, and change it, through the medium of expression. Hence it requires for an inlet, not reason or logic or a scientific power so much as a right sensibility. The true and only sufficient interpreter of it is an esthetic talent, viz., the talent of love, or a sensibility exalted and purified by love. The expression is made, in part, to mere natural feeling, such as is common to the race. Hence it has a power to work on man at his lowest point of character, and then, when his heart is engaged and propitiated by the secular charities of Jesus, it is to be transformed, regenerated, carried up into goodness, and there introduced to the higher revelations and knowledges of God, as set forth in his Divine Life. Then it knows him. Blessed are the pure in heart, for they shall see God. It is not by opinion but by love that we most truly know God. If any man love God, he is known of him. And he that loveth not, knoweth not God, for God is love.

Opinion, also, is dark and feeble in the contrast of spirit and inspiration. Christianity is called "spirit" partly because it can truly enter us and be apprehended by us only as we are in it and of it, and have its spirit in us. The letter cannot teach it, words cannot tell us what it is. We can never find it, or be found of it, till we come up out of questions and constructions, into the living spirit of Christ himself. It is also called "spirit," in part and perhaps chiefly, because it is received and receivable only through some concourse of God, or the Spirit of God. The human soul under sin, or considered simply as unreligious, is necessarily dark, because it is divorced from God, by whose inbeing it was made to have its light. It cannot make light by opinions gotten up in itself. Revolving God's idea, systematizing external cognitions, derived from his works, investigating the historic evidences of Christ, his life, his doctrine — busied in all such ways, it is rather creating darkness than light, until it receives God as an inner light, and knows him by that spiritual manifestation within, which Christ promised.

This great truth is continually present in the teachings of Christ and his apostles. If only Peter takes up the belief that he is the Messiah, the Saviour sees a discernment in him which is not of the man himself — a revelation. "Blessed art thou, Simon Bar-jonah; for flesh and blood hath not revealed it unto thee, but my Father, which is in heaven." Whenever his doctrine or parable is understood, he sees an inner light of God in that understanding. "Thou hast hid these things from the wise and prudent, and revealed them unto babes." In the same view, he promises the Comforter to his disciples, as an abiding teacher, who shall make what is now dark in respect to him, as viewed by their mere understanding, luminous and clear. They waited for him at Jerusalem according to their Master's direction, and there it would seem as if Christianity first dawned upon their conceptions. Just there, we may say, Christianity, which opinion could not reach, comes into sight, and Christ is known as the Redeemer and Saviour of the race — the Life of God manifested in the world.

Paul is continually setting forth Christianity, as a ministration of the Spirit, in the same way. It is no judgment of the flesh, it is no wisdom of this world, it is not the letter, but it is spirit and life — Christ dwelling in us. In the second chapter of his first epistle to the Corinthians, he is fuller and more definite than elsewhere, asserting the great and, as it seems to me, universal truth, that in order to be known by us, God must live in us. He does not mean to say that up to a certain time we are incapable of knowing God, or understanding Christ, and that then, being converted or having a new function communicated, we are ever after able to understand him. He only means to say that we never do in fact receive the true sense of Christianity save as we are spiritually illuminated, and in the degree of that illumination. Our theologians would have his true meaning, if they took his words as intended for themselves; to show them that they will have the knowledge of Christ not in debates alone, not in articles, systems, and opinions, such as they get up in the life of nature, but by the constant indwelling, rather, and teaching of God's own Spirit. Would to

God he might be thus received! and that we might all be able to say, with Paul, "Now we have received not the spirit of the world, but the spirit which is of God, that we might know the things that are freely given to us of God." If, ceasing to be merely natural, we become spiritual, in the true apostolic sense, we shall discern, I am sure, if not all things, many things that have as yet been hidden from us.

There is yet another remarkable contrast between opinion and life, which is seen in the fact that opinions may be written down, or retained in the memory, while the realizations of faith and love and spirit cease and disappear, as they themselves do, unable either to be retained in the memory, or to be recalled, in any manner, afterwards. Spiritual truth dies with spiritual life. It is vital, it is essential life in its own nature, and therefore must be kept alive as it began to live, by an inward and immediate connection with God. Perhaps I shall come nearest to an exact representation, if I say that spiritual truth is God himself, dwelling in the soul and manifested there. This, it seems to me, is the clear implication of John, when he represents the same truth just now asserted from Paul, under the figure of an unction. "Ye have an unction from the Holy One, and know all things — but the anointing which ye have received of him, abideth in you, and ye need not that any man teach you, but as the same anointing teacheth you of all things, and is truth, and is no lie, and even as it hath taught you, ye shall abide in him." Here the implication is that the knowledge will abide because the unction abides; therefore, no longer than the unction abides. And this, exactly, is the experience of every unfaithful disciple. His light perishes with his love. All his clear perceptions and vivid realizations of God depart, and cannot be recalled. Even the Scripture that was light, grows dark again. His opinions remain, but his soul, like a chamber shut up at noon, is forthwith darkened, as soon as the daylight of God is shut away.

It is thus made plain to us that the highest and only true realizations of God are effected, not through opinion, but through faith, right feeling, spirit, and life. With these, mere opinion holds a very clear and distinct contrast, and should manifestly occupy, under them, a very inferior place. Now opinion is one of the elements of dogma, and therefore dogma holds the same contrast, and should hold the same place. But the other element is authority, or a ruling power. Conceive opinion, then, exalted to become a rule to faith, to the perceptive power of love, to the teachings of the Spirit, and the realizations of the life — a measure, a guide, a standard, a rule of judgment, a test of character, a term of fellowship — then you have the proper conception of dogma. This, too, I conceive to be its proper meaning; also, in common use, its virtual meaning; and in this view, as it is found exalting itself above faith and the Spirit, it must, in reverence, be rejected.

I said its virtual meaning. Perhaps I ought to raise an express distinction here between its virtual and its conscious or intended meaning; for we certainly speak of scientific and dogmatic theology, when we have no thought of setting human speculations and opinions above the liberty of the Spirit and the light of faith, and when, in fact, we should heartily disclaim any such thought. Only it will generally turn out, after all, that we actually have it; for so deeply fixed is our traditional impression that systematic divinity, school theology, or whatever we call dogma, is to be the rule of our judgments and the guardian of our purity, that we never hesitate, in the church or in the council, to try all subjects of belief, practice, or character, by this standard — admitting no possibility that divine illumination may have assisted any disciple to transcend it, and really assuming that we want no such illumination ourselves, unless it be in the application of our dogma to the question in hand.

Were it not for this virtual assumption of authority in our school divinity, which makes it dogma, when really no such thing is thought of as the subjection of faith and spirit to the measures of opinion, it would be wholly unnecessary to take any stand as against dogma. Undoubtedly we have a right to investigate and form opinions in matters of religion, as in reference to all other subjects — a right, also, to assert and teach opinions — we only have not a right to make the life of nature and our natural judgments a law to the inspirations of faith and the realizations of God, in the hidden life of the Spirit. Manifestly, opinions, taken as mere actings of our intellectual nature, cannot compass matters of so high a quality. We cannot, by any mere phosphorescence of thought, throw out from within ourselves that daylight which our soul desires, and which, in the manifested radiance of God, it may ever have. Neither is that possible which is continually assumed without, apparently, even the suspicion of a doubt, that theology, taken as a work of analysis and speculative generalization, is competent to produce a body of judgments that will be a true and proper science of God. If there is ever to be anything produced here that can reasonably be called a science, it will more resemble an experience than the dry judgments and barren generalizations hitherto called theology. To have science of a matter is to know it, and there are many of the humblest babes of faith, in corners of obscurity here and there, who really know more, and have a truer science of God, than some who are most distinguished among the Christian doctors.

Besides, if we ever to have any sufficient or tolerable comprehensive theology, it can never be matured save through the medium of an esthetic elevation in the sensibilities of our souls, which only the closest possible union of the life to God can produce. For the Scriptures offer us the great truths of religion not in propositions and articles of systematic divinity. They only throw out in bold and living figures, often contrary or antagonistic in their forms, the truths to be communicated. Language is itself an instrument wholly incapable of anything more adequate. Therefore what we want, in the receiving of light from the scripture, is a living, ingenuous, patient, pure sensibility — a heart so quickened by the Spirit of God as to be even delicately perceptive of God's meaning in the readings and symbols he gives us. And then, having gotten the truth, we want modesty enough not to take our spiritual discernings into our natural judgment, to be shaped and manipulated there — modesty enough not to assume that we can go beyond the Scriptures, and body into science and fixed articles of divinity what they, for want of any sufficient medium, never attempted. So that, after all, our ripe comprehensive theology, when we find it, will be so convoluted with spirit, and so mixed with faith, that it will be as much a life, a holy breadth and catholicity of spirit, as a theory. It will be as far from possible representation in any of the niggard forms of abstract science, or the debated articles of school divinity, as can be conceived.

It is not my design, then, as you perceive, wholly to discard opinion, science, systematic theology, or even dogma in the best possible sense of the term. I would only set the judgments of the natural life in their proper place — or rather in a place that is not most improper; for, in proper truth, all the thinkings, judgments, analyzings, opinions, and the faculties by which they are wrought, should themselves be filled with the same quickening Spirit, and exalted by the same faith which animates the heart; with that, also, bathed in the radiance and indwelling light of God, so as to be themselves organs and vehicles of essential truth and life. Then every faculty is promoted, and the whole man becomes spirit, acting not as in mere nature, but as in the life of God; without eagerness, partiality, prejudice, or care — acting as in rest. And then it will be, not science stretching itself as before to compass the unimaginable and infinite worlds of faith, but science indeed, the quiet reading of God through the heart. The noise and commotion before made in the busy clatter of opinions,

ceases, and the tumult is heard no more. We dwell in the light, in the stillness, so to speak, of the light of God; for light is a silent element — all
vivacity, another name for motion, but silent.

But it is not in this highest, truest state of spiritual life and union to
God, that the gospel finds us. Our faith is imperfect, only initiated, possibly not even that; and since the world we live in, too, is full of false learning, corrupt opinion, and deceitful pretenses of knowledge, we must be
allowed to cultivate theology with what measures of grace we have, and
struggle up through our imperfect mixtures of natural judgment and spiritual discernment, into the full day of light and love. Though our theolo-
gies and opinions and supposed scientific conclusions, in as far as they are
of the mere life of nature, have no more of authority, and are no more
entitled to a Christian standing than our speculation in geology, they have
yet a far higher consequence, because they are related to matters of
graver import, and are sure to be connected with results of deeper consequence.

That I may produce a just impression of my subject, and deliver it of
any appearance of partiality or extravagance, let me enumerate here some
of the uses that are served by Christian theories, and the scientific forms
of truth elaborated by the Christian symbols and teachers.

In the first place, they have an immense pedagogic value. I mean by
this that, like the old system of Moses, they are schoolmasters to bring us
to Christ. Doubtless they often deserve, and with much greater emphasis,
to be called "beggarly elements," yet there are uses to be served by them
still. The world is not in the spirit, but in the life of nature. There it must
be met, and somewhat on its own level. If it were addressed only out of
the inner light, and in terms of the highest and purest Christian experience, it would be no better than if it were called in an unknown tongue.
But Christian theology comes to it with a view or theoretic outline of the
gospel which is itself made up, for the most part, speculatively, within the
life of nature. It enters into the thinking power, and begins a motion
there. If it is lame in itself, as all systems are, still it will have a value.
Probably it will have some connection with the age, and will set forth
Christ, in a scheme of thought that has some reference to the present
habit and want. In this way, Christianity gets into the mental system of
the world, and through that into the heart. A good scheme is far better
than a bad, but even a bad will be better than none at all; for if Christi-

anity were known and presented only from the point of highest spiritual experience, it would never find a place of contact; therefore, no place to begin its regenerative work. And yet there is more of the true light of Christ in one hour of highest communion with him, than the best scheme of theological opinions has ever been able to offer.

A similar and very important influence is exerted by the catechetic discipline of children, or their exercise in Christian doctrine. Here might seem at first view to be one place where dogma, in its proper sense of authority, is appropriate. But it will be found, after all, that the soul of a child will not be fastened to Christ by spikes of dogma driven by parental authority. The truest power of discipline is that which is most divine, the fragrance of a divine life filling the house. Still there is wanted a human view of Christ and his truth, a conception of principles, opinions, and to some extent of theoretic matter, which, if they are catechetically given, will work in the childish mind as moving powers of thought, and so as preparatives and grounds of a true Christian faith.

Secondly, there is an instinct of system in our nature, which must have its liberties and opportunities in religion as in all subjects. Our mind adheres to unity, demanding that all events and opinions shall conform to system and support, as a whole, what we sometimes call the unity of reason. Hence we are continually drawing our knowledges, consciously or unconsciously, toward unity; and if we succeed but poorly in our attempts, the little success we have comforts us, and our endeavor comforts us still more. Manifestly it is wholly impossible for us in the mere life of nature, and by force of opinion, to grasp the universe of religion, and mold it into the system of a science. Still, if only we set the world pulling at these high themes by guesses and yearnings after knowledge, they may possibly draw themselves up, at last, by God's help, into those higher realizations which are fitly called science. I suppose it has been generally observed that curiosity abates when faith enters, and that the instinct of system lulls in its activity as spiritual life quickens in the soul. And the reason seems to be that when it is connected thus with the life of God, and receives him in his power, it virtually receives all system — even the true system of God himself — and has it by a sense deeper than consciousness, or at least in a manner that is beyond definite conception. It has the sympathetic touch, if I may so speak, of all things, and blesses itself in the sense of a unity vaster than thought can reach. And it will be seen that, in this view, scientific theology stimulates the soul in reaching after God. It is the alphabet in which nature begins to stammer; which exercises and also exasperates her curious impulses, preparatory to a true knowledge of God in his fullness.

Thirdly, there is a value in scientific theology, considered as a speculative equipment, for meeting the assaults of unbelief, false learning, and skepticism. I am well aware of the unfruitfulness of mere polemic argumentations with infidels and skeptics. Few are the cases where such argumentations have produced conviction, and led to a hearty embrace of Christ. And yet there is an effect of inestimable value one remove farther off and more general, viz., in the impression produced that Christianity has something to say, that it can take its place on a level even with science, and stand scrutiny there, holding its ground invincibly against all opponents. Were it not for this, had it nothing to speak of but experiences and spiritualities, it would be disrespected by the uninitiated, as a scheme that begins and ends in unintelligible vagaries.

Fourthly, Christianity must be handled under forms of science and speculation, because in that manner only can it form a valid connection with truths of fact and philosophy. Christianity does not come into the world armed against all other knowledge, to destroy it. It claims, on the contrary, its right to possess and appropriate and melt into unity with itself, all other truth; for whatever truth there is in the universe belongs to the Lord of Christianity, and holds a real consistency, both with him and it. Therefore Christianity must open its bosom, bring its holy affinities into play, repel the false, attract the true, and gather to its poles all particles of knowledge and science, as the loadstone gathers the particles of iron. Hence Christianity fell into immediate contact with all human philosophies and opinions, and a process of attrition began, in which it was, at last, to wear itself into union with all real truth. The same process is now going on between Christianity and the revelations of science. Thus, for example, it was seriously apprehended that the modern doctrines of astronomy would make as great havoc of Christianity as they certainly did of many of the church dogmas. But the God of Calvary and of the firmament, the love of one and the grandeur of the other, are gradually melting into union. We have still immense masses of theologic rubbish on hand, which belong to the Ptolemaic system, hugh piles of assumption about angels that have never sinned and angels that have, about other worlds and the reach of Christ's atonement there, which were raised up, evidently, on the world when it was flat, and must ultimately disappear as we come into a more true sense of the astronomic universe. So also geology, opening to view new conceptions of the cosmogony of the universe, is destined gradually to assimilate with the Christian truth and become a part of it. For, as God is one, he is sure, at last, to be found in agreement with himself. And then we shall know the Christian truth as much more perfectly as we better conceive the truth of things. Science without will favor simplicity and rest within. As the idols of superstition or false science are displaced, as the range of intellection is broader and more clear, Christianity will better know her place, her office, and her nature. And if she has many times been corrupted and shackled by the false wisdom of man, she will emerge at last, in the strength and freedom of her youth, as much more at home in the broad universe of her Lord, as much readier to fulfill a mission of victory and grandeur, as she better knows herself and the orbit in which she moves.

Once more, considering that Christian character is imperfect, liable to the instigation of passion, to be overheated in the flesh and think it the inspiration of God, Christian theology and speculative activity are needed as providing checks and balances for the life, to save it from visionary flights, erratic fancies, and wild hallucinations. It was partly for the want, I suppose, of some such influence as this, that Papias, Tertullian, Irenæus, the sober Clement, even, and a large class of the early teachers ran into so many absurd and fanciful errors. The intellectual life needs to be kept in high action, else under pretense of living in the Spirit we are soon found living in our fancies and our passions — just as the kite rises gracefully and sleeps in equipoise on the upper air only in virtue of a pull upon the cord below; and if it be maintained that the cord only pulls downward, and not upward, it does yet hold the bosom of the paper voyager to the breeze, without which it would soon be pitching in disorderly motions to the ground. It appears, in other words, that we have two distinct methods of knowledge, a lower method in the life of nature, and a higher in the life of faith. Therefore we are not to set them in mutual opposition, as has generally been done heretofore, by the rationalists on one side, and the mystic on the other; but we are to assume that a healthy working of our religious nature is that which justifies uses, exercises, all. Regarding the realm of reason and the realm of faith as our two Houses of Assembly, we are to consider nothing as enacted into a law which has not been able to pass both houses. For if a man will reduce all religious truth to the molds and measures of the natural understanding, receiving nothing by faith which transcends the measures of the understanding, he acts, in fact, upon the assumption that he has no heart; and as he cannot perceive by the understanding what is perceivable only by the faith of the heart, he ignores all living truth, and becomes a skeptic or a rationalist. If, on the other hand, what power of reason or science he had is wholly disallowed and renounced, so as to operate a check no longer on the contemplations of faith, or assist in framing into order the announcements of feeling, then faith and feeling are become a land of dreams, and the man who began as a Christian ends as a mystic. Faith must learn to be the light of nature, nature to apply her cautions and constraining judgments. The heart and the head must be as two that walk together, never so truly agreed as when they agree to help each other.

Accordingly, it is one of the chief problems of Christianity to settle the true relationship of reason and faith, the truth of reason and the truth of the life; a great and truly magnificent problem, in the working of which all the past ages of the church have, under God, been engaged. To settle this, and bring us out at last into a true and healthy conception of the natural and the spiritual as related one to the other, seems to me to be the real burden of the past history of the church. For if the descent into dogma, of which I have spoken, has been a most sorrowful experience, which few will be able to deny — if it has even been a fall, answering, in one view, to the first fall of the race, still this experience, this fall, it were even wrong not to believe will at last turn out for the furtherance of the gospel. God suffers no barren experience — this will not be such. On the contrary, if we are to return, as I fervently hope, to the simple life-given truths of the first teachers, we must expect to go back enriched by this dark experience. Indeed, those eminent disciples who have risen up, here and there, to recall us to the simple, original truth of Christ, seem to me to have failed on this very account, that they have had no sufficient perception of the benefits to be received from this exercise of man upon the Christian truth. And so, beginning an unreasonable war upon the uses of reason, they have failed, of necessity. Contrary to this, it is my hope that God is about to bring us back to the original, simple age of spirit and life, and yet in such a way that we shall have our benefit in what we have suffered, and shall see that all the sorrows we have passed through, and the confusions we have wrought, were necessary, in a sense, to the complete intelligence and final establishment of the church.

LANGUAGE AND THEOLOGY [1]

EDITOR'S INTRODUCTION

When Bushnell published his three historic addresses, as given at Harvard, Yale, and Andover in 1848, he prefixed to them a lengthy essay on the nature of theological language. "If these views of language have been historically introductory to me," he observed, "it is hardly probable that others will enter fully into my position without any introduction at all." [2] Yet many of his critics paid scarcely any attention to the "preliminary dissertation." Most of those who did examine it pronounced it unsound and detrimental to the cause of Christianity.[3] In a ponderous sixty-page review of *God in Christ*, the editors of the *Christian Observatory* called the dissertation "the oddest feature" of that book.[4] After adding a few trivial remarks, they disdainfully dismissed it with the charge "that the drift of the whole is to bring logic into contempt" and "to make definitions useless." [5] According to David N. Lord, Bushnell's theory was "in every respect a complication of misconceptions and absurdities." [6] Charles Hodge of Princeton Seminary saw "nothing either new or objectionable" in the theory, but he accused the author of drawing extravagant conclusions from it.[7]

1. "Preliminary Dissertation on the Nature of Language, as Related to Thought and Spirit," *God in Christ* (Hartford, 1849), 12–50; 53–59; 62–63; 65–67; 69–84; 91–97.
2. *Ibid.*, 102.
3. For a judicious appraisal of Bushnell's linguistic theory in light of the major criticisms brought against it, see Donald A. Crosby, "Horace Bushnell's Theory of Language: A Historical and Philosophical Study" (unpublished Ph.D. dissertation, Columbia University, 1962), Chap. 7.
4. "Review [of] *God in Christ*," *Christian Observatory*, III (1849), 242.
5. *Ibid.*, 243.
6. "Dr. Bushnell's Dissertation on Language," *Theological and Literary Journal*, II (July 1849), 102.
7. "Bushnell's Discourses," *Biblical Repertory and Princeton Review*, XXI (1849), 265.

That is only a token of the criticism that greeted the dissertation on language. However, Bushnell did not surrender his linguistic theory. Barbara Cross remarked that Bushnell "did not construct his later works on his semantic theories," thus implying that he lost faith in the theory presented in the dissertation.[8] The evidence does not bear out her statement. In *Christ in Theology* (1851), Bushnell argued vigorously for the very same theory which he had maintained in all his previous writings.[9] In *The Vicarious Sacrifice* (1866), he reasserted it.[10] Finally, near the end of his life, in 1869, he defended it in a long article, entitled "Our Gospel a Gift to the Imagination." [11] Thus there is abundant evidence that Bushnell did not abandon his theory of language.

❖   ❖   ❖   ❖

I do not propose, in the dissertation that follows, to undertake a full investigation of language. I freely acknowledge my incompetence to any such undertaking. What I design is, principally, to speak of language as regards its significancy, or the power and capacity of its words, taken as vehicles of thought and of spiritual truth. What I may offer concerning other topics involved in the general subject, such as the origin of language; the phonology of words, or the reason why certain things are named by certain sounds, and not by others; letters and the written forms of words; laws of grammar; questions of ethnology, and the like; will be advanced in a purely incidental way, and with no other design than to make my theory of the *significance* of words more intelligible and clear. I cannot promise that I shall fall into no mistakes which the learned philologists and grammarians will detect, though I have little fear that they will discover any important error in what I advance, in regard to the philosophy of words, taken as *instruments of thought*, which is the particular subject under discussion.

To understand the precise power of words, or the true theory of their power, without some reference to their origin, will be difficult or impossible; for it is, in fact, the mode of their origin that reveals their power. And yet what we say of their power may be true, in general, if what we say of their origin should not hold in every particular.

It is undoubtedly true, as many have asserted, that human language is a

8. *Horace Bushnell, Minister to a Changing America* (Chicago, 1958), 113.
9. "Language and Doctrine," *Christ in Theology* (Hartford, 1851), 15–89.
10. *The Vicarious Sacrifice, Grounded in Principles of Universal Obligation* (New York, 1866), 455–60.
11. *Hours at Home*, X (December 1869), 159–72.

gift of God to the race, though not, I think, in the sense often contended for. It is by no means asserted, in the Scriptures to which they refer, that God himself pronounced the sounds, or vocal names, by which the objects of the world were represented, nor that he framed these names into a grammar. It is only implied in what is said that he first called into action the instinct of language in our father, by directing his mind to the objects round him, "to see what *he* would call them." He was himself, in this view, the occasional cause of the naming process; and considering the nature of the first man to have been originally framed for language he was the creative cause; still the man himself, in his own freedom, is the immediate, operative cause; the language produced is as truly a human, as a divine product. It is not only *for* the race, but it is also *of* the race — a human development, as truly as knowledge, or virtue, or the forms of the social state.

But, if we believe the Scriptures, there is far less depending on this particular history than many seem to suppose. For, in whatever manner the first language came into being, it is expressly declared, afterwards, to be in existence no longer. Thus when it is affirmed in the history of Babel and the dispersion, that God there confounded the language of the race, that they might "not understand" each other and might be "scattered abroad over the earth," it is plainly testified, howsoever the first language came into being, that it exists no longer. Accordingly, the attempt so eagerly prosecuted in former times, to ascertain what living language is descended from the first language, is really an attempt, under countenance of the Bible, to prove the Bible untrue. And so, when our modern ethnologists undertake, as they say, in behalf of the Scriptures to establish the unity of the human race by tracing all human languages to some common source, through a comparison of terms, or names, found in them all, they would seem to controvert the authority of the Scriptures by their argument quite as effectually as they sustain it. No fair construction can be given to the history of the dispersion, as recorded by Moses, without understanding him to affirm the virtual destruction of the one language of the race by a miracle. According to the representation given, they are here thrown back once more on their linguistic instincts; and we are to look for the development of new languages, radically distinct from each other, such as the free movement of small families or circles, instigated each by peculiar circumstances and causes, may produce. Nor have our ethnologists been able as yet, with all their supposed discoveries, to disprove at all the original distinctness of many of the existing languages.

Within certain circles of language, they seem to have a degree of success; but when they pass to certain larger circles — from the Indo-Germanic languages, for example, to the American or the Chinese — they find the matter offered to their theories wholly intractable and unreducible. So, I will even dare to prophesy, it always will be. I will also venture, with as much deference to the great learning of our investigators in this field as properly becomes one who is only a spectator of their works, to suggest the inquiry, whether it is not likely sometime to be discovered that the very mode of the argument hitherto used is involved in mistake. For if common terms are found sprinkled through many languages, and are taken to indicate a common origin in the languages where they are found, do not the diverse terms made use of as names of things in the same languages indicate quite as conclusively, and even more conclusively, the original distinctness of these languages? There would be common terms, of course, in languages radically distinct; such as have been conveyed by emigrations, wars, and the mixture of races; such as relate to objects, measures, numerals, and dates employed in the intercourse of commerce. On the other hand, it is impossible to conceive how different names for the same thing, and that a thing every day spoken of by every body, could have come into use after having once had the same name — how *oak* became *quercus*, for example, or *quercus*, *oak*; how *house* became *domus*; *cloud*, *nubes*; *light*, *lux*; or the contrary. What do such diversities indicate, in fact, and that on the broadest scale, but that sometime or other there have been distinct namings of things; or, what is nowise different, the existence of distinct original languages? It is often true, in the speculations of the philosophers and literati as in medicine and, I suppose I must add, in theology, that they go by a fashion. Have we no reason to anticipate that a contrary fashion will sometime come into vogue among them, and that we shall sometime find them arguing for original diversities of language as strenuously as now for the original unity of language? This, I judge, is the view, in fact, of Adelung,[1] and, in a less decided form, of William von Humboldt,[2] two of the most competent and most respected investigators in this field.

1. [ED.] Johann Christoph Adelung (1732–1806), German grammarian and philologist; author, *Grammatisch-Kritisches Wörterbuch der Hochdeutschen Mundart* (1774–86).

2. [ED.] Wilhelm von Humboldt (1767–1835), brilliant German philologist, whose monumental treatise was *Über die Kawisprache auf der Insel Java, nebst einer Einleitung über die Verschiedenheit des menschlichen Sprachbaues und ihren Einfluss auf die geistige Entwickelung des menschengeschlechts* (3 vols., 1836).

At the same time it cannot be pretended, by those who are most sanguine in the hope of sometime reducing all existing languages to a common origin or parentage, that the investigations hitherto made have yielded any definite token of success except within certain acknowledged limits of affinity. The fact that there are living languages between which no real affinity can be discovered, still exists in its integrity. And therefore we must either admit the existence of races originally distinct, or else we must refer these languages to the Scripture solution of a miracle.

And now the question rises, in what manner were these distinct languages produced? It is not a question about language in general, or some one language in particular, but about the languages. If we say that God, by direct pronunciation of words, taught man language, we must mean that he taught in this manner as many distinct languages as there are, else our solution is too narrow for the problem. And as probably no one will imagine that God has at any time pronounced to the different families of the race so many languages, we fall back, most naturally, upon the view just given of the formation of the first language, and take up the belief that all these different languages are so many free developments of the race; though all from God, in the sense that he has created in all human beings a certain free power of self-representation or expression, which is itself a distinct capacity for language, and, in one view, language itself.

Nor is there any so great impossibility or mystery in this matter of originating a language as many seem to suppose. I hope it will not offend the romantic or marveling propensity of my readers, if I affirm that a new language has been created and has perished, in Connecticut, within the present century. A very distinguished citizen, whose name is familiar to the country at large, himself a scholar and a keen philosophic observer, had a pair of twin boys, who were drawn to each other with such a mysterious and truly congenital fondness as to be totally occupied with each other, and thus to make little or no progress in learning the language of the family. Meantime, they were constantly talking with each other in a language constructed between them, which no one but themselves could understand. In this language they conversed at their plays as freely as men at their business, and in a manner that indicated the most perfect intelligence between them. At an early age one of them died; and with him died, never to be spoken again, what beyond any reason for doubt was the root of a new original diversity of human speech — a new tongue. Nor is there any reason to doubt that incipient and rudimental efforts of nature in this direction are often made, though in cases and modes that escape attention. Indeed, to believe that any two human beings, shut up wholly to each other, to live together until they are of a mature age, would not construct a language, is equivalent, in my estimation, to a denial of their proper humanity.

Let us trace the manner in a supposed experiment; for, in this way, the true conception of language as a human product, and also as a vehicle of thought, will be exhibited with more clearness and facility than in any other. The experiment can be made only in a small circle, as in a family, or between two or three individuals; for the sounds of a new language could never settle into a current use and significance where many persons, or a large community, are concerned; because they do not exist together in terms of sufficient closeness and mutuality to allow the growth of common uses. Perceiving this, even Caesar confessed his inability, with all the authority he had, to give currency to but a single word.

We suppose, then, two human persons to be thrown together, who as yet have never heard the use of words, and of course have no language. Considered simply as human, they have a certain ground or preparation in their very nature of speech. In one view, language is in them potentially beforehand, only it is not developed into actual existence; they are linguistic natures, so to speak, only it is not yet clear what kind of tongue they are going to create. This, in fact, is the opinion of Humboldt, and also of many of the most competent philologists. "Speech," he says, "according to my fullest conviction, must really be considered as inherent in man: language could not have been invented without its type pre-existing in man." [3] This being true, we are then to see it formed or developed afterward, and become a historical fact. As to the manner in which the process goes on, I find no conception of it given which is satisfactory, or which adequately explains a universal fact pertaining to the significance and power of language as an instrument of thought and spiritual expression.

There is no difficulty in perceiving how our two unlanguaged men will proceed, when thrown together in the manner supposed, as far as the naming of sensations or physical objects is concerned. For the object is always present as a mediator or interpreter between them, so that when a sound is uttered as a name for it, or in connection with it, they may always know to what the sound or name refers. Thus all sights, sounds, smells, tastes, and touches, or feelings, or what is the same, their objects,

3. [ED.] *Cf.* Humboldt, "Über das vergleichende Sprachstudiums [1822]," in *Deutscher Geist: Ein Lesebuch aus zwei Jahrhunderten*, Oskar Loerke, ed. (new enlarged ed., 1953), 367.

are easily named, and their names will come into currency without difficulty, when sounded as representatives of the objects. As to the sounds
adopted, they will generally be determined arbitrarily, or, at least, by
causes so occult or remote that we must regard them as arbitrary. There
may have been reasons why one says *tree*, and another *arbor;* one *rock,*
and another *saxum;* one *star*, and another *stella;* one *sun*, and another *sol;*
but if there are such reasons, they are too abstruse to be investigated.
Sometimes when *sounds* are the objects named, they will very naturally
be imitated; as in *hoarse* and *hiss*. Still, no theory of sound as connected
with sense in the names of things will be found to hold extensively
enough to give it any moment. In the languages radically distinct,
we shall find that the sounds or names which stand for the same objects
have generally no similarity whatever; whence it follows irresistibly
that nothing in the laws of voice or sound has determined the names
adopted.

We have now seen how our two language-makers will get on, in the
naming of things or physical objects. In this manner they will make out a
string of *nouns* or names, which may be called a noun-language. It will
comprise the names of all physical objects and demonstrations, including,
of course, the names of actions; for verbs, prior to the formation of
grammar, are only the nouns of actions. Thus far we have generated only
a physical language, or terms of physical import. And thus far, even, animals are capable of language: they can learn, though not as easily and on
as large a scale as we, to associate names or sounds with outward things
and actions.

There now remains to be formed another sphere of language, wholly
distinct, which the animals cannot learn, viz.: the language of intelligence;
that which, under an outward form, carries an inward sense, and so avails
to serve the uses of mind. It has been easy for our language-makers to
agree in the use of sounds standing for outward objects and acts, because
these outward objects and acts can be so fixed upon, or the mind so directed towards them, that a mutual understanding may be had in regard
to the object which it is designed to name, before the name to be adopted
is uttered. But if, now, one of them has a thought or emotion in his mind,
or wishes to speak of a spiritual being or world, this, it will be seen, is not
capable of being shown or pointed at, because it lies out of sense. The
thought or emotion cannot be taken out and exhibited to the eye: how,
then, can the two parties come to any such understanding as will enable
them to name it? Here is a difficulty, and it is the great difficulty to be

surmounted in the production of intellectual language. And if we are to understand the nature of language as an instrument of thought and spiritual truth, or to judge of its capacity for uses of this kind, it will be just here, in the solution of this difficulty relating to the genesis of language, that we shall get the desired key to its significance in such uses.

How, then, shall our experimenters proceed? Obviously they cannot advance at all save through the mediation of things; that is, of objects and acts in the sensible world, which may come in to their aid as signs of thought, or interpreters between them. It is only as there is a Logos in the outward world, answering to the logos or internal reason of the parties, that they can come into a mutual understanding in regard to any thought or spiritual state whatever. To use a more familiar expression, there is a vast analogy in things which prepares them, as forms, to be signs or figures of thoughts, and thus, bases or types of words. Our bodily mechanism, and the sensible world we live in, are in fact made up of words, to represent our thoughts and internal states; they only want naming, and then, passing into sound, to be re-produced or have their images called up by sounds, they drop out, so to speak, their gross material quality, and become words of spirit, or what the poet calls "winged words" — cursitating forms of life that fly out in sound upon the air, as interpreters and messengers of thought between the minds of men.

Thus, if the mind of one of our two strangers is laboring with any thought or emotion, he will strike at some image or figure in the sensible world that is itself a fit representation of his thought or emotion — a form prepared in nature to be its type. Turning the attention of the other party upon this image, and signifying by gesture, probably, that he is trying to mirror some internal state in it, he puts the other party on generating that internal state, or the conception of it. The image becomes, in fact, a common sign or conception of the same internal state — they understand each other. So that now the name, when it is sounded, will stand not merely as the name of the object or image physically taken, but the name, also, of that thought which it represented. And thus an intellectual word is generated.[4]

I do not mean by this to imply that our language-makers will be acting as philosophers in this process, reflecting on their own states, and then finding images to figure them, or stand as words for them. On the contrary, they will be struggling out into speech in the simplicity of children, guided not by reflection, but more by instinct. A very large share

4. [ED.] See Bushnell, Manuscript entitled "There is a Moral Governor" (May 1832), 4–6; Manuscript entitled "Revelation" (1839), 12–20.

of the signs by which they interpret their thoughts one to the other will consist of bodily gestures and actions — all as natural to the internal activity as a blush, or any flash of passion, to the inner state, represented and depicted by it in the face. For the body is a living logos, added to the soul to be its form, and play it forth into social understanding. It will also be found that a very large share of the words which represent our emotions and thoughts are in fact, as their etymology declares, derived from the psychological expressions or demonstrations made through the body. Or when thoughts and emotions are represented by figures drawn from the physical creation above us and around us, the principle is the same: it is not done artificially, but by the simple force of nature. The soul that is struggling to utter itself, flies to whatever signs and instruments it can find in the visible world, calling them in to act as interpreters, naming them at the same time, to stand ever after as interpreters in sound, when they are themselves out of sight.

It is hardly necessary to suggest that, when a physical object or action has gotten a name beforehand, in the noun-language of physics, our two experimenters will sometimes recall the name or word, using it now as a figure, in a secondary sense, to represent a thought or feeling. But here the process of manufacture, philosophically speaking, is the same. If the word becomes devoted to the secondary use, it will stand as in the cases above described — a name of some physical form or appearance, which form or appearance shadows forth a thought or truth of the mind — then, by use, the regular suggestive of that thought or truth, and its representative in the current utterances of speech.

We find, then, that every language contains two distinct departments: the physical department — that which provides names for things; and the intellectual department — that which provides names for thought and spirit. In the former, names are simple representatives of things, which even the animals may learn. In the latter, the names of things are used as representatives of thought, and cannot, therefore, be learned save by beings of intelligence — (*intus lego*) — that is, beings who read the inner sense, or receive the inner contents of words; beings in whom the Logos of the creation finds a correspondent logos, or reason, to receive and employ the types it offers, in their true power.

For the benefit of the mere English reader, who is wholly unexercised in subjects of this nature, it may be important to say that what is here advanced in theory is fully supported by reference to the actual history of our words. We cannot always, or in every instance, show what physical object or act lies named in our intellectual words to give them their power; though in a great majority of cases, the words carry their origin in their face; and where they do not, it is only to be supposed that the physical history of the word or name is lost.

Thus, the word *spirit* means, originally, *breath*, or air in motion; that being the symbol, in nature, of a power moving unseen.

The word *religion* is *re*, back, and *ligo*, to bind — the conception being that man is made to be free, but bound back in terms of obligation to his Maker.

In the same manner, *expectation* is a looking forth, and *hope* a reaching forth, in which we see how accurately the original physical meaning of the word governs and distinguishes the internal meaning; for we look out for (expect) the coming of things both good and bad, but reach after (hope for) only those that we desire.

In the same way we have *prefer*, to set before; *abstraction*, drawing apart; *reflection*, turning back; *obedience*, before-hearing, as when a servant stands before his master, listening to receive his commands; *glory*, brightness, *grace*, outward beauty or concinnity; *faith*, a tie or ligature; *right*, straight.

Or sometimes a word takes a historical origin. Thus, the word *sincerity* is supposed to be the same as *sine*, without, and *cera*, wax; the practice of the Roman potters being to rub wax into the flaws of their unsound vessels when they sent them to market. A sincere (without-wax) vessel was the same as a sound vessel, one that had no disguised flaw.

The English reader is to understand that all the terms in language which are devoted to spiritual and intellectual uses have a physical or outward sign underlying their import, as in the cases here named. Of this the scholar has never a doubt, although he cannot always, or in every instance, trace out the physical sign or base of the word, so as to be certain of it. All things out of sense get their names in language through signs and objects in sense that have some mysterious correspondence or analogy, by which they are prepared beforehand to serve as signs or vehicles of the spiritual things to be expressed.

But as yet we have no grammar; we have only nouns to represent the objects, physical and intellectual, about which we may wish to communicate. We have what Klaproth [5] calls, "the stuff or matter of language," and "grammar is to be the fashioning or form."

5. [ED.] Heinrich Julius Klaproth (1783–1835), orientalist; author, *Asia Polyglotta* (1823; with language atlas).

I do not say that grammar, or the framing of words into sentences, is to be a matter wholly subsequent in time; for we shall see, by and by, that the relations of things in space are such as must, by necessary consequence, give laws of grammar at last to the words by which they are named; and, of course, we are to suppose a rudimental tendency to grammar in the first efforts of speech. But this tendency will complete its aim, or produce a complete grammar, only under conditions of time and use.

Thus a *warm*, that is, a sensation of warmth, being always spoken of in connection with some object in which the warmth resides, will become an appendant word, or ad-jective.

Adverbs will be formed, out of original nouns or names of things, in a similar way.

Prepositions and conjunctions, though indicating no such fact to the mere English reader, are all originally names of things or actions, and are reduced to their present humble condition of servitude by the process which constructs a grammar. Thus the word *through*, and the word *door*, when traced historically, coalesce in the same origin. Nor could anything be more natural, in stringing nouns together before any precise grammar is formed, to speak of going *door* any wall or obstacle; which, if it were continued, would shortly make the word *door* into a preposition, as we actually see in the word *through*.

In the same way the preposition *by* is supposed to be the relic of a verb or noun of action which signified pressing close upon, or rubbing.

So the conjunction *if* is known to be the imperative mood of the verb *to give*, and is written in the old English, *gif*, with the particle *that* after it. "I will do this *gif that* (if) you will do the other."

In the same way it is discovered, to the satisfaction of Horne Tooke [6] and other philologists, that the conjunction *and* is the same as the imperative mood of *add*, or *an-add* (*on-add*) contracted. "Love and (*on-add*) truth."

It would carry me too far to go at large into illustrations of the process by which the original noun-words are wrought into grammar. My object in adducing these few examples is simply to indicate the manner of the process far enough to remove any suspicion of mistake in the conclusion at which we had before come, that all the terms of language are originally names of things or sensible appearances. As regards the connection of subject and predicate in sentences, or, what is the same, the grammatical

6. [ED.] Horne Tooke (1736–1812), English etymologist, who wrote *Diversions of Purley* (1786; expanded in 1798).

structure of sentences, it must suffice to say that verbs are orginally mere names of acts, or phenomena of action, not distinguished from what are called nouns, or names of things, until use settles them into place in propositions or forms of affirmation. A *shine* and a *run* are names of appearances, just as a *sun* and a *river* are names of appearances. And when these names are strung together, in the use, the *sun* and the *shine*, the *river* and the *run*, the idea of subject and predicate becomes associated, and the grammatical relation of subject and predicate is developed as a law of speech between them. I speak not here of the order of subject and predicate in sentences, for the order will differ in different languages. I only indicate the manner in which the relative qualities of subject and predicate are developed in language. Nature having them in her own bosom, existing there in real grammatical relation, not only gives us the words, but shows us how to frame them into propositions. And in the same way it will be observed, in the hints just given concerning other parts of speech or grammatic elements, that they really have their birth in the grammar of the world. The prepositions, for example, the *over*, the *under*, the *through*, the *by*, are all so many actual relations; and when the subjects and predicates are brought into speech, these come also with them. And then, when propositions are advanced which relate to thought or spirit, where in one view the *over*, the *under*, the *through*, the *by*, are totally irrelevant, thought and spirit not being under the laws of space, still there is a mysterious relation in these outward analogies of space to the workings of the mind, such that the external grammar of creation answers to the internal grammar of the soul, and becomes its vehicle.

As a further illustration of the same general view, I would refer the reader to a beautiful theory — if it should not, rather, be called discovery — of Professor Gibbs relating to case in grammar, or more particularly to "case in the Indo-Germanic languages." The exposition of this theory will be found in the *Christian Spectator*, Vol. IX.[7] Here it is shown that as words themselves, or the bases of words, are found in space, so they are declined or formed into grammar under the relations of space. Thus it is ascertained that there is one case which represents the *where* of a predicate, a second the *whence*, a third the *whither*, a fourth the *by*, or *through what place*. This, in regard to words taken in their most external and physical senses. And then, precisely as physical objects become types or bases of words having an intellectual significance, so, or

---

7. [ED.] Josiah W. Gibbs, "Historical and Critical View of Cases in the Indo-European Languages," *Quarterly Christian Spectator*, IX (1837), 109-34; 415-31.

in virtue of the same kind of analogy, the relations of space under which we find these objects, ascend with them to partake in their elevation, and shape their fitness to the uses of the mind. Thus, in the department of mind or spirit, four cases are found answering to the four just named, employed no longer to denote external relations but the internal relations of thought and action — an internal *where, whence, whither,* and *by* or *through what place.* Professor Gibbs does not undertake to verify these deductions, except in the particular families of languages under examination. Still, it is very obvious that such results in grammar do not take place apart from some inherent law or system pertaining either to mind or to outward space, or to one as related to the other. Indeed, it is impossible, with such a revelation before us, not to take up at once the sublime conviction just now named, that grammar itself is in some sense of the outer world — in the same way as the terms or names out of which language is constructed. In this view, which it is not rash to believe will sometime be fully established, the outer world is seen to be a vast menstruum of thought or intelligence. There is a logos in the forms of things, by which they are prepared to serve as types or images of what is inmost in our souls; and then there is a logos also of construction in the relations of space, the position, qualities, connections, and predicates of things, by which they are framed into grammar. In one word, the outer world, which envelops our being, is itself language, the power of all language. Day unto day uttereth speech, and night unto night showeth knowledge; there is no speech nor language where their voice is not heard — their line is gone out through all the earth, and their words to the end of the world.

And if the outer world is the vast dictionary and grammar of thought we speak of, then it is also itself an organ throughout of Intelligence. Whose intelligence? By this question we are set directly confronting God, the universal Author, no more to hunt for him by curious arguments and subtle deductions, if haply we may find him; but he stands EXPRESSED every where, so that, turn whichsoever way we please, we behold the outlooking of his intelligence.[8] No series of Bridgewater treatises,[9] piled even to the moon, could give a proof of God so immediate, complete, and conclusive.

8. [ED.] See Bushnell, "Revelation," 29–32.

9. [ED.] Francis Henry Egerton (1756–1829), Earl of Bridgewater, left eight thousand pounds to the Royal Society to be used in promoting studies in religious apologetics. The resulting works were known as the Bridgewater treatises, eight of them appearing between 1833 and 1840.

In such a view of the world, too, and its objects, there is an amazing fund of inspiration elsewhere not to be found. The holding of such a view is, in fact, sufficient of itself to change a man's intellectual capacities and destiny; for it sets him always in the presence of divine thoughts and meanings; makes even the words he utters luminous of Divinity, and to the same extent, subjects of love and reverence.

The Christian public of our country are well aware that the very distinguished scholar whose theory of "Case" I just now cited, has never been celebrated as a rhapsodist, or enthusiast; and I know not any stronger proof, therefore, of the inspiring force derivable from a full insight of this subject, than when he breaks out in the midst of a dry grammatical analysis, in the following truly eloquent paragraph: —

> There can be no exercise, in the whole business of instruction, more useful to the mind, than the analysis of sentences, in the concentrated light of grammar and logic. It brings one into the sanctuary of human thought. All else is but standing in the outer court. He who is without, may, indeed, offer incense; but he who penetrates within, worships and adores. It is here that the man of science, trained to close thought and clear vision, surveys the various objects of his study with a more expanded view, and a more discriminative mind. It is here that the interpreter, accustomed to the force and freshness of natural language, is prepared to explain God's revealed Word with more power and accuracy. It is here that the orator learns to wield, with a heavier arm, the weapons of his warfare. It is here that every one who loves to think beholds the deep things of the human spirit, and learns to regard with holy reverence the sacred symbols of human thought.[10]

This paragraph, taken in connection with the illustrations of the article just referred to, has the inspiring force even of a lyric. Rightly spoken is it, when language is represented thus, as a "sanctuary of thought." For in what do we utter outselves, what are the words and the grammar in which we speak, but instruments of a divine import and structure? Such a discovery, received in its true moment, were enough to make a thoughtful Christian stand in awe, even of his own words.

We have now seen in what manner our two language-makers will proceed to construct a tongue. It is not my intention to say that the process will go on in the exact order here described — first, physical terms; second, intellectual; third, a grammar. The several departments of the work

10. [ED.] Gibbs, "Historical and Critical View of Cases in the Indo-European Languages," *Quarterly Christian Spectator*, IX, 120.

will be going on together, under the guidance of the Word or divine Logos, in the forms, images, activities, and relations of the outward world. For he is in the world, and the world was made by him, though it knows him not. It speaks in words he gave, and under a grammar that he appointed, and yet it knows him not.

I have suggested the fact that a very large share of our intellectual words are based on bodily gestures and demonstrations. I know of no method in which I can better indicate the simple, instinctive, inartificial process of word-making and grammar-making, than by calling upon the reader to conceive a human person charged with thought and passion — many thoughts and many passions — uttering himself instinctively by the voice, and at the same time by pantomime, indigitation of symbols, and changes of look. The voice will attend or follow the action, naming off its demonstrations as bases of words; the action will supply and interpret the voice; or pointing to signs in the inanimate world adjacent, summon these to act as interpreters, and become bases of words; and then, as all this transpires in space, the laws of space will be making a grammar for the words, and determining their law. The resulting tongue will represent, of course, both the man's own liberty and the world in which he moves. And then, as one or more persons beside must be concerned, at the same time, the process will be doubled or trebled; and between so many forces all concurring, a tongue or language will at last be matured that will represent the parties, their instincts, characters, and temperaments; all the circumstances and accidents, too, of the outward state.

If it be objected to this view that some existing languages have no grammar, being nothing but a collection of monosyllabic names or sounds, I must be permitted to doubt whether any such language exists. It may be that no laws of inflection, or conjugation, or even of composition, have yet been discovered in the Chinese language, for example; nevertheless it must be clear that some law of relation, some condition of subject and predicate pertains to that tongue, more exact than to have the words somewhere in the Chinese empire, and that law or condition, whatever it be, is in fact a grammar. And it will also be found, when philosophically investigated, that this Chinese grammar, whatever it may be, really represents the great universal grammar of the soul and the creation.

How far the views of language here offered coincide with theories advanced by distinguished modern philologists, I am scarcely able to say. They may have been wholly anticipated, or they may be already exploded. It would be singular, if the scholars who are spending their lives in philological studies, should not detect some mistakes or crudities in my illustrations.

The very distinguished scholar, Frederic Schlegel,[11] if I rightly conceive his theory, traces not merely the forms or bases of words to the creative Logos, but also the names or vocal sounds themselves. Thus he speaks of "words which in the unsearchable interior of Deity are spoken, where, as in holy song expressed, depth calleth unto depth." Descending, then, to the account of language given in the second chapter of Genesis, he receives it as teaching that God gave to Adam, literally and vocally, the rudiments of speech. "But," he adds, "under this simple sense there lieth, as does through all that book of twofold import, another and far deeper signification. The name of any thing or living being, *as it is called in God,* and designated from eternity, holds in itself the essential idea of its innermost being, the key of its existence, the deciding power of its being or not being; and so it is used, in sacred speech, where it is, moreover, in a holier or higher sense, united to the idea of the Word. According to this deeper sense and understanding, it is in that narration shown and signified that, together with speech, entrusted, communicated, and delivered immediately by God to man, and through it, he was installed as the ruler and king of nature."

But, unfortunately, this very transcendental theory will account for but one language, and we certainly know that there are more than one. Besides, what reasonable man can suppose that "names" taken as vocal sounds "are called in God," and that the discourse of divine thought is transacted by means of internal pronunciations? How plain is it, also, that "the name of anything holds in itself, the essential idea of its innermost being," and becomes "united to the idea of the Word," not as a sound, but simply as having in the sound, or named by the sound, a physical type or base which is the real supporter and law of its meaning, and the reason of its connection with the Logos. In other words, the truth is here inverted by Schlegel; what he supposes to be from the name, is plainly communicated to the name.

Some of the Germans are endeavoring, in general coincidence with the scheme of Schlegel, to elaborate a theory of names, taken as sounds, by which they will be seen to represent the most interior qualities of the ob-

11. Frederick von Schlegel (1772–1829) was an early German Sanscrit scholar, also philologist. With his brother, August Wilhelm, he founded the literary journal *Athenaeum,* which became the medium of the Romantic school of writers. Among other works, he wrote *Von der Sprache und Weisheit der Indier* (1808), and *Philosophie der Geschichte* (2 vols., 1829).

jects named. They go into philosophic experiments on sounds, and find reason, as they think, to believe that all objects express their true nature by means of the vibrations they impart to the air — that is by their sound. That precise sound, accordingly, is their name in language. This most subtle and beautiful theory, however, will be seen at a glance to have no real countenance in facts. What endless varieties of name or vocal sound are employed in the different languages of the world, to signify the same objects! How, then, do these vocal sounds represent the interior nature, or proceed from the interior nature, of their objects? Indeed, where the objects named are themselves sounds, the names have yet, in most cases, no agreement whatever. Thunder, for example, is the same sound the world over, and it is such a sound as we might imagine would almost certainly be imitated in the name given it. And yet, if we turn only to the American families of language, we are surprised to find that thunder is called, in the Chickasaw, *elloha;* in the Creek, *tenitka;* in the Huron, *inon;* in the Cadoes, *deshinin;* in the Nootka, *tuta.* Before such facts, filling, I may say, the whole domain of language, all theories about the representative nature of names, taken as sounds, would seem to be idle in the last degree.

Mr. Locke presents a view of language which, if we regard the mere words in which it is given, would seem even to be identical with that which I have advanced. He says, —

> *It may also lead us a little towards the original of all our notions and knowledge,* if we remark how great a dependence our words have on common sensible ideas; and how those which are made use of to stand for actions and notions, quite removed from sense, have their rise from thence, and from obvious sensible ideas are transferred to more abstruse significations, and made to stand for ideas that come not under the cognizance of our senses, *e.g.* to imagine, apprehend, comprehend, adhere, conceive, instill, disgust, disturbance, tranquillity, &c., are all words taken from the operations of sensible things, and applied to certain modes of thinking. Spirit, in its primary signification, is breath; angel, a messenger; and I doubt not but, if we could trace them to their sources, we should find in all languages the names which stand for things that fall not under our senses, to have had their rise from sensible ideas. By which we may give some guess what kind of notions they were, *and whence derived, which filled their minds who were the first beginners of languages;* and how nature, even in the naming of things, unawares suggested to men the *originals and principals of all their knowledge;* whilst to give names which might make known to others any operations they felt in themselves, or any other ideas that come not under the cognizance of

the senses, they were fain to borrow words from ordinary known ideas of sensation; by that means to make others the more easily to conceive those operations they experimented in themselves, which made no outward appearance.[12]

It is remarkable that while Mr. Locke seems even to set forth, in these terms, the precise theory of language I have given, he is yet seen really to hold it in no one of its important consequences. He even denies, shortly after, that there is any "natural connection between words and ideas," and declares that the significance of words is given "by a perfectly arbitrary imposition" — as if there were no analogy whatever between the bases or types of words and the thoughts they are seized upon to represent. Doubtless the true solution of this mixture of light and obscurity in his notions of language is to be found in the fact that he was too much occupied with his theory of knowledge as derived from sensation, really to notice the true import and scope of his own suggestions. This also seems to be indicated as a fact, by the clauses I have placed in italics.

The late Dr. Rauch, in his work on "Psychology," gives an account of language that is sufficiently acute, and is generally coincident with the view here advanced. On the particular point, however, which is labored in this article, the significance of language, he is less satisfactory; coming, in fact, to no results that are of any great practical moment in determining the true method of moral and religious inquiry. He grounds the possibility of language on the "identity" of reason and nature, not on the *analogy* or outward analogical relation of the latter to the former.[13] And that he has not mistaken his English word, as some might imagine, appears, I think, from the important fact that he makes no distinction between the terms of mere sense, and terms of thought or intellectual significance. Nature appears, in his view, to be counterpart to reason, in such a sense that the names of sensation and the names of thoughts, or intellectual states, fall into the same category, to be interpreted by the same law. Whereas, if there be any importance in the view I would present, it consists in showing that all terms of intellect or spirit come under a wholly different law, both as regards their origin and their interpretation, from the terms of sense or the mere names of things. This will appear more fully in the illustrations that follow.

---

12. [ED.] John Locke, *An Essay Concerning Human Understanding*, 24th ed. (2 vols., London, 1824), I, Book III, Chap. 1, § 5.

13. [ED.] Frederick A. Rauch, *Psychology; or, a View of the Human Soul*, 3d ed. (New York, 1844), 256.

We pass now to the application of these views of language, or the power they are entitled to have, in matters of moral and religious inquiry and especially in Christian theology.

There are, as we discover, two languages, in fact, in every language. Or perhaps I shall be understood more exactly if I say that there are, in every human tongue, two distinct departments. First, there is a literal department, in which sounds are provided as names for physical objects and appearances. Secondly, there is a department of analogy or figure, where physical objects and appearances are named as images of thought or spirit, and the words get their power, as words of thought, through the physical images received into them. Thus, if I speak of my *pen*, I use a word in the first department of language, uttering a sound which stands for the instrument with which I write. But if I speak of the *spirit* of a man, or the *sincerity* of a Christian, I use words that belong to the second department of language, where the sounds do not stand for the mental ideas as being names directly applied to *them*, but represent, rather, certain images in the physical state, which are the natural figures or analogies of those mental ideas. How it was necessary, in the genesis of language, that it should fall into this twofold distribution, has been shown already. The man who knows his tongue only by vernacular usage is aware of no such distribution. Many who are considered to be educated persons, and are truly so, are but half aware of it. At least, they notice only now and then, when speaking of matters pertaining to thought and spirit, that a word brought into use has a physical image in it. For example, when speaking of a good man's *heart*, they observe that the word has a physical image connected with it, or that it names also a vital organ of the body. Then they either say that the word has two meanings, a physical and a spiritual, not observing any law of order or connection by which the physical becomes the basis or type of the spiritual; or they raise a distinction between what they call the *literal* and *figurative* uses of the word. But this distinction of literal and figurative, it does not appear to be noticed, even by philologists, runs through the very body of the language itself, making two departments; one that comprises the terms of sensation, and the other the terms of thought. They notice, in the historical investigation of words, that they are turning up all the while a subsoil of physical bases; and, though they cannot find in every particular case the physical term on which the word is built, they attain to a conviction that every word has a physical root, if only it could be found; and still the natural necessity that all words relating to thought and spirit should be figures, and as such get their significance, they do not state. They still retain the impression that some of the terms of thought are literal, and some figurative.

This is the manner of the theologians. They assume that there is a literal terminology in religion as well as a figurative (as doubtless there is, in reference to matters of outward fact and history, but nowhere else), and then it is only a part of the same mistake to accept words not as signs or images, but as absolute measures and equivalents of truth; and so to run themselves by their argumentations, with a perfectly unsuspecting confidence, into whatever conclusions the *logical forms* of the words will carry them. Hence, in great part, the distractions, the infinite multiplications of opinion, the errors and sects and strifes of the Christian world. We can never come into a settled consent in the truth, until we better understand the nature, capacities, and incapacities of language as a vehicle of truth.

In order, now, that I may excite our younger theologians especially to a new investigation of this subject, as being fundamental, in fact, to the right understanding of religious truth, I will dismiss the free form of dissertation, and set forth under numerical indications a series of points or positions inviting each their attention, and likely, though with some modifications, perhaps, to be finally verified.

1. Words of thought and spirit are possible in language only in virtue of the fact that there are forms provided in the world of sense, which are cognate to the mind, and fitted, by reason of some hidden analogy, to represent or express its interior sentiments and thoughts.

2. Words of thought and spirit are, in fact, names of such forms or images existing in the outward or physical state.

3. When we investigate the relation of the form, or etymological base, in any word of thought or spirit, to the idea expressed, we are able to say (negatively) that the idea or thought has no such form, or shape, or sensible quality, as the word has. If I speak of *right* (*straight, rectus*), it is not because the internal law of the conscience, named by this word, has any straightness or lineal quality whatever. Or if I speak of *sin, peccatum,* ἁμαρτία, where in so many languages, as I might also show in a great variety of others, the image at the root of the word is one of lineal divarication (as when an arrow is shot at the mark, and misses or turns aside), it is not because sin, as a moral state of being or a moral act, has any lineal form in the mind. Thoughts, ideas, mental states, we cannot suppose have any geometric form, any color, dimensions, or sensible qualities whatever.

4. We can also say (positively), in reference to the same subject, that

there is always some reason in every form or image made use of, why it should be used; some analogic property or quality which we feel instinctively, but which wholly transcends speculative inquiry. If there is no lineal straightness in rectitude, no linear crookedness or divarication in sin, taken as an internal state, still it is the instinct of our nature to feel some sense of correspondence between these images and the states they represent. . . .

Here we come to our limit. All we can say is that by a mystery transcending in any case our comprehension, the divine Logos, who is in the world, weaves into nature types or images that have an inscrutable relation to mind and thought. On the one hand is form; on the other is the formless. The former represents, and is somehow fellow to, the other; how, we cannot discover. And the more we ponder this mystery, the closer we bring it to our understanding, the more perfectly inscrutable will it appear. If we say that the forms of the reason answer to the forms of nature and the outward life, that is true; but then there are no forms in the reason, save by a figure of speech, and the difficulty still remains.

5. There are no words, in the physical department of language, that are exact representatives of particular physical things. For whether we take the theory of the nominalists or the realists, the words are, in fact and practically, names only of genera, not of individuals or species. To be even still more exact, they represent only certain sensations of sight, touch, taste, smell, hearing — one or all. Hence the opportunity in language for endless mistakes and false reasonings in reference to matters purely physical. This subject was labored some years ago with much acuteness and industry by one of our countrymen, Mr. Johnson, in a "Treatise on Language, or the Relations of Words to Things." [14] The latter part of his title, however, is all that is justified; for to language in its more comprehensive sense, as a vehicle of spirit, thought, sentiment, he appears to have scarcely directed his inquiries.[15]

6. It follows that as physical terms are never exact, being only names of genera, much less have we any terms in the spiritual department of language that are exact representatives of thought. For, first, the word here

14. [ED.] Alexander Bryan Johnson, *A Treatise on Language: or the Relation which Words Bear to Things* (New York, 1836). Republished as *Alexander Bryan Johnson's A Treatise on Language*, edited, with a critical essay on his philosophy of language, by David Rynin (University of California Press, Berkeley, 1947).

15. [ED.] "Bushnell is in partial error," said David Rynin, "for Johnson deals at length with language as a vehicle of thought, . . . but his judgment is correct so far as language as a vehicle of spirit and sentiment is concerned, whatever is to be understood by that" (*ibid.*, 357).

used will be the name only of a genus of physical images. Then, secondly, it will have been applied over to signify a genus of thoughts or sentiments. And now, thirdly, in a particular case it is drawn out to signify a specific thought or sentiment which, of course, will have qualities or incidents peculiar to itself. What, now, can steer a word through so many ambiguities and complications, and give it an exact and determinate meaning in the particular use it is applied to serve? Suppose, for example, one desires to speak of the *bitterness* displayed by another on some given occasion. In the first place, this word *bitterness*, taken physically, describes not a particular sensation common to all men, but a genus of sensations; and as some persons have even a taste for bitter things, it is impossible that the word, taken physically, should not have an endless variety of significations, ranging between disgust and a positive relish or pleasure. If, now, it be taken as the base or type of an intellectual word, it will carry with it, of necessity, as great a variety of associations; associations so unlike that it will be impossible to clothe it with the same precise import, as a word of sentiment. Then, secondly, men are so different, even good and true men, in their personal temperament, their modes of feeling, reasoning, and judging, that moral bitterness, in its generic sense, will not be a state or exercise of the same precise quality in their minds. Some persons will take as bitterness in general what others will only look upon as faithfulness, or just indignation. And, then, thirdly, in the particular case to which the word is to be applied, different views and judgments will be formed of the man, his provocations, circumstances, duties, and the real import of his words and actions. Accordingly, as one declares that he was bitter, another will receive the declaration as no better than a real slander. And so it must of necessity be. It is impossible so to settle the meaning of this word *bitterness*, as to produce any exact unity of apprehension under it. And the same is true of the great mass of words employed in moral and spiritual uses — such as love, gentleness, contentment, patience, wisdom, justice, order, pride, charity. We think we have the same ideas in them, or rather (which is more likely) we think nothing about it; but we find continually that when we come to particular uses, we fall into disagreements, often into protracted and serious controversies; and whether it be said that the controversy is about words or things, it is always a controversy about the real applicability of words.

What, then, it may be asked, is the real and legitimate use of words when applied to moral subjects? for we cannot dispense with them, and it is uncomfortable to hold them in universal skepticism, as being only instruments of error. Words, then, I answer, are legitimately used as the signs of thoughts to be expressed. They do not literally convey or pass over a thought out of one mind into another, as we commonly speak of doing. They are only hints, or images, held up before the mind of another, to put *him* on generating or reproducing the same thought; which he can do only as he has the same personal contents, or the generative power out of which to bring the thought required. Hence there will be different measures of understanding or misunderstanding, according to the capacity or incapacity, the ingenuousness or moral obliquity of the receiving party — even if the communicating party offers only truth, in the best and freshest forms of expression the language provides.

There is only a single class of intellectual words that can be said to have a perfectly determinate significance, viz., those which relate to what are called necessary ideas. They are such as time, space, cause, truth, right, arithmetical numbers, and geometrical figures. Here the names applied are settled into a perfectly determinate meaning, not by any peculiar virtue in *them*, but by reason of the absolute exactness of the ideas themselves. Time cannot be anything more or less than time; truth cannot, in its idea, be anything different from truth; the numerals suffer no ambiguity of count or measure; a circle must be a circle; a square, a square. As far as language, therefore, has to do with these, it is a perfectly exact algebra of thought, but no farther.

It will perhaps be imagined by some — indeed, it is an assumption continually made — that words of thought, though based on mere figures or analogies in their original adoption, gradually lose their indeterminate character, and settle down under the law of use, into a sense so perfectly unambiguous that they are to be regarded as literal names, and real equivalents of the thoughts they signify. There could not be a greater mistake. For, though the original type or historic base of the word may pass out of view, so that nothing physical or figurative is any longer suggested by it, still it will be impossible that mere use should have given it an exact meaning, or made it the literal name of any moral or intellectual state. The word *sin* is of this description, and most persons seem to imagine that it names a given act or state, about which there is no diversity of understanding. Contrary to this, no two minds ever had the same impression of it. The whole personal history of every man, his acts, temptations, wants, and repentances; his opinions of God, of law, and of personal freedom; his theory of virtue, his decisions of the question, whether sin is an act, or a state, of the will, or of the heart: in fact, his whole theology and life will enter into his impression of this word *sin*, to change the quality and modify the relations of that which it signifies. It will also be found, as a matter of fact, that the interminable disputes of the theologians on this particular subject originate in fundamental differences of view concerning the nature of sin, and are themselves incontestible proofs that, simple as the word is, and on the lips of every body (as we know it to be), there is yet no virtual agreement of meaning connected with the word. The same, as just now intimated, is true of *hope, fear, love,* and other like familiar terms, which we fancy have a meaning so well settled. They have a dictionary meaning that is settled; but yet, hope, fear, love, is to every man what his own life-experience, and his theories and mental struggles have made it, and he sees it, of necessity, under a color quite peculiar to himself; so peculiar that he will even advance concerning it, what another cannot find the truth of, or receive. And this is true of all the intellectual terms in language, with the exception of a class just named, relating to necessary and absolute truths. Besides these, there is no word of thought, or spirit, that exactly measures its ideas, or does any thing more than offer some proximate notion, or shadow of the thought intended. . . .

7. Words of thought or spirit are not only inexact in their significance, never measuring the truth or giving its precise equivalent, but they always affirm something which is false, or contrary to the truth intended. They impute *form* to that which really is out of form. They are related to the truth, only as form to spirit — earthen vessels in which the truth is borne, yet always offering their mere pottery as being the truth itself. . . . A very great share of our theological questions, or disputes, originate in the incapacity of the parties to separate truths from their forms, or to see how the same essential truth may clothe itself under forms that are repugnant. There wants to be a large digestion, so to speak, of form in the teacher of theology or mental philosophy, that he may always be aware how the mind and truth, obliged to clothe themselves under the laws of space and sensation, are taking, continually, new shapes or dresses — coming forth poetically, mystically, allegorically, dialectically, fluxing through definitions, symbols, changes of subject and object, yet remaining still the same; for if he is wanting in this, if he is a mere logicker, fastening on a word as the sole expression and exact equivalent of a truth, to go on spinning his deductions out of the form of the word (which yet have nothing to do with the idea), then he becomes a one-word professor, quarreling, as for truth itself, with all who chance to go out of his word; and, since words are given not to imprison souls but to

express them, the variations continually indulged by others are sure to render him as miserable in his anxieties, as he is meager in his contents, and busy in his quarrels. . . .

8. But if we are liable thus to be carried away by the forms contained in our words, into conclusions or impressions that do not belong to the truths they are used to signify, we are also to peruse their forms with great industry, as being at the same time a very important key to their meaning. The original type or etymology of words is a most fruitful study. Even when they pass into meanings that seem to be contrary one to another, it will yet be found, in almost every case, that the repugnant meanings are natural growths, so to speak, of the same vital root; as some kinds of trees are seen to throw out leaves having several different shapes. The etymologists have been hard pressed, often, by ridicule, and it is not to be denied that they have sometimes produced fancies in place of facts. As little is it to be denied that words do now and then present no aspect of agreement in their senses with the types out of which they spring. They appear to have suffered some kind of violence — to have fallen among thieves, and been left half dead from the injury they have suffered. And yet there is a wonderful light shed upon words, in most cases, by the simple opening of their etymologies. Distinctions are very often drawn at a stroke, in this way, which whole chapters of dissertation would not exhibit as well. Sometimes a dark subject is made luminous at once by the simple reference to an etymology; and then we are even amazed to see what depths of wisdom, or spiritual insight, have been hid, as it were, in our language, even from ourselves. . . .

9. Since all words, but such as relate to necessary truths, are inexact representations of thought, mere types or analogies, or, where the types are lost beyond recovery, only proximate expressions of the thoughts named; it follows that language will be ever trying to mend its own deficiencies, by multiplying its forms of representation. As, too, the words made use of generally carry something false with them, as well as something true, associating form with the truths represented, when really there is no form; it will also be necessary, on this account, to multiply words or figures, and thus to present the subject on opposite sides or many sides. Thus, as form battles form, and one form neutralizes another, all the insufficiencies of words are filled out, the contrarieties liquidated, and the mind settles into a full and just apprehension of the pure spiritual truth. Accordingly we never come so near to a truly well-rounded view of any truth as when it is offered paradoxically; that is, under contradic-

tions; that is, under two or more dictions, which, taken as dictions, are contrary one to the other.

Hence the marvelous vivacity and power of that famous representation of Pascal: "What a chimera, then, is man! What a novelty! What a chaos! What a subject of contradiction! A judge of every thing, and yet a feeble worm of the earth; the depositary of truth, and yet a mere heap of uncertainty; the glory and the outcast of the universe. If he boasts, I humble him; if he humbles himself, I boast of him; and always contradict him, till he is brought to comprehend that he is an incomprehensible monster." [16]

Scarcely inferior in vivacity and power is the familiar passage of Paul — "As deceivers, and yet true; as unknown, and yet well known; as dying, and behold, we live; as chastened, and not killed; as sorrowful, yet always rejoicing; as poor, yet making many rich; as having nothing, yet possessing all things" [2 Cor. 6: 8–10]. . . .

Precisely here, too, I suppose, we come upon what is really the true conception of the incarnation and the trinity. These great Christian mysteries or paradoxes come to pass under the same conditions or laws which pertain to language. All words are in fact only incarnations, or insensings of thought. If we investigate the relations of their forms to the truths signified, we have the same mystery before us; if we set the different but related forms in comparison, we have the same aspect of repugnance or inconsistency. And then we have only to use the repugnant forms as vehicles of pure thought, dismissing the contradictory matter of the forms, and both words and the word are understood without distraction — all by the same process.

Probably the most contradictory book in the world is the gospel of John; and that for the very reason that it contains more and loftier truths than any other. No good writer, who is occupied in simply expressing truth, is ever afraid of inconsistencies or self-contradictions in his language. It is nothing to him that a quirk of logic can bring him into absurdity. If at any time he offers definitions, it is not to get a footing for the play of his logic, but it is simply as multiplying forms or figures of that which he seeks to communicate — just as one will take his friend to different points of a landscape, and show him cross views, in order that he may get a perfect conception of the outline. Having nothing but words in which to give definitions, he understands the impossibility of definitions as determinate measures of thought, and gives them only as being *other*

16. [ED.] Cf. *The Pensées of Pascal*, trans. by W. F. Trotter, Everyman ed. (London, 1932), 121.

forms of the truth in question, by aid of which it may be more adequately conceived. On the other hand, a writer without either truth or genius, a mere uninspired, unfructifying logicker, is just the man to live in definitions. He has never a doubt of their possibility. He lays them down as absolute measures, then draws along his deductions, with cautious consistency, and works out thus what he considers to be the exact infallible truth. But his definitions will be found to hang, of necessity, on some word or symbol, that symbol to have drawn every thing to itself, or into its own form, and then, when his work is done, it will be both consistent and false — false because of its consistency.

10. It is part of the same view, that logic itself is a defective and often deceitful instrument. I speak not here of logic as a science, but of that deductive, proving, spinning method of practical investigation commonly denoted by the term *logical*. It is very obvious that no turn of logical deduction can prove anything, by itself, not previously known by inspection or insight. And yet, there is always a busy-minded class of sophists or speculators who, having neither a large observation nor a power of poetic insight, occupy themselves as workers in words and propositions, managing to persuade themselves and others that they are great investigators, and even discoverers of truth. . . .

It seems to be supposed, or rather assumed, by the class of investigators commonly called logical, that after the subject matter of truth has been gotten into propositions, and cleared, perhaps, by definitions, the faculty of intuition, or insight, may be suspended, and we may go on safely to reason upon the forms of the words themselves, or the "analogy the words bear to each other." And so, by the mere handling of words and propositions, they undertake to evolve, or, as they commonly speak, to *prove* important truths. They reason, not by or through formulas, but upon them. . . .

It will also be observed that our mere reasoners and provers in words, in order to get their formulas arrayed for action, always rule out, or clear away, those antagonistic figures, paradoxes, and contrarious representations, by means of which only a full and comprehensive expression of the truth is possible. They are great in the detection of disagreements, or what they call contradictions; and the finding out of such elements, or the reducing of another to this bad dilemma, by their constructive process, they suppose to be a real triumph of intelligence — which is the same as to say that they can endure none but a one-sided view of truth.

It will almost always happen, also, to this class of investigators, that, when reasoning of man, life, self-active being, God, and religion, they will take up their formulas under the conditions of cause and effect, or space and time, or set them under the atomic relations of inorganic matter. Discussing the human will, for example, or the great question of liberty, the writer will be overpowered by the terms and predicates of language; which being mostly derived from the physical world, are charged, to the same extent, with a mechanical significance. And then we shall have a sophism, great or small, according to his capacity — a ponderous volume, it may be, of formulas, filled up, rolled about, inverted, crossed and twisted — a grand, stupendous, convoluted sophism — all a mere outward practice, however, on words and propositions, in which, as they contain a form of cause and effect in their own nature, it is easily made out that human liberty is the liberty of a scale-beam, turned by the heavier weights. Meantime, the question is only a question of consciousness, one in which the simple decision of consciousness is final — to which, argument, whether good or bad, can really add nothing, from which nothing take. . . .

11. In the reading or interpretation of an author, writing on intellectual and moral subjects, we are to observe first of all whether he takes up some given word or figure, and makes it a law to his thinking. If some symbol that he uses today stands by him also tomorrow, rules his doctrine, shapes his argument, drawing every thing into formal consistency with it, then we are to take up the presumption that he is out of the truth, and set ourselves to find where his mistake is. . . .

12. If we find the writer in hand moving with a free motion, and tied to no one symbol, unless in some popular effort, or for some single occasion; if we find him multiplying antagonisms, offering cross views, and bringing us round the field to show us how it looks from different points, then we are to presume that he has some truth in hand which it becomes us to know. We are to pass round accordingly with him, take up all his symbols, catch a view of him here, and another there, use one thing to qualify and interpret another, and the other to shed light upon that, and, by a process of this kind, endeavor to comprehend his antagonisms, and settle into a complete view of his meaning. . . .

There is no book in the world that contains so many repugnances, or antagonistic forms of assertion, as the Bible. Therefore, if any man please to play off his constructive logic upon it, he can easily show it up as the absurdest book in the world. But whosoever wants, on the other hand, really to behold and receive all truth, and would have the truth-world overhang him as an empyrean of stars, complex, multitudinous, striving antagonistically, yet comprehended, height above height, and deep under deep, in a boundless score of harmony; what man soever, content with no small rote of logic and catechism, reaches with true hunger after this, and will offer himself to the many-sided forms of the Scripture with a perfectly ingenuous and receptive spirit; he shall find his nature flooded with senses, vastnesses, and powers of truth, such as it is even greatness to feel. . . . Never was there a book uniting so many contrarious aspects of one and the same truth. The more complete, therefore, because of its manifoldness; nay, the more really harmonious, for its apparent want of harmony.

How, then, are we to receive it and come into its truth? Only in the comprehensive manner just now suggested; not by destroying the repugnances, but by allowing them to stand, offering our mind to their impressions, and allowing it to gravitate inwardly towards that whole of truth in which they coalesce. . . .

13. The views of language and interpretation I have here offered suggest the very great difficulty, if not impossibility, of mental science and religious dogmatism. In all such uses or attempted uses, the effort is to make language answer a purpose that is against its nature. The "winged words" are required to serve as beasts of burden; or, what is no better, to forget their poetic life, as messengers of the air, and stand still, fixed upon the ground, as wooden statues of truths. Which, if they seem to do; if, to comfort our studies of dogma, they assume the inert faces we desire, and suffer us to arrange the fixed attitudes of their bodies, yet, as little Memnons touched and made vocal by the light, they will be discoursing still of the free empyrean, disturbing, and scattering, by their voices, all the exact meanings we had thought to hold them to, in the nice corporeal order of our science.

In algebra and geometry, the ideas themselves being absolute, the terms or names also may be; but in mental science and religion no such exactness is possible, because our apprehensions of truth are here only proximate and relative. I see not, therefore, how the subject matter of mental science and religion can ever be included under the fixed forms of dogma. Definitions cannot bring us over the difficulty; for definitions are, in fact, only changes of symbol, and if we take them to be more, will infallibly lead us into error. In fact, no man is more certain to run himself into mischievous error, than he who places implicit confidence in definitions. After all, definitions will be words, and science will be words, and words, place them in whatever shapes we may, will be only shadows of truth. . . .

It ought not to be necessary to remind any reader of the Bible that religion has a natural and profound alliance with poetry. Hence, a very large share of the Bible is composed of poetic contributions. Another share, equally large, is that which comes to us in a form of history and fact; that is, of actual life, which is equally remote from all abstractions and, in one view, equally poetic; for history is nothing but an evolution or expression of God and man in their own nature and character. The teachings of Christ are mere utterances of truth, not argumentations over it. He gives it forth in living symbols, without definition, without *proving* it, ever, as the logicians speak, well understanding that truth is that which shines in its own evidence, that which *finds* us, to use an admirable expression of Coleridge, and thus enters into us. . . .

We find little, therefore, in the Scriptures, to encourage the hope of a complete and sufficient Christian dogmatism, or of a satisfactory and truly adequate system of scientific theology. Language, under the laws of logic or speculation, does not seem to be adequate to any such use or purpose. The Scriptures of God, in providing a clothing for religious truth, have little to do with mere dialectics, much to do with the freer creations of poetry; and that for reasons, evidently, which ought to waken a salutary skepticism in us in regard to the possibility of that which so many great minds have been attempting with so great confidence for so many hundreds of years. With due respect, also, I will venture to ask whether the actual results of this immense engineering process which we call dogmatic and polemic theology — as surely polemic as dogmatic — does not give some countenance to the doubt I am suggesting? . . .

There is, however, one hope for mental and religious truth, and their final settlement, which I confess I see but dimly, and can but faintly express or indicate. It is that physical science, leading the way, setting outward things in their true proportions, opening up their true contents, revealing their genesis and final causes and laws, and weaving all into the unity of a real universe, will so perfect our knowledges and conceptions of them, that we can use them, in the second department of language, with more exactness. There is, we have also seen, in what we call nature — that is, in its objects — an outward grammar of relations, which constructs the grammar of language; or what is not far different, the logic of propositions. In the laws of nature, I suppose, there is in like manner an internal grammar, which is certain, as it is evolved, to pass into language, and be an internal grammar in that, systematizing and steadying its uses. And then language will be as much more full and intelligent as it has more of God's intelligence, in the system of nature, imparted to its symbols. For undoubtedly the whole universe of nature is a perfect analogon of the whole universe of thought or spirit. Therefore, as nature becomes truly a universe only through science revealing its universal laws, the true universe of thought and spirit cannot sooner be conceived. It would be easy to show, in this connection, the immense force already exerted over the empire of spiritual truth, by astronomy, chemistry, geology, the revelations of light and electricity, and especially of the mysterious and plastic workings of life, in the animal and vegetable kingdoms. We are accustomed to say that this is not the same world to live in that it was fifty years ago. Just as true is it, that it is not the same world to *think* in that it then was — of which, also, we shall, by and by, take notice.

If, then, it please any one to believe, notwithstanding the present incapacities of dogmatism, that when, through science, we are able to see things physical in their true force and relations, having also within us, inbreathed by the spirit of God, a comprehensive heart and feelings sufficiently cleared of prejudice to behold, in the universal mirror of God, his universal truth — if, I say, any one please to believe that now the Christian world may arrive at some final and determinate apprehensions of Christian doctrine, I will not object. But if they do, observe, it will only be that they have settled at last into a comprehensive reception of the universal symbolism, and not that they have invented a few propositions, so intensely significant and true, as to dispense with all besides.

14. It is important to notice, as connected with the subject of language, that dogmatical propositions, such as are commonly woven into creeds and catechisms of doctrine, have not the certainty they are commonly supposed to have. They only give us the seeing of the authors, at the precise standpoint occupied by them, at the time, and they are true only as seen from that point — not even there, save in a proximate sense. Passing on, descending the current of time, we will say, for two centuries, we are brought to a different point, as when we change positions in a landscape, and then we are doomed to see things in a different light, in spite of ourselves. It is not that the truth changes, but that we change. Our eye changes color, and then the color of our eye affects our seeing. We are different men, living as parts in a different system of things and thinkings, denyings, and affirmings; and as our contents and our antagonisms are

different, we cannot see the same truths in the same forms. It may even be necessary to change the forms, to hold us in the same truths.

I could name phrases that have been brought into the creeds of many of our New England churches, within the present half century, which are already waxing old, and are doomed, within the next half century, to ask a re-modification.

Besides, in the original formation of any creed, catechism, or system of divinity, there is always a latent element of figure, which probably the authors know not of, but without which it is neither true to them, nor to anybody. But in a long course of repetition the figure dies out, and the formula settles into a literality, and then, if the repetition goes on, it is really an assent to what is not true; for that which was true at the beginning has now become untrue — and that, however paradoxical it may seem, by being assented to. . . .

At the same time, it is remarkable with what ease a man who is sensible of the fluxing nature and significance of words may assent to almost any creed, and that with a perfectly sincere doubt whether he does not receive it in its most interior and real meaning; that is, whether going back to the men who made it, taking their standpoint, and abating what belongs to the form of a truth, in distinction from the truth itself, he does not come into the real senses or interior beliefs they clothed in these forms. Perhaps it is on this account that I have never been able to sympathize at all with the abundant protesting of the New England Unitarians against creeds. So far from suffering even the least consciousness of constraint, or oppression, under any creed, I have been readier to accept as great a number as fell in my way; for when they are subjected to the deepest chemistry of thought, that which descends to the point of relationship between the form of the truth and its interior formless nature, they become thereupon so elastic, and run so freely into each other, that one seldom need have any difficulty in accepting as many as are offered him. He may regard them as only a kind of battle-dooring of words, blow answering to blow, while the reality of the play, viz., *exercise,* is the same, whichever side of the room is taken, and whether the stroke is given by the right hand or the left.

The greatest objection that I know to creeds — that is, to creeds of a theoretic or dogmatic character — is that they make so many appearances of division where there really is none, till the appearances make it. They are likely, also, unless some debate or controversy sharpens the mind to them, and keeps them alive, to die out of meaning, and be assented to, at last, as a mere jingle of words. Thus we have, in many of our orthodox formulas of trinity, the phrase "the same in substance," and yet how many are there, even of our theologians, to whom it will now seem a heresy to say this with a meaning. And the clause following, "equal in power and glory," will be scarcely less supportable, when a view of trinity is offered which gives the terms an earnest and real significance.

On these accounts, the best creed is that which stays by the concrete most faithfully, and carries its doctrine, as far as possible, in a vehicle of fact and of real life. This is the peculiar excellence and beauty of what is called the "Apostles' Creed." If, however, creeds of theory, or systematic dogma, must be retained, the next best arrangement would be to allow assent to a great number of such creeds at once; letting them qualify, assist, and mitigate each other. And a virtual allowance of this is, in fact, one of the best points in our Saybrook Platform, which accepts the acknowledgment, either of its own Articles, or of the "Doctrinal Articles of the Church of England," or of the "Westminster Confession," or of the "Confession agreed on at the Savoy"; and if it be indifferent which of the four is received, there can be no objection, certainly, if all are received. And it is in just this way that the Scripture has its meaning filled out, qualified, fortified, secured against subsiding into falsity, or becoming a mere jingle of sounds. We have so many writers set before us, each in his own habit, and giving his own form of the truth; offering the truth some at one pole and some at the other, that, when we receive and entertain them all, making, in fact, a creed of them all, they act as complementary forces, and by their joint effect keep us ever in the fullest, liveliest, and most many-sided apprehension of the Christian truth.

15. I have said nothing of the manner in which the user of language imparts himself to it. Undoubtedly every human language has, in its words and forms, indelible marks of the personal character and habit of the men by whom it was oringinally produced. Nay, it may even be said that every language carries in its bosom some flavor of meaning or import derived from all the past generations that have lived in it. Not more truly does it represent the forms of nature than it does within or under these forms the contents, also, of history. And therefore what is called usage has a certain importance when we seek the import or right use of words. But not any such importance as the lexicographers, and the Blairizing critics, have given it. Usage is a guide to use, but never a limit upon use. We have our freedom, as our fathers had, and as good a right to use words with new meanings, certainly, as to have new thoughts.

And just here it is that we come upon a matter which, if it be too mysterious to be investigated, is yet too important to be overlooked. In every writer distinguished by mental life, words have a significance and power breathed into them, which is wholly peculiar — whether it be in the rhythm, the collocations, the cadences, or the internal ideas, it may be impossible to guess. But his language is his own, and there is some chemistry of life in it that belongs only to him, as does the vital chemistry of his body. This holds of every writer who can properly be called a living soul. . . .

16. That I may not seem to be offering to the public, doctrines the real import of which I have not considered myself, something must be said of the consequences likely to result to religion from the admission of views such as I have here presented. Only be it observed that their truth depends in no degree on any expectations of good, or any vaticinations of evil, which the faith of one or the panic of another may raise.

Unquestionably, the view of language here presented must produce, if received, a decided mitigation of our dogmatic tendencies in religion. It throws a heavy shade of discouragement on our efforts in this direction. It shows that language is probably incapable of any such definite and determinate use as we have supposed it to be in our theological speculations; that for this reason dogma has failed hitherto, and about as certainly will hereafter. Taking away, thus, the confidence of the speculative theologer, it will limit, proportionally, his eagerness. It will also reduce the very excessive eminence he has, at present, in the public estimation, requiring a re-adjustment of the scale that now pertains between this and the historical, literary, and practical departments of Christian study. Or, better still, showing that the advancement and the real amount of true theology depends, not on logical deductions and systematic solutions, but principally on the more cultivated and nicer apprehension of symbol, it may turn the industry of our teachers more in this direction, giving a more esthetic character to their studies and theories, and drawing them as much closer to the practical life of religion.

Without being at all aware of the fact, as it would seem, our theologic method in New England has been essentially rationalistic; though not exactly in the German sense. The possibility of reasoning out religion, though denied in words, has yet been tacitly assumed. Not allowing ourselves to be rationalists *over* the Scriptures, we have yet been as active and confident rationalists *under* them as it was possible to be — assuming, always, that they address their contents to the systematic, speculative reason of men, into which they are to be received, and by which they are to be digested into formulas — when they are ready for use. We have had a certain negative way of declaring against the competence of the natural man to understand spiritual things, but it has been done principally in that way only, and as a convenient method of cutting off speculative arguments that could not be speculatively answered. It has not been held, as a practical, positive, and earnest Christian truth, that there is a PERCEPTIVE POWER in spiritual life, an unction of the Holy One, which is itself a kind of inspiration — an immediate, experimental knowledge of God, by virtue of which, and partly in the degree of which, Christian theology is possible. No real doubt has been held of the perfect sufficiency of formulas; or of natural logic, handled by the natural understanding, to settle them. The views of language here offered lead to a different method. The Scriptures will be more studied than they have been, and in a different manner — not as a magazine of propositions and mere dialectic entities, but as inspirations and poetic forms of life; requiring, also, divine inbreathings and exaltations in us, that we may ascend into their meaning. Our opinions will be less catechetical and definite, using the word as our definers do, but they will be as much broader as they are more divine; as much truer, as they are more vital and closer to the plastic, undefinable mystery of spiritual life. We shall seem to understand less, and shall actually receive more. No false *pre-cision*, which the nature and conditions of spiritual truth forbid, will, by cutting up the body of truth into definite and dead morsels, throw us into states of excision and division equally manifold. We shall receive the truth of God in a more entire organic and organific manner, as being itself an essentially vital power. It will not be our endeavor to pull the truth into analytic distinctions, as if theology were a kind of inorganic chemistry, and the last end of discovery, an atomic theory; but we shall delight in truth, more as a concrete, vital nature, incarnated in all fact and symbol round us — a vast, mysterious, incomprehensible power, which best we know when most we love.

Striving ever outward, towards the infinite, and not inward or downward, upon speculative minima or atoms, we shall be kept in a humbler and far less positive state of mind. Our judgments of others will be less peremptory, and as we are more modest, we shall be as much more patient and charitable. And our views of language, as an instrument wholly inadequate to the exact representation of thought, will operate immediately to favor the same result.

If any should be apprehensive that the views here offered may bring in an age of mysticism, and so of interminable confusion, they will greatly misconceive their import, and also the nature of mysticism itself. A mystic is one who finds a secret meaning, both in words and in things, back of their common or accepted meaning — some agency of LIFE, or LIVING THOUGHT, hid under the forms of words and institutions, and historical events. Hence all religious writers and teachers who dwell on the representative character of words and things, or hold the truths of religion, not in mechanical measures and relations, but as forms of life, are so far mystics. Thus Neander gives it, as a characteristic of the apostle John — "that a reference to communion with the Redeemer, in the inward life, and in the present, predominates over the reference to the future, and to outward facts; he dwells upon the elements of the inner life, the facts of Christian consciousness, and only slightly adverts to outward matters of fact and ecclesiastical arrangements. In accordance with this spirit, he exhibits all the particular incidents in the outward history of Christ, only as a manifestation of his indwelling glory, by which this may be brought home to the heart; he always avails himself of these narratives, to introduce what the Redeemer declared, respecting his relation to mankind, as the source of life. John is the representative of the truth which lies at the basis of that tendency of the Christian spirit, which sets itself in opposition to a one-sided intellectualism, and ecclesiastical formality — and is distinguished by the name of mysticism." [17]

I make no disavowal, then, of the fact that there is a mystic element, as there should be, in what I have represented as the source of meaning in language, and also in the views of Christian life and doctrine that follow. Man is designed, in his very nature, to be a partially mystic being; the world to be looked upon as a mystic world. Christ himself revealed a decidedly mystic element in his teachings. There is something of a mystic quality in almost every writing of the New Testament. In John, it is a character. In "the dialectic" Paul, there are very many passages quite as mystical as any in John.

Now, the very cautious and salutary skepticism I have maintained concerning the insufficiency and the partially repugnant character of words, leaves as little room as possible to apprehend any danger of wildness, or confusion from the entrance of a mystic element, thus qualified and guarded. There is nothing, in fact, that we so much need, as an apostle

17. [ED.] John Augustus William Neander, *History of the Planting and Training of the Christian Church*, trans. from the third German edition by J. E. Ryland (Philadelphia, 1844), 317-18. Through this work, among others, Bushnell came in contact with Schleiermacher's teaching on the Christian consciousness.

John among our other apostles; and I fervently hope that God will some-time send us such a gift. The very last thing to be feared is, that our loss-and-gain style of religion, the stern, iron-limbed speculative logic of our New England theology, will receive some fatal damage from a trace of the mystic element. It will produce no overturnings, sap no foundations, dissolve no formulas, run to no license or extravagance. It will enter only as life came into the bones; which, though they rose up into a limbered and active state, and were hidden somewhat from the eye by an envelope of muscle and skin, were yet as good bones as before; probably as much better and more systematic, as there was more of the life-order in them and about them.

The two principal results, then, which I suppose may follow, should these views of language be allowed to have their effect in our theology, are a more comprehensive, friendly, and fraternal state than now exists between different families of Christians; and, as the confidence of dogma is mitigated, a more present, powerful, and universal conviction entering into the Christian body, that truth, in its highest and freest forms, is not of the natural understanding, but is, rather, as Christ himself declared — spirit and life. We shall have more of union, therefore, and more of true piety enlightened by the spirit of God — neither of which involves any harm or danger.

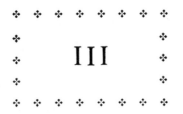

III

CHRISTIAN COMPREHENSIVENESS [1]

When Bushnell began his ministry at the North Church, the congregation was about evenly divided between Taylorites and Tylerites. The young pastor was thus forced to become a peacemaker. Efforts at reconciliation began the more hopefully, because by personal conviction he could not agree fully with either school of thought. Accordingly he endeavored to unite the church through what he later characterized as "the comprehensive method," a method which presupposed elements of truth and error in both Taylorism and Tylerism.[2] Recalling that situation twenty years later, he said: "I took my stand openly on all the vexed questions, preaching both sides." [3] By this means he endeavored to bring both parties to see the need for a more comprehensive truth than either yet possessed and to want to remain together in the church in order to find it. The end result justified his procedure. A few rigid Tylerites or conservatives resisted the process of reconciliation and withdrew from the church, but most of the members responded to it and grew in breadth of insight and in mutual affection with the passing years.

As a result of this experiment, Bushnell became so convinced of the merit of the comprehensive method of resolving tensions and enlarging Christian insight that he elaborated its fundamental principles in the essay of 1848. Strangely, it has received little attention. The two best known older works on him — Cheney's *Life and Letters* (1880), and Munger's *Horace Bushnell* (1899) — give it no consideration whatever. That is true also of Barbara Cross's recent volume, *Horace Bushnell* (1958). Almost

---

1. "Christian Comprehensiveness," *New Englander*, VI (1848), 81–88; 90–97; 105–06.
2. See *supra*, 3.
3. *Twentieth Anniversary: A Commemorative Discourse* (Hartford, 1853), 14.

the only published exception is Irving H. Bartlett's short article of 1957.[4] This neglect is regrettable, for the essay on "Christian Comprehensiveness" reflects some of the distinctive elements in Bushnell's theological method.

As the essay of 1848 reveals, Bushnell was impressed with Cousin's view of the history of thought. On the presupposition that human reason comprised three inseparable elements — the idea of the finite, of the infinite, and of their relation — Cousin held that there must be three (and only three) corresponding epochs in history, the first being primarily concerned with the infinite; the second, with the finite; and the third, with the finite-infinite.[5] In each epoch, all the major elements of culture — industry, politics, art, philosophy, religion — will be interpreted from the ruling perspective.[6] With respect to philosophy, for example, idealism will dominate the first epoch; empiricism, the second; and eclecticism (Cousin's system), the third. The three philosophic systems can arise only in that order. "After the subjective idealism of the school of Kant, and the empiricism and sensualism of that of Locke, have been developed and their last possible results exhausted, no new combination is in my opinion possible but the union of these two systems by centering them both in a vast and powerful eclecticism." [7] In other words, eclecticism completed the triadic sequence and constituted the final philosophy. Hegel's influence upon Cousin is manifest.

Bushnell was by no means a technical Cousinian; indeed, he pointed out the Frenchman's oversimplified theory of the development of thought. Nevertheless, Cousin definitely influenced Bushnell. For instance, his idea that the emergence of polar opposites in philosophy is a necessary prerequisite to the growth of philosophic thought has its parallel in Bushnell's notion that the rise of antithetical creeds has prepared the way for the achievement of a more comprehensive creed. Or again, just as Cousin

---

4. "Bushnell, Cousin, and Comprehensive Christianity," *Journal of Religion*, XXXVII (1957), 99–104. A few doctoral studies have recognized the theological significance of Bushnell's 1848 essay. See Harold R. Heininger, "The Theological Technique of a Mediating Theologian — Horace Bushnell" (unpublished Ph.D. dissertation, University of Chicago, 1933), 161–70; Irving H. Bartlett, "The Romantic Theology of Horace Bushnell" (unpublished Ph.D. dissertation, Brown University, 1952), 136–39; John E. Howell, "A Study of the Theological Method of Horace Bushnell and Its Application to His Cardinal Doctrines" (unpublished Ph.D. dissertation, Duke University, 1963), Chap. 2.

5. Victor Cousin, *Introduction to the History of Philosophy*, trans. by Henning G. Linberg (Boston, 1832), 180, 191, 214–22.

6. *Ibid.*, 202.   7. *Ibid.*, 414.

held that every great system of philosophy contained some element of truth worth preserving in a higher synthesis, so Bushnell believed that almost every one of the historic creeds of the church, no matter how repugnant to one another, stood for an element of truth which should find its place in a more inclusive Christian confession.

❖   ❖   ❖   ❖

We are not among those who regard the Christian sects as equivalent to so many schisms. . . . Doubtless there is such a thing as schism, divisions that are wrought by evil passions, therefore dishonorable, hurtful, and criminal; and such is the weakness of our nature that there are doubtless vestiges of schism in all Christian bodies. Still it is our privilege, on the whole, and being our privilege, our duty, to regard the Christian sects, not as divisions, but as distributions rather; for it is one of the highest problems of divine government in the church, as in all other forms of society, how to effect the most complete and happy distribution — such a distribution as will meet all wants and conditions, content the longings, pacify the diversities, and edify the common growth of all. Thus it may be said that the present distribution of the church, abating what is due to causes that are criminal, makes it more completely one; just as an army, set off into companies and battalions, some trained to serve as infantry and some as horse, some with artillery and some with the rifle, undergoing each a form of exercise and discipline peculiar to itself, becomes thereby not several and distinct armies, but because of the orderly distribution made, a more complete and perfect whole — in the field, an engine of greater power, because it unites so many forms of action and bears so many sorts of armor.

At the same time, it is not to be denied that this manifold distribution of the church has its propriety, in causes and events that imply a crude state, or a state of only partial development. Therefore, while we do not regret the distribution, or proclaim it as the public shame of religion, we may well desire a riper state, in which the Christian body shall coalesce more perfectly and draw itself towards a more comprehensive and catholic polity. The work of distribution and redistribution has already gone far enough, as most Christians appear to suppose. We see, indeed, that unity is rising, now, as a new ideal upon the Christian world. They pray for a closer fellowship; they flock together from the ends of the world to consult for unity. A proper and true catholic church is before the mind, as an object of longing and secret hope, as never before — it is named in distant places, and by men who have had no concert, save through the Spirit of God and the spirit of the age. And if these are signs of capacity for a more catholic state, it may also be seen, in the few persons rising up here and there to speak of a more comprehensive faith, or to handle questions of polity and doctrine in a more comprehensive spirit, that there are powers coming into the field, which possibly God has trained for the preparation of a new catholic age. Probably never until now has the world been ready to conceive the true idea of a comprehensive Christianity. Nor is it ready now, save in part. The idea itself is yet in its twilight, dimly seen, only by a few — by none save those who are up to watch for the morning.

Our object in this article is to say what we are able of a subject formerly so remote from the world. We confess that, in our own apprehension, we seem rather to stammer than to speak plainly. Still, as it is by stammering that we learn to speak, we go to our rudimental effort suffering no pride to detain us.

What we mean by comprehensiveness, or a comprehensive Christianity, may be illustrated, in part, from the manner and teachings of Christ himself, who is the Lord of Christianity. In nothing did Christ prove his superhuman quality more convincingly, than by the comprehensiveness of his spirit and his doctrine. He held his equilibrium, flew into no eccentricities, saved what was valuable in what he destroyed, destroyed nothing where it was desirable rather to fulfill than to destroy. . . . It is by this singular comprehensiveness, in the spirit of Christ, that the grandeur of his life and doctrine is most of all conspicuous. For by this it was that he set himself in advance, most clearly, of his own and of all subsequent times. With men, if they ever attain to any thing of a comprehensive aim, it is only in what may be called the second age of the church or society, the historical and critical age. In the first age, they see truth; in the second they consider the seeings of others and their import. In the first age they regard the forms of truth as identical with truth itself; therefore they stand, every man for his own form, having no choice but to live or die by it, and no thought, perhaps, but to make others live or die by it too. But in the second age, opinions become a subject of comparison, their laws are inquired after, their forms become plastic and are seen melting into each other. Under contrary forms are found common truths, and one form is seen to be the complement of another — all forms, we may almost say, the complement of all others. But it was in no such philosophic and critical method that Christ attained to so great comprehensiveness. He found it rather in the native grandeur of his own spirit. Speaking not as a critic but as a seer, his simple seeing placed him thousands of years in advance of us, under all the lights of history. We seem now to be just beginning to spell out in syllables, and by a laborious criticism, that which Christ seized upon as an original intuition.

But we must enter, if possible, into the more interior merits of our subject. It was given out a few years ago, by the distinguished French philosopher M. Cousin, that there are, in philosophy, three possible schools of opinion, which must each have an era to itself — one that begins with the ideal, or absolute; a second that begins with the empiric, or conditional; a third which seeks to adjust the relations of the two, producing an ideal-empiric, or, as he would call it, an eclectic school. Besides these three, he declares that it is even impossible to invent another. And the latter of the three he regards as the ripe school, one that will contain the last and fully matured results of philosophic inquiry. Now as human life lies between the infinite and the finite, as regards thought and the objects of thought, having contact in fact with both, there is certainly a show of truth in the theory offered. The history of opinions too may be made, without any great violence, to yield it a complexion of favor. Still it is easy to show in what manner other and more various oppositions may arise, and how they may be multiplied almost without number. They are in fact so multiplied, both in philosophy and in religious doctrine.

Having it, then, for our subject in this article to investigate, as far as we are able, the causes out of which religious oppositions arise, and to suggest the true remedy, let us first of all glance at the methods in which the Christian world falls into so many repugnant attitudes.

Doubtless it is true in part, as M. Cousin suggests, that many of these repugnances are due to the fact that the *material* of thought is itself divided between what is absolute or ideal, and what is actual or empirical; so that a mind viewing any subject partially, that is from one pole, is likely to conflict with one viewing it from the other, and both with one who endeavors to view it from both poles at once.

But there are divisions, or repugnances, that are due as much to the *incomprehensibility* of the matter of thought as to the twofold nature of its contents. The matter of thought is infinite in quantity, as well as ideal or empirical in quality. Hence it results that, as the minds of men are finite, they can only pull at the hem of the garment, and must therefore be expected to pull in different ways, accordingly as they fall upon the hem on one side or on the other. For as the garment is, to each, nothing but the hem, in that part where he has hold of it, he is likely to make up his sect or school according to the view he has. But after long ages of debate, wherein every part of the hem is brought into view, then it is possible, certainly, for any disciple, who will look through the eyes of *all,* to form to himself some view of it that is broader and more comprehensive.

Then again there are reasons for the rise of repugnant views, in thought and religious doctrine, which lie in what may be called the contents of *persons.* For it is not merely the contents of thought, but quite as much the contents of the thinkers, that give birth to contrary opinions and sects. We speak here of personal temperament, or of national temperament, working in the subject; of that which history has produced, or waits to have produced; of impulses, wants, all of which need as much to have their day and be tried, as the subject matter of thought itself. For example, the Pelagian doctrine of will, or self-supporting virtue, and the Quaker doctrine of quietism, may arise, in no small degree, from varieties of personal temperament. And since temperament is as much a reality as thought itself, what can ever display the manifold forms of a perfect and complete doctrine, unless temperament also is allowed to have its trial? So also prelacy was produced by historic causes, that is, by impulses and sympathies historically prepared. So also of independency or equality. It was something in the convenience of political power, or private ambition, or Christian experience, that produced these repugnant methods of organization, and set them in conflict. And now, since they are both set before the mind, as exhibited on trial, it is possible to decide with greater confidence on the method most congenial to the Christian scheme—perhaps on a method that combines the excellences of both.

There is yet one more source of repugnant and partial opinion, which is quite as fruitful as the others; namely, *language.* No matter whether we speak of philosophic doctrine, or of that which is derived from revelation, every opinion or truth must come into the world and make itself known, under the terms of language. And all the processes of ratiocination, under which opinions are generated, are processes that are contained within the laws of language. But language cannot convey any truth whole, or by a literal embodiment. It can only show it on one side, and by a figure. Hence a great many shadows, or figures, are necessary to represent every truth; and hence, again, there will seem to be a kind of necessary conflict between the statements in which a truth is expressed. One statement will set forth a given truth or subject matter under one figure, and a second under another, and a third, possibly, under yet another. The doctrine of atonement, for example, is offered, in Scripture, under a great variety of figures, and a history of the doctrine, up to this moment, consists in a great degree of the theologic wars of these figures, doing battle each for the supremacy. For as soon as any figure of truth is taken to be the truth itself, and set up to govern all the reasons of the subject, by its own contents as a figure, argument itself settles into cant, and cant is enthroned as doctrine. For cant, in rigid definition, is the perpetual chanting, or canting, of some phrase or figure, as the fixed equivalent of a truth. And as most men who speculate, both in philosophy and religion, are not fully aware of the power of words, or how, if they place a truth under one word in distinction from another, it will assuredly run them into dogmas that are only partially true; successive dogmas in theology or philosophy are perpetually coming upon the stage, and wearing themselves down into cant to die — in which, though they resemble themselves to the swans, it is yet with a difference; for the swans only sing when they die, but these sing themselves to death. The number of contrary theories that may be gathered round a given subject are limited, of course, only by the number of figures adjacent to it.

Instead, therefore, of the single cause for repugnant or opposing theories, discovered by M. Cousin, we find as many as four classes of causes; one that lies in the twofold quality of the contents of thought; a second in the infinite quantity of the contents; a third in the contents of persons, including society and history; a fourth in the containing powers of language, as an instrument of thought and speculation.

On the whole, it does not appear that the theory of M. Cousin is sufficient. It is less defective as relating to questions of philosophy or philosophic systems, for which it was specially intended, but it is defective even here; for nothing is more certain than that the thoughts and speculations of men are shaped by causes which do not lie in the quality of the subject matter of thought. Far more extensively true is this in matters of theology or revealed religion, where so much depends on questions of fact or interpretation — questions that are not determinable by any philosophic or *a priori* method. Still the doctrine he advances that all questions of philosophy lie between two poles or extremes, is one that has a vast and almost universal application. So also of his doctrine that, inasmuch as men are after truth and not after falsehood, it may generally be assumed that under all extremes advanced there dwells a truth. And these will hold equally well in matters of theology.

Holding this view, it may seem to follow also, as asserted by M. Cousin, that there can arise, about any subject or question, only three *schools* of opinion — the schools of the extremes, and a third school, which undertakes to settle their relation, or comprehend them in a common view. And perhaps there can not in any legitimate way. Still it will be found, in historical fact, that men do not always proceed in a legitimate way. Other causes act upon them, which do not lie in the subject matter of inquiry. As we see them in actual controversy, they describe a history which may be well enough represented by the five stages or modes which follow.

First comes up into the light one extreme and, with or without controversy, it is adopted. After awhile a second school, looking the dominant opinion or practice in the face, begins to see that there is something wrong or false in it, and rises up as an assailant, to assert the second extreme. Now comes the war between extremes. The parties are certain, both, that they have the truth. They regard each other, in their present half-seeing state, as wholly repugnant and contrary. The war goes on, therefore, as a war between simple truth and falsehood, which no terms of peace can reconcile, and which permits no issue but one of life or death. Probably the new extreme will prevail and the old subside into a secondary place.

Meantime, there is likely to appear a neutral school, made up of those who are disposed to peace, and deprecate war, and who can not escape the feeling that there is something extravagant or excessive (as there certainly is) in both the militant schools. These are the moderate men who praise moderate things — the wooden-headed school, who dread nothing with so great reason as a combustion of any sort. Hence it is the real problem with them to divide distances, and settle themselves down as nearly midway between the poles as possible. Sometimes they are called in derision, men of the fence, but they call themselves, and more correctly, *neuters*, that is, neithers; for the real study and problem of their school is negative. It is not to find the truth as a positive form and law, but it is simply to find a position halfway between the two schools before them — to be about as much and about as little one as the other. They are prudent, but not wise. They make a show of candor, without so much as a thought of the truth. But as men grow weary of controversy, and the passions that give zest to it for a time are seen to die out, and give place, at last, to a sense of disgust; as extremes held singly are seen moreover to bring a sense of defect and weariness by themselves, the neutrals are very likely to get their turn and become the reigning school. The public are

sick — why must their ears be stunned by the perpetual din of controversy? So falling into the sick list of neutrality, one after another, the two
schools of the extremes are gradually thinned away and seem about to be
forgotten. But for some reason it begins at length to be felt that there is a
very peculiar inspidity in this neutral state. There is nothing sufficiently
positive in it to waken a resonant feeling in the soul. Plausibilities have
taken the place of truths, and the diet is too thin to feed the blood. After
spending thus a whole age or generation midway between somewhere and
nowhere, or rather between two somewheres, they begin to feel that neu-
tralities, after all, are more sickening than controversies, and they are willing, possibly to go back and resume the old quarrel of the extremes, if it
is only for the health of the exercise.

There is also what is sometimes called a liberal school, which differs
widely from the neutral, as having aims of a more generous quality. For
while the timorous neutral is engaged to settle his position midway between extremes, the liberal is extending an equal indulgence to both. The
former is moved by prudence to himself, the latter by charity to others.
The virtue of one is moderation, that of the other tolerance. One lets go
the truth to consult distances, the other admits that possibly we are all too
distant from the truth and see it too dimly to be over positive concerning
it. Now most of the arguments and motives to liberality are of a reasonable and generous quality, and where the liberal spirit is connected with a
rigid and earnest devotion to truth, it is a condition of health to itself and
a mark of respect to others. But how easy is it to be indulgent to others, if
first we are indifferent to the truth. And if liberality itself is made to be
the virtue and hung up as the flag of a school, it is very sure to prove
itself, ere long, to be anything but a virtue. Or if still it be called by that
name, it will show itself to be the most unilluminated, most impotent and
insipid of all virtues. Having no creed, in fact, save that other men shall
be welcome to theirs — earnest in nothing save in vindicating the right of
others to be earnest, counting it charity not to be anxious for the truth,
but to be patient with all error, smiling indulgently upon all extremes, not
caring how the truth may fare between them — the liberal school makes a
virtue of negation, and freezes itself in the mild and gentle temperature it
has mistaken for charity. The word *liberal* is in fact a negative word,
there is nothing positive in it. And, as words are powerful, no body of
men, however earnest at the beginning, can long rally under this word as
a flag, without making it a sacrament of indifference, and subsiding, thus,
into a state which involves a disrespect to all the sacred rights of truth.

But as life can not long be endured where earnestness is lost, so the liberalist will begin, ere long, to feel that his supposed charity does not bless him. And now he will gird himself again for war, seize upon some post and fortify it, and though it do not cover a half acre of ground, he will swear to die fighting for something, as better than possessing nothing.

Having now the schools above named before us, first the schools of the extremes, with their wars; then the neutral or the liberal school or both, succeeding and bringing in an age of dearth that cannot longer be supported; we may see how a fifth school rises to complete the cycle and gather unto the truth, her own true catholic brotherhood. There rises up now a man, or a few men, who looking again at the two extreme schools, begin to ask whether it is not possible to comprehend them — that is to receive, hold, practice all which made the extreme opinions true to their disciples? The very thought gives compass or enlargement to the soul in which it is conceived. It ascends, as it were, to a higher position, to look down upon the strifes of the race and use them as the material of its exercise, conveniencies to its own final establishment and victory. In this effort to comprehend extremes, it offers no disrespect, but the highest respect, rather, to the great and earnest spirits that have stood for the truth and fought her battles, giving them all credit for their courage and devotion, and considering them, in fact, as the right and left wing of the field, which it now remains to include in one and the same army. It is in fact a disciple of the extremes, taking lessons of both, and ceasing not till it has gotten whatever good and whatever truth made their opinions sacred to themselves. In the endeavor to comprehend extremes, it comprehends also both the views of the neutral and the liberal schools. The neutral was sure that there was some extravagance, some defect of equilibrium in the extremes, and this he thought to restore, by dividing distances and holding neither. The comprehensive school restores it by holding both and bringing both to qualify and moderate each other. The liberal saw charity perishing in the earnest battle of the extremes, and required of itself a more indulgent spirit. The comprehensive school finds not only a defect of charity, but, what is more, a real ground for charity, in the fact that both extremes are only standing for the two poles of truth; earnest because they have the truth, and only quarreling because they have not breadth enough to see that they are one. In the comprehensive school it will be a first conviction, that all serious, earnest men have something in their view which makes it truth to them; therefore that all serious, earnest men, however repugnant in their words, have yet some radical agreement, and if the place can be found, will somewhere reveal their brotherhood. Therefore they are not only to tolerate, but to love and respect each other. Nay, they are each to ask, what has the other, which is necessary to its own completeness in the truth? And thus the comprehensive school, finding its liberality in the higher pursuit of truth, will have it not as a negation and exercise it not as a sacrament of indifference. It will be moderate without pursuing moderation, liberal without pursuing liberality, both because it follows after the truth, giving heed to all earnest voices, and bowing as a disciple to all her champions.

It is not our design, in giving out this distribution of schools, to place them all upon an equal footing. The first two and the last, the two extreme or partisan schools and the comprehensive school *must* appear in their order — they constitute the necessary conditions of mental progress in the truth, and truth can not find a complete and full development without them. The other two, the neutral and the liberal, *do* appear casually, or incidentally, and often hold an important figure in the real history of sects and opinions, and no sufficient view of the actual history of opinions can be given without some reference to them. They may both be regarded, perhaps, as spurious modes of the comprehensive school, actuated by some dim and undiscovered sense of the fact that there is doubtless a higher, broader truth, which, if it were known, would reveal an aspect of extravagance in the partisan strifes of the world. In this view, they may be looked upon as rudimental efforts preparatory to the development of a true comprehensiveness. And therefore the proper dignity of a comprehensive effort, guided by intelligent convictions and fixed laws of criticism, could not appear without some notice of the contrast between it and them.

Having it for our design, in this article, to recommend the comprehensive spirit in religion, we are tempted first of all to speak of it as related to character itself; for this is the radical interest of the subject, and the illustrations we may offer here will be familiar to all our readers, even to those who are unexercised in the higher abstractions of theology.

The endeavor to comprehend all antagonisms and hold the just equilibrium of truth is the highest and most ingenuous that a human soul can propose — one that God only can perfectly realize. Yet whosoever has but conceived such a thought gives some evidence therein of a resemblance to God, and he is, according to the measure of his success, a truly great character. A comprehensive character is, in fact, the only really great character possible among men. And, being that which holds the fullest agreement and sympathy with God, it is one, we are persuaded, that is specially valued and cherished by him. We shall find also, by inspection, that all the defective modes of character in Christian men are due to the fact that some partial or partisan view of duty sways their demonstrations. Sometimes one extreme is held, sometimes the other, and accordingly we shall see that, excepting cases where there is a fixed design to brave the laws of all duty, the blemished characters go in pairs.

Thus one man abhors all prejudice, testifies against it night and day, places all his guards on the side opposite, and, as prejudgments of some kind are the necessary condition of all judgments, it results, of course, that he falls into an error quite as hurtful and more weak, ceasing to have any fixed opinion, or to hold manfully any truth whatever. Another, seeing no evil but in a change of opinions, holds his opinions by his will and not by his understanding. And as no truth can penetrate the will, he becomes a stupid and obstinate bigot — standing for truth itself, as if it were no better than falsehood. . . .

So in all the possible views or aspects of Christian character, you will come nearest to what is great and Christ-like, if you seek to unite whatever repugnant extremes are before you — to be modest and yet bold; conciliatory and yet inflexible; patient in suffering, sharp in rebuke; deferential to all men, independent of all; charitable towards the erring, severe against the error; at once gentle and rigid, catholic and exclusive, all things to all men, and one thing only to yourself. The more numerous and repugnant the extremes of character (excepting those which are sinful), you are able to unite in one comprehensive and harmonious whole, the more finished and complete your character will be. . . .

Passing on now to matters of faith and doctrine, we shall see the same only more distinctly. And as all the extremes of practice go by pairs, so we shall find that sects and dogmas are set off in pairs about given points, and fighting each for its own opinion or pole — thus that all the Christian sects stand to represent, in some sense, all the Christian truths. Which, if we can manage to comprehend, as we know they are acknowledged and comprehended by Christ in the unity of his own body, then we shall complete ourselves in Christian doctrine, and realize the idea of a true Christian catholicity.

We do not, of course, maintain that there is no error in the Christian sects. A want of catholicity, or comprehensiveness, is itself error. To see any thing partially, or at one pole, is to see it insufficiently, thus in defective forms and proportions. Thus all sects and schools hold mixtures of

error, created by only half seeing what they see. Besides they are all instigated, in part, by evil passions and blinded by false prejudices, so that
they not only fall into error by half seeing, but sometimes by wrong seeing also. Still it will generally be found, if we set ourselves to a careful
scrutiny of the tenet or opinion which is distinctive in a given sect or
school, that there is some real truth in it, however repugnant at first view
to us — something which makes it true to the school, and the school earnest in maintaining it. As a matter of fact too, we have almost never seen
a dogma advanced by any body of men, however monstrous, which, if it
were dissolved and viewed in its contents historically, would not yield
some important truth.

Thus, among the first efforts of the church to frame a doctrine of
atonement, the death of Christ is often represented, and especially by
Irenæus and Origen, as a ransom paid to the devil. No representation
probably could be more abhorrent, when taken on its face, to the feelings
of all modern Christians. But if we can have patience to withhold our
judgment long enough to take down the drapery of the language, or dissolve its figures, thus to separate the real truth of feeling they may have
received, under a form of dogma so abhorrent to our speculative views of
the subject; in a word, if we can accurately conceive their historic state
of mind when advancing this rude theory of atonement, the first which
unilluminated reason had produced, we shall find no difficulty in allowing
that they held a warm and living truth, under a form so badly misshapen.

No doctrine is sooner rejected, or more derided for its absurdity, than
the doctrine of the real presence. But when taken with all the negations
added, in regard to the sensible form of the elements in the supper, it
would be difficult to show that any thing more is left than what every
believing Christian ought to admit, viz., that the recipient of the supper is
to meet therein a grace which is above sensation, and feast himself in the
participation of the divine nature. Out of this great truth of the presence,
passing into a human philosophy, the doctrine of transubstantiation, and
of a sacrifice, probably grew. The injuriousness of the doctrine is due not
to the fact that it contains no truth, but to the fact, rather, that the disciple is like to be confused and astounded as before a miracle wrought by
the priest, and thus to miss of the truth. The exaggeration, or over-
statement, smothers the truth contained. Meantime, is it not also possible
that the Protestant often misses the same truth, under the doctrine of
Zwingli? He comes, we will suppose, to do an act, to use a symbol that
will assist him to remember his Lord. But if he is wholly occupied with

his own act, there is no communion. He is only magnetizing himself. Communion implies reciprocity, and if he may not and does not receive the real Christ, there is no reciprocity. If, therefore, Christ does not offer himself there to be received, by a presence above sensation, or if the disciple does not believe it, then he is blinded by his rationalism as the Romanist by his superstition. Two things are necessary to the Christian idea of the supper: an act of reception, which is an act of faith, and a matter to be received, which is a matter offered to faith. If the Romanist omits the faith, how often, both in practice and also in theory, does the Protestant omit the matter of faith. When both poles are united, when Christ the matter of faith is offered to faith, and faith receives the matter offered, then is the Lord's body discerned.

The Quaker doctrine of an inner light, however derided, contains a great and sublime truth. And, if it be taken as antagonistic to the doctrine that all true knowledge is derivable to the soul through sense, whether as occupied with nature, or instructed by revelation, it might be difficult to say which is nearer to the truth. If one nullifies the word, the other nullifies the soul as the candle of the Lord. Or if the world is dark without Christ, so, if the light that is in us be darkness, how great is that darkness — even having Christ before us. Without the inner light, revelation can not certify its truth; for there is nothing in the soul to measure and discriminate truth. Without revelation visiting the soul from without, or through the senses and the understanding, the inner light of conscience and reason is provoked to no distinct announcement of itself. There is a divine Word in the soul's own nature, but it shineth in darkness and is not comprehended, till the Word becomes flesh and is represented historically without. And even then, the natural man discerneth not the things of the Spirit, until the inner life of the soul is quickened to perceptiveness by the inbreathing of God. The Quaker and the Scripturalist, therefore, are both right and both wrong — right in what they assert, wrong in what they deny. Unite the positive contents of both, and we have the Christian doctrine.

The same may be said, in substance, regarding the Absolute Religion of Mr. Parker;[1] for this is only a modified Quakerism — a Quakerism whose inspiration lies in natural ideas and instincts, and not, to any extent, in spiritual gifts. Nor is any thing more true than that the soul is constituted for religion, much as he has represented. It is a great and divine truth

1. [ED.] See Theodore Parker, *A Discourse of Matters Pertaining to Religion*, edited with a preface by Thomas W. Higginson (Boston, 1907), 214 and *passim*.

also — one that revelation itself presupposes and actually affirms. But if Mr. Parker had taken pains to inquire why God has set us in a sphere of sensation, amid objects of knowledge and scenes of experience — why he did not make us mere absolutes ourselves, in a world of geometries and bare intellectualities — he might have been led to suspect that the same reasons which determined to this, might require also historic revelations and even miracles. For if it be needful to live in a phenomenal world, if the absolutes of the soul are nothing worth, until they are brought forth into actual discourse, and represented and mirrored in the objects and scenes of experience; if seeing and hearing, trial and work, are wanted to assist the absolute religion, why may not a Divine Word in the flesh be as needful as a Divine Word in the world? At the same time, Mr. Parker is not to be answered by denying the religious nature of the soul. If the soul were not a religious nature, the historic word would be worthless; and so, without the historic word, the religious nature, as a glance at the nations of mankind abundantly shows, will only baffle itself in its sins, and become a blinded and bewildered instinct.

Many persons are inexpressibly shocked by the Calvinistic dogma of unconditional election and reprobation, or of absolute decrees. But if they could suspend their mind long enough to sound its depths and measure its real contents, they would find a great and holy truth enveloped in it, one that is even fundamental to God's empire, and necessary to the highest power of his government over souls — the same which has given to Calvinism a religious energy so peculiar. If it be understood that God enters into the actual historical world of men, to pick out unconditionally one for life and another for death, there is abundant reason to be shocked by such a doctrine. But if we go above the actual to contemplate God, before the foundation of the world, as dealing with intelligibles, or possibles, perusing systems of possibles, foreknowing them and their contents, not as actual, or historical, but as intelligible; then instituting, or by a fiat of will actualizing the best and wisest, we shall see that, in putting that best system on foot, he has made it certain that all the contents of the system will emerge, historically, in due time. He has done it by an absolute unconditional decree; for, if he had not put the system on foot, nothing in it would ever become a historical fact. And having done so, every thing in it will, and he will not be disappointed. What he saw in the intelligible will emerge in the historical, exactly as he saw it. But not so as to exclude conditions in the actual. For the intelligible system he selected was a system linked together by innumerable causes and relations; comprising activities to be exerted by himself, laws pronounced, works of grace performed, acts and choices of the subjects as they, in their own freedom or self-activity, would determine; results of character and destiny, such as his own good activity, and theirs, both good and evil, would produce. And here is the great truth of Calvinism. Having this intelligible system before him, with all its ingredients, conditions, and results, God by an absolute decree institutes the system; which is the same as to say that whatsoever it contains, will come to pass — come to pass, that is, under the conditions, so as not to infringe upon the responsibility of any subject, and so as to justify him and his goodness in all. In this grand truth of Calvinism, God's WILL becomes a reality. The world is felt to be in his hands. He asks no leave to reign. He reigns not blindly, or as a being baffled by unknown contingencies. Trembling before his sovereignty, we find it still a benign sovereignty, a rock of confidence and love. Unable to ascend above the actual and historical, the Arminian sees no other way to save the conditions of freedom and just responsibility, but to deny a truth so essential to God's government. Probably the Calvinist, equally unable to get above the actual, asserts his doctrine of divine will and unconditional decrees as holding under and within the sphere of actual history. One destroys the government of God, the other makes him a tyrant. And yet they are both asserting great and fundamental truths. Unite the Arminian and the Calvinist, comprehend both doctrines, and we have the Christian truth.

In these illustrations, it has been our object to show that in dogmas regarded with the utmost repugnance there is generally to be found some important truth, if only we have patience to look for it. In the same illustrations, we have also advanced the general purpose we have in hand, viz., to show that all the Christian truths stand in opposites, or extremes that need to be comprehended. That something of this kind is true in matters of natural science, is known to all. In the astronomic forces, in the chemical resolution of substances, in light and electricity, we discover nature lying between her poles, and science becoming a doctrine, when it comprehends them both. And, in this, we have only a symbol of what relates to mind and spirit, the doctrine of man and the doctrine of God.

Accordingly, the first thing to be done in theology is to reveal the poles, or the repugnant forms of truth. In all matters of moral judgment, or intellectual opinion, there must be something in the nature of controversy, to prepare the way. The elements to be combined or comprehended will thus be brought to light, and set up as distinct objects of contemplation. Then the man or the teacher that follows, holding himself aloof from the controversy, and looking calmly on as a spectator, to ask what do these combatants mean? — what great truth have they each in mind, for which they are doing battle? — will most uniformly find that they have one which is somehow reconcilable with the opposite. Accordingly, there is no one who has so great advantage, in arriving at the truth, as he who follows after a controversy, if only he has the independence of men and the implicit love of truth necessary to improve his position.

Our churches, for example, have been recently agitated by a warm and earnest controversy in reference to the doctrine of spiritual regeneration. Ask what the antagonist parties are after, and it will be found that one is after the truth of divine agency and spiritual dependence, the other after the liberty and responsibility of the subject. In this case neither of the parties intends to deny what the other really wishes to maintain. Both assert our dependence, both our ability; but one a dependence which to the other destroys all ability, one an ability which to the other destroys all dependence. Never was there a better opportunity to settle the true comprehensive doctrine on this difficult subject, than when such a controversy going before has set up, in full view, the antagonistic elements to be united. But if we are to use the advantage offered, we must not be in haste to enroll ourselves as disciples or partisans. We must ascend to a higher and calmer position, where we may see at once all the material offered us, and use it as material to be comprehended in a single view or doctrine. Then possibly we may find that a soul, under the bondage of evil, is able to renew himself in good in and through dependence — able to work because God worketh in him. It will not be said that he has a natural ability which means nothing, nor a natural ability which means that he can do all by himself. It will not be found that God must dispense an ictic grace *before* he can put forth any right motion, which absolves the sinner from any attempt; nor that he can regenerate himself, and is dependent on God only by consent or courtesy. But it will be seen that he *can* do nothing out of God — any thing in God.

In the great question put in issue by the Unitarians concerning the trinity, or the nature of God, it is difficult, in a single paragraph, to indicate the true comprehensive doctrine. But we are ready to express our firm conviction that the Unitarians will not be found to have stood forth in the maintenance of a pure error, when insisting on the strict unity of God. There was a kind of trinity maintained, and still is, by many, which amounts to a practical triplicity, and breeds a mental confusion in the worshiper that is both painful and hurtful. For this there was no remedy but to assert the absolute unity of the divine nature, and the position here assumed is impregnable. No doctrine of trinity that infringes upon this can ever be maintained. Does it therefore follow, since God is one, that there is no conceivable tripersonality which can be vindicated? Others may thus judge, but for ourselves we have no difficulty in perceiving either the meaning, or the practical need of such a doctrine. For if there be a practical confusion in the triplicity held by many, there is a practical impotence in the bald philosophic unity and its representations when rigidly adhered to, that is even more injurious to the life of religion. While our Unitarian friends, therefore, are reposing in all confidence on their impregnable doctrine of the divine unity, it becomes them to remember that if they are not reasoned out of it they may yet be frozen out, which is quite as bad. For without a trinity subjective to us and filling the forms of the mind, God is necessarily distant, unconversible, and without any adequate warmth to sustain our religious vitality. Of this we feel quite as sure as we do of God's objective unity. If in saying this we seem to speak enigmatically, it is all we can say at present. We only express, in addition, our confident belief in the possibility of a doctrine that shall comprehend all which the Christian world, on both sides of this great question, are contending for. For it would be singular — a philosophic anomaly passing belief, that all Christendom should have been standing for so many centuries for that which, after all, is a pure phantasm or hallucination. It is not in mankind to go after naked error in this way. Even when they stumble worst, it will be found that they have yet some semblance of truth. . . .

We might go on with illustrations of this kind, till a great multitude of the controverted doctrines of Christianity are seen yoked with their opposites, in friendly embrace — pantheism with theism, absolute religion with revealed religion, supralapsarianism with sublapsarianism, absolute decrees with self-active freedom, salvation by grace with salvation by works, inability with ability, natural depravity with natural innocence, the bondage of sin with the freedom of the sinner. In all these repugnances we have only the two poles of truth, which, if we can manage to comprehend in one and the same mental view, we arrive at the proper integrity of the Christian doctrine. Indeed, we may lay it down as true, in general, that all the Christian sects, in all their manifold repugnances of doctrine, are only concerned to exhibit the great elemental truths of Christianity. They all have errors, they all partially mistake, as it is human to do, and yet they all have some form of truth to maintain, which, when it is viewed comprehensively, and carefully distinguished under the forms of language, will fall into the same great scheme of Christian doctrine and assist to fill out the body thereof. So that when a man is able to comprehend the reality of all sects, casting away the unreality, he will be a full-grown proper Christian man.

Dismissing here subjects of doctrine, we go on to speak of polities and organizations. Polities are not so much essential truths, or doctrines, as means to ends. They embody each some practical aim or idea, and offer each some valuable contribution to the comprehensive church of the future. Whether they will ever coalesce in any practical unity or mutual acknowledgment of each other, bringing in their treasures to enrich the common body, many will doubt; but, if a hope so beautiful must be renounced as visionary, we shall easily convince ourselves, by a study of their contents, that they have each some kind of wealth which makes their existence valuable, even now, to the world. Or, if some of them have no longer a sufficient reason for the maintenance of a distinct existence, it is only because they have already emptied their treasures into the world's history. Possibly such an opinion may some time be held of them all; for it may be that they are all designed to serve only temporary uses. And then, when they have all emptied themselves into history, and history contains the product of all, what forbids that a new church may emerge that shall comprehend the uses of all?

And if any such result is ever to appear, where sooner than here in these United States? Why else are we thrown together in this manner — Christians of all names and sects, living in the same neighborhoods, fellow citizens under the same laws, holding equal terms before the laws, united in business, intermarried in families? No such spectacle as this has ever been exhibited before, since Christianity entered the world, and yet it seems to be the design of God that it shall, ere long, be so in all the other nations of mankind. The extension of liberty must bring the same results to pass every where. It seems to be God's purpose that all these multiform sects and polities shall either dissolve each other and lodge their contents at last in a grand comprehensive unity, or else wear themselves into similar shapes by their mutual attrition. And how else could a properly catholic state, which is the hope of us all, be constructed? [2] . . .

In offering these thoughts to the public, we are well aware that some may be scandalized or alarmed by their free spirit. But such will relieve

2. [ED.] Owing to limitations of space, we have omitted a lengthy discussion of what the various denominational polities (including Quaker, Baptist, Presbyterian, Methodist, Episcopal, and Roman Catholic) might contribute toward the comprehensive church of the future.

their apprehensions, if they consider that we ask no compromise of opinions and do not even speak of liberality as a special Christian virtue. We simply require it of all Christians to look for the truth, and the truth only. And if we require them to look beyond themselves and across their own boundaries, we see not that there is any thing specially frightful in this, if they look for nothing but the truth. Or if we prepare a previous conviction, in their minds, that there is somewhat of truth in all Christian bodies, does any one doubt that there is? And if it should happen that all these bodies look upon the truth on a side peculiar to themselves, what harm can it do us to pass round and look through their eyes? The method taken by the late Evangelical Alliance, at London, was truly a dangerous method and closely allied to licentiousness; for it chose out only common truths in which all the parties could agree, and consented to let all other truths pass into shade as of minor consequence.[3] We recognize, contrary to this, the great principle that truth is a whole and is to be sought only as a whole — any where, every where, and by all means. Let no one fear the debauching of his Christian integrity in so doing.

Others probably will look upon our labor in this matter as a useless expenditure of breath, and the hope we encourage as altogether visionary and romantic. It would be, if we held the expectation that the church of God is ever to become a political unity. Or if we proposed to the Christian sects to come together and work out a comprehensive unity, by any deliberative effort, in the manner of compromise and composition. Or if we looked for the realization of any such result as we speak of, by any given method, within any given space of time. Our object is simply to set before the Christian sects the comfortable truth that our antagonisms are to a great degree comprehensible — parts only or partialities, having each their complement in all the others. Thus to beget a more fraternal feeling and soften the asperities and prejudices that hold us asunder. Thus to set all thinking minds on an endeavor after the broadest and most catholic views of truth, in the confident hope that God will thus enlarge their souls, draw them together, towards a more complete brotherhood, and finally into a full consent of worship. This, if we rightly understand, is what the Scriptures mean by seeing eye to eye. We now see shoulder to shoulder, but when we can look into the eye, every man of his brother, and see what he sees, we shall be one.

And if any one asks, when shall these things be? we may well enough

3. [ED.] For a critical analysis of the basic shortcomings of the Evangelical Alliance, which convened at London in 1846, see Bushnell, "The Evangelical Alliance," *New Englander*, V (1847), 102–25.

refer him to the geologists for an answer. For if God required long ages of heaving and fiery commotion to settle the world's layers into peace and habitable order, we ought not utterly to despair if the geologic era of the church covers a somewhat longer space of time than we ourselves might prescribe. Enough for us that we show the laws of commotion and the methods of final pacification. Enough for us that the views we have advanced, if accepted and held by our fellow Christians, will be found to contain the philosophic causes of a better day, drawing us all into a closer assimilation and, as sure as causes must have their effects, into a final embrace in the truth. Confident of this, and leaving times and seasons to God, we do not seem to propose to the world unpractical schemes, or romantic expectations.

PART TWO

❖

Theological Reconstruction

NATURE AND THE SUPERNATURAL [1]

EDITOR'S INTRODUCTION

By 1850, Horace Bushnell had become seriously concerned over the accelerating trend toward naturalism, a trend which he attributed mainly to the impact of modern scientific method. Christianity was in danger, he warned, "from what may be called a bondage under the method of science, — as if nothing could be true, save as it is proved by the scientific method." [2] He considered this question briefly in his Dudleian Lecture, given at Harvard in 1852, but he explored it definitively in *Nature and the Supernatural*, published six years later.

Bushnell's main purpose in that book has often been misrepresented. This is evident, for example, in an address given by Theodore Thornton Munger at the Bushnell Centennial in 1902, on "The Secret of Horace Bushnell." [3] The "secret and law" of Bushnell's thought, said Munger, was that he went to nature to find God. "Driven by his own nature into nature — among her laws and processes and intelligences — he finds himself in God." [4] In his effort to vindicate this thesis, Munger appealed chiefly to *Nature and the Supernatural*, contending that therein Bushnell employed the term "nature," not in its usual restricted sense, "but nature as going beyond into universal being, even God, who is included in its category." [5] He further argued that "Bushnell, outrunning his day, conceived God as immanent in his works — the soul and life of them. . . .

1. *Nature and the Supernatural, as Together Constituting the One System of God* (New York, 1858), Chap. II (36–37, 42–52, 58–62); Chap. III (64–65, 76–82, 84–90).
2. *Ibid.*, 20.
3. *Bushnell Centennial. Minutes of the General Association of Connecticut at the One Hundred and Ninety-Third Annual Meeting Held in Hartford, June 17–18, 1902* (Hartford, 1902), 35–46. The address was republished in *The Outlook*, LXXI (August 10, 1902), 1063–68. The latter source will be cited here since it gives a slightly revised version of the address as printed in the *Minutes of the General Association*.
4. *The Outlook*, LXXI (August 10, 1902), 1068.   5. *Ibid.*, 1066.

Therefore if one would know how God feels and acts, one must go to nature, and to humanity as its culmination." [6]

That is an amazing misrepresentation of Bushnell's thought. In the first place, he did not use the term "nature" to designate the whole of reality or universal being; on the contrary, he explicitly contended that there are "two distinct orders and degrees of being, which, together, constitute the real universe." [7] In the second place, Bushnell did not hold — as Munger implied — to the idea of divine immanence in the sense that God's operations are subject to one universal law. Although he insisted upon a completely lawful universe, he declared that the universe involved the operation of three distinct and non-interchangeable kinds of law: (1) the law of nature, (2) the moral law, and (3) the law of "God's last end." [8]

It is important to understand Bushnell's main design in writing *Nature and the Supernatural*. Certainly it was not to urge men to go first of all to nature to find God. Bushnell acknowledged that God "is beautifully expressed in a small way in nature," but he insisted that God "is even more visibly, convincingly, and gloriously expressed in Christianity than he is in all the world." [9] Far from urging men to go to nature to discover God, he actually pointed to the peril of becoming preoccupied with nature. The peril was pantheism. Nor, again, was it Bushnell's main purpose to seek to reconcile the two orders of nature and the supernatural. Yet Williston Walker expressed a commonly held notion when he wrote: "In this painstaking study [*Nature and the Supernatural*] Doctor Bushnell strove to show that nature and the supernatural are not antagonistic and exclusive realms." [10] It is granted that Bushnell sought to show the complementary relation of nature and the supernatural. However, this was but a subsidiary part of a more basic intention, which was twofold: (1) to demonstrate the inadequacy of a religion framed within the terms of "mere nature"; and (2) to establish an intellectual footing for belief in a universe which included the supernatural as the primordial ground and redemptive agency of the world of nature. With respect to his constructive purpose, he wrote:

> I shall make out a conception both of nature and of supernatural redemption by Jesus Christ, the incarnate Word of God, which exactly meets the magnificent outline-view of God's universal plan, given by the great apostle to the Gentiles — "And He is before all things, and by Him (*in* Him, it should be,) all things consist [*cf.*

6. *Ibid.*, 1068.   7. *Nature and the Supernatural*, 86.
8. *Ibid.*, 261–71.   9. *Ibid.*, 508.
10. "Horace Bushnell," in *Christian Nurture*, revised by Luther A. Weigle (New York, 1916), xxvii.

Col. 1:16–17]." Christianity, in other words, is not an afterthought of God, but a forethought. It even antedates the world of nature, and is "before all things" — "before the foundation of the world." Instead of coming into the world, as being no part of the system, or to interrupt and violate the system of things, they all *consist*, come together into system, in Christ, as the center of unity and the head of the universal plan.[11]

Although Bushnell sought to counteract an excessive naturalism, he did not condemn science as such; on the contrary, he regarded it as a necessary instrument for the advancement of truth. With the exception of Darwin's theory of the transmutation of species, he was remarkably hospitable to the whole range of scientific discovery.[12] Observing that "truth is one," since it is "based in God's all comprehensive intelligence," he urged that religion "must seek to put itself in harmony with every sort of truth, else it cannot be true itself." [13] Thus he held that the biblical account of such events as the creation, the flood, and the fall must be reinterpreted in light of scientific knowledge.[14] Still, this does not alter the fact that Bushnell's main purpose in *Nature and the Supernatural* was to defend Christianity against the growing tendency to translate it into naturalistic categories.

In formulating his view of the two orders of being — nature and the supernatural — Bushnell borrowed heavily from Coleridge. In the *Aids to Reflection*, the poet-philosopher wrote:

Nature is the term in which we comprehend all things that are representable in the forms of time and space, and subjected to the relations of cause and effect; and the cause of the existence of which, therefore, is to be sought for perpetually in something antecedent. . . . It follows, therefore, that whatever originates its own acts, or in any sense contains in itself the cause of its own state, must be spiritual, and consequently supernatural.[15]

In his later writings, as well as in *Nature and the Supernatural*, Bushnell revealed the strong influence of Coleridge.[16]

❖ ❖ ❖ ❖

11. *Nature and the Supernatural*, 31.

12. Bushnell, "Science and Religion," *Putnam's Magazine*, I (January–June 1868), 265–75.

13. *Ibid.*, 272.

14. *Ibid.*, 266–71. According to Frank H. Foster, Bushnell accepted the Bible "as it was handed to him without special question" (*The Modern Movement in American Theology* [New York, 1939], 60). That statement is groundless.

15. "Aids to Reflection," *Complete Works of Samuel Taylor Coleridge*, William G. T. Shedd, ed. (7 vols., New York, 1868), I, 263. See also *ibid.*, 154, 272–73.

16. See, for example, "Progress," *Hours at Home*, VIII (January 1869), 206.

Chapter II

Definitions — Nature and the Supernatural

In order to the intelligent prosecution of our subject, we need first of all
to settle on the true import of certain words and phrases, by the undistin-
guishing and confusing use of which, more than by any other cause, the
unbelieving habit of our time has been silently and imperceptibly determined. They are such as these: "nature," "the system of nature," "the
laws of nature," "universal nature," "the supernatural," and the like. The
first and last name, "nature" and the "supernatural," most need our attention; for, if these are carefully distinguished, the others will scarcely
fail to yield us their true meaning.

The Latin etymology of the word *nature* presents the true force of the
term, clear of all ambiguity. The nature (*natura*) of a thing is the future
participle of its being or becoming — its *about-to-be,* or its *about-to-
come-to-pass* — and the radical idea is, that there is in the thing whose
nature we speak of, or in the whole of things called nature, an about-to-
be, a definite futurition, a fixed law of coming to pass, such that, given the
thing, or whole of things, all the rest will follow by an inherent necessity.
In this view, nature, sometimes called "universal nature," and sometimes
"the system of nature," is that created realm of being or substance which
has an acting, a going on or process from within itself, under and by its
own laws. Or if we say, with some, that the laws are but another name
for the immediate actuating power of God, still it makes no difference in
any other respect with our conception of the system. It is yet *as if* the
laws, the powers, the actings, were inherent in the substances, and were
by them determined. It is still to our scientific separated from our religious contemplation, a chain of causes and effects, or a scheme of orderly
succession, determined from within the scheme itself.

Having settled, thus, our conception of nature, our conception of the
supernatural corresponds. That is supernatural, whatever it be, that is
either not in the chain of natural cause and effect, or which acts on the
chain of cause and effect, in nature, from without the chain. Thus if any
event transpires in the bosom, or upon the platform, of what is called nature, which is not from nature itself, or is varied from the process nature
would execute by her own laws, that is supernatural, by whatever power
it is wrought. . . .

But the real import of our distinction between nature and the supernatural, however accurately stated in words, will not fully appear till we show it in the concrete; for it does not yet appear that there is, in fact, any such thing known as the supernatural agency defined, or that there are *in esse* any beings, or classes of beings, who are distinguished by the exercise of such an agency. That what we have defined as nature truly exists will not be doubted, but that there is any being or power in the universe who acts, or can act, upon the chain of cause and effect in nature from without the chain, many will doubt and some will strenuously deny. Indeed the great difficulty heretofore encountered, in establishing the faith of a supernatural agency, has been due to the fact that we have made a ghost of it; discussing it as if it were a marvel of superstition, and no definite and credible reality. Whereas it will appear, as we confront our difficulty more thoughtfully and take its full force, that the moment we begin to conceive ourselves rightly, we become ourselves supernatural. It is no longer necessary to go hunting after marvels, apparitions, suspensions of the laws of nature, to find the supernatural; it meets us in what is least transcendent and most familiar, even in ourselves. In ourselves we discover a tier of existences that are above nature and, in all their most ordinary actions, are doing their will upon it. The very idea of our personality is that of a being not under the law of cause and effect, a being supernatural. This one point clearly apprehended, all the difficulties of our subject are at once relieved, if not absolutely and completely removed.

If any one is startled or shocked by what appears to be the extravagance of this position, let him recur to our definition; viz., that nature is that world of substance whose laws are laws of cause and effect, and whose events transpire, in orderly succession under those laws; the supernatural is that range of substance, if any such there be, that acts upon the chain of cause and effect in nature from without the chain, producing thus results that, by mere nature, could not come to pass. It is not said, be it observed, as is sometimes done, that the supernatural implies a suspension of the laws of nature, a causing them, for the time, not to be — that, perhaps, is never done — it is only said that we, as powers, not in the line of cause and effect, can set the causes in nature at work in new combinations otherwise never occurring, and produce, by our action upon nature, results which she, as nature, could never produce by her own internal acting.

Illustrations are at hand without number. Thus nature, for example, never made a pistol or gunpowder, or pulled a trigger; all which being done, or procured to be done, by the criminal, in his act of murder, he is

hung for what is rightly called his unnatural deed. So of things not criminal; nature never built a house, or modeled a ship, or fitted a coat, or invented a steam engine, or wrote a book, or framed a constitution. These
are all events that spring out of human liberty, acting in and upon the
realm of cause and effect to produce results and combinations which mere
cause and effect could not; and, at some point of the process in each, we
shall be found coming down upon nature, by an act of sovereignty just
as peremptory and mysterious as that which is discovered in a miracle,
only that a miracle is a similar coming down upon it from another and
higher being, and not from ourselves. Thus, for example, in the firing of
the pistol we find materials brought together and compounded for making
an explosive gas, an arrangement prepared to strike a fire into the substance
compounded, an arm pulled back to strike the fire, muscles contracted to
pull back the arm, a nervous telegraph running down from the brain, by
which some order has been sent to contract the muscles; and then, having
come to the end of the chain of natural causes, the jury ask, Who sent the
mandate down upon the nervous telegraph, ordering the said contraction?
And, having found, as their true answer, that the arraigned criminal did
it, they offer this as their verdict, and on the strength of the verdict he is
hung. He had, in other words, a power to set in order a line of causes and
effects, existing elementally in nature, and then, by a sentence of his will,
to start the line, doing his unnatural deed of murder. If it be inquired
how he was able to command the nervous telegraph in this manner, we
can not tell, any more than we can show the manner of a miracle. The
same is true in regard to all our most common actions. If one simply lifts
a weight, overcoming, thus far, the great law of gravity, we may trace
the act mechanically back in the same way; and if we do it, we shall
come, at last, to the man acting in his personal arbitrament, and shall find
him sending down his mandate to the arm, summoning its contractions
and sentencing the weight to rise. In which, as we perceive, he has just so
much of power given him to vary the incidents and actings of nature as
determined by her own laws — so much, that is, of power supernatural.

And so all the combinations we make in the harnessing of nature's
powers imply, in the last degree, thoughts, mandates of will, that are at
some point peremptory over the motions by which we handle, and move,
and shape, and combine the substances and causes of the world. And to
what extent we may go on to alter, in this manner, the composition of the
world, few persons appear to consider. For example, it is not absurd to
imagine the human race, at some future time, when the population and

the works of industry are vastly increased, kindling so many fires, by putting wood and coal in contact with fire, as to burn up or fatally vitiate the
world's atmosphere. That the condition of nature will, in fact, be so far
changed by human agency, is probably not to be feared. We only say
that human agency, in its power over nature, holds, or may well enough
be imagined to hold, the sovereignty of the process. Meantime, it is even
probable, as a matter of fact, that infections and pestilential diseases invad-
ing, every now and then, some order of vegetable or animal life, are referable in the last degree to something done upon the world by man. For
indeed we shall show, before we have done, that the scheme of nature
itself is a scheme unstrung and mistuned, to a very great degree, by man's
agency in it, so as to be rather unnature, after all, than nature; and for just
that reason demanding of God, even for system's sake, in the highest
range of that term, miracle and redemption.

Suffice it, for the present, simply to clear, as well as we are able, this
main point, the fact of a properly supernatural power in man. Thus some
one, going back to the act by which the pistol was fired, will imagine,
after all, that the murderer's act in the firing was itself caused in him by
some condition back of what we call his choice, as truly as the explosion
of the powder was caused by the fire. Then why not blame the powder,
we answer, as readily as the man — which most juries would have some
difficulty in doing, though none at all in blaming the man? The nature of
the objection is purely imaginary, as, in fact, the common sense, if we
should not rather say the common consciousness of the word decides; for
we are all conscious of acting from ourselves, uncaused in our action. The
murderer knows within himself that he did the deed, and that nothing
else did it through him. So his consciousness testifies — so the consciousness of every man revising his actions — and no real philosopher will ever
undertake to substitute the verdict of consciousness, by another, which
he has arrived at only by speculation, or a logical practice in words. The
sentence of consciousness is final.

Hence the absurd and really blamable ingenuity of those would-be
philosophers who, not content with the clear, indisputable report of consciousness in such a case, go on to ask whether the wrong-doer of any
kind was not acting, in his wrong, under motives and determined by the
strongest motives, and since he is a being made to act in this manner,
whether after all he really acted himself, any more than other natural
substances do when they yield to the strongest cause? Doubtless he acted
under motives, and probably enough he felt beside that half his crime was

in his motive, being that which his own bad heart supplied. The matter of the strongest motive is more doubtful; but if it be true, in every case, that the wrong-doer chooses what to him is the strongest motive, it by no means follows that he acts in the way of a scale-beam, swayed by the heaviest weight; for the strength of the motive may consciously be derived, in great part, from what his own perversity puts into it; and, what is more, he may be as fully conscious that he acts, in every case, from himself, in pure self-determination, as he would be if he acted for no motive at all. Consciously he is not a scale-beam, or any passive thing, but a self-determining agent; and if he looks out always for the strongest motive, he still as truly acts from his own personal arbitrament as if he were always pursuing the weakest.

It does not, however, appear, from any evidence we can discover, that human action is determined uniformly by the strongest motive. That is the doctrine of Edwards, in his famous treatise on the will,[1] but as far as there is any appearance of force in his argument, it consists in the inference drawn, or judgment passed, *after* any act of choice, that the inducing motive *must have been* the strongest because it prevailed. Whereas, appealing to his simple consciousness, he would have found that he had never a thought of the superior strength of the motive chosen, *before* the choice; and that, when he ascertained the fact of its superiority, it was only by an inference or speculative judgment drawn from the choice —

1. The fortunes of this Treatise [*Freedom of the Will* (1754)], in the world of morals and religion, have been quite as remarkable as the puzzle it has raised in the world of letters. The immediate object of the writer was gained, and the faith of God's eternal government, assailed by a crazy scheme of liberty which brought in open question the divine foreknowledge and the proper self-understanding of God in his plan, was effectually vindicated. So far the argument availed to serve the genuine purposes of religion. But, from that day to this, passing over to the side opposite, it has been turned more and more disastrously against the Christian truth, and even against the first principles of moral obligation. Priestly was an implicit believer in the doctrine, holding it as the foundation principle of a scheme of necessity which could hardly be said to leave a real place for duty in the world. And now, in our own day, it has descended to the level of the subterranean infidelity, and become a familiar and standing argument with almost every moral outcast who has thought enough in him to know that he is annoyed by the distinctions of virtue. Having turned philosopher on just this point and shown that we are all governed by the strongest motive, he asks with an air of triumph: Where, then, is the place for blame? What do we all but just what we are made to do? Could Edwards return to look on the uses now made of his argument, his saintly spirit might possibly be stirred with some doubts of its validity. [ED.] Concerning "strongest motive," see *The Works of Jonathan Edwards*, Vol. I: *Freedom of the Will*, Paul Ramsey, ed. (New Haven, 1957), 141–42, 160–61.

just as some harvester, noting the heavy perspiration that drenches his body in the field, will judge from such a sign that he must be dissolving with heat; when the real sense of his body, wiser and truer than his logic, is that he is being cooled. And what, moreover, if it should happen that Edwards, in his inference, is only carrying over into the world of mind a judgment formed in the world of matter; subjecting human souls to the analogy of scale-beams, and concluding that since nature yields to the strongest force, the supernatural must do the same. Meantime, what is the consciousness testifying? Here is the whole question. There is no place here for a volume, or even for the amount of a syllogism. Find what the consciousness testifies, and that, all tricks of argument apart, is the truth.

Taking, then, this simple issue, the verdict we are quite sure is against the doctrine of Edwards; viz., that, in all wrong or blamable action we consciously take the weakest motive and most worthless; and, partly for that reason, blame our own folly and perversity. It may be that the good rejected stands superior only before our rational convictions, while the enticement followed stirs more actively our lusts and passions. Still we know, and believe, and deeply feel, at the time — we even shudder it may be in the choice, at the sense of our own perversity — that we are choosing the worst and meanest thing, casting away the gold and grasping after the dirt. Probably a good many crude-minded persons, little capable of reporting the true verdict of their consciousness, would answer immediately, after any such act of choice, that they made it because the motive was strongest; for every most vulgar mind is so far under the great law of dynamics as to judge that whatever force prevails must be the strongest. Besides, how could he be a reasonable being if he chose the weakest motive; therefore it *must be* that he chose the strongest. So it stands, not as any report of consciousness, but simply as a *must be* of the logical understanding. Whereas the real sin of the choice was exactly this and nothing else, that the wrong-doer followed after the weakest and worst, and did not act as a reasonable being should; and that is what his consciousness, if he could get far back enough into the sense of the moment, would report. Nor does it vary at all the conclusion that a wrong-doer chooses the weakest motive, to imagine with many loose-minded teachers that the right is only postponed, and the wrong chosen for the moment, with a view to secure the double benefit, both of the right and the wrong; for the real question at the time is, in every such case, whether it is wisest, best, and every way most advantageous, to make the delay and try for the double benefit; and no man ever yet believed that it was. Never was there a case of wrong or sinful choice, in which the agent believed that he was really choosing the strongest, or weightiest and most valuable motive.[2]

So far, then, is man from being any proper item of nature. He is under no law of cause and effect in his choices. He stands out clear and sovereign as a being supernatural, and his definition is that he is an original power, acting not in the line of causality but from himself. He is not independent of nature in the sense of being separated from it in his action, but he is in it, environed by it, acting through it, partially sovereign over it, always sovereign as regards his self-determination, and only not completely sovereign as regards executing all that he wills in it. In certain parts or departments of the soul itself, such as memory, appetite, passion, attention, imagination, association, disposition, the will power in him is held in contact, so to speak, with conditions and qualities that are dominated partly by laws of cause and effect; for these faculties are partly governed by their own laws, and partly submitted to his governing will by their own laws; so that when he will exercise any control over them, or turn them about to serve his purpose, he can do it, in a qualified sense and degree, by operating through their laws. As far as they are concerned, he is pure nature, and he is only a power superior to cause and effect at the particular point of volition where his liberty culminates, and where the administration he is to maintain over his whole nature centers.

2. A certain class of theologians may, perhaps, imagine that such a view of choice takes away the ground of the divine foreknowledge. How can God foreknow what choices men may form, when, for aught that appears, they as often choose against the strongest motive as with it? He could not foreknow any thing, we answer, under such conditions, if he were obliged to find out future things as the astronomers make out almanacs, by computation. But he is a being, not who computes, but who, by the eternal necessity even of his nature, intuits every thing. His foreknowledge does not depend on his will, or the adjustment of motives to make us will thus or thus, but he foreknows every thing first conditionally, in the world of possibility, before he creates, or determines any thing to be, in the world of fact. Otherwise, all his purposes would be grounded in ignorance, not in wisdom, and his knowledge would consist in following after his will, to learn what his will has blindly determined. This is not the Scripture doctrine, which grounds all the purposes of God in his wisdom; that is, in what he perceives by his eternal intuitive foreknowledge of what is contained in all possible systems and combinations before creation — "Whom he did foreknow, them he also did predestinate" — "elect, according to the foreknowledge of God." If, then, God foreknows, or intuitively knows, all that is in the possible system and the possible man, without calculation, he can have little difficulty, after that, in foreknowing the actual man, who is nothing but the possible in the world of possibles, set on foot and become actual in the world of actuals. So far, therefore, as the doctrine of Edwards was contrived to support the certainty of God's foreknowledge, and lay a basis for the systematic government of the world and the universal sovereignty of God's purposes, it appears to be quite unnecessary.

It is also a part of the same general view that, as all functions of the soul but the will are a nature, and are only qualifiedly subjected to the will by their laws, the will, without ever being restricted in its self-determination, will often be restricted as regards executive force to perform what it wills. In this matter of executive force or capacity, we are under physiological and cerebral limitations; limitations of association, want, condition; limitations of miseducated thought, perverted sensibility, prejudice, superstition, a second nature of evil habit and passion; by which, plainly enough, our capacity of doing or becoming is greatly reduced. This, in fact, is the grand, all-conditioning truth of Christianity itself; viz., that man has no ability, in himself and by merely acting in himself, to become right and perfect; and that, hence, without some extension to him from without and above, some approach and ministration that is supernatural, he can never become what his own ideals require. And therefore it is the more remarkable that so many are ready, in all ages, to take up the notion, and are even doing it now, as a fresh discovery, that these stringent limitations on our capacity take away the liberty of our will. As if the question of executive force, the ability to make or become, had any thing to do with our self-determining liberty! At the point of the will itself we may still be as free, as truly original and self-active, as if we could do or execute all that we would; otherwise, freedom would be impossible, except on the condition of being omnipotent; and even then, as in due time we shall see, would be environed by many insuperable necessities. . . .

Finding now, in this manner, that we ourselves are supernatural creatures, and that the supernatural, instead of being some distant, ghostly affair, is familiar to us as our own most familiar action; also that nature, as a realm of cause and effect, is made to be acted on from without by us and all moral beings — thus to be the environment of our life, the instrument of our activity, the medium of our right or wrong doing toward each other, and so the school of our trial — a further question rises; viz., what shall we think of God's relations to nature? If it be nothing incredible that we should act on the chain of cause and effect in nature, is it more incredible that God should thus act? Strange as it may seem, this is the grand offense of supernaturalism, the supposing that God can act on nature from without; on the chain of cause and effect in nature from without the chain of connection, by which natural consequences are propagated — exactly that which we ourselves are doing as the most familiar thing in our lives! It involves, too, as we can see at a glance, and shall hereafter show more fully, no disruption by us of the laws of nature, but only a new combination of its elements and forces, and need not any more involve such a disruption by him. Nor can any one show that a miracle of Christ, the raising, for example, of Lazarus, involves any thing more than that nature is prepared to be acted on by a divine power, just as it is to be acted on by a human, in the making of gunpowder, or the making and charging of a firearm. For, though there seems to be an immense difference in the grade of the results accomplished, it is only a difference which ought to appear, regarding the grade of the two agents by whom they are wrought. How different the power of two men, creatures though they be of the same order; a Newton, for example, a Watt, a Fulton; and some wild Patagonian or stunted Eskimo. So, if there be angels, seraphim, thrones, dominions, all in ascending scales of endowment above one another, they will, of course, have powers supernatural, or capacities to act on the lines of causes in nature, that correspond with their natural quantity and degree. What wonder, then, is it, in the case of Jesus Christ, that he reveals a power over nature appropriate to the scale of his being and the inherent supremacy of his divine person.

And yet it will not do, our philosophers tell us, to admit any such thing as a miracle, or that any thing does, or can, take place by a divine power, which nature itself does not bring to pass! God, in other words, can not be supposed to act on the line of cause and effect in nature; for nature is the universe, and the law of universal order makes a perfect system. Hence a great many of our naturalists, who admit the existence of God, and do not mean to identify his substance with nature, and call him the Creator, and honor him, at least in words, as the Governor of all things, do yet insist that it must be unphilosophical to suppose any present action of God, save what is acted in and through the preordained system of nature. The author of the *Vestiges of Creation*,[3] for example, looks on cause and effect as being the eternal will of God, and nature as the all-comprehensive order of his Providence, beside which, or apart from which, he does, and can be supposed to do, nothing. A great many who call themselves Christian believers really hold the same thing, and can suffer nothing different. Nature, to such, includes man. God and nature, then, are the all of existence, and there is no acting of God upon nature; for that would be supernaturalism. He may be the originative source of nature; he may even be the immediate, all-impelling will, of which cause and effect

---

3. [ED.] Robert Chambers, *Vestiges of the Natural History of Creation* (1843), 118.

are the symptoms; that is, he may have made and may actuate the machine, in that fated, foredoomed way which cause and effect describes, but he must not act upon the machine-system outside of the foredoomed way; if he does, he will disturb the immutable laws! In fact, he has no liberty of doing any thing, but just to keep agoing the everlasting trundle of the machine. He can not even act upon his works, save as giving and maintaining the natural law of his works; which law is a limit upon him, as truly as a bond of order upon them. He is incrusted and shut in by his own ordinances. Nature is the god above God, and he can not cross her confines. His ends are all in nature; for, outside of nature, and beyond, there is nothing but himself. He is only a great mechanic, who has made a great machine for the sake of the machine, having his work all done long ages ago. Moral government is out of the question — there is no government but the predestined rolling of the machine. If a man sins, the sin is only the play of cause and effect; that is, of the machine. If he repents, the same is true — sin, repentance, love, hope, joy, are all developments of cause and effect; that is, of the machine. If a soul gives itself to God in love, the love is but a grinding-out of some wheel he has set turning, or it may be turns, in the scheme of nature. If I look up to him and call him Father, he can only pity the conceit of my filial feeling, knowing that it is attributable to nothing but the run of mere necessary cause and effect in me, and is no more, in fact, from me, than the rising of a mist or cloud is from some buoyant freedom in its particles. If I look up to him for help and deliverance, he can only hand me over to cause and effect, of which I am a link myself, and bid me stay in my place to be what I am made to be. He can touch me by no extension of sympathy, and I must even break through nature (as he himself can not), to obtain a look of recognition.

How miserable a desert is existence, both to him and to us, under such conditions — to him, because of his character; to us, because of our wants. To be thus entombed in his works, to have no scope for his virtues, no field for his perfections, no ends to seek, no liberty to act, save in the mechanical way of mere causality — what could more effectually turn his goodness into a well-spring of baffled desires and defeated sympathies, and make his glory itself a baptism of sorrow. Meantime the supposition is to us a mockery, against which all our deepest wants and highest personal affinities are raised up, as it were, in mutinous protest. If there is nothing but God and nature, and God himself has no relations to nature, save just to fill it and keep it on its way, then, being ourselves a part of nature, we are only a link, each one, in a chain let down into a well, where nothing else can ever touch us but the next link above! Oh, it is horrible! Our soul freezes at the thought! We want, we must have, something better — a social footing, a personal, and free, and flexible, and conscious relation with our God; that he should cross over to us, or bring us over the dark Styx of nature unto himself, to love him, to obtain his recognition, to receive his manifestation, to walk in his guidance, and be raised to that higher footing of social understanding and spiritual concourse with him, where our inborn affinities find their center and rest. . . .

Chapter iii

Nature is not the System of God — Things and
Powers, How Related

God is expressed but not measured by his works; least of all by the substances and laws included under the general term, nature. And yet how liable are we, overpowered, as we often are, and oppressed by the magnitudes of nature, to suffer the impression that there can be nothing separate and superior, beyond nature. The eager mind of science, for example, sallying forth on excursions of thought into the vast abysses of worlds, discovering tracks of light that must have been shooting downward and away from their sources, even for millions of ages, to have now arrived at their mark; and then discovering also that, by such a reach of computation, it has not penetrated to the center, but only reached the margin or outmost shore of the vast fire-ocean whose particles are astronomic worlds, falls back spent, and having, as it were, no spring left for another trial, or the endeavor of a stronger flight, surrenders, overmastered and helpless, crushed into silence. At such an hour, it is any thing but a wonder that nature is taken for the all, the veritable system of God; beyond which, or collateral with which, there is nothing. For so long a time is science imposed upon by nature, not instructed by it; as if there could be nothing greater than distance, measure, quantity, and show, nothing higher than the formal platitude of things. But the healthy, living mind will sooner or later recover itself. It will spring up out of this prostration before nature, to imagine other things, which eye hath not seen, nor ear heard, nor science computed. . . .

What I propose, then, in the present chapter, coincidently with the strain of remark here indulged, is to undertake a negative, showing (what, in fact, is decisive upon the whole question) that the surrender of so many minds to nature and her magnitudes is premature and weak; that nature plainly is not, and can not be, the proper and complete system of God; or, if we speak no more of God, of the universe. . . .

The atheist denies the existence of any being or power above nature; the pantheist does the same — only adding that nature is God, and entitled in some sense to the honor of religion. Now, to show the existence of a God supernatural, a God so far separated from nature and superior to it as to act on the chain of natural cause and effect from without the chain, the new science of geology comes forward, lays open her stone registers, and points us to the very times and places where the creative hand of God was inserted into the world, to people it with creatures of life. Thus it is an accepted or established fact in geology that our planet was, at some remote period, in a molten or fluid state, by reason of the intense heat of its matter. Emerging from this state by a gradual cooling process, there could of course be no seeds in it and no vestiges or germs of animal life. It is only a vast cinder, in fact, just now a little cooled on the surface, but still red hot within. And yet the registers show, beyond the possibility even of a doubt, that the cinder was, in due time and somehow, peopled with creatures of life. Whence came they or the germs of which they sprung? Out of the fire, or out of the cinder? The fire would exterminate them all in a minute of time, and it will be difficult to imagine that the cinder, the mere metallic matter of the world, has any power to resolve itself, under its material laws, into reproductive and articulated forms of life.

Again, these ancient registers of rock record the fact that, here and there, some vast fiery cataclysm broke loose, submerging and exterminating a great part of the living tribes of the world, after which came forth new races of occupants, more numerous and many of them higher and more perfect in their forms of organization. Whence came these? By what power ever discovered in nature were they invented, composed, articulated, and set breathing in the air and darting through the waters of the world?

Finally man appears, last and most perfect of all the living forms; for, while so many successive orders and types of living creatures, vegetable and animal, show us their remains in the grand museum of the rocks, no vestige, or bone, or sign of man has ever yet been discovered there. Therefore here again the question returns, Whence came the lordly occupant? Where was he conceived? In what alembic of nature was he distilled? By what conjunction of material causes was he raised up to look before and after, and be the investigator of all causes?

Having now these facts of new production before us, we are obliged to admit some power out of nature and above it, which, by acting on the course of nature, started the new forms of organized life, or fashioned the germs out of which they sprung. To enter on a formal discussion of the theory, so ambitiously attempted by some of the naturalists, by which they are ascribed to the laws of mere nature or to natural development, would carry me farther into the polemics of geology and zoology than the limits of my present argument will suffer. I will only notice two or three of the principal points of this development theory, in which it is opposed by insurmountable facts.[4]

First of all, it requires us to believe that the original germs of organic life may be and were developed out of matter by its inorganic forces. If so, why are no new germs developed now? and why have we no well-attested facts of the kind? Some few pretended facts we have, but they are too loosely made out to be entitled for a moment to our serious belief. Never yet has it been shown that any one germ of vegetable, or animal life, has been developed by the existing laws of nature, without some egg or germ previously supplied to start the process. Besides, it is inconceivable that there is a power in the metallic and earthy substances, or atoms, however cunningly assisted by electricity, to generate a seed or egg. If we ourselves can not even so much as cast a bullet without a mold, how can these dead atoms and blind electric currents, without any matrix, or even governing type, weave the filaments and cast the living shape of an acorn, or any smallest seed? There can be no softer credulity than the skepticism which, to escape the need of a creative miracle, resorts to such a faith as this.

But, supposing it possible, or credible, that certain germs of life may have been generated by the inorganic forces, the development scheme has it still on hand to account for the existence of man. That he is thus composed in full size and maturity is impossible; he must be produced, if at all, in the state of infancy. Two suppositions, then, are possible, and only two; and we find the speculations of the school vibrating apparently between them. First, that there is a slow process of advance in order,

4. Whoever wishes to see this subject handled more scientifically and in a most masterly manner, may consult the "Essay on Classification" prefixed to the great work of Mr. Agassiz on Natural History, where the conceit that our animal and vegetable races were started in their several eras by physical agencies, without a creative Intelligence, is exploded so as to be forever incapable of resuming even a pretense of reason. [ED.] From 1848 to 1873 Louis Agassiz (1807–73) taught natural history at Harvard University. For a recent edition of the essay referred to by Bushnell, see Louis Agassiz, *Essay on Classification*, Edward Lurie, ed. (Cambridge, Mass., 1962).

through which the lowest forms of life gradually develop those which are higher and more perfect, and finally culminate in man. Or secondly, that there is a power in all vital natures, by which, at distant but proper intervals, they suddenly produce some order of being higher than they, much as we often see in those examples of propagation which we denominate, most unphilosophically, *lusus naturae*, and that so, as the last and highest *lusus*, if that were a scientific conception, man appears; being in fact the crown, or complete fulfillment, of that type of perfection which pertains to all, even the lowest forms of life. In one view the progress is a regular gradation; in the other it is a progress by leaps or stages.

As regards the former, it is a fatal objection that no such plastic, gradual movement of progress can be traced in the records of the geologic eras. All the orders, and genera, and species, maintain their immovable distinctions; and no trace can any where be discovered, whether there or in the now living races, of organic forms that are intermediate and transitional. Tokens may be traced in the rocks of a transitional development in some given kind or species, as of the gradual process by which a frog is developed; but there is no trace of organized being midway between the frog and the horse, or of any insect or fish, on its way to become a frog. Besides, it is wholly inconceivable that there should be *in rerum natura* any kind of creature that is midway, or transitional, between the oviparous and mammal orders. Still further, if man is the terminal of a slow and plastic movement, or advance, what has become of the forms next to man, just a little short of man? They are not among the living, nor among the dead. No trace of any such forms has ever been discovered by science. The monkey race have been set up as candidates for this honor. But, to say nothing of the degraded consciousness that can allow any creature of language, duty, and reason, to speak of his near affinity with these creatures, what one of them is there that could ever raise a human infant? And if none, there ought to be some intermediate race, yet closer to humanity, that can do it. Where is this intermediate race?

Just this, too, is the difficulty we encounter in the second form of the theory. There neither is nor can be any middle position between humanity and no humanity. If the child, for child there must be, is human, the mother and father must either be human or else mere animals. If they have not merely the power of using means to ends, but the necessary ideas, truth, right, cause, space, time, and also the faculty of language, that is of receiving the inner sense of symbols, which is the infallible test of intelligence (*intus lego*), then they are human; otherwise they are animals. No matter, then, how high they may be in their order; their human child is a different form of being, with which, in one view, they have nothing in common. And he is, by the supposition, born a child; the son of an animal, but yet a human child. And then the question rises, what animal is there, existing or conceivable, what accident, or power in nature, that can nurse or shelter from death, that feeblest and most helpless of all creatures, a human infant? Neither do we find, as a matter of fact, that the animal races advance in their nursing and protecting capacity accordingly as they advance in the scale of organization. The nearest approach to that kind of tending and protective capacity necessary to the raising of a human infant, any where discernible in the animal races, is found in the marsupial animals; which are yet far inferior, as regards both intelligence and organization, to the races of dogs, elephants, and monkeys. Nay, the young salmon, hatched in the motherhood of the river, being cradled in the soft waters, and having a small sac of food attached underneath, to support the first weeks of their infancy, are much better off in their nursing than these most advanced races. Any theory, in short, which throws a human child on the care of an animal parentage, is too nearly absurd to require refutation.

But there is a scientific reason against this whole theory of development, which appears to be irresistible; viz., that it inverts the order of causes, and makes exactly that which distinguishes the fact of death, the author and cause of life. For it is precisely the wonder, as was just now shown, of the living creatures, or vital powers, that instead of being under the laws of mineral substances, they are continually triumphing over them. Never do they fall under and submit to them, till they die, and this is death. Thus, when a little nodule of living matter called an acorn is placed in the ground, it takes occasion, so to speak, from its new conditions, begins to quicken, opens its ducts, starts its pumps into action, sets at work its own wondrous powers of chemistry, and labors on through whole centuries, composing and building on new lengths of wood, till it has raised into the sky, against gravity and the laws of dead chemistry, a ponderous mass of many tons weight; there to stand, waving in triumph over the vanquished chemists of the ground, and against the raging storms of ages; never to yield the victory till the life grows old by exhaustion. Having come now to the limit of its own vital nature, the tree dies; whereupon the laws of inorganic matter, over which it had triumphed, fall at work upon it in their turn, to dissolve it; and between them and gravity, pulling it down upon the ground, it is disintegrated and reduced to inorganic dust. Now what the theory in question proposes is, that this same living nodule was originally developed, organized, and gifted with life, by the laws of dead matter — laws that have themselves been vanquished, as regards their force, by its dominating sovereignty, and never have been able to do any thing more than to dissolve it after it was dead.

We are brought, then, to the conclusion, which no ingenuity of man can escape, that the successive races of living forms discovered by geology are fresh creations, by a power out of nature and above it acting on nature; which, it will be remembered, is our definition of supernaturalism itself. And this plainly is no mere indication, but an absolute proof that nature is not the complete system of God. Indeed, we may say what might well enough be clear beforehand, that if man is not from eternity, as geology proves beyond a question, then to imagine that mere dead earth, acted on by its chemical and electric forces, should itself originate sense, perception, thought, reason, conscience, heroism, and genius, is to assert in the name of science what is more extravagant than all the miracles even of the Hindu mythology. . . .

But we come to a point more positive and decisive; viz., that we do positively know existences that can not be included in nature, but constitute a higher range, empowered to act upon it. This higher range we are ourselves, as already shown by our definition of nature and the supernatural. . . . By that definition we are now prepared to assume and formally assign the grand twofold distinction of *things* and *persons*, or *things* and *powers*. All free intelligences, it was shown, the created and the uncreated, are, as being free, essentially supernatural in their action; having all, in the matter of their will, a power transcending cause and effect in nature, by which they are able to act on the lines and vary the combinations of natural causalities. They differ, in short, from every thing that classes under the term nature, in the fact that they act from themselves, uncaused in their action. They are powers, not things; the radical idea of a power being that of an agent or force which acts from itself, uncaused, initiating trains of effect that flow from itself.

Of the two great classes, therefore, named in our distribution, one comprehends all beings that are able to originate new trains of effects — these are the Powers; and the other is made up of such as can only propagate effects under certain fixed laws — these are Things. At the head of one class we conceive is God, as Lord of Hosts; who, in virtue of his all-originating power as Creator, is called the First Cause; having round him innumerable orders of intelligence which, though caused to exist by him, are as truly first causes in their action as he — starting all their trains of consequences in the same manner. In the other class we have the immense catalogue of what are called the natural sciences — the astronomical bodies, the immaterial forces, the fluids and solids of the world, the elements and atoms of chemistry, the dynamics of life and instinct — in all of which, what are called causes are only propagations of effects under and by fixed laws. Hence they are second causes only; that is, causes whose causations are determined by others back of them; never in any sense originative or first causes. The completeness of the distribution will be yet more clear, and the immense abyss of distance between the two orders or classes more visibly impassable, if we add such points of contrast as the following:

Powers, acting in liberty, are capable of a double action — to do, or not to do (God, for example, in creating, man in sinning); things can act only in one way, viz., as their law determines.

Powers are perfectible only by exercise, after they are made; things are perfect as made.

Powers are perfected, or established in their law, only by a schooling of their consent; things are under a law mechanical at the first, having no consent.

Powers can violate the present or nearest harmony, moving disorder in it; things are incapable of disorder, save as they are disordered by the malign action of powers.

Powers, governed by the absolute force or fiat of omnipotence, would in that fact be uncreated and cease; things exist and act only in and by the impulsion of that fiat.

We have thus drawn out and set before us two distinct orders and degrees of being, which together constitute the real universe. So perfectly diverse are they in kind, that no common terms of law or principle can for one moment be imagined to include them both; they can be one system only in some higher and broader sense, which subordinates one to the other, or both to the same final causes. One thing is thus made clear; viz., that nature is not, in any proper sense, the universe. We know that it is not, because we find another kind of existence in ourselves, which consciously does not fall within the terms of nature. Probably the disciples of naturalism will make answer to this course of argument, by complaining that we gain our point thus easily by means of our definition, which definition is arbitrary — drawing a distinction between nature and the supernatural, or between things and powers, that is not usual.[5] Whether it be usual or not is not the question, but whether it is grounded in reality and witnessed immediately by our own consciousness. If it has been the prime sophism of the naturalists to assume the universality of nature, and still more if they have carried the assumption so far as to hold, in fact and even formally, that men are only things — under the same laws of eternal necessity with things, and equally incapable of obligation, thus a part of the system of universal nature — we certainly have as good a right to raise definitions that meet the truth of consciousness, as they to overlook and hide them in plain defiance of consciousness. There may be something fatal in such definitions, but there certainly is nothing arbitrary.

Receiving it now as a truth sufficiently established that nature, or the realm of things, is not the system of the universe, that there is beside a realm of powers, it is difficult to close the survey taken, without glancing for a moment at the relative weight and consequence of the two realms. When such a question is raised, there are many who will have it as their feeling, whether they say it in words or not, that the world of things preponderates in magnitude; for what are we doing, a great part of us, whether men of action or men of science, but chasing the shows of our senses, and magnifying their import, by the stimulation of our egregious idolatry? And yet it would seem that any most extempore glance at the world of powers would suffice to correct us, and set the realm of things, vast as it is, in a very humble place. First, we recognize in the grand inventory our own human race. We call them persons, spirits, souls, minds, intelligences, free agents, and we see them moving out from nature and above it, consciously superior; streaming into it in currents of causality from themselves; subduing it, developing or detecting its secret laws, harnessing its forces, and using it as the pliant instrument of their will; first causes all, in a sense, and springs of action, side by side with the Creator, whose miniatures they are, whose footsteps they distinguish, and whose recognition they naturally aspire to. Next adjacent to these we have the intelligent powers of the astronomic worlds, and all the outlying populations of the sky; so numerous that we shall best conceive their number, not by counting the stars and increasing the census obtained by some factor or multiplier greater than the mind can definitely grasp, but by imag-

5. [ED.] Noah Porter, of Yale, for example, did consider Bushnell's definition of nature arbitrary; cf. his "Nature and the Supernatural," *New Englander*, XVII (1859), 231.

ining the stellar spaces of infinity itself interfused and filled with their
prodigious tides of life and motion. All these, like us, are creatures of admiration, science, will, and duty; able to search out the invisible in the
visible, and find the footsteps of God in his works. Then again, also, we
recognize a vast and gloriously populated realm of angels and departed
spirits, who, when they are sent, minister, unseen, about us; mixed, we
know not how, in the surroundings of our state, with unsaintly and demoniacal powers of mischief, not sent nor suffered even to come, save
when they are attracted by the low affinities we offer as open gates to
their coming. To which, also, we are to add those unknown, dimly imagined orders of intelligences, of which we are notified in the terms of
revelation — seraphim, living creatures, thrones, authorities, dominions,
principalities, and powers.

Now all these living armies or hosts of God, and God the Lord of
Hosts, capable of character, society, duty, love — creators all, in a sense
of things that otherwise could never be, first causes all of their own acts
and doings, able to adorn what is and contrive what is not, and carry up
the worlds themselves in ascending scales of improvement — can we look
on these and imagine that nature includes the principal sum and constitutes
the real system of being? Are not these other forms of being the transcendent forms, and if we will inventory the universe, are they not all, in
fact, that gives it an assignable value? If God himself be a real existence,
what is he, by the supposition, but the major term of all existence — the
all-containing substance, a being so great that we scarcely need refer to
the free populations just named, to sink all that is below him, and is called
nature, into comparative insignificance. But when we regard him as the
Uncreated Power at the head of his immense family of powers, all systematized or sought to be systematized, all perfect in good or else to be
perfected under one law, viz., the eternal, necessary, immutable law of
right — a law which he first of all accepts himself, in which his own character of beauty and truth and even his felicity is based, and which therefore he ordains for all, to be the condition of their character, as of his
own, building nature itself to it, as a field of exercise and trial; then do
we, for once, catch a true glimpse of the significance of nature. It is no
more that universe the philosophers speak of; it is raised in dignity by the
relation it fills, and, for a like reason, sunk in quantity to comparative
nothingness. Its distances no longer occupy us, its magnitudes appall us no
more, the astronomic splendors are tinsel; nothing is solid, or great, or
high, but those transcendent powers whose eternities are the main sub-

stances of the worlds. Nature, in short, is only stage, field, medium, vehicle, for the universe; that is, for God and his powers. These are the real magnitudes, because they contain, at once, the import and the final causes, or last ends, of all created substance. The grand, universal, invisible system of God, therefore, is a system that centralizes itself in these, subordinating all mere things, and having them for its instruments.

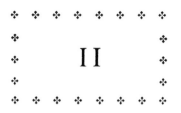

THE INCARNATION AND THE TRINITY

1. Concio ad Clerum [1]

EDITOR'S INTRODUCTION

On August 15, 1848, the General Association of Connecticut met at Yale, where Bushnell delivered the *Concio ad Clerum* on "The Divinity of Christ." Many of the clergy had gathered in a mood of anxiety, for the speaker's orthodoxy was already in doubt. After citing ten marks of Christ's divinity, Bushnell plunged into two subjects of long-standing controversy between the Congregationalists and the Unitarians: (1) the person of Christ, and (2) the trinity. We need not repeat his argument here, for the full text of the *Concio* is reproduced below.

What was the public reaction? "Nobody who heard that address," wrote Leonard Bacon, "could say that the preacher was a Unitarian. Yet there was room to ask: 'Is he orthodox?' " [2] Judging from later events, many of those present answered that question with an emphatic no. Before publishing the *Concio* and the two allied addresses, Bushnell carefully revised and expanded all three of them, with the hope of muting some of the anticipated criticisms. But to no avail. The "evil notoriety" which had gone before them grew tenfold after they appeared in *God in Christ*. The book satisfied neither liberal nor orthodox churchmen, but the latter wielded the verbal hatchet the more fiercely. Of those speaking

1. "Concio ad Clerum: A Discourse on the Divinity of Christ; Delivered at the Annual Commencement of Yale College, August 15, 1848," *God in Christ* (Hartford, 1849), 121–81.
2. "Concerning a Recent Chapter of Ecclesiastical History," *New Englander,* XXXVIII (1879), 704.

from outside the Congregational family, none used more cutting language than did Charles Hodge of Princeton Seminary.[3] Flatly pronouncing the book "a failure," he accused its author of being "only half out of the shell."

Our chief concern here, however, is with the reaction of Connecticut Congregationalists. They raised an uproar which lasted five years (1849–54) and which at times severely tested established ecclesiastical discipline. In order to indicate the nature and scope of the criticisms lodged against Bushnell, we must review briefly the main developments in the controversy.[4]

The most determined assailant of Bushnell was the Association of Fairfield West, which included some able but rigidly orthodox clergymen, such as Theophilus Smith, Edwin Hall, and Lyman H. Atwater (later, teacher of moral philosophy at Princeton University).[5] About three months after *God in Christ* was published, that Association, on May 30, 1849, adopted resolutions warning "That opinions are extensively propagated among us, tending to undermine the faith of ministers and churches, in the doctrines of the Trinity, Incarnation, and Atonement as they are received by all orthodox churches." [6] The Association further declared that it was "the duty of district associations and consociations" [7]

3. "Bushnell's Discourses," *Biblical Repertory and Princeton Review*, XXI (1849), 259–98.

4. For an older account which seems generally reliable, see Edwin Pond Parker, *The Hartford Central Association and the Bushnell Controversy* (Hartford, 1896). Our analysis, however, is based on original sources, including unpublished minutes.

5. For illuminating commentaries on the Bushnell controversy from the standpoint of the Association of Fairfield West, see Lyman H. Atwater, "Horace Bushnell," *Presbyterian Review*, II (1881), 114–44; Charles Hodge, "Recent Doctrinal and Ecclesiastical Conflicts in Connecticut," *Biblical Repertory and Princeton Review*, XXV (1853), 598–637.

6. *Minutes of the General Association of Connecticut, at the Meeting in Salisbury, June, 1849* (New Haven, 1849), 15.

7. At the time of the Bushnell controversy, Connecticut Congregationalism was maintained under a system of discipline set forth in the Saybrook Platform, adopted in 1708. The "Articles" of the Platform authorized three types or forms of organization: (1) District Consociations, (2) District Associations, and (3) the General Association. The District Consociation (one or more per county) comprised the ministers and the churches of a given district. Its function was to promote the general well-being of its members; also, on the direction of the District Association, it was responsible for constituting a Council to try any minister accused of heresy within its jurisdiction. The District Association was composed of ministers only, and its duties were: to promote ministerial fellowship; to examine and recommend candidates for the ministry; to examine any of its members accused of heresy, and, if the facts warranted, to direct the District Consociation involved to call a Council

to apply discipline "so far as it may be necessary, for removing such heresies from among them." [8]

Anticipating that an overture on the matter would come before the next annual session of the General Association of Connecticut, the Hartford Central Association (to which Bushnell belonged), on June 4, appointed a committee of five — Noah Porter, Walter Clarke, Joel Hawes, Charles B. McClean, and Merrill Richardson — with Porter as chairman, to examine *God in Christ* and determine whether the author had published views which were fundamentally erroneous.[9]

As expected, when the General Association met at Salisbury the following June, the Fairfield brethren offered their resolutions for adoption. The Association, however, took no action except to say that "it belongs exclusively to the district associations, to institute Christian discipline in cases of error among their own members." [10]

From the beginning, the Porter committee found itself fundamentally divided in its attitude toward *God in Christ*. Finally, on September 18, 1849, it asked Hartford Central to choose between a majority and a minority (Hawes and Clarke) report. In summary, the majority said:

> We are satisfied, that whatever errors the book may contain, it furnishes no sufficient ground for instituting a judicial process with him [Bushnell]. . . . We regret his departure, in some of his statements, from the formulas of the church. We adhere to these formulas; but we regard him, notwithstanding the exceptions which he has taken to them, as holding to what is essential to the scheme of doctrine which they employ. . . . He could not, in our view, be properly or justly subjected to the charge of heresy, and a consequent trial, or be denied the confidence of his brethren in the ministry.[11]

In contrast, the minority summarily declared: "On the questions of the Trinity, the Personality of Christ, and the Atonement, the book before us

to conduct the trial. The General Association, a statewide body, was composed of delegates chosen by the District Associations. It convened annually to promote the welfare of Congregationalism, but it was without judicial or legislative authority. See "The Saybrook Articles," in H. Shelton Smith, Robert T. Handy, and Lefferts A. Loetscher, *American Christianity: An Historical Interpretation with Representative Documents* (2 vols., New York, 1960–63), I, 224–29.

8. *Minutes of the General Association, June, 1849*, 15.

9. Manuscript "Records of the Hartford Central Association [1843–1901]," 31 (MS. in Congregational House, Hartford, Connecticut). Bushnell himself suggested the appointment of the committee, and all the members of it except Joel Hawes were acceptable to him. See Bushnell's letter to Leonard Bacon (June 6, 1849). (MS. in Yale University Library).

10. *Minutes of the General Association, June, 1849*, 15.

11. "Records of the Hartford Central Association," 42–43. Punctuation supplied where necessary for clarification.

holds views which deny and subvert the essential facts of our common faith." [12] After an exhaustive debate on the two reports, the majority report was adopted (October 23, 1849).[13]

The stage was now set for vigorous controversy. In January of 1850, Fairfield West, feeling "much amazed and grieved" at the decision, addressed a remonstrance to Hartford Central, setting forth the alleged errors of *God in Christ*, and entreating that body "to redress the injury" done to the cause of Christ.[14] On March 5, Hartford Central politely but firmly declined to reopen the case "until new evidence of a decisive character shall be presented to us." [15] Whereupon, Fairfield West at once resorted to public pressure. It mailed a printed copy of its *Remonstrance and Complaint* (which included Hartford Central's answer) to all the Congregational ministers in Connecticut, and also sent a circular letter to all the district associations except Hartford Central, "earnestly requesting them to meet and consider this subject [the Bushnell case], and let us know the conclusion to which they come." [16]

Having received considerable support, Fairfield West came before the next session of the General Association (held at Litchfield in June 1850) with a long memorial, the basic design of which was to get the Association to pronounce as fundamental the four doctrines which *God in Christ* supposedly denied: (1) the trinity, (2) the humanity of Christ, (3) vicarious atonement, and (4) justification by faith. In the end, on recommendation of a committee of thirteen, the Association did go so far as to declare that those four doctrines were, as described by the Westminster Assembly, "*fundamental* articles of the Christian religion," and that their denial was "heresy." [17] The Association did not, however, say whether *God in Christ* had actually denied the articles in question. Nevertheless, it tended to encourage Fairfield West, for it not only pointed out that any district association had a right to remonstrate with any other association believed to be sheltering heresy, but it also declared that an effort should be made by the suspected body "to satisfy" the complainants.[18]

With that much support from the General Association, Fairfield West immediately requested Hartford Central either to reopen the Bushnell

12. *Ibid.*, 55.   13. *Ibid.*, 56.

14. *Remonstrance and Complaint of the Association of Fairfield West, to the Hartford Central Association: Together with the Reply of the Hartford Central Association* (New York, 1850), 33.

15. *Ibid.*, 35.   16. *Ibid.*, 4.

17. *Minutes of the General Association of Connecticut, at the Meeting in Litchfield, June, 1850* (New Haven, 1850), 18.

18. *Ibid.*, 17.

case or else endeavor to satisfy the complaining party on the points at issue. In May 1851, Hartford Central replied by reaffirming its belief in the essential soundness of *God in Christ* and refusing to enter into a debate on doctrinal questions with Fairfield West. The defenders also put in a timely word: "We deem it best for the interests of Zion, that all measures tending to divide our churches and ministers, and to make a schism in the spiritual body, be laid aside."

Fairfield West merely intensified its efforts. Its next move was to make out a case for heresy in Bushnell's latest publication, *Christ in Theology* (1851). Having minutely examined that book, the Association published its results in a ninety-five-page pamphlet,[19] and in March 1852 mailed a copy of it to every Congregational minister in Connecticut.[20] When the General Association met at Danbury in June, Fairfield West came forward with still another memorial, this time in the form of seven questions. The most ominous question was number six: "When any of our District Associations persist, after due labor used, in violating any of the fundamental principles which lie at the basis of our ecclesiastical union, and our mutual confidence and fellowship, ought not the General Association itself to interfere, in the use of appropriate means, until the offense is removed?"[21] The memorial was tabled, pending the reading of a communication from Bushnell, who protested that the General Association had no authority whatever to intervene in his case. The Association acknowledged that it was "not a legislative or judicial body"; but at the same time it declared that in view of "the present state of public feeling" with respect to *God in Christ* and *Christ in Theology*, "all the parties concerned should, in the interest of Christian charity, remove, as far as possible, every obstacle, whether real or supposed, to a full and fair investigation, according to our ecclesiastical rules."[22]

There were only two authorized ways whereby Bushnell could be brought to stand trial. One of these had been closed when the Hartford Central Association cleared him of fundamental error. There was, however, another road to a trial. Under Article 4 of the Hartford North Con-

19. *Appeal of the Association of Fairfield West, to the Associated Ministers Connected with the General Association of Connecticut* (New York, 1852).

20. The *Appeal* carried an announcement saying that it could be bought at various cities in Connecticut and at Boston.

21. *Memorial of the Association of Fairfield West, to the General Association of Connecticut, June 15, 1852* (n.p., 1852), 8.

22. *Minutes of the General Association of Connecticut, at their Meeting in Danbury, June, 1852* (New Haven, 1852), 8–9.

sociation, to which the North Church belonged, any minister suspected of heresy could be brought before the Consociation for trial if at least three members of his church would sign a written complaint against him.[23] However, since no member of the North Church would take that step, the second road to a trial also was closed. Thus unless established ecclesiastical order were violated, Bushnell's pursuers could not bring him to trial. Nonetheless, the action taken by the General Association at Danbury led Bushnell's congregation to fear that he might be harassed indefinitely. To put an end to such treatment, they — without any support from Bushnell — voted unanimously, on June 27, 1852, to withdraw North Church from the Hartford North Consociation.[24]

Not even this step, however, stopped the anti-Bushnell campaign. When the General Association convened at Waterbury (1853), it was presented with a complaint signed by fifty-one ministers, accusing Hartford Central of sheltering heresy and of subverting the doctrinal basis of fellowship in the General Association. Bitterly resenting the charge, Hartford Central answered the complainants in a scathing document, saying: "First, they actually misquote and abundantly misconstrue and pervert the language of Dr. Bushnell, to render their accusation of fundamental error plausible, and secondly, they charge his peculiarities, be they more or less erroneous, upon us." [25] Acrimonious debate followed. The complainants tried to persuade the General Association to instruct Hartford Central to present Bushnell for trial, but they did not succeed. The Association did, however, pass the following resolution:

> *Resolved,* That the opinions imputed to Dr. Bushnell by the complainants, and the imputation of which is no doubt warranted, if the constructions are just which they conscientiously give to certain quotations from his published books, are opinions with which the ministers in the churches of Connecticut, as represented in this General Association, have no fellowship and the profession of which on the part of candidates for the ministry, ought to prevent their receiving the license or approbation of any of our Associations; and further, that where a minister is reasonably charged with holding

23. Bushnell, *Twentieth Anniversary: A Commemorative Discourse* (Hartford, 1853), 26, note 2.

24. Mary B. Cheney, *Life and Letters of Horace Bushnell* (New York, 1880), 261. This action placed North Church on a par with twenty-nine other non-consociated churches in Connecticut.

25. "Records of the Hartford Central Association." This document is placed in the back of the record book, and is unpaginated.

those opinions, definite charges and specifications should be preferred against him before the proper body, which body should make arrangements to secure for the charges an impartial hearing and decision.[26]

This resolution clearly signifies that the majority of the Congregational ministers in Connecticut were emphatically opposed to Bushnell's theological views and would do everything possible, consistent with ecclesiastical regulations, to extirpate them. However, the Waterbury meeting marked the climax of the Bushnell case, so far as the General Association was concerned. When the Association gathered at New Haven (1854), some members of Fairfield West still sniped at Bushnell, but their parting shot had little influence on the delegates.

Bushnell was never put on trial for his alleged heresies. Nevertheless, he was made to suffer for his views in other ways perhaps no less grievous to bear. Many of his ministerial brethren rebuffed him. "The pulpits of Hartford and the neighborhood," said a friend, "were barred against him as they would have been against an avowed Unitarian or Universalist. . . . The expression of any sympathy with him brought a man at once under suspicion." [27] Bushnell wrote to Leonard Bacon of New Haven, "I hope you are not all going to cast me out as a reprobate, if so let me know it." [28] This refusal of fellowship, which increased as the controversy progressed, deeply wounded him. He overcame this isolation eventually, but it took him many years to do so.

From the standpoint of doctrine, the questions at issue in the *Concio* were chiefly two. First, Bushnell was accused of denying that Jesus had a human soul.[29] That charge rested on inference, not on any direct remark by him. His main concern was to counteract the current tendency of the trinitarians to deny that Jesus' divine nature had any direct part in his sacrificial life and death. Bushnell's target was New England Nestorian-

26. *Minutes of the General Association of Connecticut, at their Meeting in Waterbury, June, 1853* (New Haven, 1853), 10.

27. Amos S. Chesebrough, "Reminiscences of the Bushnell Controversy," *Bushnell Centenary. Minutes of the General Association of Connecticut at the One Hundred and Ninety-Third Annual Meeting Held in Hartford, June 17, 18, 1902* (Hartford, 1902), 50–51.

28. Letter to Leonard Bacon (March 30, 1849). (MS. in Yale University Library.) In this same letter Bushnell reported that Professor Eleazar T. Fitch, preacher to the church in Yale College, had just broken off an engagement to exchange pulpits with him.

29. See, for example, *Appeal of the Association of Fairfield West*, 31–34; "Review [of] *God in Christ*," *Christian Observatory*, III (1849), 257–59.

ism.[30] Thus he declared: "I only deny that his [Jesus'] human soul, or nature, is to be spoken of, or looked upon, as having a *distinct* subsistence, so as to live, think, learn, worship, suffer, by itself." [31]

Second, Bushnell was accused of denying an immanent trinity.[32] The Fairfield West Association said: "Dr. B. declares that his scheme requires him to controvert all arguments which go to prove a Trinity immanent in the Godhead." [33] The truth is that he expressly refused to take a position either for or against an immanent trinity.[34] At this time he viewed the persons of the trinity in terms of their "instrumental" value in expressing God to the world, and he left open the question of their ontological ground.

❖   ❖   ❖   ❖

It is laid upon me, by the General Association of Connecticut, to discuss before you, this evening, the DIVINITY OF CHRIST — a duty which I most willingly undertake, because I think the time has now come when a re-investigation of the subject will be more likely than at any former period, to issue in a practical settlement, or approach to settlement, of the questions involved. It will be understood, in this discussion, that I speak *ad clerum*, and not *ad populum*. I am not of course responsible for the difficulty of the subject, as I am not for the subject itself. I am only responsible for the thoroughness of the argument; a responsibility which I must endeavor to meet as best I am able. And if the reasonings necessary to a sufficient exhibition of the subject are sometimes remote or distant from the range of popular thought, I must not therefore withhold. On the contrary, I must yield to the high necessities of the subject, and regard nothing else; least of all, any desire I might feel to accommodate the ease and patience of my audience. However, I will endeavor to make the argument as simple and clear as I am able — only reminding you that the subject we investigate is God's own nature; which, to say nothing of ease or the enter-

30. Frank H. Foster, *A Genetic History of the New England Theology* (Chicago, 1907), 409–10.

31. *God in Christ*, 163. See also *Christ in Theology* (Hartford, 1851), 92–107.

32. *Remonstrance and Complaint*, 9–10; *Appeal*, 19–30; Chauncey A. Goodrich, *What Does Dr. Bushnell Mean?* (Hartford, 1849), 18–20; "Review [of] *God in Christ*," *Christian Observatory*, III, 244, 267; Charles Hodge, "Bushnell's Discourses," *Biblical Repertory and Princeton Review*, XXI (1849), 277–81.

33. *Appeal*, 20. Fairfield West misquoted Bushnell. What he actually said was: "My position required me to controvert all arguments which either prove or disprove an immanent trinity" (*Christ in Theology*, 133).

34. *Christ in Theology*, 117–21.

tainment of a leisure hour, it were the greatest presumption in me, and the greatest levity in you, to suppose it possible, by any human argument, to render even comprehensible. God exceeds our measure, and must, until either he becomes less than infinite or we more than finite. If we can apprehend him so as to be clear of distraction, and of terms that are absolutely cross to faith itself, it is all that can be hoped.

The text that I have chosen for my theme, is:

> *"For the Life was manifested, and we have seen it, and bear witness, and shew unto you that Eternal Life which was with the Father, and was manifested unto us"* (1 Jn. 1:2).

If we raise the question whether Christ is divine, or only a mere human person appearing in his proper humanity, this passage of scripture furnishes the simplest and most beautiful answer that can be given in words. It declares that Christ was a manifestation of the Life of God, that Eternal Life that was with the Father before the manifestation. Accordingly we are to see, in the language, not merely that the reality of Christ is God, but we have an indication in the term *was manifested* of that which is the real end of his mission, and the proper solvent of whatever inquiries may be started by his person as appearing in the flesh, or under the historic conditions of humanity. In this view, my whole discourse will only be a development of the text, and therefore I need not stay upon it longer.

By the *divinity* of Christ, I do not understand simply that Christ differs from other men, in the sense that he is better, more inspired, and so a more complete vehicle of God to the world than others have been. He differs from us, not in degree, but in kind; as the half divine parentage under which he enters the world most certainly indicates. He is in such a sense God, or God manifested, that the unknown term of his nature, that which we are most in doubt of, and about which we are least capable of any positive affirmation, is the human. No person, I think, would ever doubt for a moment the superhuman quality of Jesus, if it were not for the speculative difficulties encountered by an acknowledgment of his superhuman quality. Instead, therefore, of placing the main stress of my discourse on the direct argument for Christ's divinity, I shall barely name or catalogue a few of the proofs, and then proceed to the difficulties raised by such a view of his person. I allege:

1. What is said of his pre-existence. "I came out from God." "I came forth from the Father, and am come into the world." "I came down from heaven." "Ye are from beneath, I am from above." "The glory which I had with thee before the world was." If these passages do not

affirm the pre-existence of Christ in the plainest manner conceivable, I mistake their import. And, in this view, they are totally repugnant to the idea of Christ's simple humanity.

2. The miraculous birth of Christ is either a fable, or else it denotes the entrance into humanity of something that is distinct from it. This argument holds only with those who admit the truth of the history — a question which cannot be argued here. I will only say that this event of history, so flippantly rejected by some, has, to me, the profoundest air of verity; setting forth, as it does, in the most artless form, that which corresponds philosophically with the doctrine of a divine incarnation elsewhere advanced. If God were ever to be incarnate in the world, in what other manner, so natural, beautiful, and real, could he enter into the life of the race?

3. The incarnation itself plainly asserted. "The Word was made flesh." "That which we have seen with our eyes, which we have looked upon, which our hands have handled of the word of Life." "He that was in the form of God, and was made in fashion as a man." Who can imagine, without great violence, that language of this nature is applicable to any mere man? To make it even supportable, the man, so called, must be different from all other men, to such a degree that you may far more easily doubt his humanity than his divinity.

4. What is said of the import, or the contents of his person, in passages like these: "In whom dwelt all the fullness of the Godhead bodily." "The church which is his body, the fullness of him that is all in all." "The express image of his person." "The image of the invisible God." "Complete in him which is the Head of all principality and power." How expressions of this nature, transcending so manifestly all human measures, can yet be interpreted so as to consist with the simple humanity of Jesus, I willingly confess my inability to conceive.

5. What Christ himself declares concerning his relations to the Father. "I and the Father that sent me." "Ye neither know me nor my Father." "That which I have seen with my Father." "The Father is in me and I in him." "He that hath seen me hath seen the Father." How can we imagine any mere man of our race daring to use language like this concerning himself and God? Nay, he even goes beyond any one of the expressions here cited. He has the audacity (for what else can we call it, regarding him simply as a man?) to promise that he and the Father — they two — will come to men together, and be spiritually manifest in them — "WE will come unto him and make OUR abode with him."

6. The negatives he uses concerning himself, as related to the Father, are even more convincing still, if possible. Thus, when he ways, "My Father is greater than I," how preposterous for any mere human being of our race to be gravely telling the world that God is greater than he is! So, also, it is often argued from those numerous expressions of Christ in which he calls himself the "Son of Man," that he there concedes his humanity. Undoubtedly he does (for he does not appear to use the language in the lighter significance of the old prophets), but what kind of being is this who is *conceding* his humanity? Could there be displayed, by any human creature, a bolder stretch of presumption than to declare that God is superior to him, or to call himself "the Son of Man" by condescension?

7. Christ assumes a relation to the world which is most offensive, on the supposition that he is a merely human being. Nor does it mitigate in the least the egregious want of modesty displayed in his attitude, to say that he was specially inspired; for, in all other cases, the inspiration of the man has made him humbler in spirit than he was before — made him even to sigh before the purity of God — "Woe is me, for I am a man of unclean lips!" Imagine, now, a human being, one of ourselves, coming forth and declaring to the race — "I am the light of the world." "I am the way, the truth, and the life." "I am the living bread that came down from heaven." "No man cometh unto the Father but by me." What greater effrontery could be conceived?

8. Christ assumes his own sinlessness, saying, "Which of you convinceth me of sin?" — never confessing a fault, never asking pardon for any transgression. His sinlessness, too, is generally conceded by those who hold his simple humanity. But what is it to be human, but to have a tentative nature — one that learns the import of things, and especially of good and evil by experiment? Accordingly, if the man Jesus never makes the experiment of sin, it must be because the divine is so far uppermost in him as to suspend the proper manhood of his person. He does not any longer act the man; practically speaking, the man sleeps in him. It is as if the man were not there, and, judging only from the sinlessness of his life, we should make no account of the human element in his nature. He acts the divine, not the human, and the only true reality in him, as far as moral conduct is concerned, is the divine. Set in connection with this conclusion, the universal unqualified determination of the race never to believe in a perfect man — always to assume the fallibility and imperfection of every human being — and the sinlessness of Jesus becomes, itself, a stubborn evidence of his superhuman character.

9. We want Jesus as divine, not as human; least of all do want him as the human, still out of humanity and above it, as held by many Unitarians. It is God that we want, to know him, to be near him, to have his feeling unbosomed to us. As to the real human, we have enough of that. And as to the unreal, superhuman human, that is, the human acted wholly by the divine, so as to have no action of its own save in pretense, what is it to us but a mockery? What can we learn from it? True, we may draw from it the ideal of a beautiful and sinless life, and in that there may be a certain power. Still, it is an ideal, presented or conceived only to be despaired of. For this beautiful life, being sinless, is really not human, after all; and *we* cannot have it, unless our nature is overborne and acted wholly by God in the same manner which, alas! is no longer possible, for we are deep in sin already. No! let us have the divine, the deific itself — the very feeling of God, God's own beauty, truth, and love. Then we shall have both the pure ideal of a life, and a power flowing out from God to ingenerate that life in us. God; God is what we want, not a man; God, revealed through man, that we may see his heart, and hide our guilty nature in the bosom of his love: God so identified with our race, as to signify the possible union and eternal identification of our nature with his.

10. As a last evidence on this subject, and one that, in my view, winds up all debates, I add the holy formula of baptism — "into the name of the Father, Son, and Holy Ghost." That the Father is God, is conceded; so, also, that the Spirit is God, and then, between these terms on either hand, we have, dropped in, *"the Son"* — a man, we are told, a mere human creature, who is one of ourselves! This, too, in a solemn formula that is appointed for the consecration of a believing soul to God. I am well aware that one or two passages are cited to countenance this very harsh construction, but they are not parallel. If we read, for example, "To the general assembly and church of the first born, and to God the judge of all, and to the spirits of just men made perfect, and to Jesus, the mediator of the new covenant" — this is only a case of mixed rhetoric, produced, in part, by the order of ideas. But in this baptismal formula we have nothing but a mere collocation of names, and one that suffers no dignified or endurable construction, unless each term is taken to import the real divinity of the subject. It appears evident to me that our Unitarian brethren impose upon themselves, in the construction they give to this formula, by collecting about the person of Christ associations that do not belong to his proper humanity — associations which really belong to our view of his

person, not to theirs. Were they to read, "In the name of the Father, A. B. the carpenter, and the Holy Ghost," they would be sensible, I think, of some very great violence done to the words by any construction which holds the strict humanity of Christ.

Indeed, it has always seemed to me that any attempt to get away from the proper divinity of Christ, as held in this formula, must be taken to proceed from a most disingenuous spirit; were it not that the practical difficulties thrown upon the souls of men, the bewilderment they have suffered, the confusion that has enveloped their religious nature, under our supposed orthodox views of the trinity, may have created such a necessity as must be allowed to excuse almost any kind of violence. And, were it not for this, I do not believe that any reader of the New Testament, least of all any true believer in it, would ever have questioned for a moment the real divinity of Christ. In fact, it never was seriously questioned until after the easy and free representations of the Scripture and of the apostolic fathers had been hardened into dogma, or converted by the Nicene theologues and those of the subsequent ages, into a doctrine of the mere human understanding; an assertion of three metaphysical persons in the divine nature. I do not say that such a mistake must not have been committed. And then, when a trinity of this kind was once inaugurated, it was equally necessary that speculation should rise up, sometime or other, to clear away the rubbish that speculation had accumulated. A metaphysical trinity must be assaulted by a metaphysical unity. And then, coming after both, and taking up the suspicion that possibly dogma is not the whole wisdom of man; seeing, in fact, that it is wholly incompetent to represent the living truths of Christianity, we may be induced to let go a trinity that mocks our reason, and a unity that freezes our hearts, and return to the simple Father, Son, and Holy Ghost of the Scriptures and the apostolic fathers; there to rest in the living and life-giving forms of the spirit. To this it is my design, if possible, to bring you; for in maintaining the essential divinity of Christ there is no difficulty whatever, till we begin to speculate or dogmatize about the humanity, or find ourselves in contact with the more commonly accepted doctrine of trinity.

I speak of the more commonly accepted doctrine. What that doctrine is, I am well aware it would be exceedingly difficult to state. Let us pause here, a moment, and see if we can find our way to any proximate conception of it.

It seems to be agreed by the orthodox that there are three persons, Father, Son, and Holy Ghost, in the divine nature. These three persons, too, are generally regarded as belonging, not to the *machina Dei*, by which God is revealed, but to the very *esse*, the substantial being of God, or the interior contents of his being. They are declared to be equal; all to be infinite; all to be the same in substance; all to be one. But as soon as the question is raised, what are we to intend by the word *person*, the appearance of agreement, and often of self-understanding, vanishes.

A very large portion of the Christian teachers, together with the general mass of disciples, undoubtedly hold three real living persons in the interior nature of God; that is, three consciousnesses, wills, hearts, understandings.[1] Certain passages of Scripture supposed to represent the three persons as covenanting, co-operating, and co-presiding, are taken, accordingly, so to affirm, in the most literal and dogmatic sense. And some very distinguished living teachers are frank enough to acknowledge that any intermediate doctrine, between the absolute unity of God and a social unity, is impossible and incredible; therefore, that they take the latter. Accordingly, Father, Son, and Holy Ghost are, in their view, socially united only, and preside in that way, as a kind of celestial tritheocracy over the world. They are one God simply in the sense that the three will always act together, with a perfect consent or coincidence. This view has the merit that it takes consequences fairly, states them frankly, and boldly renounces Orthodoxy, at the point opposite to Unitarianism, to escape the same difficulties. It denies that the three persons are "the *same* in substance," and asserts instead, three substances; and yet, because of its clear opposition to Unitarianism, it is counted safe, and never treated as a heresy. However, when it is applied to Christ and his work, then it breaks down into the same confusion as the more common view, reducing the Son to a really subordinate and subject position, in which the proper attributes of deity are no longer visible or supposable.

But our properly orthodox teachers and churches, while professing three persons, also retain the verbal profession of one person. They suppose themselves really to hold that God is one person. And yet they most certainly do not; they only confuse their understanding, and call their confusion faith. This, I affirm, not as speaking reproachfully but, as I suppose, on the ground of sufficient evidence — partly because it cannot be otherwise, and partly because it visibly is not.

1. [ED.] For a conspicuous example, see Edward Beecher, "The Doctrine of the Trinity, Rational and Scriptural," *Biblical Repository and Classical Review*, 3d series, V (October 1849), 727, 732.

No man can assert three persons, meaning three consciousnesses, wills, and understandings, and still have any intelligent meaning in his mind, when he asserts that they are yet one person. For, as he now uses the term, the very idea of a person is that of an essential, incommunicable monad, bounded by consciousness, and vitalized by self-active will, which being true, he might as well profess to hold that three units are yet one unit. When he does it, his words will of necessity be only substitutes for sense.

At the same time, there are too many signs of the mental confusion I speak of, not to believe that it exists. Thus, if the class I speak of were to hear a discourse insisting on the proper personal unity of God, it would awaken suspicion in their minds; while a discourse insisting on the existence of three persons would be only a certain proof of orthodoxy; showing that they profess three persons, meaning what they profess, and one person, really not meaning it.

Methods are also resorted to in the way of explaining God's oneness in consistency with his existence in three persons, which show that his real oneness, as a spirit, is virtually lost. Thus it will sometimes be represented that the three persons are three sets of attributes inhering in a common substance; in which method the three intelligences come to their unity in a virtually inorganic ground; for if the substance supposed be itself of a vital quality, a Life, then we have only more difficulties on hand, and not fewer; viz., to conceive a Living Person having in himself, first, the attributes of a person, and secondly, three more persons who are attributes, in the second degree — that is, attributes of attributes. It can hardly be supposed that any such monster is intended, in the way of bringing the three persons into unity; therefore, taking the "substance" as inorganic, we have three vital personal Gods, and back of them, or under them as their ground of unity, an inorganic deity. I make no objection here to the supposition that the persons are mere attributes of a substance not themselves; I ask not how attributes can be real enough to make persons, and not real enough to make substances; I urge it not as an objection, that our very idea of person, as the word is here used, is that of a living substance manifested through attributes — itself the most real and substantial thing to thought in the universe of God — I only call attention to the fact that this theory of divine unity, making it essentially inorganic, indicates such a holding of the three persons as virtually leaves no unity at all, which is more distinct than a profession of mental confusion on the subject.

But, while the unity is thus confused and lost in the threeness, perhaps I should also admit that the threeness sometimes appears to be clouded or obscured by the unity. Thus, it is sometimes protested that, in the word *person*, nothing is meant beyond a "threefold distinction"; though it will always be observed that nothing is really meant by the protestation — that the protester goes on to speak and reason of the three, not as being only somewhats, or distinctions, but as metaphysical and real persons. Or, the three are sometimes compared, in their union, to the soul, the life principle, and the body united in one person called a man — an illustration which, if it has any point or appositeness at all, shows how God may be one and not three; for the life and the body are not persons. Or, if the soul be itself the life, and the body its external development, which is possible, then in a yet stricter sense there is but one person in them all.

Probably there is a degree of alternation, or inclining from one side to the other, in this view of trinity, as the mind struggles now to embrace one, and now the other, of two incompatible notions. Some persons are more habitually inclined to hold the three; a very much smaller number to hold the one. Meantime, and especially in the former class of those who range themselves under this view of metaphysical tripersonality, mournful evidence will be found that a confused and painfully bewildered state is often produced by it. They are practically at work, in their thoughts, to choose between the three; sometimes actually and decidedly preferring one to another; doubting how to adjust their mind in worship; uncertain, often, which of the three to obey; turning away, possibly, from one in a feeling of dread that might well be called aversion; devoting themselves to another, as the Romanist to his patron saint. This, in fact, is polytheism, and not the clear, simple love of God. There is true love in it, doubtless, but the comfort of love is not here. The mind is involved in a dismal confusion, which we cannot think of without the sincerest pity. No soul can truly rest in God, when God is two or three, and these in such a sense that a choice between them must be continually suggested.

Besides, it is another source of mental confusion, connected with this view of three metaphysical persons, that though they are all declared to be infinite and equal, they really are not so. The proper deity of Christ is not held in this view. He is begotten, sent, supported, directed, by the Father, in such a sense as really annihilates his deity. This has been shown in a truly searching and convincing manner by Schleiermacher in his historical essay on the trinity. And indeed you will see at a glance that this view of a metaphysical trinity of persons breaks down in the very point which is commonly regarded as its excellence — its assertion of the proper deity of Christ.

Indeed, it is a somewhat curious fact in theology, that the class of teachers who protest over the word *person,* declaring that they mean only a *threefold distinction,* cannot show that there is really a hair's breadth of difference between their doctrine and the doctrine asserted by many of the later Unitarians. They may teach or preach in a very different manner — they probably do, but the theoretic contents of their opinion cannot be distinguished. Thus, they say that there is a certain divine person in the man Christ Jesus, but that when they use the term *person,* they mean not a person, but a certain indefinite and indefinable distinction. The later Unitarians, meantime, are found asserting that God is present in Christ, in a mysterious and peculiar communication of his being, so that he is the living embodiment and express image of God. If, now, the question be raised, wherein does the indefinable *distinction* of one differ from the mysterious and peculiar *communication* of the other, or how does it appear that there is any difference, there is no living man, I am quite sure, who can invent an answer.

Such is the confusion produced by attempting to assert a real and metaphysical trinity of persons in the divine nature. Whether the word is taken at its full import, or diminished away to a mere something called a distinction, there is produced only contrariety, confusion, practical negation, not light.

And now the question comes upon us — how shall we resolve the divinity or deity of Christ, already proved, so as to make it consist with the proper unity of God? To state the question as boldly and definitely as possible, we have two terms before us. First, we have the essential unity and supremacy of God. This we are to assume. I am willing to assume it without argument. Indeed, there is no place for argument; for if any one will say that he believes in three metaphysical or essential persons in the being of God, there is no argument that can set him in a more unsatisfactory position, whether intellectually or practically, than he takes himself. Or if any one endeavors to relieve his position, by declaring that he only means distinctions by the word *persons,* he then flies into darkness and negation for his comfort, and there he may safely be left. We take, then, as a first point, to be held immovably, the strict personal unity of God — one mind, will, consciousness. Then, secondly, we have, as a term to be reconciled with this, the three of Scripture, and the living person walking the earth, in the human form, called Jesus Christ — a subject, suffering being, whose highest and truest reality is that he is God. Such is the work we have on hand, and it must be performed so as to justify the language of Scripture, and be clear of any real absurdity.

To indicate beforehand the general tenor of my argument, which may assist you to apprehend the matter of it more easily, I here suggest that the trinity we seek will be a trinity that results of necessity from the *revelation* of God to man. I do not undertake to fathom the interior being of God, and tell how it is composed. That is a matter too high for me, and, I think, for us all. I only insist that, assuming the strictest unity and even simplicity of God's nature, he could not be efficiently or sufficiently revealed to us, without evolving a trinity of persons such as we meet in the Scriptures. These persons or personalities are the *dramatis personae* of revelation, and their reality is measured by what of the infinite they convey in these finite forms. As such they bear, on the one hand, a relation to God, who is to be conveyed or imported into knowledge; on the other, they are related to our human capacities and wants, being that presentation of God which is necessary to make him a subject of thought, or bring him within the discourse of reason; that also which is necessary to produce mutuality, or terms of conversableness, between us and him, and pour his love most effectually into our feeling.

To bring the whole subject fully before us, let us endeavor first of all to form the distinctest notion possible of God, as existing in himself, and unrevealed. Then we shall understand, the better, what is necessary to reveal him. Of course we mean, when we speak of God as unrevealed, to speak of him anterior to his act of creation; for the worlds created are all outgoings from himself, and in that view, revealments of him. God unrevealed is God simply existing, as spirit, in himself.

Who, now, is God thus existing in himself? Has he any external form, by which he may be figured or conceived? No. Is he a point without space — is he space without limit? Neither. Is his activity connected with any sort of motion? Certainly not; motion belongs to a finite creature ranging in the infinite. Is there any color, sound, sign, measure, by which he may be known? No. He dwells in eternal silence, without parts, above time. If, then, we can apprehend him by nothing outward, let us consider, as we may without irreverence, things of a more interior quality in his being. Does he, then, act under the law of action and reaction as we do?

Never. This, in fact, is the very notion of absolute being and power, that it acts without reaction, requiring no supports, living between no contrasts or antagonisms. He simply is, which contains everything. Does he, then, reason? No; for to reason in the active sense, as deducing one thing from another, implies a want of knowledge. Does he, then, deliberate? No; for he sees all conclusions without deliberation, intuitively. Does he inquire? No; for he knows all things already. Does he remember? Never; for to remember is to call up what was out of mind, and nothing is out of mind. Does he believe? No; the virtue that he exercises is a virtue without faith, and radically distinct, in that view, from anything called virtue in us. Where, then, is God? by what searching shall we find him out? by what sign is he to be known or conceived? Does he think? No, never, in any human sense of the term; for thought, with us, is only a finite activity under the law of succession and time; and besides this, we have no other conception of it. Has he new emotions rising up, which, if we could see them rise, would show us that he is? No; emotion, according to our human sense, is a mere jet of feeling — one feeling moving out just now into the foreground before others; and this can be true only of a finite nature. God, in such a sense, certainly, has no emotions.

What, then, shall we say; what conception form of God as simply existing in himself, and as yet unrevealed? Only that he is the Absolute Being — the Infinite — the I Am That I Am, giving no sign that he is, other than that he is.

"A very unsatisfactory, unpleasant, unsignificant, and practically untrue representation of God," you will say. Exactly so! that is the point I wish to be discovered. And without a trinity, and incarnation, and other like devices of revelation, we should never have a better.

Having now come down hither, as it were, upon the shore of the Absolute — that Absolute which has no shore — let us pause just here a moment, and take note, distinctly, of two or three matters that will assist us to open what remains of our subject with a better intelligence. And

1. Observe that, when God is revealed, it cannot be as the One, as the Infinite, or Absolute, but only as through media. And as there are no infinite media, no signs that express the infinite, no minds, in fact, that can apprehend the infinite by direct inspection, the One must appear in the manifold; the Absolute in the conditional; Spirit in form; the Motionless in motion; the Infinite in the finite. He must distribute himself, he must let forth his nature in sounds, colors, forms, works, definite objects and

signs. It must be to us as if Brahma were waking up; as if Jehovah, the Infinite I Am, the Absolute, were dividing off himself into innumerable activities that shall dramatize his immensity, and bring him within the modes of language and discursive thought. And in whatever thing he appears or is revealed, there will be something that misrepresents, as well as something that represents him. The revealing process, that which makes him appear, will envelop itself in clouds of formal contradiction — that is, of diction which is contrary, in some way, to the truth, and which, taken simply as diction, is continually setting forms against each other.

Thus, the God revealed, in distinction from the God Absolute, will have parts, forms, colors, utterances, motions, activities, assigned him. He will think, deliberate, reason, remember, have emotions. Then, taking up all these manifold representations, casting out the matter in which they are cross to each other, and repugnant to the very idea of the God they represent, we shall settle into the true knowledge of God, and receive, as far as the finite can receive the Infinite, the contents of the divine nature.

2. To make this same view yet more evident, observe that we ourselves being finite, under time and succession, reasoning, deliberating, thinking, remembering, having emotions, can never come into the knowledge of God, save as God is brought within our finite molds of action. There are certain absolute verities which belong to our own nature, and which, therefore, we can know as absolute, or which, I should rather say, we must know. They are such as the ideas of space, cause, truth, right, and axioms of mathematical science. But these are simple ideas, and have their reality in us. God is a BEING out of us, a Being in whom the possibilities and even facts of all other being have their spring. Taken in this view, as the absolute, all-comprehensive being, we can know him only *as* being; that is, by a revelation, or rather by revelations, giving out one after another, and in one way or another, but always in finite forms, something that belongs to the knowledge of God. And then we know God only as we bring all our knowledges together. Thus we approach the knowledge of the Absolute Being, and there is no other way possible, or even conceivable.

Or, let me give the same truth under yet another form. God, as the Absolute Being, is not under the law of action and reaction, as I have said. He does not compare, try contrasts, raise definitions, in order to know himself. He has all the poles of self-knowledge in his consciousness, and knows himself by an absolute, eternal, infinite, self-intuition. We, on the other hand, exist under the law of action and reaction, and our minds are

worked under this law, as truly as our bodies. The only absolute knowledge we have relates to the few necessary ideas just alluded to. As regards
all matters of opinion, fact, being, we are obliged to get our knowledge
under the law of action and reaction — through finites that are relative to
each other, through antagonisms, contrasts, comparisons, interactions,
counteractions. And yet in God, considered as Absolute, there are none
of these. Therefore to set our minds in action, or to generate in us a
knowledge of himself, he must produce himself in finite forms; under the
relations of space, as above and below, on this side and on that; by motion
towards, involving motion from. For instance, the Saviour, in his exaltation, goes up, by a visible ascent, into the heavens. That is, motion from
and motion towards indicate his divine exaltation. And yet, if he had
parted from his disciples on the other side of the world, he would have
moved in exactly the contrary direction. Now, the reality of the ascension, as we call it, is not the motion, but what the motion signifies,
viz., the change of state. So, when we pray for the Holy Spirit, it is
for the descent of the Holy Spirit — not that there is any descent or motion in the case; we only work our thought under the great law of action
and reaction, which belongs to the finite quality of our nature.

It was under this principle, and no other, that the special economy of
the Jewish state was appointed. The whole universe of God is a real and
proper theocracy, but here a special theocracy is organized for the purpose of raising contrasts, and by that means revealing God, or making his
sway apparent. God was the God of Egypt, Babylon, and Philistia, as
truly as of Israel. But in a uniform handling of these nations, dark and
brutish as their minds at that time were, all would miss of perceiving him
— he would be only a lost idea. Hence for the benefit of all, that is, to
make his sway apparent to all, he selects one people of the four, to receive a special discipline and have a special outward future dispensed to
them. He is to be called their God, and they his people; and it is to be
seen, by the victories he gives, and the wondrous deliverances he vouch-
safes, how superior he is to the other gods of the nations. And so he will
be known, at length, as the Great God and King above all gods. In one
view, this special theocracy has a fictitious and even absurd look; for,
when we scan the matter more deeply, we find that God reigns in Philistia as truly as in Israel, and the contrast raised is only God contrasted
with himself. Still the truth communicated through the contrast — viz.,
God, is the fundamental verity of the transaction, and the Jewish polity is
only the means he appointed to make his power known, and disclose to all

that broader and more comprehensive theocracy, which is the shelter, blessing, and joy of all.

The Scripture writers, too, are continually working this figure of contrast, even setting God, if we compare their representations, in a kind of antagonism with himself. Here, for example, is the great and broad sea — full of his goodness. Here it is a raging monster, whose proud and turbulent waves it is the glory of his majesty to hold in check. In one case, the sea represents him. In the other, he is seen triumphing over his representative. Just so in the heavens, which at one time are his very garment; while at another, it is half his grandeur that he sits upon the great circle above them, to mold and sway their motions.

Now it is in this manner only, through relations, contrasts, actions and reactions, that we come into the knowledge of God. As Absolute Being, we know him not. But our mind, acted under the law of action and reaction, is carried up to him, or thrown back upon him, to apprehend him more and more perfectly. Nothing that we see, or can see, represents him fully, or can represent him truly; for the finite cannot show us the Infinite. But between various finites, acting so as to correct each other, and be supplements to each other, we get a true knowledge. Our method may be compared to that of resultant motions in philosophy. No one finite thing represents the Absolute Being; but between two or more finite forces acting obliquely on our mind, it is driven out, in a resultant motion, towards the Infinite. Meantime, a part of the two finite forces, being oblique or false, is destroyed by the mutual counteraction of forces.

Under this same law, I suggest that we look for a solution of the trinity, and of the person of Jesus Christ. They are relatives, to conduct us up to the Absolute.

3. Observe that when God is revealed he will not, if he is truly and efficiently revealed, be cleared of obscurity and mystery. He will not be a bald, philosophic unity, perfectly comprehended and measured by us. We shall not have his boundaries, he will not be simple to us as a man is. When we have reduced him to that, and call it our reason or philosophy, we have only gotten up a somewhat larger man than ourselves, and set this larger man in the place of the Absolute Being. And if we perfectly understand him, if we have no questions about him, the colder, and in real truth the more unknown he is — the Infinite revealed away, not revealed. No; if he is revealed at all, it will be through infinite repugnances and contrarieties; through forms, colors, motions, words, persons, or personal-

ities; all presenting themselves to our sense and feeling, to pour in something of the divine into our nature. And a vast circle of mystery will be the background of all other representations, on which they will play and glitter in living threads of motion, as lightning on a cloud; and what they themselves do not reveal of God, the mystery will — a Being infinite, undiscovered, undiscoverable, therefore true. But if we could see the last boundaries of God, and hold him clear of a question within the molds of logic and cognition, then he is not God any longer, we have lost the conception of God.

Having noted these points, we shall be able, I trust, to advance more securely and with a clearer intelligence, in the development of our subject. We go back, now, to the Absolute Being, to consider by what process he will be revealed, and to see that revelation unfolded. And here I must bring to view a singular and eminent distinction of the divine nature, without which he could never be revealed.

There is in God, taken as the Absolute Being, a capacity of self-expression, so to speak, which is peculiar — a generative power of form, a creative imagination, in which, or by aid of which, he can produce himself outwardly, or represent himself in the finite. In this respect, God is wholly unlike to us. Our imagination is passive, stored with forms, colors, and types of words from without, borrowed from the world we live in. But all such forms God has in himself, and this is the Logos, the Word, elsewhere called the Form of God. Now, this Word, this Form of God, in which he sees himself, is with God, as John says, from the beginning. It is God mirrored before his own understanding, and to be mirrored, as in fragments of the mirror, before us. Conceive him now as creating the worlds, or creating worlds, if you please, from eternity. In so doing he only represents, expresses, or outwardly produces himself. He bodies out his own thoughts. What we call the creation is, in another view, a revelation only of God, his first revelation.

And it is in this view that the Word, or Logos, elsewhere called Christ, or the Son of God, is represented as the Creator of the worlds. Or it is said, which is only another form of the same truth, that the worlds were made by or through him, and the apostle John adds, that without him is not anything made that was made. Now, as John also declares, there was light, the first revelation was made, God was expressed in the forms and relations of the finite. But the light shined in darkness, and the darkness comprehended it not. The divine Word was here; he had come to his own, but his own received him not. One thing more is possible that will yield a still more effulgent light, viz.: that, as God has produced himself in all the other finite forms of being, so now he should appear in the human.

Indeed, he has appeared in the human before, in the same way as he has in all the created objects of the world. The human person, taken as a mere structure, adapted to the high uses of intelligence and moral action, is itself a noble illustration of his wisdom, and a token also of the exalted and good purposes cherished in our existence. But there was yet more of God to be exhibited in the human form of our race. As the spirit of man is made in the image of God, and his bodily form is prepared to be the fit vehicle and outward representative of his spirit, it follows that his bodily form has also some inherent, *a priori* relation to God's own nature; such probably as makes it the truest, most expressive finite type of him. Continuing, therefore, in a pure upright character, our whole race would have been a visible revelation of the truth and beauty of God. But having not thus continued, having come under the power of evil, that which was to be the expression or reflection of God became appropriated to the expression of evil. Truth has no longer any living unblemished manifestation in the world; the beauty of goodness lives and smiles no more. Sin, prejudice, passion — stains of every color — so deface and mar the race, that the face of God, the real glory of the Divine, is visible no longer. Now, therefore, God will reclaim this last type of himself, possess it with his own life and feeling, and through that, live himself into the acquaintance and biographic history of the world. "And the Word was made flesh, and dwelt among us; and we beheld his glory as of the only begotten of the Father, full of grace and truth." "The only begotten Son, which is in the bosom of the Father, he hath declared him." This is Christ whose proper deity or divinity we have proved.

Prior to this moment, there has been no appearance of trinity in the revelations God has made of his being; but just here — whether as resulting from the incarnation or as implied in it, we are not informed — a threefold personality or impersonation of God begins to offer itself to view. Just here, accordingly, as the revelation culminates or completes the fullness of its form, many are staggered and confused by difficulties which they say are contrary to reason — impossible therefore to faith. I think otherwise. In these three persons or impersonations I only see a revelation of the Absolute Being, under just such relatives as by their mutual play, in and before our imaginative sense, will produce in us the truest knowledge of God — render him most conversable, bring him closest to

feeling, give him the freest, least obstructed access, as a quickening
power, to our hearts.

To verify this view of Christ, which is now my object, I must apply it
as a solvent to the two classes of difficulties created by the incarnation:

i. To the difficulties created by the supposed relations of the divine to
the human, in the person of Jesus.

ii. To those which spring of the supposed relations of His divine person to the other divine persons, or impersonations developed in the process of revelation.

i. Under the relations of the divine to the human, we meet the objection, first of all, that here is an incarnation asserted of the divine nature;
that God, the infinite God, is represented as dwelling in a finite human
person, subject to its limitations and even to its evils; and this is incredible — an insult to reason. It may be so, and if it is, we must reject
the doctrine. But we notice, while revolving this objection, that several
other religions have believed or expected an incarnation of their deity, or
the divine principle of their worship; and that these have been the most
speculative and cultivated forms of false religion. If, then, whole nations
of mankind, comprising thinkers, scholars, and philosophers, have been
ready to expect, or have actually believed in the incarnation of their god
or highest divinity, it would not seem to be wholly cross to natural reason
to believe in such an event. On the contrary, we are rather to suspect that
some true instinct or conscious want of the race is here divining, so to
speak, that blessed visitation, by which God shall sometime vouchsafe to
give himself to the world.

Then again, it was just now made to appear that the human person was
originally and specially related to the expression of God, specially fitted
to be the organ of the divine feeling and character. It is also clear that if
God were to inhabit such a vehicle, one so fellow to ourselves, and live
himself as a perfect character into the biographic history of the world, a
result would follow of as great magnificence as the creation of the world
itself, viz.: the incorporation of the Divine in the history of the world
— so a renovation, at last, of the moral and religious life of the world. If,
now, the human person will express more of God than the whole created
universe beside (and it certainly will more of God's feeling and character), and if a motive possessing as great consequence as the creation of the
world invites him to do it, is it any more extravagant to believe that the
Word will become flesh, than that the Word has become, or produced in

time, a material universe? If so, I cannot see in what manner. Many persons, I know, do not believe that the world has been produced in time; and of course the argument I state is not for them. But I am speaking, mostly, to such as have faith to believe that the worlds were made, and find no difficulty in believing in God as a Creator. And if a miracle, a putting forth of God in time, so vast as this, is credible, why not a miracle also that has a necessity as deep, involves consequences of as great moment, and makes an expression of God as much lovelier and holier as it exhibits more of his moral excellence and grandeur — his condescension, patience, gentleness, forgiveness, in one word, his love?

I am speaking, also, to such as believe the Scriptures; and therefore it should be something to notice that they often represent the Saviour in ways that indicate the same view of his person: he is Emanuel, God with us — the Word made flesh — God manifest in the flesh — the express image of his person — the Life that was manifested — the glass in which we look to behold the glory of the Lord — the fullness of God revealed bodily — the power of God — the light of the knowledge of the glory of God in the face of Jesus Christ — the image of the invisible God. In all these, and in a very great number of similar instances, language is used in reference to Christ which indicates an opinion that his advent is the appearing of God; his deepest reality, that he expresses the fullness of the Life of God. Nor does it satisfy this language at all, to conceive that Christ is a good man, or a perfect man, and that so he is an illustration or image of God. Such a construction might be given to a single expression of the kind; for we use occasionally an almost violent figure. But this is cool, ordinary, undeclamatory language, and the same idea is turned round and round, appears and reappears in different shapes, and becomes, in fact, the hinge of the gospel — the central light of the glorious gospel of Christ, who is the image of God, shining unto men. It should also be added that probably a very great share of the difficulties that compass this subject were originally created by overlooking, or making no sufficient account of, the very class of representations here referred to; for we throw away all the solvents of the incarnation and the trinity that are given us, and then complain of our difficulties.

But the human person, it will be said, is limited, and God is not. Very true. But you have the same objection in reference to the first revelation, the Word in the world. This also is limited — at least what you have known of it is limited; besides, you have a special delight in seeing God in the smallest things, the minutest specks of being. If, then, it be incredible that God should take the human to express himself, because the human is finite, can the finite in the world, or in a living atom, express him more worthily, or do it more accordantly with reason?

But Christ, you will say, perhaps, is a living intelligent person. Taking him, therefore, as a person, I must view him under the measures and limitations of a person. Very true, if you have a right to measure the contents of his person by his body; which, possibly, you have no more right to do than you have to measure God, as revealed in any object, by the object that reveals him. For it no more follows that a human body measures God, when revealed through it, than that a star, a tree, or an insect measures him, when he is revealed through that. As regards the interior nature of Christ, or the composition of his person, we perhaps know nothing; and if his outward nature represents an unknown quantity, it may, for aught that appears, represent an infinite quantity. A finite outward person, too, may as well be an organ or type of the Infinite as a finite thing or object; and God may act a human personality, without being measured by it, as well as to shine through a finite thing or a world, without being measured by that.

But this divine person, the Christ, grows, I shall be reminded, or is said to grow in wisdom and knowledge. There must, therefore, be some kind of intelligence in him, call it human or divine, which is under a law of development, and therefore of limitation. To this I answer (1) that the language may well enough be taken as language of external description merely, or as only setting forth appearance as appearance; or (2) it may be said, which is far more satisfactory, and leaves the question where it should be, that the body of Christ evidently grew up from infancy; and that all his actings grew out, so to speak, with it; and if the divine was manifested in the ways of a child, it creates no difficulty which does not exist when it is manifested in the ways of a man or a world. The whole question is whether it is possible for the divine nature to be manifested in humanity, and as it belongs to humanity to grow, I see nothing in that to create a difficulty, more than when it is considered to be the part of humanity to inquire, reason, remember, have emotions, and move about in space; for none of these belong to the true Absolute Deity. Even to say that Christ reasons and thinks, using the words in their human sense, is quite as repugnant to his proper Deity, as to say that he learns or grows in knowledge, after the manner of a child; for to reason and to think, are, in fact, the same as to learn.

But the history of Christ, it will be said, compels us to go farther. We cannot look at the external person of Christ on the one hand, and the Absolute Jehovah on the other, and regard the former simply as a representative or expression of the other. Christ, says the Unitarian, obeys, worships, suffers, and in that manner shows most plainly that his internal nature is under a limitation; therefore he is human only. Then the common trinitarian replies, your argument is good; therefore we assert a human soul in the person of Jesus, which comes under these limitations, while the divine soul escapes; and so we save the divinity unharmed and unabridged.

Answering the latter first, I reply that in holding such a theory of Christ's obedience and sufferings, he does an affront to the plain language of Scripture. For the Scripture does not say that a certain human soul called Jesus, born as such of Mary, obeyed and suffered; but it says in the boldest manner, that he who was in the form of God, humbled himself and became obedient unto death, even the death of the cross. A declaration the very point of which is, not that the man Jesus was a being under human limitations, but that he who was in the form of God, the real divinity, came into the finite, and was subject to human conditions. Then, again, Christ himself declared, not that a human soul, hid in his person, was placed under limitations, but more — that the Son, that is, the divine person — for the word *Son* is used as relative to the Father — the Son can do nothing of himself but what he seeth the Father do; for the Father loveth the Son and sheweth him all things that himself doeth. He also prays, "O Father, glorify thou me with thine own self, with the glory that I had with thee before the world was" — a prayer which cannot be referred to the human soul, even if there was a human soul hid in his person; for that soul could speak of no glory it once had with the Father. Hence the supposition of a human soul existing distinctly, and acting by itself, clears no difficulty; for the Son, the divine part, or I should rather say, the whole Christ, is still represented as humbled, as weak, as divested of glory, and existing under limitations or conditions that do not belong to Deity.

Besides, this theory of two distinct subsistences, still maintaining their several kinds of action in Christ — one growing, learning, obeying, suffering; the other infinite and impassible — only creates difficulties a hundredfold greater than any that it solves. It virtually denies any real unity between the human and the divine, and substitutes collocation or copartnership for unity. If the divine part were residing in Saturn, he would be as truly united with the human race as now. Instead of a person whose nature is the real unity of the divine and the human, we have two distinct persons, between whom our thoughts are continually alternating; referring this to one, that to the other, and imaging all the while not a union of the two, in which our possible union with God is signified and sealed forever, but a practical, historical assertion rather of his incommunicableness, thrust upon our notice in a form more oppressive and chilling than it has to abstract thought. Meantime the whole work of Christ, as a subject, suffering Redeemer, is thrown upon the human side of his nature, and the divine side standing thus aloof, incommunicably distant, has nothing in fact to do with the transaction other than to be a spectator of it. And then, while we are moved to ask of what so great consequence to us, or to the government of God, can be the obedience and suffering of this particular man Jesus, more than of any other, it is also represented, as part of the same general scheme, that he is, after all, scarcely more than a mere nominal man — that he is so removed from the fortunes and the proper trial of a man, by the proximity of the divine, as not even to unfold a human character! And thus, while the redemption even of the world is hung upon his human possibilities, he is shown, as a man, to have probably less of human significance than any other; to be a man whose character is not in himself, but in the custody that keeps him from being himself!

There is, then, I conclude, no solid foundation for the common trinitarian theory of two distinct or distinctly active subsistences in the person of Christ. It is not scriptural. It accounts for nothing. It only creates even greater difficulties. Indeed, it is a virtual denial, we should say, of that which is in one view, the summit or highest glory of the incarnation, viz., the union signified, and historically begun between God and man.

Replying, now, both to the Unitarian and the common trinitarian together, I deny that the obedience, worship, suffering, and other subject conditions of Christ, do, of necessity, create the difficulties supposed. To name God, or even to speak of him, is, in one view, to raise a difficulty; for in so doing we are always seeking to represent the infinite by the finite; that is, by terms whose symbols and significances are relative only — subject to finite conditions and measures. But we are never troubled by any sense of absurdity or incompatibility, when we thus speak of God; for we know that our words have their truth or falsity in what they express, what they put others on thinking of God, not in their measures or boundaries, under the laws of space and time. Their reality is in what they signify, not in what they are.

And precisely so, the reality of Christ is what he expresses of God, not what he is in his physical conditions, or under his human limitations. He is here to express the Absolute Being, especially his feeling, his love to man, his placableness, conversableness, and his real union to the race; in a word, to communicate his own Life to the race, and graft himself historically into it. Therefore, when we see him thus under the conditions of increase, obedience, worship, suffering, we have nothing to do but to ask what is here expressed, and as long as we do that we shall have no difficulty. But if we insist on being more curious, viz., on understanding the composition of the person of Jesus, and the relations of the infinite to the finite in his person, we can create as much of difficulty as we please; though scarcely more than we could, if we pleased to investigate, in the same manner, the interior relations of words or the types of words to thoughts; for we can as easily perceive how Jesus is constructed for the expression of God, as how a straight line (*rectus, right*) becomes the symbol of virtue. There is a point of mystery and even of contradiction in both — a something transcendent, which no investigation will ever reach.

Therefore, to insist on going beyond expression, investigating the mystery of the person of Jesus, when it is given us only to communicate God and His love, is in fact to puzzle ourselves with the vehicle, and rob ourselves of the grace it brings. It is killing the animal that we may find where the life is hid in him, and detect the mode of its union with his body. It is taking the medicine that would cure us, and using it not as a cure but as a subject of investigation. God certainly is able to assume the human, to become incarnate in it so far as to express his union to it, and set himself as Eternal Life in historic and real connection with it. He tells us plainly that he has done it. That we may know by what law to receive and interpret his proceeding, his object is declared; viz., to express or manifest himself in the world, and thus to redeem the world.

We see at once, if it be so, that here is a matter presented, which is not psychologically or physiologically investigable, because it does [not] lie within the categories of ordinary, natural humanity. And yet, instead of turning to receive simply what is expressed of the divine, we immediately begin to try our science on the interior person of Jesus, to ascertain its contents or elements, and the mode of its composition! Nay, we must know who suffers, what worships, and all the hidden chemistries of the person must be understood! Then as to what is expressed, why, that is a matter of so little moment that many overlook it wholly.

It is as if Abraham, after he had entertained as a guest the Jehovah angel, or angel of the Lord, instead of receiving his message, had fallen to inquiring into the digestive process of the angel; or, since he came in human form and spoke with a human voice, whether he had a human soul or not; and, if so, how the two natures were put together! Let alone thy folly and thy shallow curiosity, O Abraham! we should say, hear the Lord speak to thee; what he commands thee, do, what he promises, believe! Suspend thy raw guesses at his nature, and take his message!

Or it is as if Moses, when he saw the burning bush, had fallen at once to speculating about the fire: Is this real fire? No, if it was it would burn the wood. Well, if it is not fire, then there is nothing very wonderful in it; for it is nothing wonderful that that which is not fire should not burn! Nay, is it not a very dishonest fire? he might have said; for it is not what it pretends to be — it is no real fire at all. And yet it was better, methinks, to take the bush as it was meant, to see God in it, and let the chemists look after the fire!

It is very difficult, I know, for a certain class of men, whose nature it is to live in their logic and not in simple insight, to stay content with anything which has not been verified by some word-process. Instead of putting off their shoes before the burning bush, they would put out the fire rather — by such kind of constructive wisdom as I have just now given. A poem is ill to such, if it does not stand well in the predicaments. Receiving nothing by their imagination or by their heart, the verities they embrace are all dead verities. And as dead verities cannot impregnate, they live as being dead themselves — a sterile class of souls, whom not even the life-giving mysteries of the incarnation are able to fructify. See, they say, Christ obeys and suffers, how can the subject be the supreme; the suffering man, the impassible God! Probably they toss off their discovery with an air of superior sagacity, as if by some peculiar depth of argument they had reached a conclusion so profound. They cannot imagine that even the babes of true knowledge, the simple children of Christian faith, who open their hearts to the reconciling grace of God in Christ Jesus, are really wiser and deeper than they. As if it were some special wisdom to judge that the Lord Jesus came into the world, not simply to express God, and offer him to the embrace of our love, but to submit a new riddle to the speculative chemistry and constructive logic of the race! Indeed, you may figure this whole tribe of sophisters as a man standing before that most beautiful and wondrous work of art, the "Beatified Spirit" of Guido, and there commencing a quarrel with the artist, that he should be so absurd as to think of making a beatified spirit out of mere linseed, ochers, and oxides! Would it not be more dignified to let the pigments go and take the expression of the canvas? Just so are the human personality, the obedient, subject, suffering state of Jesus, all to be taken as colors of the Divine, and we are not to fool ourselves in practicing our logic on the colors, but to seize, at once, upon the divine import and significance thereof; ascending thus to the heart of God, there to rest in the vision of his beatific glory.

I am well aware that we are never to believe, never can believe anything that is really absurd or contradictory; but we are to believe, constantly, things that, taken in their form, are contrary one to the other — contrary in diction. The highest and divinest truths are often to be expressed, or communicated only in this manner. I could name a poem of fifty lines, in which as many as four plain formal contradictions occur, all evolving truths of feeling, otherwise not in the power of any language to express. And so, the gospel of John is the most contradictory book in the world, one of which logic can make just what havoc it will — and this, because it is a book that embodies more of the highest and holiest forms of truth than any other. Accordingly, the only way to read this book is, first, to get the divine aim of Christ's mission before us, viz., to express God, then to let all the repugnant terms pour their contents into our thought and feeling, suffering whatever of repugnance there is in the vehicles to fall off and be forgotten — just as in the viewing of a picture, the colors that are used to make shades, and thus to develop the forms, are disregarded and rejected when you consider the matter of complexion; or just as the flatness of the canvas is not insisted on, as contrary to the roundness of the forms; or just as you disregard everything else when you come to the moral expression, and offer your simple feeling to that, as the living truth of all.

So in the matter of Christ's obedience, you are not so much to consider the obedience as what the obedience expresses or signifies. Man obeys for what obedience is, but the subject obedient state of Christ is accepted for what it conveys or expresses. Ask, then, what his obedience signifies, in the light and shade of his own peculiar history. Possibly it signifies what is only a highest and first truth in the character of God; viz., that he himself obeys and enthrones forever the right, honors it, enjoys it, as his own pure law; and so, or by the expression of this most powerful and divinest truth, it may be that Christ sanctifies the law that we have broken, erecting it again, in its original sacredness and majesty, before all mankind. Or if we speak of the worship paid by Christ, can anything be more clear than that Christ, in expressing what is perfect in God through the human, must use the human type according to its nature, and the conditions to which it is subject? God does not weep, but it will be no absurd thing for Jesus to weep, and that, too, in the way even of revealing or expressing God. So if he renders worship, it creates no difficulty which does not belong to his simple identification with the human, as truly as to his worship. He is only absurd when he acts the heathen, and refuses to worship in the way of expressing God. To do this effectively, he must act the human perfectly — that is, he must worship.

I do not pretend, however, to solve this matter of worship. The mystery of the divine-human must remain a mystery. I cannot fathom it. Reason itself will justify me in no such attempt. And when we come to speak of the sufferings and death, I would withhold in like manner, and require myself to look only at what the sufferings and death express. It is commonly held that God is impassible, though we never hesitate to affirm that he is displeased thus or thus, and this displeased state is, so far, of course, an un-pleased or painful state. But, even if it were otherwise, if God, in his own nature, were as unsusceptible as a rock, that fact would justify no inference concerning the person of Christ. The only question is, whether God, by a mysterious union with the human, can so far employ the element of suffering as to make it a vehicle for the expression of his own grace and tenderness — whether, indeed, God can be allowed in any way to exhibit those passive virtues which are really the most active and sublimest of all virtues; because they are most irresistible, and require the truest greatness of spirit. Therefore, when we come to the agony of the garden, and the passion of the cross, we are not, with the speculative Unitarian, to set up as a dogma beforehand, and as something that we perfectly know, that God can set himself in no possible terms of connection with suffering; nor believing with the common trinitarian that there are two distinct natures in Christ, are we to conclude that no sort of pang can touch the divine nature, and that only his human part can suffer. We cannot thus intrude into the interior of God's mysteries. We are only to see the eternal Life approach our race — Divine Love manifested and sealed; the Law sanctified by obedience unto death; pardon certified by the "Father, forgive"; peace established and testified by the resurrection from the dead. And then, if we desire more, if we must practice our physiology — why, it is better to try a human subject.

Perhaps it may be imagined that I intend, in holding this view of the incarnation, or the person of Christ, to deny that he had a human soul, or anything human but a human body. I only deny that his human soul, or nature, is to be spoken of, or looked upon as having a *distinct* subsistence, so as to live, think, learn, worship, suffer, by itself. Disclaiming all thought of denying, or affirming, anything as regards the interior composition or construction of his person, I insist that he stands before us in simple unity, one person, the divine-human, representing the qualities of his double parentage as the Son of God, and the son of Mary. I do not say that he is composed of three elements, a divine person, a human soul, and a human body; nor of these that they are distinctly three, or absolutely one. I look upon him only in the external way; for he comes to be viewed externally in what may be expressed through him, and not in any other way. As to any metaphysical or speculative difficulties involved in the union of the divine and the human, I dismiss them all, by observing that Christ is not here for the sake of something accomplished in his metaphysical or psychological interior, but for that which appears and is outwardly signified in his life. And it is certainly competent for God to work out the expression of his own feeling, and his union to the race in what way most approves itself to him. Regarding Christ in this exterior and, as it were, esthetic way, he is that Holy Thing in which my God is brought to me — brought even down to a fellow relation with me. I shall not call him two. I shall not decompose him and label off his doings, one to the credit of his divinity, and another to the credit of his humanity. I shall receive him, in the simplicity of faith, as my one Lord and Saviour, nor any the less so that he is my brother.

I am well advised of the fact that very few persons have their minds so far moderated by philosophy or reason as to be able to set any boundaries to their questions. Those who can do it, those who can think it even unreasonable to investigate the interior of this divine mystery, when it is framed only for its external significance, will find the view here given simple, intelligent, and full of comfort. But those who cannot must, of course, take the penalty. If they must still investigate what was not given to be investigated; if they must speculate still about his divine-human, its modes, its interior possibility or impossibility, refusing the spiritual brotherhood of God till they can satisfy their questions about the rhetoric he uses to express it; in a word, if their most irrational reason must sow to the wind, in its questions, it can hope to reap nothing better than emptiness and whirlwind for its answers. Enough that I have shown them a better way.

Adhering thus immovably to the simple historic unity of Christ's per-

son it will be seen that, in the reference just now made to those remarkable divine exhibitions or presentations made to Abraham and Moses, it
was not my design to assert a general parallelism between them and the
person of Christ. They were cited only as illustrations of the particular
matter there in question. These were mere theophanies — apparitions, if I
may so speak, of God. In one view, they were not historical at all; for
they do not rise out of historical elements. Christ is no such theophany,
no such casual, unhistorical being as the Jehovah angel who visited Abraham. He is in and of the race, born of a woman, living in the line of
humanity, subject to human conditions, an integral part, in one view, of
the world's history; only bringing into it, and setting in organific union
with it, the Eternal Life.

The most plausible objection that can be made to the view I am giving
of Christ's person is, that he is too exclusively divine to make an effectual
approach to our human sympathies. But it is only plausible. Obviously
nothing is gained in this respect by holding three metaphysical persons in
the divine nature; for if still the real deity of the Son is maintained (which
I fear many do unwittingly disallow, when verbally asserting it), they
have precisely the same remoteness, the same too excessive divineness to
contend with. Nor do we gain anything as regards this matter of sympathy, by supposing a distinct human soul in the person of Christ, connecting itself with what may be called the humanities of Christ. Of what so
great consequence to us are the humanities of a mere human soul? The
very thing we want, is to find that God is moved by such humanities —
touched with a feeling of our infirmities. And what can bring God closer
to our human sympathies than to behold — if only we can believe so high
a mystery — God manifest in the flesh, and historically united with our
race? Therefore, if you find that Christ really comes down to your
sphere only when a half-tint is thrown over his deity, by some confusion
practiced on his person, I may reasonably ask, whether it were not better
to add more faith in yourself, and subtract less of the divine from him
— thus to make him, indeed and in truth, the express image of God?

I have thus endeavored to verify the incarnation. I am well aware that
one who discredits everything supernatural will require something farther. But I can only intimate, here, a settled conviction that if this great
question of supernaturalism were once put upon a right basis, such as a
competent investigator might lay for it, the incarnation, which now appears to be a prodigy too violent or stupendous for belief, would be seen

to emerge as the crowning result of a grand, systematic, orderly work, which God has been forwarding in the history and heart of the race ever since the world began — that the world, in fact, would be as chaotic and as wide of the true unity of reason without an incarnation, as without a sun. Happily, most of the later Unitarians maintain the credibility of that which is supernatural — indeed, they even hold that Christ is, in some very special and supernatural sense, a manifestation of God; that the divine is, in fact, so far supreme in him, as to prevent the development of a properly human, thus to produce a really sinless character — and this differs, in reality, from the view I have presented, only as a *sub*-carnation from an *in*-carnation. God is here, behind the man, or under the man, in such a way that the man does not act himself. We have a man without a man — a perfect human character which is not unfolded by the human. And thus we have as much of mystery and contradiction, with the disadvantage that we have no countenance from the Scripture, and a doctrine, withal, that has too little body and shape to have any important resulting use.

Having thus disposed of the difficulties growing out of the relations of the divine to the human, in the person of Christ received as an incarnation, I now turn

II. To those which are involved in the relations of his person to the Father and the Holy Spirit; and, of all, to the Absolute Being.

It is a fatal objection to the Unitarian theories of this subject, as viewed under the teaching of the Scriptures, that God is nowhere represented or named as the Father, till after the appearing of Christ. It is also an objection equally fatal to the Sabellian theory, which, as commonly understood, represents that God is the Father in virtue of his creation and government of the world. For if he is the Father simply as the one God, by what accident does it happen that he never gets the appellation till after the coming of Christ? Or, if he gets it as the Creator and Governor of the world, the world was created and governed long before that day — why, then, is he still unknown as the Father? True, he is called *a* Father, just as he is called a rock, or a tower, but never *the* Father, as in the baptismal formula, and by Christ ordinarily. There is, in fact, no real and proper development of the Father which is older than Christianity, and here the designation is developed in connection with the Son and Holy Spirit as a threefold denomination of God. And this threefold denomination, again (as I think must be evident), is itself incidental to, and produced by the central fact or mystery of the incarnation, as an impersonation of God developed in time.

Thus the Divine Word, or Logos, who is from eternity the form or in the form of God, after having first bodied him forth in the creation and the government of the world, now makes another outgoing from the Absolute into the human, to reside in the human as being of it; thus to communicate God to the world, and thus to ingenerate in the world Goodness and life as from him. To make his approach to man as close, to identify himself as perfectly as possible with man, he appears, or makes his advent through a human birth — Son of Man, and Son, also, of God. Regarding him now in this light as set out before the Absolute Being (who he representatively is), existing under the conditions of the finite and the relative, we see at once that, for our sakes if not for his own, he must have set over against him, in the finite, his appropriate relative term or impersonation. A solitary finite thing or person, that is, one that has no relative in the finite, is even absurd — much more if the design be that we shall ascend, through it, to the Absolute; for we can do this only under the great mental law of action and reaction, which requires relative terms and forces, between which it may be maintained. Besides, there may have been some subjective or internal necessity in Christ himself (for we know nothing of his interior structure and wants), requiring that, in order to the proper support of his attitude, he should have in conception some finite relative impersonation. For one or both these reasons, when he appears in the human state, bringing the divine into the human, there results at one and the same time a double impersonation, that of the Father and that of the Son — one because of the other, and both as correspondent or relative terms. As Christ himself appears in the finite, he calls out into the finite with him, if I may so speak, another representative of the Absolute, one that is conceived to reside in the heavens, as he himself is seen to walk upon the earth. This he does to comfort his attitude, or more probably, to make it intelligible; for if he were to say, "Look unto me, and behold your God," then his mere human person would be taken as a proof that he is only a flagrant and impious impostor; or else, being accepted as God by those who are more credulous, they would, in fact, receive a God by apotheosis, and under human boundaries. Therefore he calls out into thought, as residing in heaven, and possessing celestial exaltation, the Father, who is in fact the Absolute Being brought into a lively, conversable, definite (therefore finite) form of personal conception, and sets himself on terms of relationship with him at the other pole; so that, while he signifies or reveals the light and love of God, in and through the human or subject life, he is able to exalt and deify what he reveals, by referring his mission to one that is greater and higher in state than himself, viz., the Father in heaven. And, in this way, double advantage is taken both of proximity and distance, in the process of revealing or expressing God. He does not say, I came forth from the One, the Absolute; from him that dwells above time, silent, never moving, without parts, or emotions, but he gives us, above, the conception of an active, choosing, feeling Spirit, and says, "I came forth from the Father."

Now there is set open a relationship between heaven and earth. To keep us from subsiding into a regard of his simple person, as limited by human boundaries, and referring all his works to a being thus limited, he intimates a connection with one who has no such boundaries, saying, "My Father is greater than I." And then again, that what he expresses may be referred to that essentially divine nature represented in his person, he exalts his attitude, saying, "I and my Father are one." Now he says, "The Father loves me," and now, "He that hath seen me, hath seen the Father." And then, again, determined to keep himself and the whole process under a cloud of mystery, so that no one shall ever feel that he has gotten the measure either of the Father or of himself, and that all may be wading ever outward through mystery, in both, towards the infinite, he says, "No man knoweth the Son but the Father, neither knoweth any man the Father, save the Son and he to whomsoever the Son will reveal him." It is a revealing process, but yet enveloped in mystery — revealing even the more, by means of the mystery.

Meantime, it is by setting ourselves before this personal history of the Father in heaven, and the Son on earth, both as representatives standing out before the Absolute Being, watching the relative history they unfold in finite forms, their acting and interacting, and discovering what is expressed thereby — cleared of all the repugnant and contradictory matter that is attributable to the vehicle, in distinction from the truth — it is thus that we are to ascend, as by a resultant of the two forces, into a lively realization, and a free, spiritual embrace of God, as our Friend, Redeemer, Peace, and Portion. A mere philosophic unity, it will be seen at a glance, is cold and dead in comparison — altogether insufficient to support the Christian uses of the soul.

But, in order to the full and complete apprehension of God, a third personality, the Holy Spirit, needs to appear. By the Logos, in the creation, and then by the Logos in the incarnation, assisted or set off by the Father as a relative personality, God's character, feeling, and truth, are now expressed. He has even brought down the mercies of his heart to meet us on our human level. So far, the expression made is moral; but there is yet needed, to complete our sense of God, the Absolute, another kind of expression, which will require the introduction or appearance of yet another and distinct kind of impersonation. We not only want a conception of God in his character and feeling towards us, but we want also to conceive him as in *act* within us, working in us, under the conditions of time and progression, spiritual results of quickening, deliverance, and purification from evil. Now action of any kind is representable to us only under the conditions of movement in time and space, which, as we have seen, is not predicable of the Absolute Being abstractly contemplated. God in act, therefore, will be given us by another finite, relative impersonation.

Accordingly, the natural image, *spirit*, that is, breath, is taken up and clothed with a personal activity. The word signifies air in motion, and as air is invisible, it becomes the symbol or type of unseen power exerted — quite transcendently, however, as regards our comprehension; for there is really no motion whatever. The word *spirit* had been used before, as in reference to the agency of God, but only in a remoter and more tropical sense, as the word Father had been; the conception of a divine personality, or impersonation, called the Holy Spirit, was unknown. We may imagine otherwise in one or two cases, as when David prays, "Take not thy holy spirit from me," but I think without any sufficient reason. Now the Divine Power, in souls, is to be developed under the form of a personal Sanctifier, related in a personal way to the Father and the Son, as they to each other. He is conceived, sometimes, as sent by the Father; sometimes, as proceeding from the Father and the Son; sometimes as shed forth from the Son in his exaltation; always as a Divine Agency, procured by the Son and representing, in the form of an operation within us, that grace which he reveals as feeling and intention towards us.

And here again, just as the Logos is incarnated in the flesh, so the Spirit makes his advent under physical signs appropriate to his office, coming in a rushing mighty wind; tipping the heads of an assembly with lambent flames; evidencing his power in souls by opening the lips of men, and playing those utterances which are themselves expressions of the mind within; endowing men with gifts above their human capacity. Now the Absolute Being, of whom we could predicate no motion or proceeding, becomes a Vital Presence, residing ever with us, to work in us all that we need, and strengthen us to that which none but a divine power can support. What we should not dare to hope, and could not otherwise conceive — the Eternal Life, declared and manifested by Christ, liveth in us.

Thus we have three persons, or impersonations, all existing under finite conditions or conceptions. They are relatives, and in that view are not infinites; for relative infinites are impossible. And yet, taken representatively, they are each and all infinites; because they stand for and express the Infinite, Absolute Jehovah. They may each declare, "I am he"; for what they impart to us of him is their true reality. Between them all together, as relatives, we are elevated to proximity and virtual converse with him who is above our finite conditions — the Unapproachable and, as far as all measures of thought or conception are concerned, the Unrepresentable God.

The Father plans, presides, and purposes for us; the Son expresses his intended mercy, proves it, brings it down even to the level of a fellow feeling; the Spirit works within us the beauty he reveals, and the glory beheld in his Life. The Father sends the Son, the Son delivers the grace of the Father; the Father dispenses, and the Son procures the Spirit; the Spirit proceeds from the Father and Son, to fulfill the purpose of one, and the expressed feeling of the other; each and all together dramatize and bring forth into life about us that Infinite One, who to our mere thought were no better than Brahma sleeping on eternity and the stars. Now the sky, so to speak, is beginning to be full of Divine Activities, heaven is married to earth, and earth to heaven, and the Absolute Jehovah, whose nature we before could nowise comprehend, but dimly know, and yet more dimly feel, has by these outgoings waked up in us, all living images of his love and power and presence, and set the whole world in a glow.

There is, then, according to the view now presented, a real and proper trinity in the Scriptures; three persons, Father, Son, and Holy Ghost — one God. If it be objected that the word *trinity* is not here, neither is the term *free agency*. There certainly can be no harm in the use of such terms as mere terms of convenience, if we are careful not to derive our doctrine from them. That there is in the Scriptures a threefoldness which contains the real matter of a trinity, is to me undeniable, and if I am right in the views now presented, it must be of the highest consequence to religion that this trinity be admitted, cordially accepted, lived in as a power

— a vitalizing element offered to our souls, as the air to the life of our bodies. Every human soul that will adequately work itself in religion, needs this trinity as the instrument of its working; for without this, it is neither possible to preserve the warmth, nor to ascend into the true greatness of God.

Neither is it any so great wisdom, as many theologians appear to fancy, to object to the word *person;* for if anything is clear, it is that the Three of Scripture do appear under the grammatic forms which are appropriate to person — I, thou, he, we, and they; and, if it be so, I really do not perceive the very great license taken by our theology when they are called three persons. Besides, we practically need, for our own sake to set them out as three persons before us, acting relatively toward each other, in order to ascend into the liveliest, fullest realization of God. We only need to abstain from assigning to these divine persons an interior, metaphysical nature, which we are nowise able to investigate, or which we may positively know to contradict the real unity of God.

Do you then ask whether I mean simply to assert a modal trinity, or three modal persons? — I must answer obscurely, just as I answered in regard to the humanity of Christ. If I say that they are modal *only*, as the word is commonly used, I may deny more than I am justified in denying, or am required to deny, by the ground I have taken. I will only say that the trinity, or the three persons, are given to me for the sake of their external expression, not for the internal investigation of their contents. If I use them rationally or wisely, then, I shall use them according to their object. I must not intrude upon their interior nature, either by assertion or denial. They must have their reality to me in what they express when taken as the wording forth of God. Perhaps I shall come nearest to the simple, positive idea of the trinity here maintained, if I call it an INSTRUMENTAL TRINITY, and the persons INSTRUMENTAL PERSONS. There may be more in them than this, which let others declare when they find it. Enough, meantime, for me, that there is this — that in and through these living persons, or impersonations, I find the Infinite One brought down even to my own level of humanity, without any loss of his greatness, or reduction of his majesty. And if they help me to this, I see not anything more of so great consequence for them to give me, even if I could read their most interior nature, and resolve all problems concerning them. I perceive, too, that God may as well offer himself to me in these persons as through trees, or storms, or stars — that they involve as little contrariety, as few limitations, and yield as much more of warmth as they have more of life. I discover, also, that this threeness helps me the more, and lifts me the higher, because it baffles me. If I think it more philosophical and simple to conceive God only as one person, that person will really be a finite conception, unwittingly though very absurdly taken as infinite. And then, as the God shrinks, the mind freezes. The simplicity it so much admired, after all, brings disappointment. The ease of this philosophic unity is itself a great fault; for it is as if we had God's measure, and saw his boundaries. He is too clear to be infinite; and, what is even worse, too clear to have his warmth in the soul. We do not rise to the Infinite by simple thought or direct contemplation, we are borne up to that height only by a resultant motion, between relative and partially repugnant forces, such as we find in the three persons of Scripture. Through a certain feeling of multiplicity and vagueness, we are able to realize God dynamically, as we could through no definite conception of him. Represented as three, God is yet one — the more magnificently one, because he is three. The soul has her sublimation, because she is held in a maze, and God is warm, because he is a mystery. Meanwhile, if our feeling is at any time confused by these persons or impersonations, we are to have it for a fixed, first truth, that God is, in the most perfect and rigid sense, one being — a pure intelligence, undivided, indivisible, and infinite; and that whatever may be true of the Father, Son and Holy Ghost, it certainly is not true that they are three distinct consciousnesses, wills, and understandings. Or, speaking in a way more positive, they are instrumentally three — i.e., three simply as related to our finite apprehension, and the communication of God's incommunicable nature.

But some one, I suppose, will require of me to answer whether the three persons are eternal, or only occasional and to be discontinued. Undoubtedly the distinction of the Word, or the power of self-representation in God thus denominated, is eternal. And in this we have a permanent ground of possibility for the threefold impersonation called trinity. Accordingly, if God has been eternally revealed, or revealing himself to created minds, it is likely always to have been and always to be as the Father, Son, and Holy Ghost. Consequently, it may always be in this manner that we shall get our impressions of God, and have our communion with him. As an accommodation to all finite minds in the universe, it may be the purpose of Jehovah to be known by this divine formula forever. That which most discourages such a belief is the declaration of Paul — "When all things shall be subdued unto him, then shall the Son also himself be subject unto him that did put all things under him, that God may be all and in all." I will not go into a discussion of these very remarkable words; for I do not care to open God's secrets before the time. Let the future bring the future, and I know it will not be amiss when it comes. Enough for me, now, that by these dear names, my God proves his warmth, and pours his fullness into my heart — that without them, torpor settles on my religious nature, and the boasted clearness of a God made level to reason, is the clearness of a wintry day.

I suppose the position I have taken would be more acceptable to some, were I to throw in the intimation given by Neander, when ascribing a similar view to the apostles. Thus he says that the trinity "has an essentially practical and historical significance and foundation; it is the doctrine of God revealed in the humanity, which teaches men to recognize in God, not only the original source of existence, but of salvation and sanctification. From this trinity of revelation, as far as the divine causality images itself in the same, the reflective mind, according to the analogy of its own being, pursuing this track, seeks to elevate itself to the idea of an original triad in God, availing itself of the intimations which are contained in John's doctrine of the Logos and the cognate elements of the Pauline theology." If now it be inquired whether, beginning with a doctrine of trinity, produced by the process of revelation, and adequately accounted for as necessary to that process, I would then turn to hunt for some "analogy" in myself, and try to climb up thus, through myself, into a discovery of an original triad in God — convincing myself, also, that John and Paul give "intimations" of such a triad, I frankly answer, no. The expression of such a hope might comfort some who would otherwise be disturbed, but it will only mislead a much greater number, who had better keep their discretion. If God has given us an instrumental triad, which is good for its purposes of revelation, there can be no greater fraud upon it than to set ourselves to the discovery of an original triad back of it, that has no instrumental character, and has nothing to do with revelation. It is just the way to confuse and lead us off from every proper use and construction of the trinity God has given us. In just this way it is, too, that the trinity has been made a source of so great controversy and so little profit, in all past ages — it has been turned into a metaphysical problem, and its instrumental character, as the representative development of God, has of necessity been hidden from the view. Besides, what wisdom are we likely to arrive at, better than the shadowy vagaries others, in past ages, have conjured up, by hunting our human spirit through, to find some Platonic triad there, which shall solve the trinity of persons in God? Let us rather baptize our over-curious spirit into the name of the Father, and of the Son and of the Holy Ghost, and teach it quietly to rest in what of God's infinite nature it may there receive. We talk of simplicity, often, when upon this matter of trinity — as we rightly may. O that we had simplicity enough to let God be God, and the revelation he gives us, a revelation! — neither trying to make him a finite person after our own human model, nor ourselves three that we may bring our humanity up to solve the mysteries of his Absolute, Infinite substance! There is no so true simplicity as that which takes the practical at its face, uses instruments as instruments, however complex and mysterious (for what is more so than a man's own body), and refuses to be cheated of the uses of life by an over-curious questioning of that which God has given for its uses.

This view of Christ and the trinity differs, I am aware, in some respects from that which is commonly held; but I hope the difference will not disturb you. I have known no other since I began to be a preacher of Christ, and my experience teaches me to want no other. If it has delivered me from agonies of mental darkness and confusion concerning God, which at one time seemed insupportable, it cannot be wrong to hope that God will make the truth a deliverance equally comfortable and joyful to some of you.

Observe, too, in closing, what an outlay God has made to communicate or manifest himself to our race. In his own Absolute nature, God is a being so vast that, when I drew out the conception of him as existing in himself, I presume it was somewhat painful to you, so remote was it from all your own personal modes of being and life, as a finite creature. And yet it will be difficult for anyone to dispute the necessity of such a conception of God, when taken as Absolute, and as viewed by abstract thought or contemplation. But what have we seen? This Transcendent Being struggling out, so to speak, into the measures of human knowledge, revealing himself through the petty modes and molds of our finite nature! He fills the whole universe with actions and reactions, such as will bring us into lively acquaintance with him. He comes into the human itself, and melts into the history of man through agonies, sorrows, and tears. He kindles heaven and earth into a glow, by the relative activities of Father, Son, and Holy Ghost. And for what? Simply to communicate himself, to express his nature and his feeling. What, then, does our everlasting God and Father plan for, but to bestow himself upon us? And it is in this view, that the Blessed Three come to me with a sound so dear, and a burden of love so rich. I see therein how earnestly my God desires to be known and pos-

sessed by me — by you as truly, by all, by every human creature. What
breathing man is there of you, around whom the Triune is not circling here
as a day of light and love? The Incommunicable is communicated,
brought down even to be fellow to you, that you may know him and love
him! He waits to be received, to clear away your darkness, to purge you
from your sin, and be in you the fullness of him that filleth all in all.

2. The Christian Trinity [1]

As indicated in the preceding editorial comment, Bushnell did not, in the
Concio of 1848, undertake to pass judgment on the question of whether
the trinity was immanently grounded in God's nature. He did not deny it
as a possibility, but neither did he affirm it as a fact. In this respect, as he
observed, his doctrine of the trinity differed from that of the Sabellians,
the Unitarians, and the orthodox. They all had endeavored to pry into the
interior nature of God and say what it was like, whereas he had abstained
from giving an opinion one way or the other. "Let the future bring the
future," he declared. "Enough for me, now, that by these dear names
[Father, Son, Holy Ghost], my God proves His warmth, and pours His
fullness into my heart." [2]

However, by the time he published *Christ in Theology* (1851) he was
becoming dissatisfied with his theory of the trinity as set forth in 1848. It
was good as far as it went, but it was incomplete on its metaphysical side.
Since that time he had carefully restudied the history of trinitarian doctrine, and had become an admirer of the Nicene Creed. "I feel obliged to
confess," he wrote, "that I had not sufficiently conceived its import, or
the title it has to respect as a Christian document." [3] His New England
brethren, he said, had unwisely cut themselves off from the Nicene tradition. Thus their doctrine of the trinity, far from being true to classical
orthodoxy, was singularly provincial, "a kind of theological *patois*, quite
peculiar to ourselves." [4] In particular he condemned them for having
repudiated the idea of "eternal generation and procession" as held by the
Nicene fathers; for in doing so, he observed, they ceased to conceive a

1. "The Christian Trinity a Practical Truth," *New Englander*, XII (1854), 485–502,
506–9.
2. *God in Christ* (Hartford, 1849), 177–78.
3. *Christ in Theology* (Hartford, 1851), 177.   4. *Ibid.*, 170.

trinity "grounded in God as act" and "began to assert a trinity of persons in the divine essence itself, which is plain tritheism." [5] He contended that although his own theory did not coincide precisely with that of the Nicene Council, it came closer to doing so than did that of New England Calvinism. "I do then peremptorily," said Bushnell "refuse to justify myself, as regards this matter of trinity, before any New England standard." [6]

Bushnell was now seeking to give an ontological dimension to his theory of the trinity. This is evident in *Christ in Theology*.[7] Comparing his own method with that of the Nicene Council, he observed that whereas the Council began on the ontological plane — "within the active life of God" — he began with the expressional activity of God in its impact upon the world. Thus his method "discovers, first, the probable need of trinity, as an instrumental verity; allowing us then to ascend, by the a posteriori method, to a conviction of *some* necessary ground for this in the divine nature back of it; and, again, more timidly and with larger reservations of modesty, to the conviction that God, eternally self-revealing in his nature, is, in that sense, eternally and immanently three." [8]

The essay of 1854, here reproduced, marks a significant advance toward classical trinitarianism, for therein the author discovers "something more interior, as a ground [for the trinity] in the eternity of God, antecedent to the revelation in time." Still further evidence of Bushnell's determination to give his theory of the trinity an ontological grounding is revealed in a sermon entitled "Our Relations to Christ in the Future Life," written near the end of his life and first published in 1872.[9] He read this discourse before Hartford Central Association, having introduced it with the remark, "Brethren, I am going to read you what is probably the last sermon I shall write." [10] At the outset he observed that those who hold the trinity "more lightly, or in a more nearly Sabellian way" commonly assume the discontinuance of it "when the uses of redemption no longer require it." Those of this opinion assume that the Son, having finally subjugated evil, will himself be ultimately subjected to God, "that God may be all in all" (1 Cor. 15:28). "God is thus reduced back to his complete normal unity. Trinity is gone, and the absolute One, the strictly Unitarian God, has the whole field to himself." [11] "There is a fatal want of depth in this conception," Bushnell protested.[12] The need

5. *Ibid.*, 172. 6. *Ibid.*, 175. 7. *Ibid.*, 167–77. 8. *Ibid.*, 176–77.
9. *Sermons on Living Subjects*, centenary ed. (New York, 1910), 442–68.
10. Mary B. Cheney, *Life and Letters of Horace Bushnell* (New York, 1880), 513.
11. *Sermons on Living Subjects*, 443. 12. *Ibid.*, 444.

for the trinity, he insisted, does not cease with the subjugation of sin and evil; it is eternally needed to maintain the full dimensions of God's attributes and to meet the requirements of finite minds. Accordingly "we shall there know God unalterably and forever as trinity — Father, Son, and Holy Ghost." [13]

Our conclusion, then, is this: Bushnell developed his doctrine of the trinity in two stages. The first is reflected in the *Concio* of 1848. The second began to emerge in *Christ in Theology*, appeared significantly in "The Christian Trinity," and culminated in "Our Relations to Christ in the Future Life." The second stage ended in a doctrine of the trinity which grounded the persons in the eternally generative action of God. Thus those who have characterized Bushnell as a Sabellian or semi-Sabellian [14] have misinterpreted his doctrine of the trinity. He was essentially a classical trinitarian.[15]

❖   ❖   ❖   ❖

It is most remarkable that our Lord Jesus Christ, at just the moment when we look to find him offering what is most of all practical and distinctive in his gospel, most necessary in that view to its power in the earth, advances just the Christian trinity and nothing else. His work is now done, and the hour of his final ascension is come. His disciples are gathered round him to receive their commission of trust and the farewell address, so to speak, of their great Leader. Now he will seize on the first truths of the kingdom and put them forward. No matter of mere theory or of idle curiosity will obtrude. He will give them counsel for the guidance of their future course — cautions, encouragements, suggestions of heavenly wisdom. He will bring out the great truth of salvation, the change to be wrought in mankind, the manner and means of the change — the way to preach and what to preach, and all that is necessary to the established polity and wise conduct of the future church about to be

13. *Sermons on Living Subjects*, 450.

14. Theodore T. Munger, *Horace Bushnell: Preacher and Theologian* (Boston, 1899), 123, 126, 155–56; Williston Walker, "Dr. Bushnell as a Religious Leader," *Bushnell Centenary. Minutes of the General Association of Connecticut at the One Hundred and Ninety-Third Annual Meeting Held in Hartford, June 17, 18, 1902* (Hartford, 1902), 27; S. D. F. Salmond, "The Theology of Horace Bushnell," *London Quarterly Review*, XCV (January–April 1901), 151; Frank H. Foster, *The Modern Movement in American Theology* (New York, 1939), 65; Claude Welch, *In His Name* (New York, 1952), 8, 26.

15. For a similar conclusion, see Fred Kirschenmann, "Horace Bushnell: Orthodox or Sabellian?" *Church History*, XXXIII (1964), 49–59.

gathered in all parts of the world by their ministry. What then does he say? — "Go ye therefore and teach all nations, baptizing them in the name of the Father, and of the Son, and of the Holy Ghost." This, and this alone, is the commission. What then does it mean, that Christ himself, the simplest and most practical and, in the higher sense, most rational of all teachers, in a parting charge to his disciples, gives them not any truth or vestige of truth over and above this one difficult, ever to be contested formula of trinity? At first view the fact appears to have no agreement either with the time or with the general manner of the teacher; but as we pause upon it and ponder it a little more deeply, we begin to suspect that this formula of trinity is given simply because it is the gospel in its most condensed term of statement, and is put deliberately forward in this manner in the foreground of the commission, as a general denomination for all that is practical in the Christian truth. And that such was the real understanding of Christ sufficiently appears in the fact, that the commission given is itself a working commission. They are to go "teaching and baptizing all nations," and the converts made are to be baptized into the name of the Sacred Three, as being the name of that power by which alone they are renewed, and are to have their spiritual cleansing accomplished. In some deeper sense of it open to him, the trinity, as we are thus left to understand, is the underlying truth, and contains the whole working matter of his gospel.

No sentiment or opinion could be farther off from the current impressions of our time. That the Christian trinity is in any sense a practical truth appears in our day to be very generally unsuspected.

Thus among the outsiders, the light-minded critics and worldly cavilers of profane literature, the trinity is taken, *ex concessis*, for a standing example of the utterly barren futilities preached and contended for as articles of religion.

The class of Unitarian believers handle the subject more seriously, and arrive at the conclusion, which they assert with peremptory confidence, that it is a stupendous theologic fiction, a plain absurdity in itself and in its effects, one of the worst practical hindrances to the power of the gospel; for how can it be less when it annihilates the simplicity of God, confuses the mind of the worshiper, and even makes the faith of God an impossible subject to the unbeliever?

Meantime how many of the formally professed believers of the doctrine are free to acknowledge that they see no practical value in it, and will even blame the preacher who maintains it, for spending his time and breath in a matter so far out of the way of the practical life, a merely curious article or riddle of the faith. And how many others, even of the more serious class of believers, would say, if they were to speak out what is in their feeling, that they take the trinity as a considerable drawback on the idea of God. They would recoil indeed from the thought, as being even a blamable irreverence, of imagining any improvement of God; but if they could think of him as a simple unit of personality, in the manner of the Unitarians, he would consciously be just so much more to their mind, and their practical relations towards him would be proportionally cleared and comforted.

An issue is thus made up, it will be seen, between the ascending Redeemer on one side, and a very general sentiment or opinion of the Christian world on the other, regarding the practical import of the Christian trinity. On the side last named, it is very commonly asserted that it has no practical value, and is only a kind of scholastic futility which, if we do not reject, we receive as a faith wholly inoperative and useless. On the side of the Son of God himself it is assumed to be, in fact, a condensed expression for all that is operative and powerful in the Christian faith. Protected by so great a name, it requires no courage in us to venture some considerations, from our human point of view, that may go to illustrate the intense practical significance of this great truth. For what Christ has given us from his higher point of authority evidently needs, in this as in other cases, to be naturalized in our human convictions by a discovery of the want on our own side, which his truth is given to supply. Indeed it has often seemed to us that nothing is ever needed, as regards the evidence of this much litigated truth, but to know it in its practical uses, and perceive the sublime facility with which it limbers the play of our thought to all that is most transcendent in divine nature and the new economy of the gospel of Christ.

In asserting the immense practical value thus of the Christian trinity we do not mean, it is hardly necessary to say, that the trinity is practical in the sense of presenting something to be done or practiced. Neither is it practical in the sense of showing in what manner something else is to be done. It is practical only as an instrument of thought, action, self-application to all the great matters of the faith. What is more practical than human language? And as by the use of language our understandings are adjusted, our feelings expressed, our information received, our mind itself developed, so by the Christian trinity it is that our sense of God is opened; what he has done for us and will do, put in terms of use; all the relations of what he does in one part of his kingdom to what he has instituted and done in another — mysteries of law and grace, letter and spirit — played into our practical apprehension, so that by mere names and signals our faith is inducted into uses before we can discover reasons and settle definitions. The trinity, in short, is so related to the gospel and our approach to God in the faith of the gospel, that the grace of it, without such a concomitant, will be fatally baffled in its access and rendered practically inefficient.

But this, again, we could not say of all the possible or existing forms of trinity; for it is not to be denied that conceptions of this great truth are held by many which are so far abhorrent from its proper simplicity, and so badly distorted by the perverse ingenuity of human speculation, as to oppose great hindrances to the practical repose of faith, and even to counteract, in a great degree, the real benefit of the doctrine. We undertake to show the practical value only of the Christian trinity, or trinity of the Christian Scriptures.

And the Scriptures offer no theoretic or scientific statement of the doctrine whatever, give us nothing pertaining to the subject in terms of logical definition. They assume the strict unity and simplicity of God, that he is one substance or entity, only one; which one they also assume, will, at least, be most effectively thought as three, a threefold grammatic personality, or three persons, Father, Son, and Holy Ghost. These persons are not even called persons, but are only set in the grammar of uses silently as such. Of course it is nowhere said or implied that they are three persons in the same sense that John, James, and Peter, are three; and the mere laws of grammar, in which they stand, support no such inference, any more than the grammar of sex supports a like inference respecting the real gender of the sun and moon. The three are persons, evidently, only in some sense that recognizes a radical unity of substance (which is not true of any three men), some tropical, or instrumental sense, that needs not any way to be, and cannot be, exactly defined. The plurality therefore, whatever it be, does not divide, but only more sufficiently communicates, the One.

Our argument does not require that we should go into any discussion regarding either the evidence, or the interior significance of the trinity. It fixes simply on the Scripture fact, a phenomenon occurrent in the Scripture, showing its practical use and necessity. And for the present we shall speak *as if* it were only a matter of form or language, accommodated in

that manner to our finite wants and uses, but before we close, shall ascend
to a point more interior, and to higher apprehensions of the subject, viz.:
to the discovery of something more interior, as a ground in the eternity
of God, antecedent to the revelation in time. Our present concern is to
show that assuming the oneness and infinity of God, trinity is needed as a
way of conceiving God, and working our piety towards him, in the matters of grace and redemption. So far, trinity may be regarded as language
for God, or as an expedient in the manner of the Sabellians. The arguments for use or practical necessity will be greatly simplified by including, in the question, nothing more than this: or at least, by including
nothing more, till we have reached a point where the transition to a
deeper view of the subject can be made with advantage.

As a grand preliminary in this mode of argument, we need to observe
that in conceiving God, we are obliged to represent him, as we do all spiritual realities, by images and figures, taken from things we know. And
then there is, of course, a sense in which the representation is true and a
sense in which it is not true, and exactly where the line is to be drawn, we
often cannot tell more exactly than simply to say that we speak in a figure. Thus we describe the heavenly state as a paradise, a garden, watered
by a river, with trees of healing on its banks; or we conceive it as a city
whose height, length, and breadth are equal, and whose walls are built of
precious stones; and then we cannot tell more exactly where truth ends
and error begins, than simply to say that the representation holds figuratively, and not literally.

Or we may take a different illustration, that will assist our subject in
other respects. We say, and most of us have no thought of difficulty in
affirming it, that God is a person, or a personal being. But a little reflection will show us, that the word *person*, thus applied, is only a figure derived from our finite human personality, and is in fact a strictly finite
word. After all, God is not a person save in a figure, as we shall see at a
glance if we ask what constitutes our idea of a person. This we shall readily answer out of our own consciousness, by saying that a person is a conscious being, an agent or intelligent self-active force — exactly what our
consciousness conceives to be included in itself. But the moment we begin
to recite the inventory of our consciousness, we find that almost every
article in it is in such a type of measure and mode that we cannot refer it
to God at all. Thus a person or agent, as we conceive the term, drawing
on our own consciousness, wills; putting forth successively new determinations of will, without which new determinations, personality is null,

and no agency at all. But God never does that: his determinations are all passed even from eternity. So a person thinks, or has successions of thought coming in, as it were, in file, one after another. God never thinks in any such sense. As all his acts are done, so all his thoughts are present contemporaneously from eternity. A person or intelligent agent reasons, drawing one proposition out of others — in this sense God never reasons. A person remembers — God never remembers; for nothing past is ever out of mind. A person hopes and conjectures — God does neither; for the future is as truly present to him, as the past. A person has e-motions, simple movings out of feeling into the foreground of the hour. God has no such temporary movings, in which one feeling jets up for the hour into eminence, and takes the foreground of his life; all movings or states of affection are in him at once, and appropriate exactly to their objects. And so we find that a very great part, certainly, of what we were affirming, in the assertion that God is a person, is in some other view not true. Literally, God is not a person; for the very word is finite in all its measures and implications, because it is derived from ourselves. Figuratively, he is a person; and beyond this, nothing can be said which is more definite, save that he is in some sense unconceived, a real agent who holds himself related personally to us, meeting us in terms of mutuality, such that we can have the sense of society with him, and the confidence of his society with us, *as if* he were in truth a literal person like ourselves. There is a value in this last illustration, beyond the mere showing under what conditions of figure we are obliged to speak of the divine nature, and what are the conditions of truth in our representation. We do not remember ever to have seen the fact noticed, but we do exactly the same thing, as regards truth or intelligent comprehension, when we say that God is a person, that we do when we say that he is three persons, and there is really no difficulty in one case that does not exist in the other. As we can say that God is a person without any real denial of his infinity, so we can say that he is three persons without any breach of his unity. Indeed, we shall hereafter see that he is set forth, and needs to be, as three persons, for the very purpose, in part, of mending a difficulty created by asserting that he is one person; that is, to save the impression of his infinity. The word *person* is, in either case, a figure, and as truly in one as in the other. And if the question be raised, what correspondent reality there is in the divine nature to meet and justify the figure, there can plainly be no literal correspondence between the infinite substance of God and any merely finite term, whether one or three; or, if we suppose a correspondence undefinable and tropical, it may as well answer to three persons as to one.

Neither is there any difficulty in removing the logical objections so pertinaciously urged against the trinity, on the ground that three distinct personal pronouns are applied to God, requiring us to regard him as a council or plurality of beings; after which it is impossible that he should be one being. Grammatic laws and relations may as well pass into figure as mere names of things. Thus, to convey a certain undefined or indefinable impression, we may apply the feminine pronoun *she* to a ship, using a grammatic term of gender for a descriptive and representative purpose. And then, to represent or connect another impression, we may give the ship a masculine name, such as Hercules or Agamemnon. Whereupon the man of logic, scandalized by so great absurdity, may begin to argue that since the ship is feminine as to gender, it cannot be masculine; or if it is masculine then it cannot be feminine. But it will be sufficient, for any one but him, to answer that we use these terms of gender only to represent some indefinable partially correspondent reality which we can signify by this short method better than by any other. So if it be urged that person means person, and number means number, by the inevitable laws of grammar, and that when we have called God three persons, it must be absurd to speak any longer of his unity, it is sufficient to answer, that there may be a representative personality and number, as well as a representative or tropical gender, and that any mere logical practice on the words will, in both cases, be equally futile and puerile. Indeed, the pronoun *he* applied to each one of the persons of the trinity, is itself a word of gender, as truly as of number and person, and it would not be as great an offense to the majority of mankind to say that God is impersonal, as to apply to him the feminine pronoun. Why then should it create so great difficulty that God is represented as a trinity of persons? Why not go into a logical practice on the gender of the pronoun, as well on the number and the grammatic personality? There may, it is true, be a much closer degree of correspondence in these latter cases, with something interior in God — of that we shall speak hereafter — but, for aught that appears, the logical process covers precisely the same *kind* of falsity in one case as in the other.

But these are matters inductive and preliminary. We come now to the question itself, What is the practical import of the trinity? Wherein consists its value? It is needed, we answer, to serve two main purposes:

1. To save the dimensions or the practical infinity of God, consistently

with his personality. God is never fully presented to the mind, or adequately conceived, except when he is conceived under these two conditions together; viz., as a being really infinite, and also as existing in terms of society and personal mutuality with us. Accordingly we shall find, on the right and left of the Christian trinity, two distinct views which are both fatally defective and mutually opposite to each other.

First, the view of the pantheists, who are instigated by a desire to establish, or adequately conceive, the infinity of God. Struggling after this they spread themselves over all space and time and substance, and looking at *the All*, as an eternal going on of spiritual development under laws of eternal necessity, they call it God. Their God is the largest thought they can raise — largest, that is, in extent and containing boundary, but he is no person. Personality has been lost in the struggle after magnitude, or rather it has been actually dismissed as untenable; because the word, logically treated and literally taken, presents God under conditions of time and date, waking up to create worlds, exercised by thoughts, remembrances, reasonings, attentions, and affections personal — all which is contrary to the rational infinity of God. The doctrine of God's personality is therefore deliberately cast away as being a logical and necessary limit on his perfection; for it is not perceived that though the word *person* is finite, it may yet have an application figurative, that is legitimate, and leaves all finite implications behind, availing only to set the infinite in terms of society with us. The result is that God, in this rejection of his personality, becomes a vast platitude; or, if not this, a dreary, all-containing abyss; a being, unconscious, a fate, a stupendous ɪᴛ, without meaning or value to our religious nature; a theme of barren rhapsody and vaporing declamation, not a friend, not a redeemer, not an object of personal affinity, love or truth.

Over against these pantheistic aberrations we have the doctrine of Unitarianism, which represents God, in opposition to pantheism, as a being personal, and because of the supposed absurdities, or rational impossibilities of trinity, one person. Clearing thus at once the dearth of pantheism and the contradictions of trinity, it presents a universal Father, one person; who, being a strict undivisible unity, is therefore no offense or stumbling block to reason.

The result is that the personality or relational state of God is saved in the completest manner; God is a person, a simple unit of reason, a Father eternal, creating and ruling the worlds and doing all things for the benefit of his children. But the difficulty now is that the dimensions are lost, the infinite magnitude is practically taken away. And precisely here, as was just now intimated, is one of the grand practical uses of trinity. The Unitarians supposed that when they had carried out their doctrine and shown that God is a simple unit of fatherhood, they had gained a great point, cleared the confusion, reduced the absurdity, and presented to the world a being so lovely in his character and so rational in his evidence that all intelligent worshipers must rejoice, and the world itself must shortly turn itself to him in love. But alas! there was a fatal difficulty which they did not suspect, and which time only could reveal; viz., that in going on to assert the one God, always under the same figure of personality, till that figure became a well-nigh literal affirmation, the dimensions of God would be reduced to the measures of the human figure, and their one God, their Great Father, would be a name without magnitude, or any genuine power of impression. We do not of course mean, when we thus speak, to imply that the Unitarian will become any the less a believer theoretically in the infinity of God; or that he will not save himself from the letting-down process, in a degree, by the great tokens of power and majesty he will trace in the worlds of matter, and the adjectives he will set about the name of God, such as eternal, infinite, all-present, all-seeing, all-powerful, the Creator, Governor, Judge of the worlds. All this he will do, and yet for some reason, he may not guess what the reason is, he will be conscious of a certain decay of impression, a diminution of tonic force in the idea of God, such as once it had, before he broke loose from the absurdities of trinity; or above all such as he discovers in the writings and history of his fathers, before they broke loose, and led their children out, as they supposed, in the paths of intelligence and reason. An impression will finally begin to crowd upon him that there is, after all, something in the trinitarian feeling not in his; that their God is more a God, higher in majesty, and heavier on the soul's feeling. And the sense of this fact will by and by appear in other and more decisive indications; as when, for example, poets, essayists, and nominally Christian teachers brought up in his doctrine, begin to be heard speaking in a heathenish and mock-classic way of "the gods." They will do it because their God, their one person or Father, has somehow lost magnitude in their impressions, and because there seems to be really more rhetorical power in the plural "gods" than there is in their boasted unity of reason-God.

It could not be otherwise. How is it possible to keep up the figure of a one personality, and be always seeing God under that figure, without finally dragging him down by the force of its finite associations, and subjecting him practically to its measures? Suppose that by reason of some analogy discovered in the rock, God were always called, as he is a few times in the Scriptures, the Rock, and conceived under no other name, does any one doubt that such an image would, by its natural associations, finally obdurate or harden, and in that manner radically vitiate, the conception of God's character? He was familiarly known to the ancient race as the "Jehovah-angel"; *i.e.*, a visitor appearing in the human form to represent and speak for God. Suppose then he had always been called "the Angel," never conceived in any other way, how plain is it that he would be gradually let down to the grade of an apparition coming and going and acting in space! What then must follow when he is spoken of and worshiped only in the type of a person, which is nothing but a metaphysically finite conception? One good point is gained, viz., the mutuality, the reciprocal relationship of God; but with that everything necessary to the grandeur, the transcendent wonder, the immeasurable vastness of God, is lost or left behind.

Setting now these two failures against one another, the failure of pantheism and the failure of Unitarianism, we perceive exactly what is the problem answered by the Christian trinity. By asserting three persons instead of one, and also instead of none, it secures at once the practical infinity of God and the practical personality of God. By these cross relations of a threefold grammatic personality, the mind is thrown into a maze of sublimity, and made to feel at once the vastness, and with that the close society, also, of God. He is not less personal than he would be under the one personality of Unitarianism, and is kept meantime, by the threefold personality, from any possible diminution under the literal measures of the figure; for God cannot become either one person or three, in any literal sense, when steadfastly held as both.

In this respect the trinity, Father, Son, and Holy Ghost, practically accepted and freely used, with never a question about the speculative nature of the mystery, with never a doubt of God's rigid and perfect unity, will be found to answer exactly the great problem of the practical life of religion; viz., how to keep alive the profoundest, most adequate sense of God's infinity, and at the same time the most vivid and intensest sense of his social and mutual relationship as a person. And this, if I am right, is more to say than could be said of any other known or possible denomination for God. Regarded simply as a literary exploit, if that were all, it is at once the profoundest practical expedient ever adopted, and the highest wonder ever accomplished in human language.

Many persons talk and reason of this matter, as if it were the easiest, most extempore thing in the world to make a valid and true communication of God, not considering either the hard limitations of language or the more stringent limitations of a finite creature's thought. In this radical and somewhat feeble assumption we have the beginning of the Unitarian attempt — as if it were nothing, could involve no mystery, no paradox to give expression to the infinite God! Who that can take Job's thought of his incomprehensible, inconceivable majesty — Canst thou by searching find out God? Canst thou find out the Almighty to perfection? It is high as heaven, what canst thou do? Deeper than hell, what canst thou know? The measure thereof is longer than the earth and broader than the sea — who, we ask, that can take up such a thought of God, will have it for a perfectly easy and simple matter to present such a being to the world? Far more equal and fit to the true import of the problem were the answers of that wise heathen who, when it was required of him to give the definition of God, demanded a certain time for thought, and when the time expired double the time, and then again the double of that, till at last, by so many delays, he had given the most expressive and truest answer possible; declaring in that manner the sense he had of God's inscrutable, inconceivable mystery. Who that has a mind really opened to the difficulties of the subject will not see beforehand that when such a being communicates himself to the world, nothing will serve his object but some wondrous compilation of apparently conflicting and paradoxical images — such exactly as we have in the Christian trinity? The very mystery, and all the conflicting terminology which the Unitarians undertook to clear and logically reduce, had even a presumption in its favor. And the new explication they attempted of these absurdities of Scripture, their "Truth made Simple," it was even as clear beforehand as it could be afterwards, would be only a substitution of the little for the great, the feeble for the sublime, a merely childish half-truth for the grand, well-rounded majesty of the triune formula. Nothing is easier than the method of a "Norton's Reasons," [1] and when implicitly followed, nothing will more certainly show the problem resolved, how it may be possible, with only a moderate force, drudged in the ploddings of unilluminated scholarship, to empty a gospel most effectually of all that is necessary to its life. It is no difficult task to make God intelligible, and set him clear of all terms that stagger

1. [ED.] Andrews Norton, *A Statement of Reasons For Not Believing the Doctrines of Trinitarians Respecting the Nature of God, and the Person of Christ, Occasioned by Professor Stuart's Letters to Mr. Channing* (Boston, 1819).

comprehension; and then, when it is done, it is not less easy to find that he is just as much diminished as he is more completely leveled to the logical understanding. Withdrawn from the imagination and reduced to the measures of logical practice, he will be, in fact, to the true Almighty Infinite God what the wax-doll Napoleon is to the mysterious living paradox of genius before whose name and coming the nations shook with dread.

Regarding the grammatic plurality, or three persons, as a necessary means, in this manner, of preserving at once the personality and practical infinity of God, we ought perhaps to notice what is really a striking confirmation of our suggestion, that the Old Testament word commonly translated God (*Elohim*) is a plural word. Over this word, particularly as it occurs in the first chapter of Genesis, in connection with the phrase, "Let us make man in our image," there has been a good deal of frivolous and impertinent debate — frivolous and impertinent of necessity because the question raised, whether these pluralities are not affirmations of trinity, is a fictitious and wholly unscholarly question. The true question is different, viz.: what is the reason — for some reason there certainly was — why this plural name occurs and becomes accepted as the name of God? Such a question opens up, it will be seen, a previous history in the word, conducting us back upon the great natural fact that plurality is a form of instrumentation for God, or the divine nature, quite as readily received, and for some purposes more adequate than a simple grammatic unity. In this respect, the plural name of the Old Testament answered some of the important conditions of the trinity of the New. The pluralities introduced by means of the Jehovah Angel, the Memra or word of the Lord, and by such uses or conceptions of the Holy Spirit as we find in the fifty-first Psalm, show also in what manner the advantages of the New Testament trinity are made up in the Old by another process — if indeed it is another, which many will deny. We pass now,

II. To another view of the Christian trinity, in which it is seen to have a practical relation to our character and our state as sinners. Here it is the instrument and co-efficient of a supernatural grace or redemptive economy. Not, as we sometimes hear, that an infinite atonement is wanted, which none but an infinite and divine person could execute — that is only a very crude and distant approximation to the truth. The need we are here to discover is broader and more comprehensive, resting in the fact that God's universal economy is, in its very conception, twofold; comprising at one pole an economy of nature, and at the other an economy of supernatural grace; requiring, in order to an easy practical adjust-

ment of our life under it, a twofold conception of God that corresponds;
for which reason the Scripture three are sometimes spoken of by Calvin
and others as composing an economic trinity.

In the department of nature we discover, as we think, a realm of complete systematic causation. All events proceed in right lines of invariable
sequence, under fixed laws. But as laws are only another name for God's
will, or the action of forces representing his will, the system of nature
becomes a symbol, in its whole development, of the regulative mind of
God. What we call the natural consequences are determinations of that
mind in the same manner. In this view it will be seen that, if the universal
economy included nothing but nature, the single term or conception *God*
would answer all our necessary uses — so far there would be no discover-
able economic need of trinity.

But the universal economy is larger and contains, of necessity, another
and partially contending factor, supernaturalism, even as the balance of
the firmament is settled between two natural factors or forces always
contending with each other. Nature is a realm so adjusted that whenever
any moral agent or race of agents cast off the law moral, a train of natural
consequences forthwith takes them in hand for discipline or retribution.
The action begun is that of disease, disorder, pain, constituting what is
fitly called a fall. The penal train is a run of justice, and the run is downward even forever; for it is inconceivable that disorder should ever of itself
beget order. As little to be conceived that we, who have broken up the
ideal harmony of nature by starting a malignant and diseased action, should
be able to will it back into a state of perfection or ideal order, which we
cannot even conceive. To provoke and raise up nature was one thing, to
smooth and restore it, another. Nothing but a force supernatural can restore the mischief, and without that any thought of our own self-
clearance and self-preparation for a state of perfected health and felicity
is even absurd.

Inasmuch, then, as the spiritual training of a race of free moral agents
included the certain fact of their sin, there was, we perceive, a grand
prior necessity, that if they are to have any advantage in existence, the
scheme of God's economy should comprehend two factors, nature and
the supernatural. And this again is the same, it will be seen, as to say that
God will institute and actuate two realms of forces, a kingdom of nature
and a kingdom of grace; for as we have seen that nature is the presiding
will of God, so also must the supernatural be; and then the perfection or

completeness of God's economy will consist in the orderly comprehension of both, under harmonizing principles of law and reason which are clear to him, but only imaginable to us.

And now the question is, conceiving that we are in the state of retributive disorder, to be recovered from it, related thus to God as the Head of the two economies, and having our salvation to seek under their joint action, how we shall be able to conceive God in any manner that will set him continually in this twofold relation towards us? If we have only the single term *God*, then we must speak of God as dealing with God, contending with the causations of God, the grace-force of God delivering from the nature-force of God. If the work includes an incarnation, as we suppose it must of necessity, then it must be God sending God into the world. Or, if it includes a renovating spirit within, then we go to God to give us God, and expect that God within will graciously master the retributive causations of God within — all of which, as we may see, is a conception too clumsy and confused to serve at all the practical necessity of our state. There is, in short, no intellectual machinery, in a close theoretic monotheism, for any such thing as a work of grace, or supernatural redemption. We should even say, beforehand, that no such thing can ever be; for how can God rescue from his own causes and open a way through his own retributions? Accordingly, it will be observed that where this Unitarian conception is held, there is also discovered an almost irresistible tively constitutes the gospel. God is the king of nature and nature is the tendency to naturalism, and so to a loss or dying out of all that distinc-inclusive name of all that constitutes his dominion. There is, in fact, no legitimate place for anything but nature. Sin is softened, depravity ignored. Nature is conceived to be ideally perfect and the palpable disorders and deformities of the world are not regarded, in the admiration offered to its beauty. The gospel is education and the run of life is a course of development in right lines, without a reversal or new creation of anything. Indeed, there is no alternative but to say as some are obliged, in fidelity to their scheme itself, to do, and have not shrunk from doing, that if we are saved at all, we must be saved by justice, or the natural law of retribution.

Now there is, we have already intimated, a higher and more comprehensive view of God's universal kingdom, in which it includes and harmonizes these two economies, viz., nature and the supernatural, and by these two factors, like the contending forces of astronomy, settles and adjusts its orbit. And the Christian trinity gives us a conception of God which exactly meets such a truth, leveling it always to the practical uses of our life.

Using the term God sometimes in a sense broad enough to comprehend all the complexities of his kingdom, we are able, when we need such aid for the practical accommodation of our faith, to lay hold of relational terms that exactly represent the two economies in their action with and upon each other. First we have the term Father, which sets him before us as the king of nature, the author and ground of all existent things and causes. Next we have the Son and the Spirit, which represent the supernatural; the Son coming into nature from above nature, incarnate in the person of Jesus, by a method not in the compass of nature, erecting a kingdom in the world that is not of the world: the Spirit coming in the power of the Son, to complete, by an inward supernatural working, what the Son began by the address he made without to human thought, and the forces he imported into nature by his doctrine, his works, his life, and his death.

Having now these terms or denominations provided, we use them freely in their cross relations, as a machinery accommodated to our sin and the struggles of our faith; putting our trust in the Son as coming down from God, offering himself before God, going up to God, interceding before God, reigning with God, by him accepted, honored, glorified, and allowed to put all things under his feet; invoking also God and Christ to send down the Spirit, and let him be the power of a real indwelling life, coursing through our nature, breathing health into its diseases, and so rolling back the penal currents of justice to set us free. Having these for the instruments of our thought and feeling and faith towards God, and suffering no foolish quibbles of speculative logic to intervene and plague us, asking never how many Gods there are, or how it is possible for one to come out from another, act before another, take us from or to another; but assured of this, at every moment, that God is one and only one forever, however multiform in his vehicle; how lively, and full, and blessed, and easy too, is the converse we receive through these living personations, so pliant to our use as finite men, so gloriously accommodated to our state as sinners.

Our argument for the twofold practical need of a trinity, and the consequent practical value of the trinity we have, is now sufficiently stated, and is brought, we think, to a point of rational conviction as decisive as the nature of the subject permits. Thus far, it will be remarked, we have nothing to do with the interior mystery of the divine nature — the argument amounts to nothing more than that God, even assuming his strict unity, must needs be *exhibited* in this way, in order to the uses stated. Finding a certain threefold designation of God given out in the Christian Scriptures, in which he is presented, in form, as three personalities, Father, Son, and Holy Ghost, we take up the subject at this point and show that taken as means of divine representation, they are necessary to the adequate impression of God, and the practical uses of a supernatural and redemptive economy.

But the question will be raised by many, at this point, whether, after all, there is any thing in God answering to these personalities? Some Unitarian, for example, having followed us to just this point and admitted the force of our argument, may require to be informed wherein the truth or reality of the triune formula consists, or what there is in God's nature to support these personalities of revelation? And to this we might well enough reply by handing back the question. Having shown the practical need of just what the Scripture gives, it is not therefore specially incumbent on us to settle all other and deeper questions that may be raised. Let him bring the matter to that issue that will best satisfy himself. Let him stop at Sabellianism, if the air is not too thin to feed his breath. Or let him vault clean over, at a single stride of logic, if he will, and rest himself in the conclusion that since the three are persons, there must be three Gods, or a council of Gods. Enough for us that we have shown him the practical need of the Scripture trinity.

But we will not so dismiss the question, lest by an evasion of responsibility, at the point reached, we may seem to regard the trinity as a matter only of words, and not in any proper sense an eternal fact. Our impression then is that a very great gain, as regards the intelligent apprehension of this subject, will be made by simply giving full place at the outset to the admission that God is not a person or personal being, save in some qualified and partly tropical sense. For we can every one see at a glance that he cannot, as an infinite being, be comprehended under any such finite term *literally taken*. And yet he is a person. Who of us, except a few speculative pantheists, doubts that he is a person, or apprehends any want of honest reality, or solid eternity in the word when he is called a person? Doubtless the word is a figure (whether we have ever so thought of it or not), but it does not follow that because it is a figure, there is therefore nothing in God to meet and support the figure. Precisely in the same way, and with as good reason, God may be a trinity of persons. There is in fact no greater difficulty in conceiving God as three persons, than there is in conceiving him as one; for he may as well be three without any breach of his unity as one without any breach of his infinity. Indeed, it may be and very probably is true, that what we mean by asserting the personality of God is simply to predicate of him that sociality, conversability, or, to coin a word yet more general, that relationality which is verified to us, and practically realized in us by the trinity.

However this may be, it is an important consideration, and one that goes far to evince the profound reality of the persons, that as God in revelation assumes all the attitudes and acts all the forms of personality, so, in a like free manner, he displays a relative action of three persons towards each other and upon the world — God and with God, sending and sent, conversing with, ascending to, proceeding from — Father, Son, and Holy Ghost. In all which the trinity is seen to be not a matter of words only, but a reality or fact in the world of action. So far at least, the case is clear. What then shall we say of this tri-personality acted by God — what account shall we make of it? Is it that God will accommodate himself in this manner to finite minds? That would reduce the trinity to an occasional matter, a voluntary expedient; which would be a supposition as painful and quite as remote from all our most earnest convictions as to believe that his personality is a merely occasional matter, an act of voluntary accommodation to our finite apprehensions, and not any part of his eternal property or idea.

What then is it that gives us the impression, when we speak of God's personality, that it is an eternal property in him, a something which appertains to the divine idea itself? It cannot be that he exists as an infinite substance in the mold of our human personality; it cannot be that there is a *core* of literal personality wrapped up in his infinite substance. It is not enough that he acts personality in a way of voluntary accommodation to men. It can be only that by some *interior necessity* he is thus accommodated in his action, to the finite; for what he does by the necessity of his nature, as truly pertains to his idea, and is as truly inherent in him, as if it were the form of his divine substance itself. And precisely here we come upon the Nicene trinity. This and all the formulas of trinity that assert the "eternal generation," affirm the unity of the persons as a unity of substance — ὁμοούσιον, "same in substance" — and then regarding the eternal going on, so to speak, of God, this living process or act (*actus purissimus*) they find him eternally threeing himself, or generating three persons. These documents do not mean that God, at some date in his almanac called eternity, begat his Son and sent forth his Holy Spirit, but that in some high sense undefinable, he is datelessly and eternally becoming three, or by a certain inward necessity being accommodated in his action to the categories of finite apprehension — adjusted to that as that to the receiving of his mystery.

This necessary act of God is sometimes illustrated by a reference to our necessary action, in the process of consciousness. Thus in simply being conscious, which we are not by act of will, but by force of simply being what we are, we first take note of ourselves; secondly, raise a conception or thought of ourselves; and thirdly, recognize the correspondence of that conception with ourselves. And this we do as long as we exist, and because we exist. And some have gone so far as even to discover in this fact a parallel and a real explication of the trinity of God. The illustration is reliable, however, only as a demonstration of the intensely inherent character of all necessary action. Were this threefolding of consciousness a matter of substance, it would not be more truly inherent than it is, regarded as an act.

If then we dare to assume what is the deepest, most adorable fact of God's nature, that he is a being infinite, *inherently related in act*, to the finite, otherwise impossible ever to be found in that relation, thus and therefore a being who is everlastingly threeing himself in his action, to be and to be known as Father, Son, and Holy Ghost from eternity to eternity; we are brought out full upon the Christian trinity, and that in the simple line of practical inquiry itself. It is nothing but the doctrine *that God is a being practically related to his creatures*. And for just this reason it was that Christ, in the commission given to his disciples, set forth his formula of trinity, as a comprehensive designation for the gospel, and a revelation of the everlasting ground it has, in the inherent properties of God. He calls it therein as emphatically as possible his "everlasting gospel," a work as old as the trinity of God, a valid and credible work, because it is based in the trinity of God. So glorious and high, and yet so nigh is God; related in all that is inmost, most inherent in his nature and eternity, to our finite want, and the double kingdom of nature and grace, by which we are to be raised up and perfected for the skies — a being who is at once absolute and relational; an all-containing, all-supporting unity, and a manifolding humanly personal love; the All in all itself, and yet *above* all, *through* all, and *in* all; *of* whom also, and *through* whom and *to* whom be glory forever. . . .

It is impossible not to admire the gospel formula, that can so flood the human soul in its narrowed and blinded state with the sense of God, and raise it to a pitch of blessing so transcendent. The amazing power of the trinity, acting thus on the human imagination, and the contribution thus made to Christian experience, cannot be over-estimated.

After we have discovered, in this manner, how closely related the Christian trinity is to Christian experience, and all the highest realizations of God, it will not be difficult to account for the remarkable tenacity of the doctrine. No doctrine is more paradoxical in its terms. None can be more mercilessly tortured by the application of a little logic, such as the weakest and smallest wits are master of. None has been more often or with a more peremptory confidence repudiated by sections of the church and teachers of high distinction. The argument itself, too, has always been triumphant regarding the mere logical result; for the fact is logically absurd, and there is no child who cannot so handle the words as to show that no three persons can be one. And yet, for some reason, the doctrine would not die! It cannot die! Once thought, it cannot be expelled from the world. And this for the reason that its life is in men's hearts, not in their heads. Impressing God in his true personality and magnitude — impressing and communicating God in the grand twofold economy by which he is brought nigh to our fallen state and accommodated to our wants as sinners, showing us God inherently related both to our finite capacity and our evil necessity, what can ever expel it from the world's thought! As soon shall we part with the daylight or the air as lapse into the cold and feeble monotheism in which some teachers of our time are ready to boast as the gospel of reason and the unity of a personal fatherhood. No; this cornerstone is not to be so easily removed. It was planted before the foundation of the world, and it will remain. It is eternally woven into the practical economy of God's kingdom, and must therefore stand firm. Look up, O man! Look up, thou sinner, in thy fall, and behold thy God, eternally Father, Son, and Holy Ghost, bringing all his vastness down to thy littleness, all the power of his will to release thee from the power of his will, acting, manifolding, circling round thee, inherently fitted, though infinite, to thy finite want, and so to be the spring of thy benediction forever!

We are fully conscious of the tameness and poverty of the illustrations by which we have endeavored to set forth this greatest of all subjects. What can a mortal say that is worthy of this transcendent mystery of

God? Even if he should sometime seem to be raised in it quite above mortality, how can he utter that which is so plainly unutterable? Well is it if he does not seem rather to have blurred than cleared the glorious majesty of the subject, by the consciously dull and feeble trivialities he has offered. Indeed we could not dare to offer a discussion so far below the real merit of the theme, were it not for the conviction that there is a lower and feebler inadequacy, in our common holding of the theme, from which it is scarcely possible to detract. To hold this grand subtonic mystery, in the ring of whose deep reverberation we receive our heaviest impressions of God, as if it were only a thing just receivable, not profitable; a dead truth, not a living; a theologic article, wholly one side of the practical life; a truth so scholastic and subtle as to have, in fact, no relation to Christian experience; nothing, we are sure, can be less adequate than this, or bring a loss to religion that is more deplorable, unless it be a flat denial of the mystery itself. In this view, we cannot but indulge a degree of hope that what we have been able to say, however insufficient or unequal to the theme, may yet have a certain value as a tract for the times, raising at least a question of respect for the doctrine, where it has been renounced, starting other and worthier contemplations of it where it is received, and preparing some, in the legitimate use, to find how glorious and blessed a gift to experience, how vast an opening of God to man, how powerful, transforming, transporting, this great mystery of God may be. We can wish the reader nothing more beatific in this life than to have found and fully brought into feeling the practical significance of this eternal act or fact of God, which we call the Christian trinity. Nowhere else do the bonds of limitation burst away as here. Nowhere else does the soul launch upon immensity as here; nowhere fill her burning censer with the eternal fires of God, as when she sings,

> One inexplicably three,
> One in simplest unity.

Who that has been able, in some frame of holy longing after God, to clear the petty shackles of logic, and the paltry quibbles of a world-wise speculation, committing his soul up freely to the inspiring impulse of this divine mystery as it is celebrated in some grand doxology of Christian worship, and has so been lifted into conscious fellowship with the great celestial minds, in their higher ranges of beatitude, and their shining tiers of glory, has not known it as being, at once, the deepest, highest, widest, most enkindling, and most practical of all practical truths!

Regarding it then as such, it is only a part of the argument by which we undertake to commend it to faith and a practical use, that we indicate, in a few brief suggestions, the manner in which its advantages may be most fully received, and with fewest drawbacks of hindrance and perplexity.

First of all, then, we must hold fast the strict unity of God. Let there be no doubt, or even admitted question, of that. Take it by assumption that God is as truly one being as if he were a finite person like ourselves, and let nothing ever be suffered to qualify the assumption; for the moment we begin to let in any such thought as that the Father, Son, and Holy Ghost are three beings, we shall be thrown out of all rest, confused, distressed, questioning what and whom to worship, consulting our prejudices and preferences, and suffering all the distractions of idolators.

Holding firm the unity in this manner, use the plurality with the utmost unconcern, as a form of thought or instrumental verity, by which you are to be assisted in receiving the most unrestricted, fullest, most real and sufficient impression of the One. We must have no jealousy of the three, as if they were going to drift us away from the unity, or from reason; being perfectly assured of this, that in using the triune formula, in the limberest, least constrained way possible, and allowing the plurality to blend, in the freest manner possible, with all our acts of worship, preaching, praying, singing, and adoring, we are only doing with three persons just what we do with one — making no infringement of the unity, with the three, more than of the infinity, with the one. Let God be three persons forever, just as he is one person forever, and as this latter is a truth accepted without difficulty, and held as the necessary truth of religion, so let it be our joy that he is a being who needs for other purposes equally dear, to be and be thought as three.

Meantime we must avoid all practices of logic on the persons. We must take them as we take the one, which if we will put our logic on the term, will immediately turn out to be only a finite being — a man. They are to be set before the mind at the outset as a holy paradox, that only gives the truth in greater power of expression that it defies all attempts at logic or definition. Seizing thus upon the living symbols, we are to chant our response with the Church and say — "God of God, Light of Light, very God of very God"; and if we cannot reason out the paradox, to like it the better that it stops the clatter of our speculative millwork, and speaks to us as God's great mystery should, leaving us to adore in silence. Not that we are here to disown our reason; God is no absurdity as three persons more than as one. Fully satisfied of this, we are only to love the grand abyss of God's majesty thus set before us, and rejoice to fall into it, there to bathe and submerge our finite love, rejoicing the more that God is greater than we knew, taller than our reach can measure, wider than our finite thought can comprehend.

Neither will it do for us to suffer any impatience, or be hurried into any act of presumption, because the trinity of God costs us some struggles of thought, and because we cannot find immediately how to hold it without some feeling of disturbance or distraction. That is one of the merits of the trinity, that it does not fool us in the confidence that we can perfectly know and comprehend God by our first thought. Simply because God is too great for our extempore and merely childish comprehension, he ought to be given us in forms that cost us labor, and put us on a stretch of endeavor. So it is with all great themes. The mind labors and wrestles after them, and comes into their secret slowly. Let no shallow presumption turn us away then from this glorious mystery, till we have given it time enough, and opened to it windows enough by our praises and prayers, to let in the revelation of its glory. Let it also be an argument of modesty with us, and a welcome commendation to our reverence, that so many friends of God and righteous men of the past ages, such as bore a greater fight than we, and grew to greater ripeness in their saintly walk, bowed themselves adoringly before this holy mystery, and sung it with hallelujahs in the worship of their temples, in their desert fastings, and their fires of testimony. And as their *Gloria Patri*, the sublimest of their doxologies, is, in form, a hymn for the ages, framed to be continuously chanted by the long procession of times, till times are lapsed in eternity, what can we better do than let the wave lift us that lifted them, and bid it still roll on! Glory be to the Father, and to the Son, and to the Holy Ghost, as it was in the beginning, is now, and ever shall be, world without end. Amen.

HUMAN ESTRANGEMENT AND ITS FALSE REMEDIES

1. The Fall and Its Consequences [1]

EDITOR'S INTRODUCTION

Not until relatively late in his theological career did Bushnell publish a definitive doctrine of human nature. In the *Discourses on Christian Nurture* (1847) he largely ignored the question, apparently thinking that enough had already been said concerning it in the heated controversies which stemmed from Channing's Baltimore sermon of 1819. Yet since he did not make his position more explicit in that volume, many reviewers of it concluded that he did not hold a radical doctrine of the fall.

That conclusion, however, was unfounded. As a matter of fact, he was in that very period protesting the Unitarian doctrine of the essential goodness of man. A good example is his letter of 1849 to his Unitarian friend in Boston, Cyrus A. Bartol, in which he lamented the failure of the Unitarians to express an "out-and-out conviction of *the fall of man.*" "You [Unitarians] seem to me to be shyer here than you need be, lest you get into the old orthodox notion of a *total* depravity, and of being damned for what God made us to be. But there is room enough for a bond-state of evil, a fall, . . . without descending into any such folly." [2] Three months later (January 23, 1850) he repeated this criticism in commenting on a volume of Bartol's sermons. The sermon on "Human Nature," he said, revealed a "chasm" between their views, since it did not start with the presupposition that man, in his fallen condition, has actually lost the principle of good and is in "a state of unnature and bondage." Christianity, he insisted, "is for mankind as a lost race, not as for a race that wants

---

1. *Nature and the Supernatural* (New York, 1858), Chap. IV (103–5; 107–28; 133–39); Chap. VI (165–84; 185–90); Chap. VII (194–96; 198–202; 214–15).
2. Mary B. Cheney, *Life and Letters of Horace Bushnell* (New York, 1880), 227–28.

to be amended or patched, but new-created in the one principle of good." [3]

In his Dudleian Lecture, delivered at Harvard in 1852, Bushnell focused his attention primarily upon the human predicament, analyzing it in great detail.[4] Man, he explained, is rooted in nature; yet in his freedom he transcends nature. Accordingly, he can and does sin. When man thus sins, the impact necessarily deforms the soul, the body, society, and the whole physical world in all its aspects. The lecture, therefore, is a remarkable preview of what Bushnell unfolded definitively in *Nature and the Supernatural*, published six years later.

❖ ❖ ❖ ❖

Chapter IV

The Problem of Existence, as Related to The Fact of Evil

It has been already intimated, or shown as a possible thing, that the race, regarded as an order of powers, may break loose from God's control and fall into sin. Will they so break loose? Regarding them simply as made and set forth on the course of training necessary to their establishment in holy virtue, will they retain their innocence? Have we any reason to think, and if so what reason to think, that they will drop their allegiance and try the experiment of evil?

It is very certain that God desires no such result. When it takes place, it will be against his will and against every attribute of his infinitely beneficent and pure character. It will only be true that he has created moral and accountable beings with this peril incident, rather than to create only nature and natural things; having it in view, as the glorious last end of his plan, finally to clear us of sin by passing us, since we will descend to it, completely through it. He will have given us, or, at least, the original new-created progenitors, a constituently perfect mold; so that, taken simply as forms of being, apart from any character begun by action, they are in that exact harmony and perfection that, without or before deliberation, spontaneously runs to good; organically ready, with all heavenly affinities in play, to break out in a perfect song. So far they are innocent and holy by creation, or by the simple fact of their constituent perfection in the

3. *Ibid.*, 231–32.   4. Manuscript entitled "Dudleian Lecture," 20–103.

image of their Maker; only there is no sufficient strength, or security in their holiness, because there is no deliberative element in it. Deliberation, when it comes, as come it must, will be the inevitable fall of it; and then, when the side of counsel in them is sufficiently instructed by that fall and the bitter sorrow it yields, and the holy freedom is restored, it may be or become an eternally enduring principle. Spontaneity in good, without counsel, is weak; counsel and deliberative choice, without spontaneity, are only a character begun; issued in spontaneity, they are the solid reality of everlasting good. Still it will not, even then, be true that God has contrived their sin as a means of the ulterior good, though it may be true that they, by their knowledge of it as being only evil, will be intelligently fixed, forever afterward, in their abhorrence of it. Nor, if we speak of sin as permitted in this view by God, will it be any otherwise permitted, than as not being prevented, either by the non-creation, or by the uncreating of the race.

It may appear to some that such a view of God's relations to sin excludes the fact or faith of an eternal plan, showing God to be, in fact, the victim of sin; having neither power to withstand it, nor any system of purposes able to include and manage it. On this subject of foreordination or predetermined plan, there is a great deal of very crude and confused speculation. If there be any truth which every Christian ought to assume, as evident beyond all question, it is that God has some eternal plan that includes every thing, and puts every thing in its place. That he "foreordains whatsoever comes to pass" is only another version of the same truth. Nor is there any the least difficulty in distinguishing the entire consistency of this with all that we have said concerning God's relations to the existence of evil — no difficulty, in fact, which does not occur in phrasing the conduct and doings even of men. . . .

Thus far we have spoken of God's relations to the existence of evil, or its possible prevention. We pass over now to the side of his subjects; and there we shall find reason, as regards their self-retention, to believe that the certainty of their sin is originally involved in their spiritual training as powers. Made organically perfect, set as full in God's harmony as they can be, in the mold of their constitution, surrounded by as many things as possible to allure them to ways of obedience and keep them from the seductions of sin, we shall discover still that, given the fact of their begun existence, and their trial as persons or powers, they are in a condition privative that involves their certain lapse into evil.

If the language I employ in speaking of this matter is peculiar, it is because I am speaking with caution and carefully endeavoring to find terms
that will convey the right, separated from any false, impression. I speak of a
"condition privative," it will be observed; not of any positive ground, or
cause, or necessity; for, if there were any natural necessity for sin, it
would not be sin. If it were caused, as all simply natural events are caused;
or, what is the same, if it were a natural effect, it would not be sin. We
might as well blame the running of the rivers, in such a case, as the
wrongdoing of men; for what we may call their wrongdoing is, after all,
nothing but the run of causes hid in their person, as gravity is hid in the
running waters. If we could show a positive ground for sin; that man,
for example, is a being whose nature it is to choose the strongest motive,
as of a scale beam to be turned by the heaviest weight, and that the
strongest motive, arranged to operate on men, is the motive to do evil,
that in fact would be the denial of sin, or even of its possibility; indeed it
is so urged by the disciples of naturalism on every side. So again if we
could, in a way of positive philosophy, account for the existence of evil
— exactly what multitudes even of Christian believers set themselves to
do, not observing that, if they could execute their endeavor, they could
also make as good answer for evil, on the judgment day of the world —
if, I say, we could properly and positively account for evil in this manner,
it would not be evil any longer. When we speak of accounting for
any thing, we suppose a discovery of first principles to which it may
be referred; but sin can be referred to no first principles, it is simply the
act of a power that spurns all inductives back of the doer's will, and
asserts itself apart from all first principles, or even against them. Therefore, to avoid all these false implications, and present the simple truth of
fact, I speak of a "condition privative"; by which I mean a moral state
that is only inchoate or incomplete, lacking something not yet reached,
which is necessary to the probable rejection of evil. Thus an infant child
runs directly toward, and will in fact run into, the fire; not because of
any necessity upon him, but simply because he is in a condition privative,
as regards the experience needed to prevent him. I said also "involves the
certain lapse into evil" — not "produces," "infers," "makes necessary."
There is no connection of science or law between the subject and predicate, such that, one being given, the other holds by natural consequence;
and yet this condition privative "involves," according to our way of ap-
prehending it, a certain conviction or expectation of the event stated.
Thus we often attain to expectations concerning the conduct of men, as

fixed as those which we hold concerning natural events, where the connection of cause and consequence is absolute. We become acquainted, as we say, with a certain person; we learn how he works in his freedom, or how, as a power acting from himself, he is wont to carry himself in given conditions; and finally we attain to a sense of him so intimate that, given almost any particular occasion or transaction touching his interest, we have an expectation or confidence regarding what he will do, about as fixed as we have in the connections of natural events. The particular thing done to him "involves," in our apprehension, as the certain fact, that he will do a particular thing consequent. And yet we have no conception that he is determined in such matters by any causation, or law of necessary connection; the certainty we feel is the certainty not of a thing but of a power in the sovereign determination of his liberty. In this and no other sense do we speak of a condition privative that involves a certain lapse into evil.

Having distinguished, in this careful manner, the true import of the terms employed, it now remains to look for that condition privative on which so much depends. And we shall discover it in three particulars.

1. In the necessary defect of knowledge and consequent weakness of a free person, or power, considered as having just begun to be. We must not imagine, because he is a power able in his action to set himself above all natural causes and act originatively as from himself, that he is therefore strong. On the contrary, even though he begins in the full maturity of his person, having a constitution set in perfect harmony with the divine order and truth, he is the weakest, most unperfect of beings. The stones of the world are strong in their destiny, because it stands in God, under laws of causation fixed by him. But free agents are weak because they are free; left to act originatively, held fast by no superior determination, bound to no sure destiny; save as they are trained into character, in and through their experience.

Our argument forbids that we should assume the truth of the human genesis reported in Scripture history; for that is commonly denied by naturalism. I may not even assume that we are descended of a common stock. But this, at least, is certain, that we each began to be, and therefore we may the more properly take the case of Adam for an example; because, not being corrupted by any causes back of him, as we most certainly are, and making a beginning in the full maturity of his powers, he may be supposed to have had some advantages for standing fast in the right, which we have not.

As we look upon him, raising the question whether he has moral strength to stand, we observe first of all that being in a perfect form of harmony, uncorrupted, clean, in one word a complete integer, he must of course be spontaneous to good, and can never fall from it until his spontaneity is interrupted by some reflective exercise of contrivance or deliberative judgment. But this will come to pass, without fail, in a very short time; because he is not only spontaneous to good, but is also a reflective and deliberative being. And then what shall become of his integrity?

Entering still further into his case, as we raise this question, we perceive that he holds a place, or point, in his action, between two distinct ranges of thought and motivity; between necessary ideas on one hand, and knowledges or judgments drawn from experience on the other. In the first place, being a man, he has necessarily developed in his consciousness the law of right. He thinks the right, and, in thinking it, feels himself eternally bound by it. We may call it an idea in him, or a law, or a category of his being. He would not be a man without it; for it is only in connection with this, and other necessary ideas, that he ranges above the animals. Animals have no necessary ideas; these, especially such as are moral, are the necessary and peculiar furniture of man. What could a man do in the matter of justice, inquiring after it, determining what it is, if the idea of justice were not first developed, as a standard thought or idea, in his mind? Who would set himself on inquiries after true things and judgments, if the idea of truth were not in him as a regulative thought, or category of his nature? Thus it is, by our idea of right, that we are set to the conceiving or thought of duty, as well as placed under obligation itself; and we could not so much as raise the question of virtue or morality, if we were not first configured to its law, and set in action as being consciously under it. Herein, too, we are specially resembled to God; for by this same idea of right, necessary, immutable, eternal, it is that he is placed in obligation, and it is by his ready and perfect homage to this that his glorious character is built. And this law is absolute or unconditional to him as to us, to us as to him — no matter what may befall or not befall us, on the empirical side of our life. No impediment, no threat, or fear, or force can excuse us; least of all can any mere condition privative, such as ignorance, inexperience, or the want of opposing motive. Simply to have thought the right is to be under obligation to it, without any motive or hope in the world of experience, and despite of all opposing motives there. Even if the worlds fall on us, we must do the right.

Pass over now from the absolute or ideal side of our existence to the contingent or empirical. Here we are dealing with effects, consequences, facts; trying our strength in attempts; computing, comparing, judging, learning how to handle things, and how they will handle us. And by this kind of experience we get all the furniture of our mind and character, save what we have as it were concreated in us, in those necessary ideas of which we have spoken, and which are presupposed in all experience. What now, reverting to the case of Adam, as a just-begun existence, is the amount of his experimental, empirical, or historic knowledge? The knowledges we here inquire after, it will be observed, are such as are gotten historically, one by one, and one after another, under conditions of time; by seeing, doing, suffering, comparing, distinguishing, remembering, and other like operations. A man's knowledge here is represented, of course, by what he has been through, and felt, and thought. What then can he know at the first moment of his being, when, by the supposition, he has never had a thought, or an experience; or, if we take him at a point an hour or a day later, none but that of a single hour or day? Being a perfectly disposed creature, the first man sets off, we will say, in a spontaneous obedience to the right, which is the absolute law of his nature and is in him originally, by the necessary conditions of his nature. But there comes up shortly a question regarding some act, confessedly not right, or some act which, being forbidden, violates his sense of right. No matter what it is, he can be as properly and will be as effectually tested by adhering to the sense of obligation, in withholding from an apple forbidden, as in any thing else. Here then he stands upon the verge of experimental wrong, debating the choice. What it is in its idea or obligatory principle, he knows; but what it is in the experience of its fruits or consequences he knows not. The discord, bitterness, remorse, and inward hell of wrong are hidden, as yet, from his view. If minatory words have been used, pronouncing death upon him in case of disobedience, some degree of apprehension may have been awakened in him anticipatively, under the natural efficacy of manner and expression, which, even prior to any culture of experience, have a certain degree of power. But how little this will amount to in a way of guard or security for his virtue; for he is a knowing creature still; wanting therefore to know, and, if it were not for this noble instinct of knowledge, would not be a man. What then is this wrong he is debating, what does it signify? He does not ask whether it will bring him evil or good; for what these are, experimentally, he does not know. Enough that here is some great secret of knowledge to be opened; how can he abstain, how refuse to break through the mask of this unknown something, and know! He is tempted thus, we perceive, not by something positive placed in his way, but by a mere condition privative, a perplexing defect of knowledge incident to the fact of his merely begun existence.

Doubtless it will be urged that no such wrong would ever be debated, if some positive desire of the nature were not first excited, some constitutional susceptibility, or want, drawn out in longing for its object. Even so, precisely that we have allowed; for what is the desire of knowledge itself but a positive and most powerful instinct of the soul? Only the more clear is it that, if the desired knowledge were already in possession, the temptation itself would be over. So if some bodily appetite were excited; how trivial and contemptible were this, or any proposed pleasure, if only the tremendous evil and woe of the wrong were already known, as it will be after years of struggle and suffering in it! The grand peril therefore is still seen to be of a privative and not of a positive nature. There must be positive impulses to be governed, or else there could not be a man, and the peril is that there is yet no experimental knowledge on hand, and can be none, sufficient to protect and guard the process.

And yet the man is guilty if he makes the fatal choice. Even if the strongest motive were that way, he is yet a being able to choose against the strongest, and he consciously knows that he ought. In any view, he is not obliged to choose the wrong, more than a child is obliged to thrust his hand into the blaze of a lamp, the experience of which is unknown. The cases are, in fact, strongly analogous, save that the wrong-doer knows beforehand, as the child certainly does not, that the act is wrong or criminal; a consideration by which he consciously ought to be restrained, be the consequences what they may. And yet, who can expect that he will forever be restrained, never breaking over this mysterious line to make the bad experiment, or try what is in this unknown something eternally before his eyes! If we rightly remember, the false prophet somewhere represents the difficulty of a certain course of virtue, by that of crossing the fiery gulf of hell upon a hair. Possibly our first man may cross upon this hair and keep his balance till he is completely over, but who will expect him to do it? He may look upon the tree of knowledge of good and evil (rightly is it named), and pass it by. He can do it; there is a real possibility as there is a real obligation; but Adam, we are told, did not, neither is there any the least probability that any other of mankind, with all his advantages, ever would.

If it should be apprehended by any that a condition privative, connected as it plainly is with such perils, quite takes away the guilt of sin, that, I answer, is by the supposition impossible. It really takes away nothing. The right and only true statement is, that the guilt of sin is not as greatly enhanced as it would be, if all the knowledge needful to the strength of virtue were supplied. We differ in this matter from those naturalistic philosophers who reduce all human wrong to weakness, and obliterate, in that manner, all the distinctions of good and evil. We really excuse nothing; we only do not condemn as severely as if the eternal and absolute obligation of right, revealed in every human bosom, were more thoroughly fortified by prudential and empiric knowledge.

It may also be objected, as contrary to all experience as well as to the nature of sin itself, that sin should impart strength, or increase the capacity of virtue. What in fact does it bring but bondage, disability, and death? Even so — this is the knowledge of sin, and no one is the more capable of holiness on account of it. It is the very point indeed of this knowledge that it knows disability, helplessness, despair. And exactly this it is that prepares the possibility of a new creation. Impotence discovered is the capacity of redemption. And then, when a soul has been truly regenerated and set in union with God, its bad experience will be the condition of its everlasting stability and strength.

It will naturally enough be objected again, by some who hold the principle of disinterested and absolute virtue here assumed, that no mere defect of empirical knowledge — the knowledge of prudence or self-interest — creates a condition privative as regards the security of virtue: what need of experience to enforce obligations that are perfect, apart from all consequences? If one is loving God, as he ought, simply for his own excellence or beauty, and living by the inspiration of that excellence, what matter is it whether he knows the practical bitterness, the woe, the hell of sin, and understands the penal sanctions of reward and penalty set against it, or not? Is he going to fall out of his love and his inspired liberty, because he is not sufficiently shut in to it by fears and apprehended miseries! There is an appearance of force in the objection, and yet it is only an appearance. For, in the first place, it is not assumed that Adam, or any other man, put to the trial of a right life, is weak in his spontaneous obedience because he is not sufficiently held to it by the prudential motives of fear and known destruction; but because his curiosity, as a knowing creature, is provoked, or will be, by not so much as knowing what the motives are, in a word, by the profound mystery that overhangs the question of wrong itself. Indeed he does not even so much as know what it will do, whether it will raise to some unknown pitch of greatness in power and intelligence or not. In the next place, it is not assumed that the prudential motives of reward and penalty will ever recover any fallen spirit from his defections and bring him into the inspired, free state of love. The office of such means and motives is wholly negative; viz., to arrest the bad soul in its evil and bring it to a stand of self-renunciation, where the higher motives of the divine excellence and love may kindle it. In the third place, it is not assumed that, when souls are recovered from evil, and finally established in holy liberty, which is the problem of their trial, they are made safe for the coming eternity by knowing how dreadfully they will be scorched by evil, in case they relapse; but their safety is that, having been dreadfully scorched already by it, they have thoroughly proved what is in it, and extirpated all the fascinations of its mystery.

2. It is another condition privative, as regards the moral perfection of powers, that they require an empirical training, or course of government, to get them established in the absolute law of duty, and that this empirical training must probably have a certain adverse effect for a time before it can mature its better results. The eternal idea of justice makes no one just; that of truth makes no one true; that of beauty makes no soul beautiful. So the eternal law of right makes no one righteous. All these standard ideas require a process or drill, in the field of experience, in order to become matured into characters, or to fashion character in the molds they supply. And this process, or drill-practice, will require two economies or courses; the first of which will be always a failure, taken in itself, but will furnish, nevertheless, a necessary ground for the second, by which its effects will be converted into benefits; and then the result — a holy character — will be one of course that presupposes both.

The first named course, or economy, is that of law; which is called, even in Scripture, the letter that killeth. The law absolute, of which we just now spoke, is a merely necessary idea; commanding us, from eternity, as it did the great Creator himself — *do right* — making no specifications and applying no motives, save what are contained in its own absolute excellence and authority. But the receiving it in that manner, which is the only manner in which it can be truly received, supposes a mind and temper already configured to it, so as to be in it in mere love and the spontaneous homage that enthrones it, because of its excellence, and God because he represents its excellence. Here, therefore, is the problem, how to produce this practical configuration. And it is executed thus: God, as a power and a force extraneous, undertakes for it, first of all, to enforce it empirically, by motives extraneous; those of reward and fear, profit and loss. He takes the law absolute down into the world of prudence, re-enacting it there and preparing to train us into it, by a drill-practice under sanctions. In one view, the sanctions added are inappropriate; for they are opposite to all spontaneity, being appeals to interest, and so far calls that draw the soul away from the more inspiring considerations of inherent excellence. The subject is lifted by no inspiration. He is down under the law, at the best, trying to come up to it by willing, *punctuatim et seriatim*, what particular things are required in the specifications made by it. If we could suppose the law thus enforced to be perfectly observed under this pressure of prudential sanctions, it would only make a dry, punctilious, and painfully apprehensive kind of virtue, without liberty or dignity. The more probable result is an habitual and wearisome selfishness; for, as long as the mind is occupied by these empirical and extraneous sanctions, it is held to the consideration of self-interest only; and the motives it is all the while canvassing are such as the worst mind can feel, as well as that which is truly upright. And yet there is a benefit preparing in this first, or legal economy, which is indispensable; viz. this, that it gives adhesiveness to the law, which otherwise, as being merely ideal, we might lightly dismiss; that the friction it creates, like some mordant in the dyeing process, sets in the law and fastens it practically, or as an experimental reality; that the woes of penalty wage a battle for it, in which the soul is continually worsted and so broken in; that it develops in short a whole body of moral judgments and convictions, that wind the soul about as cords of detention, till finally the law to be enforced becomes an experimental verity fully established. Just here the soul begins to feel a dreadful coil of thralldom round it. To get away from the law is impossible; for it is hedged about with fire. To keep it is impossible; for the struggle is only a heaving under self-interested motive, to get clear of a state whose bane is selfishness. What it means, the subject can not find. He is in a condition of bitter thralldom; his sin appears to be sin even more than ever; and the whole discipline he is under seems only to minister the knowledge of sin; he groans, as it were, under a body of sin and death that he can not heave.

And so he is made ready for the second economy, that of liberating grace and redemption. For now, in Christ, the law returns, a person, clothed in all personal beauty, and offers itself to the choice, even as a friend and deliverer; so that, being taken with love to Christ, and drawing near at his call in holy trust, the bondman is surprised to find that he is loving the law as the perfect law of liberty; which was the point to be gained or carried. And so what began as a necessary idea is wrought into a character and become eternal fact. The whole operation, it will be observed, supposes a condition privative in the subject, such that he suffers, at first, a kind of repulsion by the law, and is only won to it by embracing the goodness of it in a personal friend and deliverer.

And something like this double administration of law and liberty we distinguish in many of the matters even of our worldly life. No exactness of drill makes an army efficient or invincible, till it is fired by some free impulse from the leader, or the cause; and yet the wearisome and tedious drill is a previous condition without which this latter were impossible. No great work of genius was ever written in the way of work, or before the wings were lifted by some gale of inspiration; which gale, again, would never have begun to blow, had not the windows of thought and the chambers of light and beauty within been opened, by years of patient toil and study. The artist plods on wearily, drudging in the details of his art, till finally the inspiration takes him, and from that point onward his hand is moved by his subject, with no conscious drudgery or labor. In the family, we meet a much closer and equally instructive analogy. The young child is overtaken first by the discipline of the house, in a form of law; commanded, forbidden, sent, interdicted, all in a way of authority, and to that authority is added something which compels respect. If he is a ductile and gentle child, he will be generally obedient; but the examples are few in which the child will not sometimes be openly restive, or even stiffen himself in willful disobedience. In any case, it will be law, not co-inciding always with the child's wishes, or his opinions of pleasure and advantage; and there will be a sense of constraint, more or less irksome, as if the authority felt were repugnant and contrary to the desired happiness. By and by, however, authority changes its aspect and becomes lovely. The habit of obedience, the experience had of parental fidelity and tenderness, and the discovery made of absurdity and hidden mischief in the things interdicted, as it seemed arbitrarily, gradually abolishes the sense of law and substitutes a control not felt before, the control of personal love and respect. So that finally the man of thirty will carefully and reverently anticipate the minutest wishes of a parent, and if that can be called obedience, will obey him; when, as a child of three, he could barely endure his authority, and submitted to it only because it was duty enforced.

Such is the analogy of common life. Law and liberty are the two grand terms under which it is passed — law first and liberty afterward. And with all this corresponds what is said in the New Testament of law as re-

lated to gospel. It is said, in one view, of the laborious ritual of Moses;
yet, by this historic reference, it is designed to lead the mind back into a
more general and deeper truth. It is called "the letter that killeth," as related to "the spirit that giveth life." It is said to have its value in the development of knowledge; for by the law is "the knowledge of sin" —
"that sin by the commandment might become exceeding sinful." It is
bondage introducing and preparing liberty. "The law gendereth to bondage," but the gospel, "Jerusalem that is above, is free." "If there had been
a law that could have given life, verily righteousness should have been by
the law"; but that was impossible. "It is the schoolmaster to bring us to
Christ," and then, having embraced him, he becomes a new inspiration
in our love, after which we no more need "to be under a schoolmaster."
"The law made nothing perfect, but the bringing in of a better hope did."

There is reason to suspect that many will reject what I am here advancing. They will do it, of course, for the simple reason that they know no
other kind of virtue but that which is legal, having therefore, in their
consciousness, nothing which answers to the liberty of the Spirit. To
them, what I have here said will have an appearance of cant. Exactly contrary to which, I affirm it as the only competent philosophy, perceiving, I
think, as clearly as I perceive any thing, that the conjunction discovered
in Christianity of these two ministrations is not any casual or accidental
matter — as if men had somehow fallen under law, and God was constrained, afterward, to do something for them — on the contrary that the
whole management is from before the foundation of the world, having
respect to a grand antecedent necessity, involved in the perfecting of virtue. God never proposed to perfect a character in men by mere legal
obedience. But he instituted law originally, no doubt, as a first stage,
preparatory to a second; both of which were to be kept on foot together,
and both of which are blended in one way or another, probably, in the
training of all holy minds in all worlds.

3. There appears to be yet another condition privative, as regards our
security against sin, in the social relation of powers and their trial in and
through that relation; viz., that they are at first exposed to invasions of
malign influence from each other, which can nowise be effectually prevented, save as they are finally fortified by the defenses of character. In
this view, if I am right, a great part of the problem of existence must consist in what may be called the fencing of powers; that is, by assorting and
separating the good from the bad, and rendering one class inaccessible to
the arts and annoyances of the other.

The individual, as we have seen, is to be perfected for society; and for that reason he must needs have his trial in and through society. A still wider truth appears to be that the perfect society thus preparing is to be one and universal, comprehending the righteous populations of all worlds and ages; for the terms of duty and religion are in their nature universal; and for this reason it appears also to be necessary that the trial and training should be in some open field of activity common to *all* the powers. Accordingly, as we are made with social and, if I may use the term, commercial natures; having inlets of sympathy and impression, by which we may feel one another; capacities to receive and give, to wrong, to offend, to comfort, to strengthen, to seduce, and betray one another; so there is an antecedent probability that the terms of social exposure will involve some possibility of access, on the part of beings unseen, that are not of our race. Indeed, if it should happen that spirits are impossible to be sorted and fenced apart by walls of matter, or gulfs of distance, or abysses of emptiness, something like this would seem to be necessarily involved, till they are sorted and the gates of commerce are shut fast, by the repulsions of contrary affinities. And accordingly, till this takes place, there must be exposures to good and malign influence, more numerous than we can definitely mark or distinguish.

With this corresponds, it will be observed, all that is said in the Scriptures of the activity of ministering angels engaged to confirm and comfort us, the insidious arts of a bad spirit to accomplish our fall, and the manifold enticements and malignant possessions of evil demons generally. But I advert to these representations, it will be observed, not in a way of assuming their authenticity, for that is forbidden by the nature of my argument. I only cite them as offering conceptions to our mind, or imagination, that may be necessary to a full comprehension of what is included in the subject.

Many will object most sturdily and peremptorily, I am well aware, to the possibility of enticements and arts, practiced by unseen agents, to draw us off from our fidelity to God; alleging that such an exposure impeaches the fatherhood of God, and virtually destroys our responsibility. But what if it should happen to be involved, as the necessary condition of any properly social existence? And it might as well be urged that every temptation is an impeachment of God, which comes from sources unseen, being an approach that takes us off our guard, and upsets the balance, possibly, of our judgments, just when we are most implicitly confiding in them. Allowing such an objection therefore, responsibility would be impossible; for who of us was ever able to see distinctly by what avenues all of his temptations or enticements came? Besides, saying nothing of bad spirits, by how many methods, by air, look, sympathy, do we produce immediate impressions in each other, whose sources are never noted or suspected; conveying sentiments, drawing to this or that, fascinating, magnetizing, playing upon one another, by methods as subtle and secret, as if the mischief came from powers of darkness! And yet we never imagine that such enticements encroach at all on the grounds of our just responsibility; and all for the manifest reason that it never matters whence our enticements come, or by what arts the color of our judgments is varied and their equilibrium disturbed; still we know, in all cases, that the wrong is wrong, and knowing that is enough to complete our responsibility.

I am well aware of the modern tendency to resolve what is said on this subject in the Scripture into figures of speech, excluding all idea of a literal intermeddling of bad spirits. But that there are bad spirits, there is no more reason to doubt, than that there are bad men (who are in fact bad spirits), and as little that the bad spirits are spirits of mischief, and will act in character, according to their opportunity. As regards the possession of foul spirits, it has been maintained by many of the sturdiest supporters of revelation, and by reference to the words employed in one or two cases by the evangelists themselves, that they were only diseases regarded in that light. Others have assumed the necessary absurdity of these possessions without argument; and still others have made them a subject of much scoffing and profane ridicule. For the last half-century, and contemporaneously with our modern advances in science, there has been a general gravitation of opinion, regarding this and many other points, toward the doctrine of the Sadducees. Which makes it only the more remarkable that now at last a considerable sect of our modern Sadducees themselves, who systematically reject the faith of any thing supernatural, are contributing what aid they can to restore the precise faith of the New Testament respecting foul spirits. They do not call their spiritual visitors devils, or their demonized mediums possessed persons. But the low manners of their spirits and the lying oracles which it is agreed that some of them give, and the power they display of acting on the lines of cause and effect in nature, when thumping under tables, jolting stoves, and floating men and women through the upper spaces of rooms, proves them to be, if they are any thing, supernatural beings; leaving no appreciable distinction between them and the demoniacal irruptions of Scripture. For though there be some talk of electricity and science, and a show of reducing the new-discovered commerce to laws of calculable recurrence, it is much more likely to be established by their experiments, as a universal fact, that whatever being, of whatever world, opens himself to the visitation, or invites the presence of powers, indiscriminately as respects their character, whether it be under some thin show of scientific practice or not, will assuredly have the commerce invited! Far enough is it from being either impossible or incredible, and exactly this is what our new school of charlatanism suggests, that immense multitudes of powers, interfused, in their self-active liberty, through all the abysses and worlds of nature, have it as the battlefield of their good or malign activity, doing in it and upon it, as the Scriptures testify, acts supernatural that extend to us. This being true, what shall be expected but that where there is anything congenial in temper or character to set open the soul, and nothing of antipathy to repel; or where any one, through a licentious curiosity, a foolish conceit of science, or a bad faith in powers of necromancy, calls on spirits to come, no matter from what world — in such a case what shall follow, but that troops of malign powers rush in upon their victim, to practice their arts in him at will. I know nothing at all personally of these new mysteries; but if a man, as Townsend and many others testify, can magnetize his patient, even at the distance of miles, it should not seem incredible that foul spirits can magnetize also. This indeed was soon discovered in the power of spirits to come into mediums, and make them write and speak their oracles. It is also a curious coincidence that no one, as we are told, can be magnetized, or become a medium, or even be duly enlightened by a medium, who is uncongenial in his affinities, or maintains any quality of antipathy in his will, or temper, or character; for then the commerce sought is impossible. Beside it is remarkable that the persons who dabble most freely in this kind of commerce are seen, as a general fact, to run down in their virtue, lose their sense of principles, and become addled, by their familiarity with the powers of mischief.

In these references to bad spirits, and the matter of demonology in general, I do not assume to have established any very decisive conclusion; for the Scripture representations can not be assumed as true, and the new demons of science I know nothing about except by report. This only is made clear: that the suggestion of a condition privative in men, as regards their defense against the irruption of other powers, is one that can not be disproved by any facts within the compass of our knowledge. And since other powers doubtless exist, both good and bad, who are being sorted and fenced apart by the contrary affinities of character, nothing can be more consonant to reason than that there must be exposures to unseen mischief in our trial, till these eternal fences are raised.

We find then — this is the result of our search — that sin can nowise be accounted for; there are no positive grounds or principles back of it, whence it may have come. We only discover conditions privative that are involved as necessary incidents in the begun existence and trial of powers. These conditions privative are in the nature of perils, and while they excuse nothing, for the law of duty is always plain, they are yet drawn so close to the soul and open their gulfs, on either hand, so deep, that our expectation of the fall is really as pressing as if it were determined by some law that annihilates liberty. Liberty we know is not annihilated. And yet we say, looking on the state of man made perilous, in this manner, by liberty, that we can not expect him to stand. . . .

If it should be objected that my doctrine or hypothesis here is only another version of the scheme that accounts for sin as being the necessary means of the greatest good, it is enough to answer that I see no great reason to be concerned for it, even if it were. Still I do not perceive that it proposes to account for sin as being a means of any thing. It makes much of the knowledge of sin, or of its bitter consequences, and especially of the want of that knowledge, save as it is gotten by the bad experience itself. But the knowledge of sin is, in fact, knowing — that is the precise point of it — that it is the means of nothing good, that it is evil in all its tendencies, relations, operations, and results, and will never bring any thing good to any being. If then the knowing of sin to be the possible means of no good is itself a means of good, wherein does it appear that I am reproducing the doctrine that sin is the necessary means of the greatest good? Because, it may be answered, sin, as a fact of consciousness, is by the supposition the necessary means of the knowledge of sin. But that, I reply, is a trick of argument practiced on the word *means*. Undoubtedly sin, as a fact of consciousness, is the necessary *subject* of the knowledge of sin. If it were affirmed that the knowledge of certain sunken rocks, in the track of some voyage, is necessary to a safe passage, how easy to show, by just the argument here employed, that, since the rocks are a necessary means of the knowledge of the rocks, the rocks are therefore, and by necessary consequence, the necessary means of a safe passage!

There is still another point, the existence of Satan or the devil, and the account to be made of him, which is always intruded upon discussions of this nature, and can not well be avoided. God, we have seen, might create a realm of things and have it stand firm in its order; if he creates a realm of powers, a prior and eternal certainty confronts him, of their outbreak in evil. And at just this point we are able, it may be, to form some just or not impossible conception of the diabolical personality. According to the Manichees or disciples of Zoroaster, a doctrine virtually accepted by many philosophers, two principles have existed together from eternity, one of which is the cause of good and the other of evil; and by this short process they make out their account of evil. With sufficient modifications, their account is probably true. Thus if their good principle, called God by us, is taken as a being, and their bad principle as only a condition privative; one as a positive and real cause, the other as a bad possibility that environs God from eternity, waiting to become a fact and certain to become a fact, whenever the opportunity is given, it is even so. And then it follows that, the moment God creates a realm of powers, the bad possibility as certainly becomes a bad actuality, a Satan, or devil, *in esse;* not a bad omnipresence over against God, and his equal — that is a monstrous and horrible conception — but an outbreaking evil, or empire of evil in created spirits, according to their order. For Satan or the devil, taken in the singular, is not the name of any particular person, neither is it a personation merely of temptation, or impersonal evil, as many insist; for there is really no such thing as impersonal evil in the sense of moral evil; but the name is a name that generalizes bad persons or spirits, with their bad thoughts and characters, many in one. That there is any single one of them who, by distinction or pre-eminence, is called Satan or devil, is wholly improbable. The name is one taken up by the imagination to designate or embody, in a conception the mind can most easily wield, the all or total of bad minds and powers. Even as Davenport,[1] the ablest theologian of all the New England fathers, represents in his Catechism; answering carefully the question, "What is the devil?" — thus: "The multitude of apostate angels which, by pride, and blasphemy against God, and malice against man, became liars and murderers, by tempting him to that sin."

There is also a further reason for this general unifying of the bad powers in one, or under one conception, in the fact that evil, once beginning to exist, inevitably becomes organic, and constructs a kind of principate or kingdom opposite to God.[2] It is with all bad spirits, doubtless, as with

1. [ED.] John Davenport (1597-1669) was co-founder of the New Haven Colony (1638) and the first minister of the church established there.
2. [ED.] Bushnell here and elsewhere anticipated Walter Rauschenbusch's idea of

us. Power is taken by the strongest, and weakness falls into a subordinate place of servility and abjectness. Pride organizes caste, and dominates in the sphere of fashion. Corrupt opinions, false judgments, bad manners, and a general body of conventionalisms that represent the motherhood of sin, come into vogue and reign. And so, doubtless, every where and in all worlds, sin has it in its nature to organize, mount into the ascendant above God and truth, and reign in a kingdom opposite to God. And, in this view, evil is fitly represented in the Scripture as organizing itself under Satan, or the devil, or the prince of this world, or the prince of the power of the air — no puling fiction of superstition, as many fancy, but, rightly conceived, a grand, massive, portentous, and even tremendous reality. For though it be true that no such bad omnipresence is intended in the term Satan as some appear to fancy, there is represented in it an organization of bad mind, thought, and power, that is none the less imperial as regards resistance.

At just this point many fall into the easy mistake of supposing that the bad organization finds its head in a particular person or spirit, who has all other bad spirits submissive and loyal under his will, and is called Satan as being their king. But they press the analogy too far, overlooking the fact that evil is as truly and eternally anarchy as organization. It is much better to understand, as in reference to bad spirits, what we know holds good in respect to the organic force of evil here among men. Evil is a hell of oppositions, riots, usurpations, in itself, and bears a front of organization only as against good. It never made a chief that it would not shortly dethrone, never set up any royal Nimrod or family of Nimrods it would not sometime betray or expel. That the organic force of evil therefore has ever settled the eternal supremacy of some one spirit called devil or Satan, is against the known nature of evil. There is no such order, allegiance, loyalty, faith, in evil as that. The stability of Satan and his empire consists, not in the force of some personal chieftainship, but in the fixed array of all bad minds, and even of anarchy itself, against what is good.

As regards the naming process by which this devil or Satan is prepared, we may easily instruct ourselves by other analogies; such, for example, as "the man of sin," and "antichrist." These are the names, evidently, of no particular person. "The man of sin" is in fact *all the men of sin,* or the spirit that works in them; for the conception is that, as Christ has brought forth a gospel, so it is inevitable that sin will foul that gospel in the han-

---

"the kingdom of evil." Cf. *A Theology for the Social Gospel* (New York, 1917), Chap. 9.

dling, and be a mystery of iniquity upon it. And this mystery of iniquity, as Paul saw, was already beginning to work, as work it must till it is taken out of the way. And this working is to be the revelation of evil through the gospel, and of the gospel through evil. It includes the dogmatic usurpation, the priestly assumptions, the mock sacraments, and all the church idols, brought in as improvements — every thing contributed to, and interwoven with, the gospel, by sin as a miracle of iniquity. When that process is carried through, the gospel will be understood; not before. It is also noticeable that what the devil or Satan is to God as a spirit, that also antichrist is to Christ, the incarnate God-man. Antichrist is, in fact, the devil of Christianity, as Satan is the devil of the creation and Providence. As the devil too is singled out and made eminent by the definite article, so is antichrist spoken of in the singular as one person. And then again, as there are many devils spoken of, so also it is declared that "now there are many antichrists."

Satan then is a bad possibility, eternally existing prior to the world's creation, becoming, or emerging there into, a bad actuality — which it is the problem of Jehovah's government to master. For it has been the plan of God, in the creation and training of the powers, so to bring them on as to finally vanquish the bad possibility or necessity that environed him before the worlds were made; so to create and subjugate, or, by his love, regenerate the bad powers loosened by his act of creation, as to have them in eternal dominion. And precisely here is he seen in the grandeur of his attitude. We might yield to some opinion of his weakness, when pondering the dark fatality by which he is encompassed in the matter of evil; but when we see his plan distinctly laid, as a fowler's when he sets his net; that he is disappointed by nothing, and that all his counsels unfold in their appointed time and order, as when a general marches on his army in a course of victory; that he sets good empire against evil empire, and, without high words against his adversary, calmly proceeds to accomplish a system of order that comprehends the subjugation of disorder, what majesty and grandeur invest his person! Nothing which he could have done by omnipotence, no silent peace of compulsion, no unconsenting order of things made fast by his absolute will, could have given any such impression of his greatness and glory, as this loosening of the possibility of evil, in the purpose finally to turn it about by his counsel and transform it by his goodness and patience. What significance and sublimity is there, holding such a view, in the ecstatic words of Christ, when just about to finish his work — "I beheld Satan as lightning fall from heaven"!

Nor any the less when his prophet testifies after him — "And the great dragon was cast out, that old serpent called the devil and Satan, which deceiveth the whole world." "Now is come salvation, and strength, and the kingdom of our Lord and of his Christ."

That salvation, strength, and kingdom, be it also observed, are not patches of mending laid upon the rent garment of a broken plan, but issues and culminations of the eternal plan itself. The cross of redemption is no afterthought, but is itself the grand all-dominating idea around which the eternal system of God crystallizes; Jesus Christ, the "appointed heir of all things" — "the Lamb slain from the foundation of the world." Here stands out the final end or cause of all things, here emerge the powers made strong and glorious. Weak, at first, unperfect, incomplete, they are now completed and glorified — complete in him, who is the head of all principality and power. . . .

Chapter VI

The Consequences of Sin

It is very evident that if sin is a fact, it must be followed by important consequences; for as it has a moral significance considered in the aspect of blameworthiness, guilt, penal desert, and remorse, so also it has a dynamic force, considered as acting on the physical order and sphere of nature; in the contact and surrounding of which, its transgressions take effect. In one view, it is the fall of virtue; in the other, it is the disorder and penal dislocation both of the soul and of the world. As crime, it demolishes the sacred and supernatural interests of character; as a force, operating through and among the retributive causes arranged for the vindication of God's law, it is the disruption of nature, a shock of disorder and pain that unsettles the apparent harmony of things, and reduces the world to a state of imperfect or questionable beauty.

What I now propose, then, is the investigation of sin regarded in the latter of these two aspects; or to show what consequences it operates or provokes in the field of nature.

It is not to be supposed that sin has power to annul or discontinue any one of the laws of nature. The same laws are in action after the sin, or under it, as before. And yet, these laws continuing the same, it is conceivable that sin may effect what is really, and to no small extent, a new resolution or combination, which is, to the ideally perfect state of nature, what disorder is to order, deformity to beauty, pain to peace. This, of course, it will do, if at all, by a force exerted in the material world, and through the laws of nature.

At the point of his will, man is a force, we have seen, outside of nature; a being supernatural, because he is able to act on the chain of cause and effect in nature from without the chain. It follows then, of course, that by acting in this manner upon nature, he can vary the action of nature from what would be its action, were there no such thing as a force external to the scheme. Nature, indeed, is submitted to him, as we have seen, for this very purpose; to be varied in its action by his action, to receive and return his action, so to be the field and medium of his exercise.

Thus it is a favorite doctrine of our times, that the laws of the world are retributive; so that every sin or departure from virtue will be faithfully and relentlessly punished. The very world, we say, is a moral economy, and is so arranged, under its laws, that retribution follows at the heels of all sin. And by this fact of retribution, we mean that disease, pain, sorrow, deformity, weakness, disappointment, defeat, all sorts of groanings, all sizes and shapes of misery, wait upon wrong-doers, and when challenged by their sin, come forth to handle them with their rugged and powerful discipline. We conceive that in this way the aspects of human society and the world are to a considerable degree determined. But we do not always observe that nature is, by the supposition, just so far displayed under a variation of disorder and disease. First appear the wrongs to be chastised, which are not included in the causations of nature, otherwise they were blameless; then the laws of nature, met by these provocations, commence a retributive action, such as nature, unprovoked, would never display. The sin has fallen into nature as a grain of sand into the eye — and as the eye is the same organ that it was before, having the same laws, and is yet so far changed as to be an organ of pain rather than of sight, so it is with the laws of nature, in their penal and retributive action now begun. Sin, therefore is, by the supposition, such a force as may suffice, in a society and world of sin, to vary the combinations, and display a new resolution of the activities, of nature. The laws remain, but they are met and provoked by a new ingredient not included in nature; and so the whole field of nature, otherwise a realm of harmony, and peace, and beauty, takes a look of discord, and, with many traces of its original glory left, displays the tokens also of a prison and a hospital.

Thus far we have spoken of the power there is in sin to provoke a different action of natural causes. It also has a direct action upon nature to produce other conjunctions of causes, and so, other results. The laws all continue their action as before, but the sin committed varies the combinations subject to their action, and in that manner the order of their working. Indeed, we have seen that nature is, to a certain extent, submitted by her laws to the action of free supernatural agents; which implies that her action can be varied by their sovereignty without displacing the laws, nay in virtue rather of the submission they are appointed to enforce. I thrust my hand, for example, into the fire, producing thus a new conjunction of causes, viz., fire and the tissues of the hand; and the result corresponds — a state of suffering and partial disorganization. In doing this, I have acted only through the laws of nature — the nervous cord has carried down my mandate to the muscles of the arm, the muscles have contracted obediently to the mandate, the fire has done its part, the nerves of sensation have brought back their report, all in due order, but the result is a pain or loss of the injured member, as opposite to any thing mere nature would have wrought by her own combinations, as if it were the fruit of a miracle. So it is with all the crimes of violence, robbery, murder, assassination. The knife in the assassin's hand is a knife, doing what a knife should, by the laws which determine its properties. The heart of the victim is a heart, beating on, subject to its laws, and, when it is pierced, driving out the blood from his opened side, as certainly as it before drove the living blood through the circulations of the body. But the thrust of the knife, which is from the assassin's will, makes a conjunction which nature, by her laws alone, would never make, and by force of this the victim dies. In like manner, a poison administered acts by its own laws, in the body of the victim, which body also acts according to its laws, and the result ensuing is death; which death is attributable not to the scheme of nature, but to a false conjunction of substances that was brought to pass wickedly, by a human will. In all these cases, the results of pain, disorder, and death are properly said to be unnatural; being, in a sense, violations of nature. The scheme of nature included no such results. They are disorders and dislocations made by the misconjunction or abuse of causes in the scheme of nature. And the same will be true of all the events that follow, in the vast complications and chains of causes, to the end of the world. Whatever mischief or unnatural result is thus brought to pass by sin, will be the first link of an endless chain of results not included in the scheme of nature, and so the beginning of an ever-widening circle of disturbance. And this is the true account of evil.

But it will occur to some that all human activities, the good as well as the bad, are producing new conjunctions of causes that otherwise would not exist. Mere nature will never set a wheel to the waterfall, or adjust the substances that compose a house or a steamboat. How then does it appear that the results of sin are called dislocations or disorders, or regarded as unnatural, with any greater propriety than the results of virtuous industry and all right action? Because, we answer, the scheme of nature is adjusted for uses, not for abuses; for improvement, culture, comfort, and advancing productiveness; not for destruction or corruption. Therefore, it consists with the scheme of nature that water-wheels, houses, and steamboats should be built; for all the substances and powers of nature are given to be harnessed for service, and when they are, it is no dislocation, but only a fulfilling of the natural order.

We come, also, to the same result by another and different process; viz., by considering what sin is in its relation to God and his works. In its moral conception, it is an act against God, or the will and authority of God. And since God is every where consistent with himself, setting all his creations in harmony with his principles, it is of course an act against the physical order, as truly as against the moral and spiritual. Taken as a dynamic, therefore, it wars with the scheme of nature, and fills it with the turmoil of its disorders and perversities. Or, if we take the concrete, speaking of the sinner himself, he is a substance, in a world of substances, acting as he was not made to act. He was not made to sin, and the world was not made to help him sin. The mind of God being wholly against sin, the cast of every world and substance is repugnant to sin. The transgressor, therefore, is a free power acting against God morally, and physically against the cast of every world and substance of God — acting in or among the worlds and substances as he was not made to act.

This, too, is the sentence of consciousness. The wrongdoer says within himself, "I was not made to act thus, no laws of cause and effect, acting through me, did the deed. I did it myself, therefore am I guilty. Had I been made for the sin, it had been no sin, but only a fulfillment of the ends included in my substance." And how terribly is this verdict certified by the discovery that the world refuses to bless him, and that all he does upon it is a work of deformity, shame, and disorder. The very substances of the world answer, as it were, in groans, to the violations of his guilty practice.

Suppose, then, what all natural philosophers assume, that nature, considered as a realm of cause and effect, is a perfect system of order; what must take place in that system when some one substance, no matter what, begins to act as it was not made to act? What can follow, but some general disturbance of the ideal harmony of the system itself? It will be as if some wheel or member in a watch had been touched by a magnet and began to have an action, thus, not intended by the maker; every other wheel and member will be affected by the vice of the one. Or it will be as if some planet or star, taking its own way, were to set itself on acting as it was not made to act; instantly the shock of disorder is felt by every other member of the system. Or we may draw an illustration closer to probability, from the vital forms of physiology. A vital creature is a kind of unit, or little universe, fashioned by the life. Thus an egg is a complete vital system, having all its vessels, ducts, fluids, quantities, and qualities, arranged to meet the action of the embryonic germ. Suppose, now, in the process of incubation, that some small speck, or point of matter, under the shell, should begin, as the germ quickens, to act as it was not made to act, or against the internal harmony of the process going on, what must be the result? Either a disease, manifestly, that stops the process, or else a deformity; a chick without a wing, or with one too many, or in some way imperfectly organized. What then must follow, when a whole order of substances called men, having an immense power over the lines of causes in the world, not only begin, but for thousands of years continue, and that on so large a scale that history itself is scarcely more than a record of the fact, to act as they were not made to act? We have only to raise this question to see that the scheme of nature is marred, corrupted, dislocated by innumerable disturbances and disorders. Her laws all continue, but her conjunctions of causes are unnatural. Immense transformations are wrought, which represent on a large scale the repugnant, disorderly fact of sin. Indeed what we call nature must be rather a condition of unnature; apostolically represented, a whole creation groaning and in pain together with man, in the disorder consequent on his sin.

The conclusion at which we thus arrive is one that will be practically verified by inspection. Let us undertake then a brief survey of the great departments of human existence and the world, and discover, as far as we are able, the extent of the evil consequences wrought by sin.

We begin with the soul or with souls. The soul in its normal state, including the will or supernatural power, together with the involuntary powers subordinated to it by their laws, is an instrument tuned by the keynote of the conscience, viz. *right*, to sound harmoniously with it; or it is a fluid, we may say, whose form, or law of crystallization is the conscience. And then it follows that, if the will breaks into revolt, the instrument is mistuned in every string, the fluid shaken becomes a shapeless, opaque mass, without unity or crystalline order. Or, if we resort to the analogies of vital phenomena, which are still closer, a revolted will is to the soul, or in it, what a foreign unreducible substance is in the vital and vascular system of the egg, or (to repeat an illustration), what a grain of sand is in the eye — the soul has become a weeping organ, not an organ simply of sight. Given the fact of sin, the fact of a fatal breach in the normal state or constitutional order of the soul follows of necessity. And exactly this we shall see if we look in upon its secret chambers and watch the motions of sins in the confused ferment they raise — the perceptions discolored, the judgments unable to hold their scales steadily because of the fierce gusts of passion, the thoughts huddling by in crowds of wild suggestion, the imagination haunted by ugly and disgustful shapes, the appetites contesting with reason, the senses victorious over faith, anger blowing the overheated fires of malice, low jealousies sulking in dark angles of the soul, and envies baser still, hiding under the skim of its green-mantled pools — all the powers that should be strung in harmony loos-ened from each other, and brewing in hopeless and helpless confusion; the conscience meantime thundering wrathfully above and shooting down hot bolts of judgment, and the pallid fears hurrying wildly about with their brimstone torches — these are the motions of sins, the Tartarean landscape of the soul and its disorders, when self-government is gone and the constituent integrity is dissolved. We can not call it the natural state of man, nature disowns it. No one that looks in upon the ferment of its morbid, contesting, rasping, restive, uncontrollable action can imagine for a moment that he looks upon the sweet, primal order of life and nature. No name sufficiently describes it, unless we coin a name and call it a con-dition of unnature.

Not that any law of the soul's nature is discontinued, or that any capac-ity which makes one a proper man is taken away by the bad inheritance, as appears to be the view of some theologians; every function of thought and feeling remains, every mental law continues to run; the disorder is that of functions abused and laws of operation provoked to a penal and retributive action, by the misdoings of an evil will. Though it is become in this manner a weeping organ, as we just now intimated, still it is an organ of sight; only it sees through tears. And the profound reality of the disorder appears in the fact that the will by which it was wrought can not, unassisted, repair it. To do this, in fact, is much the same kind of impos-sibility — the phrenologists will say precisely the same — as for a man who has disorganized his brain by over-exertion, or by steeping it in opium, or drenching it in alcohol, to take hold, by his will, of the millions of ducts and fibers woven together in the mysterious network of its substance, and bring them all back into the spontaneous order of health and spiritual integrity.

No! it is one thing to break or shatter an organization, and a very different [one] to restore it. Almost any one can break an egg, but not all the chemists in the world can make one whole, or restore even so much as the slightest fracture of the shell. As little can a man will back, into order and tune, this fearfully vast and delicate complication of faculties; which indeed he can not even conceive, except in the crudest manner, by the study of a life.

It is important also, considering the moral reactions of the body, and especially the great fact of a propagation of the species, to notice the disorganizing effect of sin in the body. Body and soul, as long as they subsist in their organized state, are a strict unity. The abuses of one are abuses also of the other, the disturbances and diseases of one disturb and disease the other. The fortunes of the body must, in this way, follow the fortunes of the soul, whose organ it is. Sin has all its working too in the working of the brain. To think an evil thought, indulge a wicked purpose or passion, will, in this view, be much as if the sin had brought in a grain of sand and lodged it in the tissues of the brain. That then must be the effect, when every path in its curious network of intelligence is traveled, year by year, by the insulting myriads of sinning thought, hardened by the tramp of their feet, and dusted by their smoky trail!

But we are speaking theoretically. If we turn to practical evidences, or matters of fact, we shall see plainly enough that what should follow, in the effects of sin upon the body, actually does follow. How the vices of the appetites and passions terminate in diseases and a final disorganization of the body, is well understood. The false conjunction made by intemperate drink, deluging the tissues of the body with its liquid poisons, and reducing the body to a loathsome wreck, is not peculiar to that vice. The condition of sin is a condition of general intemperance. It takes away the power of self-government, loosens the passions, and makes even the natural appetite for food an instigator of excess. Indeed, how many of the sufferings and infirmities even of persons called virtuous are known by all intelligent physicians to be only the groaning of the body under loads habitually imposed, by the untempered and really diseased voracity of their appetites. And if we could trace all the secret actions of causes, how faithfully would the fevers, the rheumatisms, the neuralgic and hypochondriacal torments, all the grim-looking woes of dyspepsia, be seen to follow the unregulated license of this kind of sin. Nor is any thing better understood than that whatever vice of the mind — wounded pride, unregulated ambition, hatred, covetousness, fear, inordinate care — throws the mind out of rest, throws the body out of rest also. Thus it is that sin, in all its forms, becomes a power of bodily disturbance, shattering the nerves, inflaming the tissues, distempering the secretions, and brewing a general ferment of disease. In one view, the body is a kind of perpetual crystallization, and the crystal of true health can not form itself under sin, because the body has within a perpetual agitating cause which forbids the process. If then, looking round upon the great field of humanity, and noting the almost universal working of disease, in so many forms and varieties that they can not be named or counted, we sometimes exclaim with a sigh, what a hospital the world is! we must be dull spectators, if we stop at this, and do not also connect the remembrance that sin is in the world; a gangrene of the mind, poisoning all the roots of health and making visible its woes, by so many woes of bodily disease and death.

The particular question, whether bodily mortality has entered the world by sin, we will not discuss. That is principally a Scripture question, and the word of Scripture is not to be assumed in my argument. There obviously might have been a mode of translation to the second life that should have none of the painful and revolting incidents which constitute the essential reality of death. We do moreover know that a very considerable share of the diseases and deaths of our race are the natural effects of sin or wrongdoing. There is great reason also to suspect, so devastating is the power of moral evil, that the infections and deadly plagues of the world are somehow generated by this cause. They seem to have their spring in some new virus of death, and this new virus must have been somewhere and somehow distilled or generated. We can not refer them to mineral causes, or vegetable, or animal, which are nearly invariable, and they seem, as they begin their spread at some given locality, to have a humanly personal origin. That the virus of a poisonous and deadly contagion has been generated by human vices, we know as a familiar fact of history; which makes it the more probable that other pestilential contagions have been generated in the deteriorated populations and sweltering vices of the East, whence our plagues are mostly derived. On this point we assert nothing as a truth positively discovered; we only design, by these references, to suggest the possible (and, to us, probable) extent and power of that ferment, brewed by the instigations of sin, in the diseased populations of the world. What we suggest respecting the virus of the world's plagues may be true or it may not; this at least is shown beyond all question, that sin is a widespreading, dreadful power of bodily distemper and disorganization, which is the point of principal consequence to our argument.

Passing now to society and the disorganizing effects of sin there to appear, we see at a glance that if the soul and body are both distempered and reduced to a state of unnature, the great interest of society must suffer in a correspondent manner and degree. Considered as a growth or propagation, humanity is, in some very important sense, an organic whole. If the races are not all descended of a single pair, but of several or even many pairs, as is now strenuously asserted by some, both on grounds of science and of Scripture interpretation, still it makes no difference as regards the matter of their practical and properly religious unity. The genus humanity is still a single genus comprehending the races, and we know from geology that they had a begun existence. That they also sinned at the beginning is as clear, from the considerations already advanced, as if they had been one. Whence it follows that descendants of the sinning pair, or pairs, born of natures thrown out of harmony and corrupted by sin, could not, on principles of physiology, apart from Scripture teachings, be unaffected by the distempers of their parentage. They must be constituently injured, or depravated. It is not even supposable that organic natures, injured and disordered as we have seen that human bodies are by sin, should propagate their life in a progeny unmarred and perfect. If we speak of sin as action, their children may be innocent, and so far may reveal the loveliness of innocence — still the crystalline order is broken; the passions, tempers, appetites, are not in the proportions of harmony and reason; the balance of original health is gone by anticipation; and a distempered action is begun, whose affinities sort with evil rather than with good. It is as if, by their own sin, they had just so far distempered their organization. Thus far the fruit of sin is in them. And this the Scriptures, in a certain popular, comprehensive way, sometimes call "sin"; because it is a condition of depravation that may well enough be taken as the root of a guilty, sinning life. They do not undertake to settle metaphysically the point where personal guilt commences, but only suit their convenience in a comprehensive term that designates the race as sinners; passing by those speculative questions that only divert attention from the salvation provided for a world of sinners. The doctrine of physiology therefore is the doctrine of original sin, and we are held to inevitable orthodoxy by it, even if the Scriptures are cast away.

But if the laws of propagation contain the fact, in this manner, of an organic depravation of humanity or human society, under sin once broken loose, many will apprehend in such a fact some ground of impeachment against God; as if he had set us on our trial under terms of the sorest disadvantage. If we start, they ask, under conditions of hereditary damage, with natures depravated and affinities already distempered by the sin of progenitors, as truly as if we had commenced the bad life ourselves, what is our bad life when we begin it, but the natural issue of our hopeless, misbegotten constitution? It is no sufficient answer to say that no blame attaches to the mere depravation supposed, whether it be called sin or by any other name; it shocks them to hear it even suggested that a good being like God can have set us forth in our trial under such immense disadvantages. Probably enough they assail the doctrine of inherited depravity, in terms of fiery denunciation, whether taken as a dogma set up by theologians, or as being affirmed by Christian revelation itself; not observing that it is the inevitable fact also of human history and, admitting the fact of sin, a necessary deduction even of physiological science.

Now so far from admitting the supposed disadvantage incurred by this organic depravation of the race, or the mode of existence to which it pertains as a natural incident, we are led to an opinion exactly opposite. Indeed there appears to be no other way possible, in which the race could have been set forth on their trial, with as good chances of a successful and happy issue.

Thus, taking it for granted that God is to create a moral population, or a population of free intelligences, that having a begun existence, are to be educated into, and finally established in, good, there were obviously two methods possible. They might always be created outright in full volume, like so many Adams, only to exist independently and apart from all reproductive arrangements, or they might be introduced, as we are, in the frail and barely initiated existence of the infantile state, each generation born of the preceding, and altogether composing a rigidly constituent organic unity of races.

In the former case they would have the advantage of a perfectly uncorrupted nature, and, if that be any advantage, of a full maturity in what may be called the raw staple of their functions. But such advantages amount to scarcely more than the opportunity of a greater and more tremendous peril; for being all, by supposition, under the same conditions privative with the first man of Scripture, they would as certainly do the same things, descending to the same bad experiment, to be involved in the same consequent fall and disorder. They would only be more strictly original in their depravation, having it as the fruit of their own guilty choices.

And then, as regards all mitigating and restoring influences, the comparative disadvantage would be immense. Self-centered now, every man in his sin, and having no ligatures of race and family and family affection to bind them together, the selfishness of their fall would be unqualified, softened by no mitigations. Spiritual love they can not understand, because they never have felt the natural love of sex, family, and kindred, by which, under conditions of propagation, a kind of inevitable, first-stage virtue is instituted; such as mitigates the severities of sin, softens the sentiments to a social, tender play, and offers to the mind a type, every where present, of the beauty and true joy of a disinterested, spiritual benevolence. They compose, instead, a burly prison-gang of probationers, linked together by no ties of consanguinity, reflecting no traces of family likeness, bent to each other's and God's love by no dear memories. Society there is none. Law is impossible. Society and law suppose conditions of organic unity already prepared. Every man for himself, is the grand maxim of life; for all are atoms together, in the medley of the common selfishness; only the old atoms have an immense advantage over the young ones fresh arrived; for these newcomers of probation come of course to the prey, having no guardians or protectors, and no tender sentiments of care and kindred prepared to shelter them and smooth their way. Besides, the world into which they come must have been already fouled and disordered by the sin of the prior populations, and must therefore be a frame of being wholly inappropriate to their new-created innocence; or else, if not thus disordered, must have been a casement of iron, too rigid and impassive to receive any injury from sin, and therefore incapable of any retributive discipline returned upon it. There is, in short, no condition of trial which, after all, is seen to be so utterly forbidding and hopeless as just this state of Adamic innocence, independence, and maturity of faculty, which many are so ready to require of God as the only method of promise and fair advantage, in the beginning of a responsible life.

How different the condition realized where men are propagated as a race or races. Then are they linked together by a necessary, constituent, anticipative love. Moved by this love, the progenitors are immediately set to a work of care and benefaction, beautifully opposite to the proper selfishness of their sin. The delicate and tender being received to their embrace circulates their blood, will bear their name, and is looked upon, even by their selfishness, as a multiplied and dearer self. They are even made to feel, in a lower and more rudimental way, what joy there is in a disinterested love; and they pour out their fondness, in ways that even try their invention, instigated by the compulsory bliss of sacrifice. They want the best things too for their child, even his virtue; and probably enough his religious virtue; for they dread the bitter woes of wrong-doing. This is true, at least, of all but such as have fallen below nature in their vices, and ceased to hear her voice. They even undertake to be a providence, and do for their child all which the love of God, even till now rejected, has been seeking to do for themselves; commanding him away from wrong, and warning him faithfully of its dangers. Besides it is a great point, in the scheme of propagated life, that the child learns how to be grown, so to speak, into, and exist in, another will; which is an immense advantage to the religious nurture, even where the parental character is not good. He is not like a population of untutored, unregulated Adams, who have just come to the finding of a man's will in them, and do not know how to use it, least of all how to sink it obediently in the sovereign will and authority of God. The child's will grew in authority, and he comes out gently, in the reverence of a subordinated habit, to choose the way of obedience, having his religious conscience configured and trained by a kind of family conscience, previously developed. There is almost no family therefore — none except the very worst and most depraved — in which the rule of the house is not a great spiritual benefit, and a means even of religious virtue. How much more where the odor of a heavenly piety fills the house and sanctifies the atmosphere of life itself! Instead of being set forth as an overgrown man, issued from the Creator's hand to make the tremendous choice, undirected by experience, he is gently inducted, as it were, by choices of parents before his own, into the habit and accepted practice of all holy obedience; growing up in the nurture of their grace, as truly as of their natural affection. Furthermore, as corruption or depravation is propagated, under well-known laws of physiology, what are we to think but that a regenerate life may be also propagated; and that so the Scripture truth of a sanctification from the womb may sometime cease to be a thing remarkable and become a commonly ex-

pected fact? And then, if a point should finally be reached, under the sublime *palingennesia* of redemption, when Christian faith, together with its
fruits of nurture and sanctified propagation, should be nearly or quite
universal, and the world, which is now in its infancy, should roll on, millions of ages after, training its immense populations for the skies, how
magnificently preponderant the advantages of the plan of propagation,
which at first we thought could be only a plan to set us out in the wrong,
and sacrifice our virue by anticipation!

This comparison, which might otherwise seem to be a disgression, will
effectually remove those false impressions so generally prevalent concerning God's equity in the fact of natural corruption; and if this be done, a
chief impediment to all right conceptions of the human state, as affected
by sin, will be removed. In this manner, wholly apart from the Scriptures,
instructed only by the laws of physiology, we discover the certain truth
of an organic fall or social lapse in the race; we find humanity broken,
disordered, plunged into unnature by sin; but dark and fearful as the state
may be, there is nothing in it unhopeful, nothing to accuse. We are only
where we should be, each by his own act, if we were created independently; with immense advantages added to mitigate the hopelessness of our
disorder.

It is very true that, under these physiological terms of propagation, society falls or goes down as a unit, and evil becomes, in a sense, organic in
the earth. The bad inheritance passes, and fears, frauds, crimes against
property, character and life, abuses of power, oppressions of the weak,
persecutions of the good, piracies, wars of revolt, and wars of conquest,
are the staple of the world's bitter history. All that Mr. Fourier has said
of society, in its practical operation, is true; it is a pitiless and dreadful
power, as fallen society should be. And yet it is a condition of existence
far less dreadful than it would be if the organic force of natural affinities
and affections were not operative still, in the desolations of evil, to produce institutions, construct nations, and establish a condition of qualified
unity and protection. Otherwise, or existing only as separate units, in
no terms of consanguinity, we should, probably, fall into a state of utter
non-organization, or, what is the same, of universal prey. The grand woe
of society, therefore, is not, as this new prophet of science teaches, the
bad organization of society; but that good organization, originally beautiful and beneficent, can only mitigate, but can not shut away, the evils by
which it is infested. The line of propagation is, in one view, the line of
transmission by which evil passes; but it is, at the same time, a sure spring

of solidarity and organific power, by which all the principal checks and mitigations of evil, save those which are brought in with the grace of supernatural redemption, are supplied. Otherwise the state of evil, untransmitted and purely original in all, would make a hell of anarchy, unendurable and final. . . .

It now remains to carry our inquest one step farther. If sin has power, taken as a dynamic, to affect the soul, the body, and society, in the manner already indicated, reducing all these departments of nature to a state unnatural, it should not be incredible that it may also have power to produce a like disorder in the material or physical world. The immense power of the human will over the physical substances of the world and the conjunctions of its causes, is seldom adequately conceived. Almost every thing, up to the moon, is capable of being somehow varied or affected by it. Being a force supernatural, it is continually playing itself into the chemistries and external combinations of matter, converting shapes, reducing or increasing quantities, transferring positions, framing and dismembering conjunctions, turning poisons into medicines, and reducing fruits to poisons, till at length scarcely any thing is left in its properly natural state. Some of these changes, which it is the toil of human life to produce, are beneficent; and a multitude of others represent, alas! too faithfully, the prime distinction of sin; the acting of a power against God, or as it was not made to act. Could we only bring together into a complete inventory all the new structures, compositions, inventions, shapes, qualities, already produced by man, which are, in fact, the furniture only of his sin — means of self-indulgence, instruments of violence, shows of pride, instigations of appetite, incitements and institutes of corrupt pleasure, all the leprosies and leper-houses of vice, the prisons of oppression, the hospitals and battlefields of war — we should see a face put on the world which God never gave it, and which only represents the bad conversion it has suffered, under the immense and ever-industrious perversities of sin.

But we must carry our search to a point that is deeper and more significant. In what is called nature we find a large admixture of signs or objects which certainly do not belong to an ideal state of beauty, and do not, therefore, represent the mind of God, whence they are supposed to come. The fact is patent every where, and yet the superficial and hasty multitudes appear to take it for granted, that all the creations of God are beautiful of course. They either assume it as a necessary point of reverence, or deduce it as a point of reason, that whatever comes from God represents the thought of God; being cast in the mold of his thought, which is divine beauty itself. Not only do the poets and poetasters in prose go the round of nature, sentimentalizing among her dews and flowers, and paying their worship at her shrine, as if the world were a gospel even of beauty; but our philosophers often teach it as a first principle, and our natural theologians assume it also in their arguments, that the forms of things must represent the perfect forms of the divine thought, by which they were fashioned. It would seem that such a conceit might be dissipated by a single glance of revision; for God is the infinite beauty, and who can imagine, looking on this or that half dry and prosy scene of nature, that it represents the infinite beauty? The fact of creation argues no such thing. For what if it should happen to have been a part of God's design in the work to represent, not himself only as the pure and perfect One, the immutable throne of law and universal order, but quite as truly, and in immediate proximity, to represent man to himself; that he may see both what he is for, and what he is, and struggle up out of one into the other. Then, or in that view, it would be the perfection of the world, taken in its moral adaptations, that it is not perfect, and does not answer to the beauty of the creative mind, save under the large qualification specified.

And exactly this appears to be the true conception of the physical world. What does it mean, for example, that the vital organizations are continually seen to be attempting products which they can not finish? Thus a fruit tree covers itself with an immense profusion of blossoms that drop, and do not set in fruit. And then, of those fruits which are set, an immense number fall, strewing the ground with deaths — tokens all of an abortive attempt in nature, if we call it nature, to execute more than she can finish. And this we see in all the growths of the world — they lay out more than they can perform. Is this the ideal perfection of nature, or is there some touch of unnature and disorder in it? Is God the Creator represented in this? Does he put himself before us in this manner, as a being who attempts more fruits than he can produce? Or is there a hint in it, for man, of what may come to pass in himself? an image under which we may conceive himself and fitly represent himself in language? a token, also, and proof of that most real abortion, to which he may bring even his immortal nature, despite of all the saving mercies of God?

Swedenborg [3] and his followers have a way of representing, I believe,

3. [ED.] Emanuel Swedenborg (1688–1772), Swedish scientist and theologian, was the father of the New Jerusalem Church. His ideas at one time attracted considerable

that God creates the world through man, by which they understand that
what we call the creation is a purely gerundive matter — God's perpetual
act — and that he holds the work *to man*, at every stage, so as to represent
him always at his present point, and act upon him fitly to his present taste.
Not far off is Jonathan Edwards's conception of God's upholding of the
universe — it is in fact a perpetual reproduction; the creation, so called,
being to his person what the image in a mirror is to the person before it,
from whom it proceeds and by whom it is sustained.[4] Indeed this latter
conception runs into the other, and becomes identical with it, as soon as
we take in the fact, that God is always being and becoming to man, both
in counsel and feeling, what is most exactly fit to man's character and
want; for, in that view, God's image, otherwise called his creation, will be
all the while receiving a color from man, and will so far be configured to
him. Accordingly we look, in either view, to see the cosmos or outward
frame of things held to man, linked to his fortunes to rise and fall with
him, and so, under certain limitations, to give him back his doings and
represent him to himself — representing God, in fact, the more adequately
that it does.

The doctrine of types in the physical world, to represent conditions of
character and changes of fortune in the spiritual, is only another conception of the same general truth. And this doctrine of types we know to be
true in part; for language itself is possible only in virtue of the fact that
physical types are provided, as bases of words, having each a natural fitness to represent some spiritual truth of human life; which is in fact the
principal use and significance of language. Whence also it follows that if
human life is disordered, perverted, reduced to a condition of unnature
by sin, there must also be provided, as the necessary condition of language, types that represent so great a change; which is equivalent to saying that the fortunes of the outer world must, to some very great extent,
follow the fortunes of the occupant and groan with him in his disorders.

Or we are brought to a conclusion essentially the same, by considering
the complete and perfect unity of natural causes; how they form a dynamic whole, resting in an exact balance of mutual relationship, so that if
any world, or particle, starts from its orbit, or position, every other
world and particle feels the change. What then must follow when the

attention in New England. Bushnell's personal library contained many of his writings,
including *A Brief Exposition of the Doctrine of the New Church* (Boston, 1831), and
The True Christian Religion (Boston, 1843).

4. [ED.] *Cf.* Jonathan Edwards, "The Great Christian Doctrine of Original Sin Defended," *Works of President Edwards*, Sereno Dwight, ed. (10 vols., 1829-30), II,
551-55.

given force or substance man begins and for long ages continues to act as he was not made to act; out of character, against God, refusing place, and breaking out on every side from the general scheme of unity and harmony, in which the creation was to be comprehended? What can his human disorder be, but a propagating cause of disorder? What his deformity within, but a soul of deformity without, in the surroundings of the field he occupies? . . .

Chapter VII

Anticipative Consequences

In the account offered of the consequences of sin, we have spoken of these consequences as effects transpiring under laws, and so as matters *post* in respect to the fact of sin. The result stated coincides, in all but the positive or inflictive form, with the original curse denounced on man's apostasy, as represented in the Adamic history or sin-myth, as some would call it, of the ancient Scriptures. That primal curse, it is conceived, penetrates the very ground as a doom of sterility, covers it with thorns and thistles and all manner of weeds to be subdued by labor, makes it weariness to live, brings in death with its armies of pains and terrors to hunt us out of life, and so unparadises the world. Call it then a myth, disallow the notion of a positive infliction as being unphilosophical; still the matter of the change, or general world-lapse asserted in it, is one of the grandest, most massive, best-attested truths included in human knowledge. It is just that which ought to be true, under the conditions, and which we have found, by inspection also, to be true as a matter of fact.

Still there is a difficulty, or a great and hitherto insufficiently explored question, that remains. It is the question of date or time; for when we speak, as in the previous chapter, of the consequences of sin, we seem to imply that upon or after the fact of sin, the physical order of the world, affected by the shock, underwent a great change that amounted to a fall; becoming, from that point onward, a realm of deformity and discord, as before it was not, and displaying, in all its sceneries and combinations, the tokens of a broken constitution. All which, it will readily occur to any one, can not, in that form, be true. For the sturdy facts of science rise up to confront us in such representations, testifying that death, and prey, and deformed objects, and hideous monsters, were in the world long before the arrival of man. Nay, the rocks open their tombs and show us that older curses than the curse, older consequences antedating sin, had already set their marks on the world and had even made it, more than once, an Aceldama of the living races.[5]

"I need scarce say," remarks Hugh Miller, "that the paleontologist finds no trace in nature of that golden age of the world of which the poets delighted to sing, when all creatures lived together in unbroken peace, and war and bloodshed were unknown. Ever since animal life began upon our planet, there have existed, in all the departments of being, carnivorous classes, who could not live but by the death of their neighbors; and who were armed, in consequence, for their destruction, like the butcher with his knife and the angler with his hook and spear." [6] This being true, the paradisaic history, as commonly understood, is still farther off from a possible verification, unless we suppose the curse to be there reported as a fact subsequent, though latently incorporate before, because it is there discovered, and plainly could not be conceived, at that time, as the facts of future science may require.

For the true solution of this apparent collision between geologic revelations and the paradisaic history, lies in the fact which many have not considered, that there are two modes of consequence, or two kinds of consequences; those which come as effects under physical causes, and have their time as events subsequent; and those which come anticipatively, or before the facts whose consequences they are, because of intellectual conditions, or because intelligence, affected by such facts, apprehended before the time, could not act as being ignorant of them. These two modes of consequence, and particularly the latter, now demand our attention.

As regards the former — the consequences of suffering and dislocation that follow sin, as effects in time subsequent — there is happily not much requiring to be said; for the truth on that subject is familiar, and is in fact over-much insisted on by the modern teachers. . . .

We come now to the matter of the anticipative consequences; where it will be required of us to speak more carefully and to dwell longer.

5. [ED.] James Dana (1813–95), who taught natural history (geology) at Yale, was critical of Bushnell's notions at this point. Cf. "Anticipations of Man in Nature," *New Englander*, XVII (1859), 293–334.

6. *Testimony of the Rocks* (Boston, 1857), p. 99. [ED.] Hugh Miller (1805–56), a native of Scotland, was a journalist and practical geologist. His *Testimony of the Rocks* and *Footprints of the Creator* (1849) were unusually popular in the United States.

And here the first thing to be noted, as respects the consequences of sin in our particular world, is that the subsequent effects of the sin of other beings might very well bring in disorders here that anticipate the arrival of man. There had been other moral beings in existence doubtless before the creation of man.[7] So, in fact, the Scriptures themselves testify. They also testify that some such were evil and, as we are left to judge, fixed in a reprobate character, by long courses of evil. As they are shown to have had access to our world, after we came in as a race to possess it, so doubtless they had been visitors and travelers in it, if we may so speak, during all the long geologic eras that preceded our coming — hovering it may be in the smoke and steam, or watching for congenial sounds and sights among the crashing masses and grinding layers, even before the huge monsters began to wallow in the ooze of the waters, or the giant birds to stalk along the hardening shores. What they did, in this or that geologic layer of the world, we of course know not. As little do we know in what numbers they appeared, or by what deeds of violence and wrong they disfigured the existing order. We do not even know that the successive extinctions of so many animal races, and the deformities found in so many of the now existing races, were not somehow referable to the audacity of their wrongs and the bitter woe of their iniquities. . . . Finding then tokens of deformity and prey, and objects of disgust appearing in the world, long ages before it was inhabited by man, we are not hastily to infer that these are not actual consequences of sin. They may be such, in the strictest terms of retributive causality, though not as related to the sins of man. Preceding that, by long ages of time, they may yet be subsequent and penal effects, as related to older, vaster, outlying populations of sinners that had visited, or sent the shock of their sin into the world, before the human race appeared.

It is not proposed, however, to account for all the previously existing marks of evil in the world in this manner. It is most agreeable not to do it. For we shall easily convince ourselves that vast realms of consequences, and these as real as any, precede, and in rational order ought to precede, their grounds or occasions. Indeed it is the peculiar distinction of consequences mediated by intelligence, that they generally go before, and prepare the coming of events to which they relate. Whoever plants a state erects a prison, or makes the prison to be a necessary part of his plan;

7. [ED.] Evidently Bushnell was impressed with the pre-Adamite theory which was then under discussion. For an account of the literature on that theory, see Alexander Winchell, *Preadamites; or, A Demonstration of the Existence of Men Before Adam* (Chicago, 1880), Chap. 29.

which prison, though it be erected before any case of felony occurs, is just as truly a consequence of the felonies to be, as if it were erected afterward, or were a natural result of such felonies. All the machinery of discipline in a school, or an army, is prepared by intelligence, perceiving beforehand the certain want of discipline hereafter to appear, and is just as truly a consequence of the want, as if it were created by the want itself, without any mediation of intelligence. . . .

This too, so far from being any subject of wonder, is even a kind of necessary incident of intelligence. For every thing that comes into the view of intelligence, must also pass into the plans of intelligence. How can any intelligent being frame a plan, so as to make no account of what is really in his knowledge? Or how could the all-knowing God arrange a scheme of providential order, just as if he did not know the coming fact of sin, eternally present to his knowledge? Mind works under conditions of unity, and, above all, Perfect Mind. What God has eternally in view, therefore, as the certain fact of sin, that fact about which all highest counsel in his government must revolve, and upon the due management of which all most eventful and beneficent issues in his kingdom depend, must pervade his most ancient beginnings and crop out in all the layers and eras of his process, from the first chapter of creative movement onward. As certainly as sin is to be encountered in his plan, its marks and consequences will be appearing anticipatively, and all the grand arrangements and cycles of time will be somehow preluding its approach, and the dire encounter to be maintained with it. To create and govern a world, through long eras of time, and great physical revulsions, yet never discover to our view any token that he apprehends the grand cataclysm of sin that is approaching, till after the fact is come, he must be much less than a wise, all-perceiving Mind. Much room would be left for the doubt, whether he is any mind at all; for it is the way of mind to weave all counsel and order into a web of visible unity. . . .

In this and the preceding chapter, we have now traced the consequences of sin: there the consequences that must needs follow it, as effects their causes, showing what results of mischief and disorder it reveals in the soul, the body, society, and the world; here accounting for a large display of correspondent facts in the geologic history precedent, or before the arrival of man, showing that they still are as truly consequences of the fact of sin as the others, being only just those marks that God's intelligence, planning the world and shaping it, even from eternity, to the uses and issues of a trial comprehending sin, must needs display. Sin, it will be seen, is, in this view, a very great, world-transforming, world-uncreating fact, and no such mere casualty or matter by the way as the superficial naturalism or half-naturalistic Christianity of our time supposes. It is that central fact about which the whole creation of God and the ordering of his providential and moral government revolves. The impression of many appears to be, that sin is this or that particular act of wrong, which men sometimes do, but which most men do not, unless at distant intervals; and who can imagine that any thing very serious depends on these rather exceptional misdeeds, when, on the whole, the account is balanced by so many shows of virtue? The triviality and shallowness of such conceptions are hardly to be spoken of with patience. It is not seen that when a man even begins to sin he must needs cast away the principle, first, of all holy obedience, and go down, thus, into a general lapse of condition, to be a soul broken loose from principle and separated from the inspirations of God. Only a very little philosophy too, conceiving the fact that sin is the acting of a substance, man, as he was not made to act, must suffice to the discovery that, in a system, or scheme of perfect order, it will start a ferment of discord among causes, that will propagate itself in every direction, carrying widespread desolation into the remotest circles. The whole solidarity of being in the creation, physical and spiritual, is necessarily penetrated by it and configured to it. Character, causes, things prior and *post*, all that God embraces in the final causes of existence, somehow feel it, and the whole creation groans and travails for the pain of it. The true cosmos, in the highest and most perfectly ideal sense of that term, does not exist. Nature is become unnature.

2. Two False Gospels [1]

EDITOR'S INTRODUCTION

If the consequences of the fall are really as devastating as the preceding text has indicated, what is the solution to man's predicament? Preparatory to giving the Christian answer, Bushnell analyzed two false gospels: (1) natural progress, and (2) self-culture.

As his life drew toward its close, he became increasingly disturbed over the growing popularity of the idea of progress as viewed from within the terms of mere natural causation. Thus in January 1869 he published

1. *Nature and the Supernatural* (New York, 1858), 220–41

an incisive article on "Progress," critically evaluating "the very ill-considered theories and schemes of progress" as held by Darwin, Von Humboldt, Spencer, and Emerson.[2] Commenting in a satirical vein, he remarked of Emerson: "He is for progress, preaches progress, finds a gospel of progress in Nature, and would probably pray for progress if he thought Nature would hear." [3]

Bushnell, however, did not denounce the idea of progress as such; he only opposed the supposition that progress could take place on a non-theistic basis. Referring to the theorists in question, he wrote: "Their fault is that they hang their progress on causes, not on God as the fontal source and regulative end of causations. They all agree . . . in looking for a progress whose beginning and law is in itself, descending out of some blind eternity that is nowise beholden to God. They make a God, in fact, of progress itself, and appear to want no other." [4] Bushnell did not elaborate his own position; nevertheless, he said enough to indicate that he held a somewhat optimistic view of history, despite his realistic doctrine of the fall.[5] But this optimism, it must be noted, rested upon a profound faith in the redemptive power of the Christian gospel.

Bushnell offered no encouragement to those who expected to cure their moral disease by mere self-culture. As he observed, man can willfully shatter the moral integrity of his soul, but he cannot by any amount of will power restore its integrity. Restoration is of God, or there is none.

❖ ❖ ❖ ❖

Chapter VIII

No Remedy in Development, or Self-Reformation

We are now at the point of catastrophe in God's plan, where it is next in order to look about for some remedial agency, or dispensation, that shall restore the lapse and bring out those results of order and happiness that were proposed by God, as we must believe, in his act of creation. Are we then shut up to nature and the hope that she will surmount her own catastrophe, or may we believe that her inherent weakness will be complemented by a supernatural and divine movement, that shall organize a new economy of life?

The former is the ground taken by all the naturalizing classes of our

2. "Progress," *Hours at Home*, VIII (January 1869), 197–210.   3. *Ibid.*, 202.
4. *Ibid.*, 204.   5. *Ibid.*, 206–10.

time. Nothing can take place, they say, which is not operated under and by the laws of nature. To believe that any thing can take place which is from without, or from above the laws of nature, is unphilosophical and savors of credulity. That there is such a thing as misdirection they will admit, and some will admit also the fact of sin; and it will be agreed by them all that, in consequence either of misdirection or of sin, there are a great many apparent disasters and disorders in the world, or especially in human society, that want some kind of remedy. Our present object is to look into their principal remedies, or grounds of expected restoration, and try what virtue there is in them. They are two, or presented under two distinct forms, both of which may be taken as rival gospels opposite to Christianity.

By the class who formally reject, or ignore Christianity, development is regarded as the universal panacea — all the apparent evils of the world are to be cured by development.

The class who professedly teach and believe the Christian gospel, reducing it still to a mere scheme of ethics, or natural virtue, rely more on the individual will to be exerted in self-government, self-culture, and the doing of justice, mercy, and other good works.

Of these rival gospels, both from within the terms of nature, I will now speak, in their order.

1. Of development, or as it is often phrased, the natural progress of the race.

The world is just now taken, as never before, with ideas of progress. The human race, it is conceived, exists under laws of progress. The philosophers, or would-be philosophers, have even undertaken to reduce the laws of progress to a scientific statement. They conceive that all the advanced races of mankind began at the level of the savage state, and have been set forward to their present pitch of culture, civilization, wealth, and liberty, by laws of development in mere nature. The multitude go after them, embracing the welcome idea of progress only the more enthusiastically, that they are so much taken with the new word *development*, conceiving that there is great science in it, or, at least, some unknown kind of power. If there are any evils or bitter woes in society, development is going to cure them; for the laws of development are at work to produce progress, and they will as certainly do it, as the laws of matter will determine its motions. All crime and sin are going finally to be cured in this manner, and character is going finally to blossom on the broken stock of nature, even as flowers are developed out of stocks not broken, and roots not poisoned by disease. Finding thus a gospel of progress in the world itself and the mere laws of existence, what need of any such anti-quated mythology as the Christian gospel brings us? Or, if the argument is not openly stated in this manner, still it is virtually adopted; for how many that suppose Christianity to be true, still have it only as a thing by the way, a straw floating down this flood and passing on with us, to see the brave work human progress is doing. If it is not called a myth or wild tradition, still the really trusted gospel is phrenology, chemistry, and the other new sciences, with their grand economic creations, such as tele-graphs, railroads, steamboats, and the like — (not omitting the new and better Bible discovered in the oracles of necromancy); and these are going at last to raise the world, no thanks to Christianity, into a state of universal brotherhood and felicity! The lowest charlatans and some of the most cultivated savants hold much the same language, and trust in the same gospel of development.

Now that there is or should be such a thing as development, we cer-tainly admit. All the human faculties are capable of development by exer-cise or training, and every human being will, of necessity, be developed to a certain degree, both in mind and body, by the growth of years and the necessary struggles of life. But that human society was ever carried forward, by a single shade, in the matter of religious virtue, under mere laws of natural development, we utterly deny. It is even a fair subject of doubt whether any nation, or race of men, was ever advanced in civiliza-tion by inherent laws of progress. Certain it is that no individual was ever cleared of sin by development, or restored even proximately to the state of primal order and uprightness; equally so that the vast, far-spreading, organic woes of the world are forever immedicable by any such remedy.

In one view, it may be rightly said that the whole object of God, in our training, is to develop in us a character of eternal uprightness; developing also, in that manner, as a necessary consequence, grand possibilities of so-cial order and well-being; though when we thus speak we include the fact of sin and the engagement with it of a supernatural grace, to lift up the otherwise remediless fall of nature. But this, if we must have the word, is Christian development; a development accomplished by carrying us across and up out of the gulf of unnature, where the hope of all progress and character was ended. We are developed, in this sense, by and through an experience of that state of wrong, whose woe it is that it is the fall of nature, and in that sense the end of all development. But this, it will be seen, is not the popular doctrine of progress, which assumes the fact of a progress in right lines, without any call for supernatural interference, without any regenerative or new-creative process. There may be hard throes of suffering experience and bitter struggles with individual and social evils; but time, it is supposed, will teach, and experience redeem, and so the great battle of natural development will lead to final victory. In this manner, progress, it is supposed, will at last cure all the evils which we have been recapitulating as the fruit and fall of sin. That such a hope is groundless we will now undertake to show.

Consider, first, the savage state, whence it is continually assumed that history and civilization spring. The doctrine is that all the advanced nations of mankind began as savages, and that all the peoples of the world now existing are on their way up out of the savage state into civilization and a state of social virtue. Contrary to this, no savage race of the world has ever been raised into civilization, least of all into a state of virtue, by mere natural development. All which is evident by just that which distinguishes the savage state; for it is the principal and, in fact, only comprehensive distinction of the savage races, that they are such as have fallen below progress, living on from age to age without progress, and sometimes quite dying out; for the simple reason that there is no sufficient capacity of progress left to perpetuate their life in proximity with more advanced races. They are beings or races physiologically run down, or become effete, under sin; fallen at last below progress, below society, become a herd no longer capable of public organization, and a true, social life. It signifies nothing for such races to ask more time; time can do nothing for them better than extermination. It is well if even a gospel and a faith above nature can now get such hold of them as to raise them. They are, in fact, just as far off from the original unpracticed, undeveloped state of nature, as the most advanced races; and, as David said over the child, "I shall go to him but he shall not return to me," so it is possible for the living and advanced races to go downward, but never for these dead ones, unassisted, to rise. We have proofs enough that peoples advanced in culture may become savages, but no solitary example of a race of savages that have risen to a civilized state, by mere development. And the real fact is that we may much better assert a law of natural deterioration than a law of natural progress; for apart from some influence or aid of a supernatural kind, the deterioration of society, under the penal mischiefs of sin, would be universal. By the supposition it should be so; for, as all society is under sin, it is of course suffering the retributive action of penal causes, and as all discord propagates only greater discord and can not propagate harmony, it follows that the run of society under sin must be downward, from bad to worse, unless interrupted by some remedial agency from without.

It is somewhat difficult to test our particular opinion on this subject by actual examples; for we can not commonly trace the unhistoric and subtle methods in which any race of men may have been impregnated with new possibilities; sometimes by other religions, with which they are made conversant by commerce and travel; sometimes by sporadic and supernatural revelations; traces of which are discernible, not only in the extra-Jewish examples of Jethro, Job, and Cornelius, but in the literature of all the cultivated races, and sometimes, here and there, in the demonstrations even of the wild races. That the old Pelasgic race was raised by a mere natural progress to the high pitch of culture displayed by the Greek civilization, we have no reason whatever to believe. Their literature, from Hesiod downward, is sprinkled with too many traces of sentiment derived from the Jewish and Egyptian religions, to suffer the opinion that they are a nation thus advanced by the simple motherhood of nature. The Roman civilization was, in fact, a propagation of the Greek, with the advantage of a right infusion from her serious and venerable fathers, who, like Numa, communed with invisible powers in retired groves and silent grottoes. The Teutonic race, often named as an example of natural development, is known to have been set forward by the civilizations it conquered and its early conversion to the Christian faith. Meantime how many great and powerful races have become extinct. We look for the Ninevites with as little hope as for Ninus himself. The Assyrians, Babylonians, and Medes are also vanished. The Egyptians, Phoenicians, Etruscans, Romans, once the great powers of history and civilization, are extinct. The Aztec race, run down to such a state of incapacity as not even to understand their own monuments, or know by whom they were built, we rightly call savages, and look upon as having just now come to their vanishing point.

What now does it mean that so many races, empires, languages of the world, have become extinct? Is this a token of infallible development? Do we see in this the proof that all the evil and sin of the world are going at last to be surmounted and cleared by the inevitable law of progress? What would our new prophets of development say if they were told, when exulting so confidently in the glorious future of their own and all other nations, that a day will certainly be reached, when the Anglo-American race is become an extinct race, Washington a contested locality, and the Constitution of the United States a hopeless search of the world's antiquarians? Distant as such an expectation may be from our thoughts, and contrary as it may be to the illimitable progress of which we hear so often, it is only that which has happened a hundred times already, and may as well happen again.

We have spoken of the evident falsity of the supposition that all the advancement of the world begins at an originally savage state — that being, in fact, no first, but an old and decayed state rather, where long ages of deterioration under sin have finally extirpated the original possibilities of advancement. The first stage of human society was simply a stage of crudity, or crude capacity, and was not more remote from the state of high civilization than it was from the low, decrepit, animalized condition which we now designate by the term *savage*. All races begin together at the state of simple being, or crude capacity, and only make the fatal leap of sin together. After that they separate, some ascending, led up by their holy seers and lawgivers, and others, not having or not giving heed to such, going down the scale of penal deteriorations to become savages. A full half the globe is peopled thus by tribes which are either reduced to the savage condition, or else are far on their way toward it; humbled in capacity, physically deteriorated, and that to such a degree that the springs of recuperative force appear to be quite gone. Considering now the certain fact that all these had their beginning in a simply crude state, having the same high possibilities and affinities, which the races had that are now most advanced, what are we to think of mere development? This advantage or condition of crude possibility they had, many thousands of years ago, and the result is what we see. Having run down thus miserably under the boasted gospel of natural progress, what hope is there in this gospel for the final restoration of all things?

It is fatally opposed too by the geologic analogies. Here it stands, the settled verdict of science itself, that the successive eras of vegetable and animal life have not been introduced by any law of progress, or by any mere development of nature and her forces. The attempts that have been made to show this are even pitiable failures. They ask us, in fact, to believe greater miracles in the name of development than any we encounter in the gospel history. Thus we have displayed in the new creations of the rocks themselves a standing type of that moral new creation, by which the distempered and fallen races of the world are to be raised up. Lest we should think any such divine intervention incredible, and try to find some better hope for man in the gospel of development, we are here familiarized with the fact that no such law of development has been able to carry on the geologic progress of the planet, and that God has been wont, in all its ancient depopulations, to insert new germs of life creatively, and people it with living creatures fresh from his hand.

Again it is a consideration scarcely less impressive that God has managed to insert into the physiological history of animals and vegetables an always-present, living type of the process itself, by which, as transcending all mere development, his supernatural remedy operates; so that we may see it, as it were, with our eyes, and become familiar with it. I refer to that wondrous, inexplicable function of healing, discovered in the restoration or repair of animals and vegetables that are wounded or sick. When a tree, for example, is hacked, or bruised, a strange nursing process forthwith begins, by which the wound is healed. A new bark is formed on the edges of the wound, by what method no art of man can trace, the dead matter is thrown off, and a growth inward narrows the breach, till finally the two margins meet and the tissues interweave, and not even a scar is left. So in all the flesh wounds of animals, and the fractures even of bones. So too in regard to all diseases not terminating mortally; they pass a crisis, where the healing function, whatever it be, triumphs over the poison of the disease and a recovery follows, in which the whole flesh and fiber appear even to be produced anew.

Here then is a healing power whose working we can no way trace, and one that, if we look at the causes of disintegration present, appears even to accomplish what is impossible. Regarding the body as a machine — and taken as a merely material organization what is it more? — it is plainly impossible for it to heal, in this manner, and repair itself. The disordered watch can never run itself into good repair. In machines, disorder can only propagate and aggravate disorder, till they become a wreck. The physicians and physiologists call the strange healing function the *vis medicatrix*; as if it were some gentle, feminine nurse, hidden from the sight, whose office it is to expel the poisons, knit the fractures, and heal the wounds of bodies. And as names often settle the profoundest questions, so it appears to be commonly taken for granted here, that the healing accomplished is wrought by a nursing function thus named, as one of the inherent properties of vital substances. It may be so or it may not; for the whole question is one that is involved in the profoundest mystery. The healing property may be one of the incidents of life itself, or it may be a distinct power whose office it is to be the guard and medicating nurse of life, or it may be the working of a grand supernatural economy set in closest vicinage to nature, to be the physical, visible, always-present token of a like supernatural economy in the matters of character and the soul. But whatever view we take of this healing power in physiology, or whatever account we make of it, these two points are clear.

First that the healing accomplished is no fact of development. There is no difficulty in seeing how existing tissues and organs may create extensions within their own vascular sphere, and this is development. But where a new skin or bark is to be created, or a new interlocking made of parts that are sundered, the ducts and vesicles that might act in development, being parted and open at their ends, want mending themselves. Thus, when the parts of a fractured bone are knit together, and we see them reaching after each other, as it were, across a chasm, where there are no vessels to bridge it or carry across the lines of connection, development might well enough make the parts longer, but how could it make them unite across the fracture by which they are separated? The development of a tree, wounded by some violence, would only enlarge the wound, just in proportion to the enlargement of the surface which the bark should cover. A fevered body does not cure itself by development. As little can we imagine that the restored health and volume of the body is created by the development of the fever. No shade of countenance therefore is given to the hope that human development, under the retributive woes of sin, will be any sufficient cure of its disorders, or will set the fallen subjects of it forward, in a course of social progress.

This also, secondly, is equally clear, that as the mysterious healing of bodies yields the development theory no token of favor, it is only a more impressive type, on that account, of some grand restorative economy, by which the condition of unnature in souls and the world is to be supernaturally regenerated — just such a type as, regarding the relations of matter to mind, and of things natural to things spiritual, we might expect to find incorporated, in some large and systematic way, in the visible objects and processes of the world. And how much does the healing of bodies signify, when associated thus with the grand elemental disorder and breakage of sin! What is it, in fact, but a kind of glorious, every where visible sacrament, that tokens life, and hope, and healing invisible, for all the retributive woes and bleeding lacerations of our guilty, fallen state, as a race apostate from God?

Hence too probably the fact that transactions of healing are so closely connected, the world over, with sentiments of religion. Perhaps the fact is due in part to some latent association that connects diseases with sin and, to much the same extent, connects the hope of healing with some possibility of a divine medication. However this may be, the mystery of healing, as we are constituted, stands in close affinity with God and the faith of his supernatural operation. Thus it was that the priests both of the Egyptians and the Greeks were their physicians, and that their precepts and prescripts of healing were kept in their temples. Esculapius, too, the god of medicine, had his own altars and priests. At a latter period, the Essenes and the Christian monks, accounted by some to be their successors, had their pious explorations of diseases and the sacred powers of remedies; reducing medicine itself to a function of religion. Later still, Paracelsus himself began the restoration of medicine, as a kind of chemical theosophy. And as Christianity itself classes healings among the spiritual gifts, and calls the elders of the church to pray for the sick; so we find that some of our Indian tribes have traditions of one whom, as related to the Great Spirit, they call the Uncle, and who came into the world by a mysterious advent, long ages ago, and instituted the "Grand Medicine" which is, in fact, their religion.

It is difficult to resist the impression, in such demonstrations as these, of some very profound connection between the healing of bodies and the faith of a supernatural grace of healing for the disorders of souls. Else why this persistent tendency in men's opinions of healing, to associate the fevered body and the leprous mind, and seek the medication of both, in the common rites of religion?

But there is a shorter argument with the scheme that proposes to find a remedy for all the ills of character and society, in what it calls a more complete development. It is this: that no one ever dares practically to act on the faith of such a doctrine, whether in the state or the family. The civil law is, in fact, and to a very great extent, a restraint on development, and has its merits in the fact that it is. It forbids men to unfold themselves freely, in their base passions and criminal instigations, and deters them from it. Were it not for the state, protecting itself by such means against development, society would be quite dissolved. What we discover in families is even more remarkable. There are multitudes of parents that believe, as they suppose, with all their hearts, in the good day coming through the progress of human development. And as part of the same general faith, their views of education make it to consist simply in educing or developing just what is in the child's nature. But they do not act on that principle in the house, and dare not; though probably enough they are never aware of the fact. They maintain a family regimen that consists, to a great degree, not in development but in repression. To let the child have his way and act himself out freely, without restraint, is no part of their plan. Probably it never occurs to them as a rational possibility. Just contrary to this, they lay their foundations in a restriction of natural development; hoping in that manner to extirpate unruly and base instigations, and form a habit in the child of doing better things than he would most naturally do. And it is remarkable that, in the fulfilling of their office, which is so far an office of repression, they are acting as a force supernatural. According to our definition, it will be remembered that human wills are strictly supernatural in their action, and the child, we here discover, spends all the first years of his life under the regulative and repressive action of such wills. He is in them, in fact, more truly than he is in nature, and the house is a little creation made for him by their keeping. He is handled in infancy as they direct, fed as they direct when he begins to ask for food, clothed as they direct, commanded, limited, forbidden, repressed, and so is finally grown up to an age of self-regulation. The process may be called his development, but the most remarkable thing in it is that it is a restraint of development. Why this restraint? If development is going to be the gospel of the world's redemption, what makes it wise, in the common sense of the world, to restrain that gospel? Are the ills of society and the world going to be cured too soon? If development can do all that is promised, why not give it a hearty godspeed every where, and let every human creature, old and young, act out what is in him, in the speediest, most unrestricted manner possible? A glance in this direction is sufficient to show us that all we hear of inevitable progress, and the necessary laws of development, is hollow and deceitful. It is not development but new creation that can bring us the remedies we look for. Nature has powers and capabilities that want development. Reduced to real unnature (which is her present state), she also has disordered passions, base instigations, greedy appetites, ferocious animosities, propensities to cunning and falsehood, which want no development, and which, if they are developed, unrestrained, annihilate all chance of progress, and even forbid the existence of society. Mere development therefore promises nothing.

We come now —

II. To the other rival gospel, that which proposes to dispense with all supernatural aids, and to restore the disorders and the fallen character of sin by a self-cultivated or self-originated virtue.

Expectation is here rested on the human will, which in our view may be done, it will be said, with greater reason, since we make it, even by definition, a supernatural power. But there are different orders or degrees, it must be observed, of supernatural power; the human, the angelic, the divine; which all are alike in the fact that the will acts from itself, uncaused in its actions, but very unlike as regards potency, or the extent of their efficacy. What we are endeavoring, in our argument, to show, is the fact of a divine supernatural agency concerned in the upraising or redemption of man. But if man can raise himself by his own will, that is, by his humanly supernatural force, then plainly there is no need of a divine intervention from without and above nature to regenerate his fallen state. Still it will not be denied by the class of teachers most forward in maintaining this form of naturalism, that all religious virtue is dependent, in a certain sense, on the concourse and spiritual helping of God; only that concourse and helping, it will be said, belongs to the scheme of nature, and never undertakes to help us out of the retributive woes and disorders of nature; for nature is the system of God, including all he does or can rationally be expected to do. To imagine that such a mode of piety, or religious virtue, should be maintained by the human will, would be less extravagant if there were no sin, no consequent woes and disorders; though even then it would be the faith of a God imprisoned, or entombed, in the inexorable laws of nature; with whom the soul could aspire to no real converse and could have no social sympathy, more than with a wall. Before this unbending prisoner of fate, this nature-God, this dead wall, he might go on to dress up a character and fashion a merely ethical virtue; cultivating truth, honesty, justice, temperance, kindness, piling up acts of merit, and doing legal works of charity; but to call this character religious, however plausible the show it makes, is only an abuse of the term. Religious character is not legal. It is an inspiration — the Life of God in the soul of man; and no such life can ever quicken a soul except in the faith of a Living God, which here is manifestly wanting. Not even the pure angels could subsist in such a style of virtue; for it is the strength and beatitude of their holiness that it is no will-work in them, but an eternal, immediate inspiration of God. Consciously it is not theirs, but the inbreathing life of their Father.

But this ethical gospel, this religion acted as in pantomime, becomes even more insipid and absurd when the fact of sin, with all its consequences of distemper and disorder, is admitted. Now the problem is to find by what power the original harmony of nature can be reconstructed, and its currents of penal disaster turned back. Can the human will do this? That it can act upon the courses of nature we know — sin itself indeed is the staring and incontrovertible proof that it can. But it does not follow, as we have said already, that the power which has broken an egg, or shivered a crystal, can mend it. That is a thing more difficult, and demands a higher power.

Consider simply the change that is needed to restore the lapsed integrity of a soul. Its original spontaneity to good is gone, its silver cord of harmony is broken, the sweet order of life is turned into a tumult of inward bitterness, its very laws are become its tormentors. All its curious, multiform, scarcely conceivable functions, submitted by its laws to the will, are now contesting always with each other and are wholly intractable to its sovereignty. And still it is expected of the will, that it is going to gather them all up into the primal order, and reconstruct their shattered unity! Why, it were easier, a thousandfold, for man's will to gather all the birds of the sky into martial order, and march them as a squadron through the tempests of the air! Manifestly none but God can restore the lapsed order of the soul. He alone can reconstruct the crystalline unity. Which, if he does, it will imply an acting on those lines of causes in its nature, by whose penal efficacy it is distempered; and that is, by the supposition, a supernatural operation.

Besides, the work is really not done till the subject is restored to a virtue whose essence is liberty. And how is man, by his mere will, to start the flow of liberty? He may do this and do that, and keep doing this and that, carefully, punctiliously, suffering no slackness. But it will be work, work only, and the play of liberty will never come. He can never reach the true liberty till an inspiration takes him, and the new birth of God's Spirit makes him a son. The light he manufactures will be darkness, or at best a pale phosphorescence, till Christ is revealed within. His self-culture may fashion a picture with many marks of grace, but the quickening of God alone can make it live. If he relish his work in a degree, it will be the relish of conceit, not the living fountain of a heavenly joy, bursting up from unseen depths within. He will advance fitfully, eccentrically, and without balance, making a grimace here, while he fashions a beauty there; for there is no balance of order and proportion till his faith is rested in God, and his life flows out from the divine plenitude and perfection. Meantime his ideals will grow faster than his attainments, and if he is not wholly drunk up in conceit, he will be only the more afflicted and baffled, the greater his pertinacity. Oh, if there be any kind of life most sad, and deepest in the scale of pity, it is the dry, cold impotence of one who is honestly set to the work of his own self-redemption!

Do we then affirm, it will be asked, the absolute inability of a man to do and become what is right before God? That is the Christian doctrine, and there is none that is more obviously true. Wherein, then, it may also be asked, is there any ground of blame for continuance in sin? Because, we answer, there is a Living God engaged to help us, and inviting always our acceptance of his help. Nor is this any mere gracious ability, such as constitutes the joy of some and the offense of others. No created being, of any world, not even the new-informed man before his fall, nor the glorified saint, nor the spotless angel, had ever any possibility of holiness, except in the embrace of God. This is the normal condition of all souls, that they be filled with God, acted by God, holding their will in his, irradiated always by his all-supporting life. Just this it is that constitutes the radical idea of religion, and differs it from a mere ethical virtue. God is the prime necessity of all religious virtue, and is only more emphatically so to beings under sin. The necessity is constituent, not penal; it becomes penal only when communications originally given to the fallen, but now cast away by their sin, require to be restored.

There is really no difficulty in this question of disability under sin, save that which is created by the fogs of unintelligent speculation. It is taken extensively, as if it were a question regarding man's inherent, independent ability, when in fact he has no such ability to any thing. Can he obey God, or not? is he able to do God's will, or not? is the question raised; and it is understood and discussed as being a question that turns on the absolute quantities of the man, and not in any respect on relative aids and conditions without; much as if the question were whether he has weight, apart from all relative weights or attractions? or whether he can stand alone, apart from any thing to stand upon? or whether he has power to live a year, apart from all food and light and shelter and air? The true question of ability is different. It is this: whether the subject is able to rise into a holy life, taken as insphered in God, and all the attractive, transforming, and supporting influences of the grace of God? Apart from this, he certainly is not able. By mere working on himself and manipulating, as it were, his body of sin and death, he can do just nothing in the way of self-perfection; and if he could even do every thing as regards self-transformation, there would be no religious character in the result, any more than if his works were done before the moon. Religious character is God in the soul, and without that all pretenses of religious virtue are, in fact, atheistic. Such is the disability of a fallen man, taken as acting on himself; and the condition of an angel, acting in that manner, is no better;

for he could not begin to act thus without being himself fallen at the instant. But if the question be what a man has power to do, taken in the surroundings of divine truth and mercy, which in fact include the co-operating grace of the divine Spirit, the true answer is that he can do all things. He has, at every moment, a complete power as respects doing what God requires of him at that moment, and is responsible according to his power. And yet when we say a complete power, we mean not so much that he is going even then to do something himself, as that he is going to have something done within, by the quickening and transforming power of his divine Lord, in whom he trusts. His power is to set himself before power, open his nature to the rule of power, and so to live — even as we may say that a tree has power to live and grow, not by acting on itself and willing to grow, but as it is ministered unto by its natural surroundings, the soil, the sun, the dew, the air. It has only to offer itself openly and receptively to these, and by their force to grow.

Where, then, it may be asked, is the significance of free will, which we have even shown to be a power supernatural? If the disordered soul can not restore itself, or by diligent self-culture regain the loss it has made by sin, wherein lies the advantage of such a power, and where the responsibility to a life of holy virtue? Our answer is that by the freedom of the will we understand simply its freedom as a volitional function; but mere volitions, taken by themselves, involve no capacity to regenerate or constitute a character. Holy virtue is not an act or compilation of acts taken merely as volitions, but it is a new state or *status* rather, a right disposedness, whence new action may flow. And no mere volitional exercise can change the state or disposedness of the soul, without concurrent help and grace. We can will any thing, but the execution may not follow. To will may be present, but how to perform, it may be difficult to find — difficult, that is, when simply acting in and upon ourselves; never difficult, never possible to fail in doing, when acting before and toward a Divine Helper, trustfully appealed to. And this is the power of the will, as regards our moral recovery. It may so offer itself and the subordinate capacities to God, that God shall have the whole man open to his dominion, and be able to ingenerate in him a new, divine state, or principle of action; while, taken as a governing, cultivating, and perfecting power in itself, it has no such capacity whatsoever. And this is the only rational and true verdict. Say what we **may** of the will as a strictly self-determining power, raise what distinctions we may as regards the kinds of ability, such as natural and moral, antecedent and subsequent, we have no ability at all, of any kind, to regenerate our own state, or restore our own disorders. Salvation is by faith, or there is none.

There is then, we conclude, no hope of a restoration of society or of a religious upraising of man, except in a supernatural and divine operation. Progress under sin, by laws of natural development, is a fiction — there is no hope of progress, apart from the regenerative and quickening power of a grace that transcends mere natural conditions and causes. As little room is there to expect that men will be able to heal their own spiritual maladies and cultivate themselves into heaven's order, by a merely ethical regimen maintained in the plane of nature. The only remedy for the human state, under sin, is that which comes into nature as the revelation of a divine force.

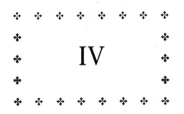

THE WORK OF CHRIST

1. The Vicarious Sacrifice [1]

EDITOR'S INTRODUCTION

In response to his spiritual illumination of 1848, Bushnell endeavored to formulate a doctrine of Christ's work which would comprehend the elements of truth for which both Congregationalists and Unitarians were contending. Accordingly, he presented at Harvard what he characterized as a "subjective-objective" view of the atonement.[2] On the subjective side, he defined the end of Christ's work, which in sum was "to re-engage the world's love and reunite the world, as free, to the Eternal Life." [3] He explicitly repudiated the traditional notion that Christ's death produced an effect on God, and thereby rendered him propitiate toward the transgressor.

Yet Bushnell wanted to go beyond a purely subjective theory. He recognized that he had not taken account of those passages of Scripture which represented Christ as our passover, our sacrifice, and our sin-offering. These "terms of the altar," or "altar forms," he believed, were necessary to the completion of his subjective theory. Their function was to represent the work of Christ as an outward transaction so as to give it greater effect within man. He characterized this altar aspect of his theory as the "objective ritual view." [4]

---

1. *The Vicarious Sacrifice, Grounded in Principles of Universal Obligation* (New York, 1866), Part I: Chap. I (37–48); Chap. V (105–11); Part II: Chap. I (129–34, 136–42); Chap. II (151–56); Chap. III (168–72, 182–84); Chap. IV (185–88, 192–95, 202–8, 212–13, 215, 220–26).

2. *God in Christ* (Hartford, 1849), 185–275; *Christ in Theology* (Hartford, 1851), 212–330.

3. *God in Christ*, 189.   4. *Ibid.*, 246.

276

The doctrine satisfied neither Unitarians nor Congregationalists. In the opinion of many Unitarians, Bushnell had added the "objective ritual view" merely as a "fetch" to save his orthodoxy. The Congregationalists generally disliked the theory. Even the majority report of the Porter committee found it seriously defective. The Fairfield men vehemently assailed it,[5] charging especially that it made nothing of Christ's vicarious suffering and sacrifice. This particular criticism may have started Bushnell on a new train of thought. At all events, his next work on the atonement, *The Vicarious Sacrifice*, centered in the principle of vicarious love. The term subjective-objective now fell into the background, but the theory followed the general pattern set forth in the Harvard discourse of 1848.

The text is reproduced from Parts I and II of *The Vicarious Sacrifice*, since Parts III and IV of this work were soon superseded by *Forgiveness and Law* (1874).

❖ ❖ ❖ ❖

PART I

NOTHING SUPERLATIVE IN VICARIOUS SACRIFICE, OR ABOVE THE UNIVERSAL PRINCIPLES OF RIGHT AND DUTY

Chapter 1

The Meaning of Vicarious Sacrifice

It is a matter of sorrowful indication, that the thing most wanting to be cleared in Christianity is still, as it ever has been, the principal thing; viz., the meaning and method of reconciliation itself, or of what is commonly called the vicarious sacrifice. This fact would even be itself a considerable evidence against the gospel, were it not that the subject matter — so vast in the reach of its complications, and so nearly transcendent in the height of its reasons — yields up easily to faith its practical significance, when refusing to be theoretically mastered, as yet, by the understanding.

There has been a litigation of the sacrifice going on for these eighteen hundred years, and especially for the last eight hundred; yet still it remains an open question with many, whether any such thing as vicarious sacrifice pertains to the work of salvation Christ has accomplished. On

5. *Remonstrance and Complaint of the Association of Fairfield West to the Hartford Central Association, together with the Reply of the Hartford Central Association* (New York, 1850), 15–19, 23–24.

one side the fact is abjured as irrational and revolting. On the other it is affirmed as a principal fact of the Christian salvation; though I feel obliged to confess that it is too commonly maintained under definitions and forms of argument that make it revolting. And which of the two is the greater wrong and most to be deplored, that by which the fact itself is rejected or that by which it is made fit to be rejected, I will not stay to discuss. Enough that Christianity in either way suffers incalculable loss; or must, if there be any such principal matter in it, as I most certainly believe that there is.

Assuming now, for the subject of this treatise, the main question stated, our first point must be to settle a just and true conception of vicarious sacrifice, or of what is the real undertaking of Christ in the matter of such sacrifice. For in all such matters, the main issue is commonly decided by adjusting other and better conceptions of the question itself, and not by forcing old ones through into victory, by the artillery practice of better contrived arguments.

This word *vicarious*, that has made so conspicuous a figure in the debates of theology, it must be admitted is no word of the Scripture. The same is true, however, of *free agency, character, theology,* and of many other terms which the conveniences of use have made common. If a word appears to be wanted in Christian discussions or teachings, the fact that it is not found in the Scripture is no objection to it; we have only to be sure that we understand what we mean by it. In the case, too, of this particular word *vicarious,* a special care is needed, lest we enter something into the meaning, from ourselves, which is not included in the large variety of Scripture terms and expressions the word is set to represent.

Thus we have — "made a curse for us" — "bare our sins" — "hath laid on him the iniquity of us all" — "made to be sin for us" — "offered to bear the sins of many" — "borne our griefs and carried our sorrows" — "wounded for our transgressions, bruised for our iniquities" — "tasted death for every man." The whole gospel is a texture, thus, of vicarious conceptions, in which Christ is represented in one way or another as coming into our place, substituted in our stead, bearing our burdens, answering for us, and standing in a kind of suffering sponsorship for the race.

Now the word *vicarious* is chosen to represent, and gather up into itself all these varieties of expression. It is the same word, in the root, as the word *vice* in vicegerent, viceroy, vicar, vicar-general, vice-president, and the like. It is a word that carries always a face of substitution, indicating that one person comes in place, somehow, of another. Thus a vice-president is one who is to act in certain contingencies, as and for the president; a viceroy, for the king. The ecclesiastical vicar, too, was a vicar as being sent to act for the monastic body, whose duties were laid as a charge upon him; and the pope is called the vicar of Christ in the same way, as being authorized to fill Christ's place. Any person acts vicariously, in this view, just so far as he comes in place of another. The commercial agent, the trustee, the attorney, are examples of vicarious action at common law.

Then if we speak of "sacrifice," any person acts in a way of "vicarious sacrifice," not when he burns upon an altar in some other's place, but when he makes loss for him, even as he would make loss for himself, in the offering of a sacrifice for his sin. The expression is a figure, representing that the party making such sacrifice for another comes into burden, pain, weariness, or even to the yielding up of life for his sake. The word "vicarious" does not say all, nor the word "sacrifice," but the two together make out the true figure of Christ and his gospel.

In this sense it is that Christianity or the Christian salvation is a vicarious sacrifice. It does not mean simply that Christ puts himself into the case of man as a helper; one man helps another without any vicarious relationship implied or supposed. Neither does it mean that Christ undertakes for man in a way of influence; one man tries to influence another, without coming at all into his place. Neither does the vicarious sacrifice imply that he simply comes under common liabilities with us, as when every citizen suffers for the wrongs and general misconduct and consequent misgovernment of the community to which he belongs; nor that he simply comes into the track of those penal retributions which outrun the wrongs they chastise, passing over upon the innocent, as the sins of fathers propagate their evils in the generations of their children coming after. The idea of Christ's vicarious sacrifice is not matched by any of these lighter examples, though it has something in common with them all, and is therefore just so much likelier to be confounded with them by a lighter and really sophistical interpretation.

On the other hand, we are not to hold the Scripture terms of vicarious sacrifice as importing a literal substitution of places, by which Christ becomes a sinner for sinners, or penally subject to our deserved penalties. That is a kind of substitution that offends every strongest sentiment of our nature. He can not become guilty for us. Neither, as God is a just being, can he be anyhow punishable in our place — all God's moral sentiments would be revolted by that. And if Christ should himself consent to such punishment, he would only ask to have all the most immovable convictions, both of God's moral nature and our own, confounded, or eternally put by.

Excluding now all these under-stated and over-stated explanations we come to the true conception, which is that Christ, in what is called his vicarious sacrifice, simply engages, at the expense of great suffering and even of death itself, to bring us out of our sins themselves and so out of their penalties; being himself profoundly identified with us in our fallen state, and burdened in feeling with our evils. Nor is there any thing so remote, or difficult, or violent, in this vicarious relation, assumed by Christ as many appear to suppose. It would rather be a wonder if, being what he is, he did not assume it. For we are to see and make our due account of this one fact, that a good being is, by the supposition, ready, just according to his goodness, to act vicariously in behalf of any bad, or miserable being, whose condition he is able to restore. For a good being is not simply one who gives bounties and favors, but one who is in the principle of love; and it is the nature of love, universally, to insert itself into the miseries, and take upon its feeling the burdens of others. Love does not consider the ill desert of the subject; he may even be a cruel and relentless enemy. It does not consider the expense of toil, and sacrifice, and suffering the intervention may cost. It stops at nothing but the known impossibility of relief, or benefit; asks for nothing as inducement but the opportunity of success. Love is a principle essentially vicarious in its own nature, identifying the subject with others, so as to suffer their adversities and pains, and taking on itself the burden of their evils. It does not come in officiously and abruptly, and propose to be substituted in some formal and literal way that overturns all the moral relations of law and desert, but it clings to the evil and lost man as in feeling, afflicted for him, burdened by his ill deserts, incapacities, and pains, encountering gladly any loss or suffering for his sake. Approving nothing wrong in him, but faithfully reproving and condemning him in all sin, it is yet made sin — plunged, so to speak, into all the fortunes of sin, by its friendly sympathy. In this manner it is entered vicariously into sacrifice on his account. So naturally and easily does the vicarious sacrifice commend itself to our intelligence, by the stock ideas and feelings out of which it grows.

How it was with Christ, and how he bore our sins, we can see exactly, from a very impressive and remarkable passage in Matthew's gospel, where he conceives that Christ is entered vicariously into men's diseases, just as he is elsewhere shown to bear, and to be vicariously entered into, the burden of their sins. I produce the passage at this early point in the discussion, because of the very great and decisive importance it has; for it is remarkable as being the one Scripture citation that gives, beyond a question, the exact *usus loquendi* of all the vicarious and sacrificial language of the New Testament.

Christ has been pouring out his sympathies, all day, in acts of healing, run down, as it were, by the wretched multitudes crowding about him and imploring his pity. No humblest, most repulsive creature is neglected or fails to receive his tenderest, most brotherly consideration. His heart accepts each one as a burden upon its feeling, and by that feeling he is inserted into the lot, the pain, the sickness, the sorrow of each. And so the evangelist, having, as we see, no reference whatever to the substitution for sin, says: "That it might be fulfilled which was spoken by Esaias the prophet, saying, 'Himself took our infirmities and bare our sicknesses' " (Mt. 8:17). And the text is the more remarkable that the passage he cites from Isaiah, is from his fifty-third chapter, which is in fact a kind of stock chapter, whence all the most vicarious language of the New Testament is drawn. Besides the word *bare* occurs in the citation; a word that is based on the very same figure of carrying as that which is used in the expression, "bare our sins," "bare the sins of many," and is moreover precisely the same word which is used by the apostle when he says, "βαστάζετε — Bear ye one another's burdens, and so fulfill the law of Christ." If then we desire to know exactly what the substitution of Christ for sin was, and how far it went — what it means for example that he bare our sin — we have only to revert back to what is here said of his relation to sicknesses, and our question is resolved.

What then does it mean that Christ "bare our sicknesses"? Does it mean that he literally had our sicknesses transferred to him, and so taken off from us? Does it mean that he became blind for the blind, lame for the lame, a leper for the lepers, suffering in himself all the fevers and pains he took away from others? No one had ever such a thought. How then did he bear our sicknesses, or in what sense? In the sense that he took them on his feeling, had his heart burdened by the sense of them, bore the disgusts of their loathsome decays, felt their pains over again, in the tenderness of his more than human sensibility. . . .

Here then we have the true law of interpretation, when the vicarious relation of Christ to our sins comes into view. It does not mean that he takes them literally upon him, as some of the old theologians and a very few moderns appear to believe; it does not mean that he took their ill

desert upon him by some mysterious act of imputation, or had their punishment transferred to his person. A sickness might possibly be transferred, but a sin can not by any rational possibility. It does not mean that
he literally came into the hell of our retributive evils under sin, and satisfied, by his own suffering, the violated justice of God; for that kind of
penal suffering would satisfy nothing but the very worst injustice. No,
but the bearing of our sins does mean that Christ bore them on his feeling, became inserted into their bad lot by his sympathy as a friend,
yielded up himself and his life, even, to an effort of restoring mercy; in a
word that he bore our sins in just the same sense that he bore our sicknesses. Understand that love itself is an essentially vicarious principle, and
the solution is no longer difficult.

See how it is with love in the case of a mother. She loves her child, and
it comes out in that fact, or from it, that she watches for the child, bears
all its pains and sicknesses on her own feeling, and when it is wronged, is
stung herself, by the wrong put upon it, more bitterly far than the child.
She takes every chance of sacrifice for it as her own opportunity. She creates, in fact, imaginary ills for it, because she has not opportunities enough
of sacrifice. In the same manner a friend that is real and true takes all the
sufferings, losses, wrongs, indignities, of a friend on his own feeling, and
will sometimes suffer even more for him than he does for himself. So also
with the patriot or citizen who truly loves his country, even though that
love is mixed with many false fires that are only fires of ambition or revenge — how does it wrench his feeling, what a burden does it lay upon
his concern, by day and by night, when that country so dear to him is
being torn by faction, and the fate of its laws and liberties is thrown upon
the chances of an armed rebellion. Then you will see how many thousands of citizens, who never knew before what sacrifices it was in the
power of their love to make for their country's welfare, rushing to the
field and throwing their bodies and dear lives on the battle's edge to save
it!

Thus it is that every sort of love is found twining its feeling always
into the feeling, and loss, and want, and woe, of whatever people, or person, or even enemy, it loves; thus that God himself takes our sinning
enmity upon his heart, painfully burdened by our broken state, and trav-
ailing, in all the deepest feeling of his nature, to recover us to himself.
And this it is which the cross and vicarious sacrifice of Jesus signify to us,
or outwardly express. Such a God in love, must be such a Saviour in
suffering — he could not well be other or less. There is a Gethsemane hid

in all love, and when the fit occasion comes, no matter how great and high the subject may be, its heavy groaning will be heard — even as it was in Christ. He was in an agony, exceeding sorrowful even unto death. By that sign it was that God's love broke into the world, and Christianity was born!

Here, then, as I conceive, is the true seed-principle of the Christian salvation. What we call the vicarious sacrifice of Christ is nothing strange as regards the principle of it, no superlative, unexampled, and therefore unintelligible grace. It only does and suffers, and comes into substitution for, just what any and all love will, according to its degree. And in this view it is not something higher in principle than our human virtue knows, and which we ourselves are never to copy or receive, but it is to be understood by what we know already, and is to be more fully understood by what we are to know hereafter, when we are complete in Christ. Nothing is wanting to resolve the vicarious sacrifice of Jesus but the commonly known, always familiar principle of love, accepted as the fundamental law of duty, even by mankind. Given the universality of love, the universality of vicarious sacrifice is given also. Here is the center and deepest spot of good, or goodness, conceivable. At this point we look into heaven's eye itself, and read the meaning of all heavenly grace. . . .

Chapter v

All Souls Redeemed, to Be in Vicarious Sacrifice

In what is called his vicarious sacrifice, Christ, as we have seen, simply fulfills what belongs universally to love; doing neither more nor less than what the common standard of holiness and right requires. And then since there can be no other standard, and no perfect world or society can be constituted under a different or lower kind of excellence, it follows incontestably that the restoration of mankind, as a fallen race, must restore them to a love that works vicariously, and conforms in all respects to the work and passion of Christ himself. Vicarious sacrifice then will not be a point where he is distinguished from his followers, but the very life to which he restores them in restoring them to God. What we call his redemption of mankind must bring them to the common standard. Executed by vicarious sacrifice in himself, it must also be issued in vicarious sacrifice in them.

The common impression, I am sorry to believe, is different. It belongs, indeed, to the staple matter of our theologic teaching on this subject that while we are to follow Christ, and copy him, and aspire to be like him, we are never to presume, and can not without great irreverence imagine, that we are to have any part with him in his vicarious sacrifice. We can not atone, it is said, or offer any satisfaction for the sin of the world; we are too little, and low, and deep in sin ourselves, and nothing but a being infinitely great and perfect, by an optional suffering that exceeds all terms of obligation on himself, can avail to smooth God's indignations, and so far even our debt, as to make forgiveness possible. Therefore we are to understand, as a first principle of the Christian salvation, that Christ, in the matter of his vicarious sacrifice, is a being by himself and is not to be followed, in any sense, by us, though followed carefully in every thing else. In this very great mistake are included three or four subordinate mistakes that require to be specially noted, and corrected by the necessary explanations.

1. That Christ, in all that pertains to his work as vicarious, acts officially, or fulfills an atoning office wholly one side of his character as a perfect character. He does not execute what belongs to the simple perfection of his love as a character fulfilling standard obligation, but performs a volunteer office in our behalf, over and above all that is obligatory on his own account. And so the vicarious sacrifice, being a matter pertaining wholly to his office, and not to his character, we of course can have no part in it, because we have no part in his office, and can have as little in the official merit by which God's account is satisfied. Now the obvious fact, that which we have seen developed in the careful illustrations of the previous chapters, is that vicarious sacrifice belongs to no office or undertaking outside of holy character, but to holy character itself. Such is love that it must insert itself into the conditions, burden itself with the wants, and woes, and losses, and even wrongs of others. It waits for no atoning office, or any other kind of office. It undertakes because it is love, not because a project is raised or an office appointed. It goes into suffering and labor, and painful sympathy, because its own everlasting instinct runs that way. There can be no greater mistake, in this view, than to imagine that Christ has the matter of vicarious sacrifice wholly to himself, because he suffers officially, or as having undertaken it for his office to supply so much suffering. He suffered simply what was incidental to his love, and the works to which love prompted, just as any missionary suffers what belongs to the work of love he is in. It was vicarious suffering in no way peculiar to him, save in degree.

No further qualification is needed, unless it be to say that effects will follow his vicarious sacrifice that can not follow such kind of sacrifice in men. And the difference will be so great that he will have accomplished all that can be fitly included in the redemption of the world, while the same kind of sacrifice, morally speaking, in men, will accomplish only some very inferior and partial benefits. A proportion stated between the incarnate Son of God and his infinitely perfect beauty on the one hand, and the very limited and sadly mixed virtue of a human person on the other, will represent as accurately as may be the comparative results of the same kind of sacrifice in both.

2. It is another of the mistakes referred to that when vicarious sacrifice is restricted wholly to Christ, and considered wholly beyond the pale of human virtue, the restriction supposes a kind of vicarious intervention for sin that is artificial, and has no root in moral obligation. Either exceeding the law of love, or else falling short of it, he fulfills a kind of substitution that we can not share because it is not in the range of our possible sentiment, or even intelligence. There is no *koinonia* for us, no "fellowship in his sufferings," because he suffers outside of all known terms of moral obligation. Whereas we may and must have fellowship, and be conformable even unto his death, because he is himself conformed in it to the one, universal, common standard of love. The true and simple account of his suffering is that he had such a heart as would not suffer him to be turned away from us, and that he suffered for us even as love must willingly suffer for its enemy. The beauty and power of his sacrifice is that he suffers morally and because of his simple excellence, and not to fill a contrived place in a scheme of legal justification. He scarcely minds how much he suffers, or how, if only he can do love's work. He does not propose to be over-good, and to suffer optionally a certain modicum beyond what perfect excellence requires, that it may go to men's account. He undertakes to furnish no superlative merit above all standard obligation, which, for just that reason, can have no perceived quality of merit. He is only just as good as he ought to be, and suffers what he ought to suffer, and has no thought of doing an artificial somewhat, in a scheme of artificial compensations, where he can be actuated by no assignable motive within the possible range of moral ideas. How far off do we place him, how poorly conceive him, when we put him thus away, and compel him to die for ends contrived, apart from all behests of character. All that is most central in his mission — the love of God in tears and deep groanings — is dried away and lost to feeling, in the sterile and dry figment we require it to be, as a mere quantitative sufficiency of pain, contributed un-

der no assignable principle, and having no moral quality whatever.

3. Another mistake that follows, when vicarious sacrifice is restricted to Christ alone, is yet more lamentable because it corrupts the idea of sacrifice itself, when imposed as a condition of human discipleship. We insist, abundantly, on the necessary law of self-denial and self-sacrifice. We quote the Master's words requiring us to follow him and bear the cross with him, or after him. There must be sacrifice, we say, every Christian comes into a life of sacrifice — only not into vicarious sacrifice; that belongs to Christ alone, suffering no participation of mortals. A qualification, or salvo, that very nearly unchristianizes Christianity itself. What is the sacrifice that must not be vicarious sacrifice, but a virtue that has even lost connection with Christian ideas? It is mere self-abnegation, a loss made for the simple sake of losing, and no such practical loss as love encounters, in gaining or serving an enemy. It has the same relation to vicarious sacrifice that penance has to repentance. It is itself a kind of penance, or torment, submitted to by the will. It does not appear to be even suspected that such kind of sacrifice is a mode of asceticism, substituted for the sacrifice of the gospel, and yet it can be nothing else, for the simple reason that it is required not to be vicarious. Sacrifice out of love, or because a full heart naturally and freely takes on itself the burdens and woes of others, has a positive character, and is itself the most intensely positive exercise that can be conceived. The other kind of sacrifice, that which must not work vicariously, is naked self-suppression, a merely dry and negative operation, in which the soul willfully chokes itself and gets no return but a sense of being famished for its pains. And how much of what is so persistently taught concerning self-denial, sacrifice, taking up the cross, is, in just this manner, a departure from all Christian ideas; a wearisome, unblessed, and forced virtue, that belongs to the false gospel of asceticism. Happily the evil is mitigated by the fact that when we go into sacrifice and suffering for others, we break away from such asceticism, without knowing it, and come into the genuine, positive kind of sacrifice with Christ himself.

4. Still another and different kind of misconception is included in the denial of vicarious sacrifice to men, in the fact that it forbids us to think of reciprocating, in any sense, the sacrifice of Christ for us, and takes away, in that manner, one of the dearest, most softening and soul-renewing exercises. What should the true love in us do so naturally, and with an instinct so free, as to take all Christ's feeling on its feeling; to suffer with him in his suffering of all kinds; to burden itself in all his bur-

dens; to be afflicted in all the losses, apostasies, and dishonors that shame his saving work; because they wound so deeply his divine sensibility. As Christ became a suffering Saviour for our sake, so the love he begets in us will take every wrong done him as done to itself, and will gladly suffer also for his sake. . . .

PART II

THE LIFE AND SACRIFICE OF CHRIST IS WHAT HE DOES TO BECOME A RENOVATING AND SAVING POWER

Chapter 1

Uses and Relations of the Healing Ministry

All the perplexed questions growing out of substitutions, imputations, legal satisfactions, and penal equivalents, have thus far been avoided. There has been no delving in our exposition, but we have been moving easily, rather, along open ranges of thought, where nothing too abstruse or difficult to serve a merely practical interest has come in our way. In this manner we have gone over a considerable tract of our field, meeting scarcely a point of debate in the subject as commonly handled. We have discovered a meaning, not difficult, for the vicarious sacrifice, and for all the Scripture phraseology relating to the same. We have seen it to be grounded in principles of universal obligation, acknowledged, or to be acknowledged, by all good minds, uncreated and created, in all worlds and ages of time.

Having reached this point, we now pass to another general department of the subject; where, continuing still in this rather untrodden, some will think, too easy level of movement, we undertake to settle a true conception of what Christ is doing in his sacrifice; viz., the end he will accomplish, the power by which he will accomplish it, and the course of life and benefaction by which he will obtain that power.

When this also is done, as I think it may be with the same facility and avoidance of perplexed questions, we may well enough comfort ourselves in the conclusion that if by and by, or from that point onward, we are obliged to go to sea in questions more perplexed and laborious, we have a considerable continent already gained behind us, where we shall have large enough room, and ranges wide enough in the truth, to afford a worthy, or even sufficient gospel by itself.

According to a current conception, Christ came into the world for the very purpose of the sacrifice, and not for ends beyond, in which the stress of his mission lay. The problem being to contribute so much of pain, or judicial suffering, as may be needed to square the account of sin, the conclusion naturally follows, when that view is taken, that he is here for the very purpose of the bleeding; that is to be substituted in our place, and take, or somehow compensate for, the release of our punishment. This, and not any thing different, is the coarsely conceived, legally quantitative vicariousness ascribed to him. We, on the other hand, regard the vicariousness in which he comes only as the mode or instinct of his love, when doing a work in the recovery and reconciliation of men. He was in vicarious sacrifice before he came into the world, having the world upon his feeling as truly as now, and only made the fact-form sacrifice because he had the burden of it on him already. The sacrifice, taken as a fact in time, was not set before him as the end or object of his ministry — that would make it a mere pageant of suffering, without rational dignity or character — but, when it came, it was simply the bad fortune such a work, prosecuted with such devotion, must encounter on its way. The missionary, going out to spend his days among a heathen people, does not go to make so much of sacrifice, including even that perhaps of life itself — that being his purpose he might better stay at home — but he makes the sacrifice when the fit hour comes, because he is in a work, and because the work requires it of him. Christ, then, we must believe, is here to do something — some great and mighty work — not to make up a necessary quantum of pain for the compensation of God's justice. The sacrifice he makes, in becoming a man of sorrows and dying a malefactor's death, will be suffered under his work, and only for his work's sake. He was not ignorant, of course, that he would suffer. He expected that dying for his work would give eloquence and power to his mission just because, not coming here to die, he would have it put upon him as the cost of his fidelity — even as Anselm carefully and rightly distinguishes when he says, "He suffered death of his own accord, not as an act of obedience, but on account of his obedience in maintaining right; for he held out so persistently, that he met death on account of it." [1]

What then is the end or object he is here to accomplish? By the supposition he is not here to square up the account of our sin, or to satisfy the

1. *Cur Des Homo*, Lib. i, Cap. ix. [ED.] For a more accurate translation of this passage, see Anselm, "Why God Became Man," in the *Library of Christian Classics*, Vol. X: *A Scholastic Miscellany: Anselm to Ockham*, ed. and trans. by Eugene R. Fairweather (Philadelphia, 1956), 113.

divine justice for us. Neither is it any principal thing that he is here to prepare a possibility of forgiveness for sin. That is, if any thing, a secondary and subordinate matter, as will be discussed hereafter, in the third part of my argument.[2] The true end or object of the sacrifice we shall find is very simple, though presented in the New Testament under manifold varieties of statement; for, widely different as the varieties are, they are all in radical agreement with each other. Taking our clue from one of the simplest and tenderest in beauty of them all — "The Son of Man is come to seek and to save that which is lost"; or from one that is widest in range and contains the highest summation of all — "To wit that God was in Christ reconciling the world to himself"; or from one most formally put, and, in a certain intellectual sense, the deepest of all — "To this end was I born, and for this cause came I into the world, that I might bear witness to the truth" — taking hold of these and all such varieties of Scripture, we conceive a transaction moving on character in souls; a regenerative, saving, truth-subjecting, all-restoring, inward change of the life — in one word the establishing of the kingdom of God, or of heaven, among men, and the gathering finally of a new-born world into it.

But the farther unfolding of this central idea we shall find requires us, for convenience' sake, to make a fourfold distribution of the field or subject matter. First, we shall naturally give attention directly to Christ's healing ministry, and the large indication there made of what he is doing and to do in his sacrifice elsewhere. Then we shall endeavor to show more exactly, in another chapter, what work he undertakes or proposes to do in souls by his sacrifice. In another and third chapter it will be shown that, for that work's sake, he undertakes to be, and in the New Testament writings is conceived as being, the Great Moral Power of God, for its accomplishment. And then, fourthly, a chapter will be added to show how he becomes that power.[3]

It is by no accident that Christ, not trained as a physician, and, as far as we can discover, never before exercised in matters of concern for the sick, opens out the grand public ministry of his Messiahship directly into an office of healing, turning the main stress of it, we may almost say, down upon the healing of bodies, from that time onward. Hence it is the more remarkable that, when so much is made, in the formulas, of his threefold function under the titles of Prophet, Priest, and King, he still

2. [ED.] Part III is not included in the present selection because the author later revised the position he took in that Part; cf. *Forgiveness and Law* (1874), Chaps. 1-2.
3. [ED.] The substance of these chapters is reproduced in the present selection.

makes no figure in them at all as a Physician or Healer. This latter he is in the literal fact of history, and a great part of his outward life is in this particular kind of engagement. The others he is, or is only to be, in some tropical, accommodated sense, where language helps its poverty by a figure more or less determinate. We discover, meantime, that while he does not disown or repel these figures, permitting himself to be called a prophet, accepted as a priest, and exalted as a king, or Messiah, in his kingdom, he does not conceive that he is specially distinguished in his lifetime, at least, in these characters; but assumes that he is to be known as the expected man of prophecy, even from the first, by the works of his healing ministry. Thus when John sends messengers to inquire, "Art thou he that should come, or look we for another?" he sends back word in the affirmative, saying, "Yes, I am the expected Healer." — "Go tell John what things ye have seen and heard, how that the blind see, the lame walk, the lepers are cleansed, the deaf hear, the dead are raised, to the poor the gospel is preached." The plain inference is that however much or little may be meant by the three particular figures above named, he is at any rate, in literal and solid fact of history, a Healer — the great expected Healer of mankind.

I do not call him the Physician, but the Healer, it may be observed; not because we need scruple to apply that name, but simply to call attention to the fact that the older designation, Healer, is the one always applied to him in the New Testament, and has, in strict construction, a quite different meaning. . . .

Why now this very remarkable devotion to the healing of bodies? Coming into the world, as we all agree, for ends so intensely spiritual — to be a deliverer of souls, and to become the Head of a universal kingdom gathered in his own glorious likeness and beatitude — why does he strike directly into this low level of labor, and concern himself in this large degree, with the diseases and disabilities of men's bodies?

It is a very common answer made to this question, that he does it from a wise consideration of the advantage he will gain by it in men's prejudices, or the power he will thus obtain over them, in the separate matter of their spiritual choices and affections. . . .

But that Christ really put himself to his works of healing for this purpose we shall not be satisfied, after all, to believe. He has too much heart in these works to permit a thought that he is in them prudentially, or to gain some ulterior and remote advantage. No, there is a deeper reason. He is here as the incarnate Lord of the worlds, and he could not even be thought in that character if, being flesh, he did not turn himself to all he meets in the flesh. And so much is there in this, that any one having deep enough insight to read such a matter beforehand would say that if the Word is to be incarnate, then he will assuredly appear to bodies, minister to bodies, claim the kindship of bodies, by a tender sympathy for their pains and a healing touch upon their diseases. Being, in this manner, Son of Man, he is brought close to man, upon his human level. He has come to be with him in that level — touched with the feeling, not of his mental or more respectable infirmities, but of those which are lowest and most loathsome. What could a fastidious Saviour do here? one who is too delicate and spiritual to concern himself with the disagreeable and often revolting conditions of bodies?

Besides, he is here in God's own love, and what shall that love grapple with, when it comes, but precisely that which is deepest in the consciousness of suffering?

No matter if he has come to be a Redeemer of souls. Souls and bodies are not so far apart as many try to believe. Where are the pains of bodies felt but in their souls? and where go the disorder and breakage of souls but directly into their bodies? How sovereign is the action of souls! how inevitable the reaction of bodies! and how nearly common are the fortunes of both! The fall of sin carries down body and soul together, and the quickening of the Spirit quickens not the soul only, but the mortal body with it. We sometimes think the body is in health, when the soul is not; and the soul in health, when the body is not; but a great many diseases work latently, a long time, before they break out, and the returning of health is often working latently, a long time, before we discover it. After all, how nearly divine a thing is health, be it in the soul or in the body; and as the fibers of both are intertwined, with such marvelous cunning, all through, how shall either fall out of God's order alone, or come back into it alone?

The whole man quivers in the shock of sin. The crystalline order of soul and body is shivered by the same blow. Diseases consequent are nothing, after that, but the fact that the harmonic condition of health is broken — nothing fitly joined together, nothing compacted by what every joint supplieth, nothing vitalized by the effectual and measurely working of all parts for each other. Why then should the Great Healer think to pass by bodies, when he comes for the healing of souls? And as all men know it, when their bodies are sick, and are ready enough to be healed — ignorant meantime altogether of the disorder in their souls, and wanting no help there — why should not the Healing Mercy apply itself, at once, where it is wanted, and not throw itself away on souls, in the attempting of a benefaction sure, at first, to be repelled?

Furthermore, if we are to understand this matter, we must carefully observe what opinion Christ himself had of men's diseases and the bad implications whence they come. How large a part of his cures are wrought on persons whom foul spirits — just now unwontedly "tormented" and stirred up to a special activity — have taken possession of. How often does he say, "Go in peace, thy sins are forgiven thee"; though perhaps nothing has been said of their sins before, and possibly nothing more is meant than that they are cured of their malady. To the simply inoffensive broken invalid, whom he found at the pool of Siloam and healed, he says, "Sin no more, lest a worse thing befall thee." Over a poor disabled woman doubled by disease, he says, in softest pity, "whom Satan has bound these eighteen years." In this manner he associates disease, even habitually, with malign causes, and very nearly identifies the burden of it with the curse and burden of sin itself. Over the young man blind from his birth, he does indeed say that "neither he nor his parents have sinned, that he was born blind," but he only means in this to repel the odious and half-superstitious impeachment, that was charging the very special suffering of the case to some special criminality in the house. Had the impeachment been that all the disabilities, and diseases, and the generally disordered health of men's bodies are due to the great public fact of sin, and the retributive causes loosened by it, his profoundly accordant conviction is proved by his mission itself. Accordingly all his healings in bodies were but so many types of the healing virtue he was dispensing, in the higher nature itself. Indeed the whole purpose of his life, comprehensively taken, was, in his own view, to work a healing general of the subject, a restoration thus to complete health and the crystal unity of heaven's vital order. Sometimes he appears to have operated for the soul through the body, and sometimes for the body through the soul, contriving in what manner to elicit faith before the cure and assuming, evidently, the fact of a reciprocal action and reaction operating naturally between them — the healing of the body helped by the faith of the soul and the faith of the soul by the healing of the body. In the large view, his operation is but one, and life, complete life, is or is to be the result.

If now any one should ask what is the particular import, or importance, of this healing work of Christ in bodies, that it should even occupy a chapter in the doctrine of his sacrifice, the very simple and sufficient answer is that it is a matter quite decisive, in respect to the nature of that substitutive office which Christ undertook to fulfill. If we want to know in what sense or manner he suffered for the sins of mankind, his immense expenditure of toil, and feeling, and disgustful sympathy, and the murderous jealousy to be encountered in healing the diseases of mankind, will furnish the exact explanation required. Indeed, if he came simply to be the manifested love of God, and to be lifted up as the brazen serpent in the wilderness, for the healing of guilty souls, nothing could be more natural in that love, having that sublime healing purpose in view, than that he should go directly into the healing of bodies in the manner described by the evangelists. But if he came to satisfy God's justice, or pacify God's wrath against sin, so to prepare a ground of forgiveness for sin, there is a very palpable twofold incongruity between his healings and such a work. First, between offering mere pain or suffering to God, and a general operation of body-cure on mankind, there is no more real agreement or consent of meaning than between doing the same and building a college, or endowing a school of surgery. And secondly, since all diseases are but issues of penal consequence, under the retributive laws God has incorporated in our human nature for the redress of our sin, what is Christ doing, in his mighty works of healing, but simply blocking or defeating the ordinances of justice, whose wrath he has come to satisfy, and whose rule to propitiate? The disagreement is radical and total, between being man's substitute under God's penalties maintained, and being man's Healer under the same discontinued, or pushed by. The question, How shall two walk together unless they be agreed? was never more apposite. The inference indeed is absolute, one way or the other, either that Christ engaged in no such work of healing, or that he came to fulfill no such office of suffering.

Meantime, the agreement between his healing ministry and the kind of vicarious action I have ascribed to him is complete. Nay, he could not come into the world, in that office, without undertaking one kind of ministry as naturally as the other; or, in fact, without feeling both to be one. . . .

Chapter II

Christ's Object is the Healing of Souls

The healings of Christ in bodies, we have just seen, are in fact an outward type of the more radical and sublime cure he undertakes, by his sacrifice, to work in fallen character. In this cure we have the principal aim and object of his mission. We may sum up thus all that he taught, and did, and suffered, in the industry of his life and the pangs of his cross, and say that the one, comprehensive, all-inclusive aim that draws him on is the change he will operate in the spiritual habit and future well-being of souls. In this fact it is, and only in this, that he becomes a Redeemer. He is here in vicarious sacrifice, not for something else, but for this.

In the unfolding of this general conception, my present chapter will be occupied. It is very commonly assumed that Christ is here for another and different main object; viz., to suffer before God's justice, and prepare, in the satisfying of that, a way of possible forgiveness for men. From this I must dissent, though without proposing here any controversy farther than may be implied in the maintenance and due illustration of my proposition above stated. What was necessary to be done for the preparation of forgiveness will be considered at a more advanced stage of the discussion. I only say, for the present, that this is no principal matter in his work, the principal matter being to inaugurate a grand, restorative, new-creating movement on character — the reconciliation, that is, of men to God. The other, the preparation of forgiveness, take what view of it we may, unless we make forgiveness the same thing as reconciliation, can be only a secondary and subordinate matter, the principal work and wonder of all being what Christ undertakes and is able to do, in the bad mind's healing and recovery to God.

That some very great and wonderful change or recasting of soul is, in some way, necessary — as well as to provide the forgiveness of sins — is generally admitted and asserted with abundant emphasis; but it is not as generally perceived that Christ has any particular agency in it. It is not denied that his teachings have great value, or that what is called his expiatory suffering for sin is effective in a degree, on men's feeling, as well as efficacious in the satisfaction of justice; and it is continually put to his credit, in this same suffering and satisfaction, that he has purchased the Holy Spirit, and sends him forth to work the needed change in souls. In this way, some compensation is made for the loss that accrues by a failure to conceive the immediate and really immense agency of Christ in such changes; still there is a loss. No conception of Christ really meets the true significance of his mission, that does not find him working centrally in the great soul-healing himself; related presently to it, in all the matter of his suffering and sacrifice. It is not his simply to forgive, or obtain the forgiveness of sin, in the lowest and most nearly negative sense of remission; his great and vastly more significant endeavor is to make the sin itself let go of the sinner, and so deliver him inwardly that he shall be clear of it. And to accomplish this requires an almost recomposition of the man; the removal of all his breakage, and disorder, and derangement, and the crystallization over again, I may so speak, of all his shattered affinities, in God's own harmony and law. And, in order to this result, whatever agencies beside concur in it, three things, included in the sacrifice and suffering of Jesus, appear to be specially needed.

1. There is a want of something done, or shown, to pre-engage the feeling, or raise a favoring prejudice in it; so that, when advance is made on God's part in a call to repentance, the subject may not be repelled, but drawn rather. Otherwise it is like to be as it was in the garden, when the culprit hearing God calling after him, fled and hid himself. No bad soul likes to meet the Holy One, but recoils painfully, shivers with dread, and turns away. But the foremost thing we see in Christ is not the infinite holiness, or sovereign purity; he takes us, first, on the side of our natural feeling; showing his compassions there, passing before us visaged in sorrow, groaning in distressful concern for us, dying even the bitterest conceivable death, because the love he bears to us can not let go of us. In a word we see him entered so deeply into our lot, that we are softened and drawn by him, and even begin to want him entered more deeply, that we may feel him more constrainingly. In this way a great point is turned in our recovery. Our heart is engaged before it is broken. We like the Friend before we love the Saviour.

2. It is another point of consequence, in the matter of our recovery, that we have some better, more tender, and so more piercing conviction of sin than we get from our natural remorse, or even from the rugged and blunt sentence of law. It is well, indeed, to be shot through with fiery bolts from Sinai, but these hard, dry wounds, these lacerations of truth, want searching and wounding over again, by the gentle surgery of love, before we are in a way to be healed. In this more subduing and more nearly irresistible convincing we have, in part, the peculiar efficacy of the cross. We look on him whom we have pierced, and are pierced ourselves. Through the mighty bosom struggle of the agony and death we look down, softened, into the bosom wars and woes Christ pities and dies for in us. And when we hear him say, ". . . of sin because ye believe not on me," we are not chilled or repelled, as by the icy baptism of fear and remorse, but we welcome the pain. As Simeon himself declared, "He is set for the fall" as well as "for the rising again"; and we even bless the fall that so tenderly prepares the rising.

In this manner it was that the conversion of Paul began at the point of that piercing word — "I am Jesus of Nazareth, whom thou persecutest." Penetrated and felled by that arrow of the divine love, his "exceedingly mad" feeling dies, and his resistance, from that moment, is gone.

3. There greatly needs to be, and therefore, in Christ, is given, a type of the new feeling and life to be restored. Abstract descriptions given of holiness or holy virtue do not signify much to those who never knew them inwardly by their effects. To conceive a really divine character by specification, or receive it by inventory, is in fact impossible. No language can give the specification, and no mind could take the meaning of it accurately, if it were given. Hence the necessity that we have some exposition that is practical and personal. We want no theologic definition of God's perfections; but we want a friend, whom we can feel as a man, and whom it will be sufficiently accurate for us to accept and love. Let him come so nigh, if possible, let him be so deeply inserted into our lot and our feeling, that we can bury ourselves in him and the fortunes of his burdened life, and then it will be wonderful, if having God's own type in his life, we do not catch the true impress from it in ourselves.

In these three points, we perceive that the suffering life and death of Jesus are the appropriate and even necessary equipment of his doing force, in what he undertakes for character. . . .

Chapter III

He Is to Be God's Power in Working Such Recovery

In ordinary cases where a work is undertaken, it signifies nothing more to say that the doer undertakes to be a power to that effect; for whatever is to be done by action supposes, of course, a power acting. But where there is something to be done not by action but by quality of being, or by the worth, and beauty, and divine greatness of a character, the action is nothing and the power to be effective thus, in simply being what it is, every thing. Therefore, when we say and show that Christ is here to new-create, or regenerate, fallen character, it is not insignificant to add that he is here to be, or become, so great a power. For the new-creation we speak of is not a work to be carried by any kind of doing or efficient activity, or even by the fiat-force of omnipotence itself, but only by such higher kind of potency as can do so great a thing, through our consent, and without infringing our liberty; do it, that is, by the felt quality of being, or holy impulsion of worth and beauty it embodies. How far it may be the way of the Holy Spirit to operate in the regeneration of character by action, or the doing method, we do not know; doubtless God will do for us by the force-principle all that may be done by it; but the force-principle is not related plainly to the doing of all which requires to be done in the matter of so great a change, unless it be in ways circuitous, and one remove distant from the will; for to operate this change by any method that overrides or even omits our concurrent choice, is not to change our character, but to demolish our personality. A great power then is wanted, which can pierce, and press, and draw, and sway, and as it were new-crystallize the soul, which still is not any kind of force. And considering what the change is which the Scripture itself proposes, we even look to see some different, higher kind of power brought into the field, and magnified as the hope of our salvation. In Christ, accordingly, we find this higher power so magnified — a power that we may call the Moral Power of God. And the representation is that Christ, by his incarnate life and passion, becomes that higher kind of power — executing in that manner, or by virtue of that kind of power, the internal new-creation for which, as was shown in the last chapter, he came into the world.

My present chapter, accordingly, will be occupied with the fact that Christ's saving mission turns upon his having become such a power. And then my next will show how he becomes such a power in the facts of his personal history.

In pursuing the subject assigned, a first matter will be to distinguish accurately what we are to understand by the supposed moral power.

Is it then that Christ is to be such a kind of power as we mean when we speak of example? Certainly not, if we take the word *example* in its most proper and common signification. An example, we conceive, is a model that we copy, and set ourselves by our own will to reproduce in ourselves. Many teachers have been rising up, in all the past ages, and propounding it as the true theory of the gospel, that Christ came forth to be a Redeemer, in the way of being an example. But no theory of the kind has ever been able, under the very meager and restricted word *example*, to get any show of general acceptance. For the truth is that we consciously want something better than a model to be copied; some vehicle of God to the soul, that is able to copy God into it. Something is wanted that shall go before and beget, in us, the disposition to copy an example.

Sometimes the example-theory has been stated broadly enough to include the demonstration of the divine love in Christ's life. Sometimes, also, this demonstration of the divine love, apart from any thing said of example, has been put forward as the object of his mission; love being regarded as the sufficient reconciling power of God on human character. But no such view has ever gained a wide acceptance; not for the reason, I must think, that God's love is not a great power on the feeling of mankind, or that, when it is revealed in Christ, it does not go far to make up the requisite power; but that consciously we need other and sturdier elements to produce impressions equal to the change proposed in our spiritual transformation. Mere love, as we commonly conceive the word, suffers disrespect. We need somehow to feel that the love is a principled love, grounded in immovable convictions of right. There is no so very intense power in love, when descending even to the greatest possible sacrifice, if we are allowed to think of it as being only a mood of natural softness or merely instinctive sympathy. Many animals will rush after one of their kind in distress, and pitch themselves into the toils of their captors, by mere sympathy of kind. To magnify love therefore, even the love of the cross, as being itself the new-creating power of God, would be a very great mistake, if the righteous rule of God is not somehow included. When Jesus in his sacrifice takes our lot upon his feeling, and goes even to the cross for us, we need also to conceive that he does this for the right, and because the everlasting word of righteousness commands him. Not all that belongs to this matter can be said as effectively here as it may be when we come, in the Third Part, to consider the relations of the sacrifice to law. So much is added here only to fasten, or sufficiently affirm, the conviction that no purely favoring, sympathetic kind of intervention, however self-sacrificing, can be any sufficient power on character to be a salvation.

By the moral power of God, or of Christ as the manifested reality of God, we understand comprehensively the power of all God's moral perfections, in one word, of his greatness. And by greatness we mean greatness of character; for there is no greatness in force, no greatness in quantity, or height, or antiquity of being, no greatness any where but in character. In this it is that so great moral power is conceived to be developed, in the self-devoting sacrifice of Christ's life and death. . . .

I have only to add, as a considerable argument for the moral view of Christ and his sacrifice, in distinction from all others, that the time of his coming coincides with this only. Had he come having it for his principal object to satisfy God's justice and be substituted, in that manner, for the release of transgression, there appears to be no reason why he should have delayed his coming for so many ages. If the effect was to be on God, God was just as capable at the very first of feeling the worth of his sacrifice, as at any time afterward; and, if this was to be the salvation, why should the salvation be delayed? But if he came to be the moral power of God on men, nothing is so difficult as the due development of any such moral power; because the capacity or necessary receptivity for it, has itself to be prepared. Thus, if Christ had come to the monster age before the flood, when raw force was every thing, and moral greatness nothing, his death and passion, all the significance of his suffering and sacrifice, would have been lost, and probably would not even have been preserved in the remembrance of history. The world was too coarse, and too deep in the force-principle of violence, to apprehend a visitation so thoughtful and deep in the merit of character. There was no room or receptivity, as yet, for Christ in the world. A long-drawn scheme of economy is previously needed, to prepare that receptivity; a drill of outward sacrifice and cere-mony, a providential milling of captivities, deliverances, wars, plagues, and other public judgments; commemorated in hymns, interpreted and set home by the preaching of a prophet ministry; till finally there is a cul-ture of mind or of moral perception produced that is sufficiently ad-vanced to receive the meaning of Christ in his sacrifice, and allow him to get an accepted place in the moral impressions of mankind. Conceiving, in this manner, that he came to be the moral power of God on character, there is good and sufficient reason for his delay. He came as soon as he could, or, as the Scripture says, "in the fullness of time"; came in fact at the very earliest moment when it was possible to get hold of history.

Indeed, so very slow is the world in getting ready for the due impres-sion of what lies in moral power, that only a very partial opening to it is prepared even now. The world is still too coarse, too deep in sense and the force-principle, to feel, in any but a very small degree, the moral power of God in the Christian history. Slowly and sluggishly this higher sense is unfolding, but there is a perceptible advance, and we may antici-pate the day when there will be a sense opened wide enough for Christ, in his true power, to enter; thus to fill, and new-create in good, all souls that live. Then, and not till then, will it be known how grand a fact the moral power of God in the person of his Son may be.

Chapter iv

How He Becomes So Great a Power

In his descent to the flesh, we might naturally expect that Christ would bring all deific perfections with him, and have them expressed in his person. And this indeed is true; but with the large qualification that they will be expressed only by degrees, and under conditions of time; that is, under such laws of expression as pertain to humanity. In one view, God is emptied of his perfections in becoming incarnate, and has them all to acquire and bring into evidence, by the same process of right living that obtains character and weight for men. Otherwise the incarnation would be no real fact. It must be with Christ as with men, and moral power, as we commonly use the term, among men, is the power that a man finally gets, by the courses and achievements of a great and worthy life, to impress and sway other men. . . .

And this, exactly, is what we are to understand by the moral power of God in the gospel of his Son. It is a new kind of power — the greatest and most sovereign power we know — which God undertakes to have by obtaining it, under the human laws and methods. Hence the incarnation. God had a certain kind of power before; viz., that which may be called attribute power. By attributes we mean what we attribute to God, when we think God, or unfold our idea of God as the Absolute Being. As being infinite and absolute, we ascribe to him certain attributes, or perfections. Such attributes or perfections are a kind of abstract excellence, such as we bring out, or generate, by our own intellectual refinements on the idea of God, to answer to our own intellectual demands. Still, as God is infinite, the perfections are distant. We hardly dare think them, if we could, into our finite molds. We almost reason them away. Thus God, we say, is omnipotent, therefore he will bring to pass exactly all that he desires; and does, in fact, desire nothing but what comes to pass. Again, God is eternally sovereign; therefore he regrets nothing, as we do; for what he wills he does. Again, God is omniscient, knowing every thing beforehand; therefore every thing is immovably fixed beforehand. Still again, God is infinitely happy; therefore he is impassible and can not suffer in feeling any way. Yet once more, God is immutably just; and must therefore have his justice satisfied by the necessary quantum of suffering. And so it turns out that in making up an attribute power we very nearly think away, or annihilate, all that creates an effective impress on our sentiment and character. We make him great, but so also make him thin and cold. We feel him as a platitude more than as a person. His great attributes became dry words, a kind of milky way over our heads — vast enough in the matter of extension, but evanescently dim to our feeling.

This result had been mitigated somewhat by his works and word and Providence, before the coming of Christ. But the tendency still was to carry back all the more genial impressions thus unfolded, and merge them in the attribute-power by which, as an unseen, infinite being, we had before contrived to think and to measure his character. Till, finally, in the fullness of time, he is constrained to institute a new movement on the world, in the incarnation of his Son. The undertaking is to obtain, through him, and the facts and processes of his life, a new kind of power; viz., moral power; the same that is obtained by human conduct under human methods. It will be divine power still, only it will not be attribute-power. That is the power of his idea. This new power is to be the power cumulative, gained by him among men as truly as they gain it with each other. Only it will turn out, in the end, to be the grandest, closest to feeling, most impressive, most soul-renovating, and spiritually sublime power that was ever obtained in this or any other world. . . .

How then does it come? — let us see if we can trace the process. When the holy child is born, he has no moral power at all. The halo which the painters show about his head is not there. He is simply the child of two very humble people, in a very mean provincial town. There was a good deal more circumstance and prospect in Washington's infancy than in his; and yet the moral power of that little one's name, George, had nothing of the ring that a great life and history will afterwards give it. Nor is it any thing if the name is called Emanuel; nobody will see any meaning in that, at present. The meaning itself is yet to be obtained.

There had been some remarkable prophecies over the child, not much regarded, of course, till afterwards. A few very pleasant facts are given concerning his childhood and youth, which will signify a great deal more as recollections than they do to present observation. His look and manner, as he grows up, are winning to every body. He is subject to his parents and a model of filial duty. His custom is to be always at the synagogue worship. On a certain occasion, when he is but twelve years old, he astonishes the doctors of the temple by his wonderful questions; and there it is that he drops the remarkable intimation, specially noted by his mother, that he "must be about his Father's business"; in which, as we can see, he already begins to be a little conscious of his great calling; which makes it all the more remarkable that he still struggles on eighteen years longer, hurried by no forwardness or impatience, till the full idea of his great ministry takes possession of his life. During this whole period he confesses no sin, and as far as we can judge, rectifies no mistake; and, if these negative facts had been noted by any body, as plainly they could not be, his piety would certainly have been seen to be of a most singular and even superhuman order.

On the whole, it does not appear that previous to entering on his public ministry when he was thirty years old, he has done any thing more than to beautifully and exactly fulfill his duties. His name is good, true, lovely; but as far as possible from being a name above every name. A certain moral power is felt in him, of course, by those who are with him, but what he is to be, in this respect, is as yet quite hidden from discovery.

But the time has now come for his great ministry to begin. The dim presentiment of his work, which he called his "Father's business" opens into a definite, settled, consciousness of his call. As it were by the revelation of the Spirit, he clearly perceives what he is to do, and what to suffer; that he is to go down into the hell of the world's corporate evil, to be wounded and galled by the world's malice, and bear the burden of the world's undoing as a charge upon his love; and so, by agonies of sacrifice, including a most bitter death, to reconcile men to God and establish the eternal kingdom of God in their hearts. The work attracts him, and yet his soul, or at least his natural human feeling, recoils. Smitten, as it were, by a kind of horror, he is hurried off into the wilderness, to wrestle with his temptations; groaning there alone, under the heavy load he is to bear, and bowing his reluctant humanity to the call, by the discipline of fasting. He comes out victorious, but as a victor spent. The angels of God recruit him by their tender and cheering ministry, and he goes to his work.

No man of the race, it is quite safe to say, ever went to the calling of his life against impediments of natural sensibility so appalling. Men do often make great and heroic sacrifices in a cause already undertaken, but he undertakes the forlornest, most appalling sacrifice, fully perceiving what it is to be beforehand. Men have the brave will raised in them afterwards, by the heat of encounter; he has his victory at the beginning, alone, in a desert, where only love and God, in the moods of silence, come to his aid. In this simple beginning of Christ, there is character enough to create a moral power never before conceived, never since realized. But it does not appear that even the facts of his temptation were made known till some time after — when, or how, we can only guess. He goes into his work, therefore, as a merely common man, a Nazarene carpenter, respected for nothing save as he compels respect by his works and his words.

Meantime John has been testifying, as a prophet, of another who is to come, or is even now at hand, whose shoes even he is not worthy to untie, and by whom the kingdom of heaven is to be set up on earth. And this other, viz., Jesus, comes to him shortly after to be baptized; when he breaks out, in prophetic vision, as soon as he perceives him coming, "Behold the Lamb of God, that taketh away the sins of the world." The consecrating dove lights upon him in his baptism, and a voice out of heaven declares, "This is my beloved Son, in whom I am well pleased." And yet even John is so little impressed, or so little believes in what he hears shortly after of his miracles and his doctrine, that he sends to inquire, as if he might still be only an ordinary man, possibly an impostor, "Art thou he that should come, or look we for another?" As yet he has not made impression enough for God's love and power by his ministry, beautiful and wonderful as it is, to even hold a prophet's opinion of him up to the pitch of his own prophetic testimony!

But he goes on with his ministry for three years; traveling on foot, sleeping in desert places and upon the mountain tops, associating mostly with the poor and humble, who have scarcely cultivation enough to yield him any fit return of sympathy, or even to be duly impressed by his miracles. The learned and select are alienated from him, partly for this reason. They deny his miracles, or they charge them openly to his conspiracy with devils. . . .

And yet, over against all these affecting and subduing demonstrations in his life, there were a great many things, we know, which at the time seemed even to discourage confidence in him. For example he was baffling always the expectations of his friends; they could hardly name an expectation, and they had abundance of them, which he did not forthwith take away by the notification of some loss, or cross of dejection, which to them wore a look totally opposite to every feeling they had respecting the great Messiah. Not to multiply instances in which he tried their confidence by other methods, we pass directly to the two great closing facts of his life, his agony and crucifixion. His work is now done, and nothing remains but to let others bring him to the murderous end they are planning to accomplish. His whole feeling is now loose upon him, respited by no occupation; and the dreadful burdens of concern for men, which his divine love, too strong for the body, rolls down upon him, press him, as it were, to the ground. He beholds the corporate curse, too, of the world's evil and madness just ready to burst upon his person, and though he is not moved by fear, his pure innocence struggles heavily, with instinctive horror, before that retributive frenzy, which is going to baptize itself in his blood! No so grand mystery of divine feeling was ever before or after set before the gaze of mortals. But his friends are at no point of view where they can even begin to conceive it. His person, his errand, his work, are as yet wholly beyond the reach even of their guesses. They have seen strange gleams of quality in him, they have been drawn, repelled, impressed, astounded, and thoroughly posed by his mystery, and they only try to settle the whirl of their brain by calling him a great prophet, Messiah, the Christ, thinking him virtually always as a man. And now in the agony, just after his triumphal entry into the city, when they look to see him rise and take on his kingship, he collapses in weakness, without any visible reason; falling on the ground, groaning, writhing, dripping in bloody sweat, like grapes in the wine-press, and calling on God and men for help, in meeting some unknown calamity that he does not name. It is as if he were just at the end of his pretensions, and struggling, as a convict might, under his impending doom. All heart is taken away from his disciples at once; their confidence in him is fatally broken; as we can plainly see in the fact that when he is arrested, an hour or two after, they forsake him utterly. Peter makes one or two wild slashes for him with his sword, and then he too is gone; only he will hang about the hall when the trial goes on, carefully denying his discipleship.

In this manner Jesus goes to his cross; and the manner of his trial and death, though supported with a transcendent dignity on his part, that makes him even the chief figure in the scene, are yet so thoroughly contemptuous and ignominious, that the poor disciples are obliged to confess to themselves, if not to others, that their much loved Messiah is now stamped as another exploded pretender! A great reaction begins, however, to be visible in the minds of the multitude. As the Roman governor himself, before whom he was dragged to a mock trial for sedition, was quite shaken out of self-possession by the dignity of his manner under the questioning — quailing visibly in the sense of a mysterious something in the man, justifying, equivocating, consenting, condemning, giving him up to his accusers, and washing his hands to be clear of the innocent blood — so in the death-scene of the cross, slave's death though it be, in the outward ignominy of the form, the multitude grow serious, and drop out their jeers in awe of his felt majesty, and finally go home, at another swing of oscillation, smiting their breasts in dumb confession of their murderous crime. They had expected nothing of him, and for just that reason they are the more easily impressed by the strange power in him — under such ignominy, dying in such majesty. Not so with his disciples. They had expected every thing of him, and now that he is dead, every expectation is blasted. Even their profound respect, unwilling as they are to shake it off, and tenderly as they would fain cling to it still, is yet a really blasted confidence, now that he is dead under such ignominy. The two senators, Nicodemus and Joseph, come with their spices, revealing what impressions they have felt of his wonderful character, and daring now to show their respect just because he is dead. Finally, on the third-day morning, it is rumored among the disciples that he is risen, but their soul is under such a weight of stupor that they can not believe it. And two of them we find trudging back homeward to Galilee, sad and heavy-hearted, and weeping, as it were, in doleful refrain — "We thought it had been he that should have redeemed Israel!"

Where now is the power? We have been exploring a large field, hunting down along the whole course of Christ's life, expecting, looking to see, the great name rolled up into volume and majesty, but that any thing we have found should have power to new-create the moral sentiments and affinities of mankind, we can hardly believe. We have seen, between the infancy and the death, a great many strange things, and a great many lovely. Coruscations of glory have been shooting out, all along the remarkable history. But there have been severities, and repellences, and discouraging tokens, blended so continually with the story, and the end of it is so dark, if not weak, that we get no such densely compacted unity of impression, as belongs to a great moral power. We are put in a maze, or even a thrilling kind of mystery, but that all-the-while cumulative power and weight, that great name which is to be a gospel of life in men's hearts, does not appear. And yet there is, it may be, a certain latent heat in the facts we have noted, that is finally to become sensible heat, or blaze into splendor. No life becomes a power till we somehow get the clue of it. A great many human characters are very much of a riddle till they come on to the crisis of fact, where their objects, and ends, and secret aims, are all discovered, and where the seeming faults and contrarieties, that were mysterious, get their solution — all to be approved in the admirable and wise unity that could not sooner appear.

Christ only differs here from such mysterious, peculiar men in the fact that he dies before the clue is given. It is only the resurrection and ascension back into glory that bring us out the true point of understanding. Now his most extraordinary nature and mission for the first time come distinctly into thought. Now, since he has gone up visibly into heaven, we begin to understand what he meant when he said that he came down from heaven. We conceive him as the incarnate Word, and begin to look upon his glory as the glory of the only begotten of the Father, full of grace and truth. In him now there may be more than we saw, a greater name and power; for the righteousness and love of God are in him, and it puts a new face on his whole life, that he is here to save the world.

We begin back now at the point of his infancy and we follow him onward again, going over all the points we have named, but with results how different! Every thing falls into place, and every step onward is the unfolding of power. The wonderful authority becomes more wonderful; in the right of a superior nature to give it sanction, the severity becomes majesty; knowing who the teacher is, what before was truth brightens into a glorious wisdom; the soft-looking innocence of the life becomes a kind of general transfiguration; the agony that seemed to be wanting in magnanimity becomes the love-groan, as it were, of his mysterious nature; the crushing defeat of the death breaks into immortal victory. Whatever, in a word, seemed weak, distracted, contrarious, takes on a look of progressive order, and falls into chime as a necessary factor in his divinely great character. And so the merely human beginning grows into what is more and more visibly superhuman, dying into boundlessness and glory, as the sun when it sets in the sea. The rising and the ascension put us on the revision, and helped us to conceive who he was; but now he is so great that the rising does not raise him any more, and the ascension does not glorify him. . . .

The historical exposition of the moral power of Christ, or of the process by which it is obtained, is now finished, and yet certain points of rational consequence remain to be suggested, which could not be crowded into the body of it without creating an appearance of distraction. The view of Christ's mission I have been trying to establish excludes the possibility, it will be seen, of any dogmatic formula in which it may be adequately stated. It is not a theorem, or form of thought, but a process, and the process includes all the facts of a life. . . .

In this manner, four points in particular may yet be made in regard to the process and effect of his life, that will render the power of it still more intelligible, and so far more impressive.

1. That the kind of moral power obtained by Christ is different from any which had been obtained by men, more difficult, deeper, and holier. He founds no school of philosophy, heads no revolution, fights no great battle, achieves no title to honor, such as the world's great men have achieved. Men consciously feel that a strong power is somehow gathering about his person, but will only know by and by what it is. It is the power, in great part, of sorrow, suffering, sacrifice, death, a paradox of ignominy and grandeur not easily solved. Honor, in the common sense of that term, can make nothing of it. Fame will not lift her airy trumpet to publish it, and would only mock it if she did. If we call him a hero, as some are trying to do, then all other heroes appear to be scarcely more than mock heroes in the comparison. . . .

2. It is a very great point, as regards the kind of power Christ is obtaining, that he humanizes God to men. I have already spoken of the necessary distance and coldness of a mere attribute power, such as we ourselves generate when trying to think God as the Absolute Being. The incarnate life and history of Jesus meet us here, at the point of our weakness. God is in Christ, consenting to obtain the power by which he will regain us to himself, under our own human conditions. He is in our plane, acting with us and for us, interpreted to our sympathies by what he does and is, in social relationship with us. His perfections meet us in our own measures, not in the impossible measures of infinity; and so he becomes a world-king in the world, and not above it and far away from it. We know him, in just the same way as we know one another. . . .

3. It is another great article of his power that he is able to raise, at once, the sense of guilt and attract the confidence of the guilty. By his purity of life, by the sublime reach of his very simple doctrine, by his terrible warnings and reproofs, by his persistent coupling of disease, in all his healings, with sin, by the sorrows and the suffering patience of his life, by the bitter ignominy of his death, followed by the Spirit coming after his resurrection, to show the things of his life to men in their true light of meaning — by all these piercing demonstrations he stirs the conviction of guilt, as never it was stirred before, and yet with no such consequences of revulsion from God as belongs to the natural action of guilt. . . .

4. To another and last point, where the moral power obtained by Christ gets even its principal weight of impression; viz., to the fact made

evident by his vicarious sacrifice, that God suffers on account of evil, or with and for created beings under evil — a fact very commonly disallowed and rejected, I am sorry to add, even by Christian theology itself, as being rationally irreconcilable with God's greatness and sufficiency.

It was very natural that the coarse, crude mind of the world, blunted to greater coarseness and crudity by the chill of guilt in its feeling, should be over-much occupied in conceiving God's infinity and the merely dynamic energies and magnitudes of his nature; the sovereignity of his will, his omnipotent force, his necessary impassibility to force external to himself, his essential beatitude as excluding all inflictions of pain or loss. Hence it has been very generally held even to this day, as a matter of necessary inference, that God is superior in every sense to suffering. Our theologians are commonly shocked, as by some frightful word of derogation, when the contrary is affirmed, and when they come to the matter of Christ's suffering they are careful to show, regarding it as a necessary point of reverence, that it was only the human nature that suffered, not the divine, suffering by itself. Besides, it will even be admitted, perhaps unwittingly, by those who dare to obtrude in this manner upon the interior mystery of Christ's person, where all reasonings about the physical suffering must be at fault, that even God himself, as well out of Christ as in the incarnate person of Christ, does incur a profoundly real suffering — not physical suffering, as I now speak, yet a suffering more deep than any physical suffering can be.

The principal suffering of any really great being and especially of God is because of his moral sensibility, nay, because of his moral perfection. He would not be perfect, if he did not feel appropriately to what is bad, base, wrong, destructive, cruel, and to every thing opposite to perfection. If the sight of wrong were to meet the discovery of God only as a disgusting spectacle meets a glass eye, his perfection would be the perfection of a glass eye and nothing more. None of us conceive him in this manner, but we conceive him as having a right sensibility to every thing. We say that he is displeased, and what is displeasure but an experience opposite to pleasure? so far a kind of suffering. We say that he "loathes" all baseness and impurity, and what is closer to a pain than loathing? We say that he "hates" all unrighteousness, and what is hatred but a fire of suffering? Is he not a "long-suffering" God, and is there no suffering in long suffering? Is he not a patient God, and what is patience but a regulated suffering? So of compassion, pity, sympathy, indignations suppressed, wounds of ingratitude, bonds of faith violated by treachery. So far we all admit the fact of divine suffering, no matter how sturdily we deny it in theory. The suffering is moral suffering, it is true, but it is the greatest and most real suffering in the world — so great that a perfect being would be likely, under it, to quite forget physical suffering, even if it were upon him. Making then so vast an admission, what does it signify afterward to turn ourselves round, in what we conceive to be our logical sagacity, and raise the petty inference that God, being infinite, must be impassible!

But we must not omit, in this connection, to notice a fact, as regards the moral suffering of God, that is not commonly admitted, or even observed, like the others just referred to. Thus we conceive that God is a being whose moral nature is pervaded and charactered, all through, by love. Some teachers even go so far as to insist that the Scripture declaration — "God is love" — is no rhetorical figure, but a logical and literal teaching; that God's very substance, or essence, is love. And yet love is an element, or principle, whether substance or not, so essentially vicarious that it even mortgages the subject to suffering, in all cases where there is no ground of complacency. As certainly as God is love, the burdens of love must be upon him. He must bear the lot of his enemies, and even the wrongs of his enemies. In pity, in patience, in sacrifice, in all kinds of holy concern, he must take them on his heart, and be afflicted for them as well as by them. In his greatness there is no bar to this kind of suffering; He will suffer because he is great, and be great because he suffers. Neither is his everlasting beatitude any bar to his suffering; for there is nothing so essentially blessed as to suffer well. Moral greatness culminates in great and good suffering; culminates also in blessedness, for there is a law of compensation in all moral natures, human as well as divine, divine as well as human, by which their suffering for love's sake becomes always a transcendent and more consciously sovereign joy. There ought to be no incredible paradox in this; for it is a fact every day proved — always to be known by mortal experience.

Now it is this moral suffering of God, the very fact which our human thinking is so slow to receive, that Christ unfolds and works into a character and a power in his human life. His compassions burdened for guilty men, his patient sensibilities, sorrows, sacrifices, the intense fellow-feeling of his ministry, his rejected sympathies, wrongs, ignominies — under and by all these it is that he verifies, and builds into a character, the moral suffering of the divine love.

2. Forgiveness and Law [1]

"I have always been trying to mend," wrote Bushnell in the last year of his life.[2] Very true. Nowhere is the fact more evident than in the development of his doctrine of Christ's work. That doctrine was of more concern to him than any other, and as new light dawned upon it he readily mended an older view. The question that baffled him most was how to give Christ's work a truly objective character. From the first he had sensed the inadequacy of a subjective theory of the atonement and had endeavored to remedy its defect by the device of the "altar forms." That was no real remedy, however, for while the altar forms supplied an objective imagery, they did not actually objectify the work of Christ. Bushnell himself later acknowledged "that while the form of the thought is objective, the real change is subjective — not a change in God, but a change rather in the sinner himself." [3]

A close scrutiny of the Harvard address will reveal that there was already a latent element in Bushnell's doctrine of the atonement which, if fully developed, would give it a more objective character. This was his insistence that forgiveness should be granted only on such terms as would keep alive in the transgressor a vivid sense of the sanctity of God's law and government.[4] "In a word," he declared, "we must be made to feel, in the very article of forgiveness, when it is offered, the essential and eternal sanctity of God's law — his own immovable adherence to it, as the only basis of order and well-being in the universe." [5] Much in this same vein appears also in *The Vicarious Sacrifice*, as when, for example, he wrote: "When Jesus in his sacrifice takes our lot upon his feeling, and goes even to the cross for us, we need also to conceive that he does this for the right, and because the everlasting word of righteousness commands him." [6] Surely, whether Bushnell recognized it or not, those expressions reflected an important element in the Edwardean theory of the atone-

1. *Forgiveness and Law, Grounded in Principles Interpreted by Human Analogies* (New York, 1874), Chap. I (33–92); Chap. II (93–95, 97, 99–103, 107–9, 111–21, 133–34, 139, 147–50, 158–62, 173–76).

2. Mary B. Cheney, *Life and Letters of Horace Bushnell* (New York, 1880), 553.

3. *Christ in Theology* (Hartford, 1851), 245.

4. *God in Christ* (Hartford, 1849), 216–37.   5. *Ibid.*, 218.

6. *The Vicarious Sacrifice, Grounded in Principles of Universal Obligation* (New York, 1866), 171.

ment. Thus while he accented the subjective aspect of his theory, much that he said concerning the necessity to honor and sustain the divine law could have been interpreted in its objective import.

In view of Bushnell's persistent searchings for further light on the atonement, it is not surprising that he finally became dissatisfied with the position taken in the Harvard discourse and in *The Vicarious Sacrifice*. The seeker professed the "arrival of fresh light" on two questions: (1) the pre-condition of man's true forgiveness of his enemy, and (2) the role of law and commandment in the process of redemption. While preparing a sermon on "Christian Forgiveness," [7] he suddenly saw that any real forgiveness of one's enemy demanded a personal sacrifice so great as to be actually self-propitiating in its effect. Since that was true of man, he concluded that it must be true also of God. He revised his doctrine of Christ's work so as to include the element of divine self-propitiation. Thus his doctrine now acknowledged that God must be reconciled to man, as well as man to God.

With respect to the second question, he saw that law and commandment have need of each other in effecting change in human character.[8] The former is a factor in nature, and the latter is a factor in the supernatural realm. Penal causations are the power in the first, and supernatural operations are the power in the second. By the law there is a knowledge of sin, and by the commandment (grace) there is deliverance from it. In their co-action they serve to recover an estranged race to the Father.

As a result of this fresh light, Bushnell wrote *Forgiveness and Law* to take the place of Parts III and IV of *The Vicarious Sacrifice*. He intended to reconstruct the older treatise so as to present a more adequate doctrine of the atonement, but his death in 1876 prevented that achievement.

Did Bushnell's "fresh light" represent a real advance over what he had said in *The Vicarious Sacrifice?* One student of his theology has said no.[9] A Scottish theologian, on the other hand, has declared that *Forgiveness and Law* marked "a notable advance" in Bushnell's doctrine of the work of Christ.[10] Perhaps a more satisfactory answer can be given if the ques-

7. *Christ and His Salvation* (New York, 1864), 372–92.

8. In *The Vicarious Sacrifice* (Part III) Bushnell had already advanced this general conception.

9. Ralph O. Harpole, "The Development of the Doctrine of Atonement in American Thought from Jonathan Edwards to Horace Bushnell" (unpublished Ph.D. dissertation, Yale University, 1924), 185.

10. S. D. F. Salmond, "The Theology of Horace Bushnell," *London Quartely Review*, XCV (January–April 1901), 158.

tion is framed differently. If one asks whether the root principle of Bushnell's theory of divine self-propitiation is latent in *The Vicarious Sacrifice,* the answer would seem to be yes. For God's disposition to make the
supreme sacrifice stemmed from his vicarious love (John 3:16). As Bushnell remarked, there is "a cross in God's perfections from eternity." [11] If,
on the other hand, one asks whether Bushnell saw the bearing of this
principle upon God's self-propitiation when he wrote *The Vicarious Sacrifice,* the answer must be no. He therefore spoke accurately when he said
that he had received "fresh light." Consequently it seems correct to conclude that *The Vicarious Sacrifice* contained the germ of the new element in Bushnell's doctrine, but that it remained hidden until he articulated it in *Forgiveness and Law.*

❖   ❖   ❖   ❖

Chapter 1

Forgiveness and Propitiation, Without Expiation

The argument of my former treatise[1] was concerned in exhibiting the
work of Christ as a reconciling power on men. This was conceived to be
the whole import and effect of it; just as, in our current theology, it is
conceived to be a work that reconciles God — sometimes a propitiation,
such as mitigates or conciliates the dispositions of God in the forgiveness
of sins; and sometimes, with far less appearance of possibility, an expiation that satisfies the justice of God, and allows him to yield the forgiveness legally.

I now propose to substitute, for the latter half of my former treatise,[2] a
different exposition; composing thus a whole of doctrine that comprises
both the reconciliation of men to God and of God to men. I have still as
little question now as before that the main significance of the gospel is in
what it does, or undertakes to do, for the reconciliation of men. Indeed, a
great part of the texts cited for atonement, so called, conceiving it as a
conciliation of God, have their whole meaning, if rightly understood, at
the other pole of the subject. And nothing is now so much wanted, to set
the gospel in its true proportion, as a just reclamation of these texts in the
meaning they have lost.

When we speak, as I am now to speak, of the propitiation of God, hav-

11. *The Vicarious Sacrifice,* 73.
1. [ED.] *The Vicarious Sacrifice* (1866).   2. [ED.] *Ibid.,* Parts III and IV.

ing it as our assumed undertaking to show the fact of such a propitiation antecedently related to the forgiveness of sins, we seem to be thrusting ourselves on a matter high above our reach, and in its own nature altogether improbable. There is even a look of offense and mortal presumption in the proposal itself. I am also pressed with the conviction that my single arguments first named will seem inconclusive, or even weak; for there is no determinate position here to be taken that will turn the question logically by itself. I have never handled a subject where all the parts and complexities of evidence are so necessary to be had in sight together, in order to any just impression. In this view, let me ask of my reader to go quite through my chapter, and get all my points in view, before he begins to set his opinions adversely in finalities of judgment passed before the time.

There is, it is true, one great principle or fundamental fact which runs through the whole subject as presented, and is, in a sense, the universal solvent of it, but that will not be seen at any single glance, and can not bring God into the range of a probable partakership with us, in the necessities of propitiation, till it has been long enough canvassed to reveal what is in it. The fact of which I speak is the grand analogy, or almost identity, that subsists between our moral nature and that of God; so that our moral pathologies and those of God make faithful answer to each other, and he is brought so close to us that almost any thing that occurs in the workings or exigencies of our moral instincts may even be expected in his.

It has been a question whether to begin this discussion at the Scripture texts, in which propitiation is asserted — as I formerly thought it was not, save in a certain objective way of accommodation — but as the view I am to advance opened first at the question of forgiveness by men toward men, I will start my argument from that point, and bring in the Scripture proofs farther on, where they will have some complexions of thought prepared to soften their incredibility.

I

In the New Testament it will be observed that forgiveness by God and forgiveness by men are set forth mutually, one by the help of the other. "Forgiving one another, even as God for Christ's sake (ἐν Χριστῷ) hath forgiven you." "Forgive us our trespasses as we forgive them that trespass against us." One kind of forgiveness matches and interprets the other; for they have a common property. They come to the same point when they are genuine, and require also exactly the same preparations and conditions precedent. It is not commonly supposed, I know, that forgiveness by men requires any thing done which is in the nature of propitiation. But we had best make nothing of that; for, in fact, the matter of forgiveness by men is so indeterminately thought, or so nearly unattempted by analysis, that we really do not know what is in it, or how it comes, or what it does. We talk of it in a certain loose way, but have really no moral casuistry by which we regulate our practice in it.

What then do we mean by forgiveness when we speak of forgiving an enemy or wrong-doer? — what, that is, by a man's forgiveness of a man? I suppose that a great many persons never had a thought of it as signifying more than the mere passing of the word. They even choke at this, and only stammer it in undertone when it is passed. As if the mere getting out of the word "I forgive" were the consummation of their duty-struggle in the question.

Nothing is more evident, to any one who cares to understand what is to be done in such a matter, than that the mere passing of the word *forgive* constitutes no new relation. It may be that the forgiving party only says it just to be quit of his adversary. He does it as a mere letting go or waiving of the man, not as a true taking hold of him rather for eternal brotherhood's sake. He is only thinking quite commonly, in this letting go, how to be let go himself, and have his obligation ended. Sometimes it will be even thought, if not spoken aloud, "Yes, I forgive him, but I hope never to see him again." Or it will be said, "Yes, I forgive, but I can never forget." Or, again, "Yes, and I do not much care whether he repents of his wrong or not, if only I can be quit of all connection with him." I can not specify, and need not, all the loose ways and turns of mock sentiment by which this grace of forgiveness is corrupted and made to be no grace at all, but only a plausible indifference under the guises of grace. It is how often but a kind of hypocrisy under which the forgiving man is hidden from his own discovery.

All this in a way of transition; the cases referred to are only cases where irresponsible, self-serving, worldly men, whether nominally Christian or not, cheapen the duty of forgiveness by light performance, or slip it by evasions and tricks of words. But there are troubles of mind in respect to this matter of forgiveness that are real, and are encountered by the best and holiest men. They mean to be forgiving, and live in the habit of it universally. Is it not the love of God that they have accepted as their ruling principle and joy — love, that is, to every body, including even their enemies? Yes, but the love of God prepares not even him to forgive by itself, as we shall by and by see. Not more certainly will it prepare any best and most loving of mankind to forgive. We take up certain modes of speaking which imply that love is a kind of total virtue, and will carry all other graces and virtues with it. And it will, in the sense of causation, or of being their causative spring. But it does not follow that it will dispense forgivenesses without also preparing the necessary antecedent propitiations. A good man lives in the unquestionable sway of universal love to his kind. If then one of them does him a bitter injury, will he therefore launch an absolute forgiveness on him? If he were nothing but love — if he were no complete moral nature — he might. But he is a complete moral nature, having other involuntary sentiments that come into play alongside of love, and partly for its sake — the sense of being hurt by wrong, indignations against wrong done to others, disgusts to what is loathsome, contempt of lies, hatred of oppression, anger hot against cruel inhumanities — all these animosities, or revulsions of feeling, fasten their grip on the malefactor's sins and refuse to let go. And they do it as for society and the law-state of discipline; composing a court of arbitrament that we call moral opinion, which keeps all wrong-doing and wrong-doers under sanctions of public opprobrium and silent condemnation. Filling an office so important, they must not be extirpated under any pretext of forgiveness. They require to be somehow mastered, and somehow to remain. And the supreme art of forgiveness will consist in finding how to embrace the unworthy as if they were not unworthy, or how to have them still on hand when they will not suffer the forgiveness to pass. Which supreme art is the way of propitiation — always concerned in the reconciliation of moral nature separated by injuries.

How it is that the forgivenesses of good men so often miscarry, will be sufficiently explained by the exposition here given. It does not follow that they are to be impeached for obstinacy or insincerity. They meant to forgive and make clean work of their forgiveness. But their old mind returns upon them and their old animosities are rekindled, as if only banked in their fires and not extinguished. They look on the faces and hear the voices of the men they undertook to forgive, and their disgusts come back on them. The old words rattle as if in new offenses, and there is no moral gong at hand by which they can be drowned. Now the difficulty very often is that the forgiven party has never been so qualified by grace that he could fitly be forgiven. But that is no sufficient excuse; for the forgiving party can be right even if there is no forgiveness passed. In most cases the true account of the matter is that the forgiving party did not find how to be fitly propitiated, and was not qualified antecedently

by such a state of preparation as his own moral nature and necessities demanded. What he so honestly meant to do, therefore, he is not unlikely
mortified by and by to discover is not effectually done.

True forgiveness, then, that which forgives as God in Christ hath forgiven, is no such letting up simply of revenge against the wrong-doer as
was first described — no shove of dismission, no dumb turning of the
back. Neither is it any mere setting of the will to do a deed of love, as we
often discover in really good men — no drumming of the hard sentiments
and revulsions and moral condemnations to sleep. Perhaps they were not
meant to go to sleep, but to stay by rather in such welcome as the new
cast of a right propitiation will suffer.

And in order to this, two things are necessary; first, such a sympathy
with the wrong-doing party as virtually takes his nature; and secondly, a
making cost in that nature by suffering, or expense, or painstaking sacrifice and labor. The sympathy must be of that positive kind which wants
the man himself, and not a mere quiet relationship with him; wants him
for a brother, considers nothing to be really gained till it has gained a
brother. The sympathy needs to be such as amounts to virtual identification, where there is a contriving how to feel the man all through, and
read him as by inward appreciation, to search out his good and evil, his
weaknesses and gifts, his bad training and bad associations, his troubles
and trials and wrongs — so to understand and, as it were, be the man himself; having him interpreted to the soul's love, by setting all tenderest,
most exploring affinities in play, finding how to work engagement in him,
and learn what may best be touched or taken hold of in a way to make
him a friend. Taking the wrong-doer thus upon itself, it will also take, in
a certain sense, his wrong to be foreign; for its longing is after some most
real identification with the fellow nature sought after. Thus we see that
to really forgive, and make clean work of it, requires a going through
into good, if possible, with the wrong-doer, and meeting him there, both
reconciled. And when it is done thoroughly enough to configure and
new-tone the forgiving party as well as the forgiven, he is so far become
himself a reconciled or propitiated man, as truly as the other is become a
forgiven or restored man. Or if the man so propitiated is repelled in the forgiveness he offers, he is, humanly speaking, but as one that came unto his
own and his own received him not.

But there remains, as was just now intimated, a second indispensable
condition by which the advances of sympathy, finding their way into and
through wrong-doers and enemies, will become a more nearly absolute

power in them, and a more complete propitiation for them; viz., in the making cost and bearing heavy burdens of painstaking and sorrow to regain them and be reconciled to them. The injured party has a most powerful and multiform combination of alienated and offended sentiment struggling in his nature. And, in one view, it is right that he should have. He could not be a proper man, least of all a holy man, without them. His integrity is hurt, his holiness offended, his moral taste disgusted. He is alienated, thrown off, thrust back into separation, by the whole instinct of his moral nature. The fires of his purity smoke. His indignations scorch his love, and without any false fire of revenge, which is too commonly kindled also, he seems to himself to be in a revulsion that he has no will to subdue. He is a wounded man whose damaged nature winces even in his prayers. So that if he says "I forgive," with his utmost stress of emphasis, he will not be satisfied with any meaning he can force into the words. Is he therefore to be blamed, that he has so many of these dissentient feelings struggling in him to obstruct his forgivenesses? No, not in the sense that he has them, but only in the sense that he does not have them mitigated or propitiated so as to be themselves in consent, or subjected by sacrifice. Let him find how to plough through the bosom of his adversary by his tenderly appreciative sympathy, how to appear as a brotherly nature at every gate of the mind, standing there as in cost, to look forgiveness without saying it, and he will find, however he may explain it or not explain it, that there is a wonderful consent in his feeling somehow, and that he is perfectly atoned (at-oned) both with himself and his adversary.

To explain this whole matter analytically I acknowledge to be difficult. Let me give it in the concrete in three or four examples. The first, which is very simple, I will give more at large that we may note in transition some of the points which are likely to occur, on the way to a complete forgiveness.

Thus you had, we may suppose, a partner in trade whom you had taken up out of his very dejected lot of poverty. Discovering talent and what you thought was character in him, you took him into confidence, to share your fortunes with you. Before you suspected danger from him, he had used the name and credit of your company, under cover of his legal rights, in a most faithless and cruel violation of trust, such as plucked you down out of wealth, and reduced you to a lot of poverty so nearly complete that you had not even bread for your children. But your industry and worth brought you up again finally to affluence; while the vices into

which he fell brought him down to want and hopeless destitution. Meantime, in all the intervening years you have been remembering his wrong,
which you could not well forget. His name has been, of course, a name
significant of bitter wrong in your house, and so connected with pain as
to be seldom or never spoken — a word as it were for the dumb. You
have said inwardly, "I must forgive," and you have meant, on principle,
to do it, perhaps really supposed it to be done; but there is, nevertheless,
to this day a sting in that name, and you do not like to hear it. To meet
him on the street, or catch the look of his face, pains you, and you inwardly shudder as you pass him, at the discovery that, Christian man as
you are, you are certainly not reconciled to him, and see not how you
ever can be. But you are shortly to find how you can be. The poor man,
going down under his vices, loses name and figure and is all but forgotten.
But you hear that his family are suffering in bitter want. Did you not say
that you could forgive, and what is come now but your opportunity?
You send them in supplies and means of comfort, once and again, conceal-
ing always your name, lest it may seem to be your revenge. By and by his
son is arrested for crime, and who but you will volunteer to give the
needed bail? and that requires your name. At length some infectious disease falls on the forlorn being and his family, and who will peril life, in
giving help and watch to people so completely out of consideration? But
you said your forgiveness long ago, and what shall you do to make it
good but go in to minister and be their saviour? The poor fellow turns
himself to the wall when he sees you and weeps aloud, saying not a word,
but just covering his face with his hands and smothering his broken-
hearted shame as he best can. Where now, on your part, is the reluctance
and revulsion that so often stifled your forgiveness? Gone, all gone, forever! The word itself is become the sweetest of all words. By your painstaking endeavor, and the peril you have borne for your enemy, you are so
far reconciled in your own nature that you can now completely forgive,
whether he can rightly be forgiven or not. He can not be till he comes
into a genuinely right mind, though still you none the less truly forgive.
The forgiveness in you is potentially complete, even though it should
never be actually sealed upon him. You have taken his sin upon you in the
cost you have borne for his sake, and what you have borne thus freely for
him quells that unreducible something, that dumb ague of justice that was
disallowing your forgivenesses. It is even as if there had been a great sacrifice transacted in your soul's court of sacrifice, by which your condemnations that were blocking your sensibilities have been smoothed and

soothed and taken away. Under so great patience and cost, the forgiving charities are all out in your feeling, fresh and clean, and swinging the censers of their worship to pay the fragrant honors due.

Take another example, that is short and sharp, but unites all the elements, either by implication or expressly. A noted English preacher, traveling on horseback in the country, is stopped by a footpad demanding his purse. Asking, "Will you let me pray?" he immediately descends and begins a prayer. It is fervently made for both parties, and begins forthwith to be answered by a thought occurrent that contains the answer; an answer that makes heavy cost for him, and mortgages much that is most precious in life's comforts to the robber. Rising to his feet he questions how a life so unjust and wicked was begun, charges it kindly to some sorrowful defect of nurture, some atmosphere of positively bad example. Still the wrong and danger of it are none the less evident, for it is, how plainly, a life that is both against God and against society. "Come now," he says, "let me offer you something better. Go home with me and take employment in my service. I will see that no human being, not even my family, shall know of this affair as long as we live." Accepting the offer, the man took service with his benefactor, and his crime was never known till it was reported, in a voluntary confession from his own lips, on the day of his master's funeral. The cost made by this man of God, in taking thus an unknown robber into his family, and trusting his and their lives to his fidelity, was about as heavy as it well could be. How complete also was the resulting forgiveness, we can see from the double trust that followed; the master trusting the man, and the man the master, for so many years of trial, in a matter always secret between them.

But we have a larger field of forgivenesses, and we are always in it; and here it is even our instinct to make cost freely, in order to keep our intractable ugly nature pliant to this gentle ministry. We have much to forgive that is not done against ourselves, but against our friends and fellow disciples, against purity and truth and love, against God, and Christ, and religion. And the offenses done, in so many ways and relations, are often dreadfully revolting — cruelties to the weak, violences to the just, vices all disgust, mockeries of what is holy, insults to Christ, so that we are set burning, as it were, in a kind of divine animosity, such as the Psalmist utters in what some hastily reprobate as the scandalous zeal of passion, when he says, "I hate them with perfect hatred, I count them mine enemies." He might have been a very great fanatic in that key, but he probably was not. God himself is in offense in just that way, and ought to be; only he will have it for his merit that, being thus exasperated, he can, without self-blame, mitigate his offense and train it to forgiveness. Much easier and more natural, at least, is it for us to end off our duty to the incorrigible and wicked in our condemnations. Our drift in this direction is so strong that we sometimes let our prayers scorch heaven over them. We forget that we are to gain them and bring them into God's forgiveness and ours by making cost for them. Perhaps we are sometimes willing to have their sins make large amount of cost for them — counting this, it may be, our righteousness. No, it is a great mistake, and we really do not mean it. What we want, after all, is not to have them get their deserts, but to have them recovered to God and forgiven. And that we shall not obtain for them till we begin to bear their sin, suffer patiently their unworthiness, and work and wait in all painstaking on their insensibility; and then, when our hard way of natural condemnation is duly softened, there is at least a chance that theirs may be. No, it must not be forgotten, that beautiful word of the Master, "Whosesoever sins ye remit, they are remitted unto them." We get other men's sins remitted of God, when we are deep enough in cost to remit them ourselves. And this exactly is the secret of those times of religious fervor in communities which are so great a mystery to many. The whole Christian mind has forgotten to be a judging and become a forgiving mind. And it has become a forgiving mind by the key of sacrifice and painstaking cost into which it has fallen. This, observe, is the cross, and when a community is in it, forgiveness runs full circle, and the church-state is a state of life.

Now in these three examples given for illustration, we see how it is that forgivenesses in men are ripened and fully brought to pass only as propitiations are. Also that our human instinct puts us therefore always on making cost when we undertake to really forgive. Also that human forgivenesses are possible to be consummated only by the help of some placation or atonement, or cost-making sacrifice. The forgiving party must be so far entered into the lot and state of the wrong-doing party, as to be thoroughly identified with him, even to the extent of suffering by him and for him. Some alternative must be taken by the man who will truly forgive, that has power to liquefy the indifferences, or assuage the stern, over-loaded displeasures, of his moral and morally injured, morally revolted nature. He may settle into a callous and dull state, by just staying at his point of uncaring self-content — but his callousness will be simply disendowed sensibility, and not forgiveness. If the offense he suffers from the wrong of his enemy is ever to be cleared, his forgivenesses will be drawn out only by such freedom in the matter of cost as opens the sluices of his feeling, and waters the dry rock about which his indignations are smoking. Suffering, in short, is with all moral natures, the necessary correlate of forgiveness. The man, that is, can not say "I forgive," and have the saying end it; he must somehow atone both himself and his enemy by a painstaking, rightly so called, that has power to recast the terms of their relationship. So far from its being an absurd thing to speak of a propitiation as the necessary pre-condition of forgiveness, no human creature will ever keep himself reconciled to his kind without finding how in some of its degrees to practice it. Instead of being a great theologic mystery, it is even the common exigent of life. Doubtless we may live in the consuming thirst of our great world-fever and just go along, with no secret heart's love reaching after any body, but whosoever longs to live in the bright cordiality of brotherhood, and have the true enjoyment of his kind, must atone himself into the gentleness and patience of love all the way.

Doubtless it may seem to some to be a hard lot put upon us, which requires us to be not only well-doers, but atoners also — the world itself to be a kind of mutually atoning world — so that we have it put upon us, not only to suffer for our own sins, but also for the sins of those who do us injury. This, I say, will seem quite hard to many. But it will depend on what kind of world we require God to give us. If it must be a world made up of facilities, and favors, and all kinds of pleasantness, with no hurts suffered, no wrongs done, no liabilities of damage, no responsibilities of sacrifice, in a word, if there is to be no tragedy, or tragic side, in our life, but all sides smoothly rounded alike, then of course a plan that is to keep us all, and about all the time, at making cost in this manner for the forgiving of bad people, may take on a look very forbidding and tedious. And yet after all there is no imaginable world, I am quite sure, that has a thousandth part of the tedium in it which one would have that is wholly made up of delectations. Insipid, uneventful, flat, with no great sentiments in it, no heroic side in duty, nothing heroic any where, nothing to condemn that touches us, nothing to forgive because we are not touched — why, such a world would even die of inanity. No, let us have tragedy and a strong, large mixture of it. And then if we chance to be good — good enough to make loss for our enemies — what luxury shall we have in our forgivenesses and the great sentiments heaved up in us as in mighty exaltations, by our experience! Of course it is not to be charged against God that he makes the bad necessities of our very tragic life. The bad part of it is all from ourselves, and the grand atonings planned for, to be

the universal element, are just that cost of experience in which we are
most ennobled and blessed. Let me have the chance of forgiving my
enemy, and I have more enlargement of life, a more uplifted consciousness, than if I owned the world in fee.

II

Finding, in this manner, how our own moral nature, as such, becomes
alienated and averted from them that do us wrong and trample the rights
of others, and how it tones itself to a completely forgiving state only by
acts of cost or sacrifice which are, in proper verity, propitiations of itself,
it should not surprise us to find the analogy running far enough to comprehend all other moral natures, even the highest. And here, as I conceive,
we get our initiatory point for the true understanding of the Christian
propitiation. We have only to go back on the pathologies of our own
moral nature, to make the discovery that we ourselves instinctively make
sacrifice to gain our adversary; in doing which we also gain ourselves. I
said that we do it instinctively, but I only mean that our moral instincts
are so far cast in this mold as to induce this kind of action, when we are in
the highest key of supernatural life and exaltation. I wish I could believe
that we are always in this key; for it is the infelicity of my argument, in
this great subject, that I am required to hang it on a fact, which alas! too
many have no witness of in their own experience. And my fear is that the
analogy I suggest will be quite insignificant to them, because they run
their life on so low a key, and make it so nearly selfish, that the exalted
consciousness, which is itself so near akin to God, is not on hand to second what I say. How shall it seem reasonable, or even properly intelligent, to propose the verification of God's way in forgiveness by our own,
or the fact of his propitiation in order to his forgivenesses by the propitiation we instinctively make ready in our own, when the mind that is
addressed lives in no element of forgiveness and propitiation, and has
nothing in experience to make so high an ascription seem any thing better
than a dull extravagance. Let the caution here given be taken without
offense.

Still it will be something for such to observe how expressly and even
formally the indorsement of revelation is given us for just this free appeal
to the human analogies. Thus when Christ requires us to forgive as God
forgives, his apostle turns the doctrine boldly round, requiring us to forgive "even as God for Christ's sake hath forgiven us." By these words
"for Christ's sake," *en Christō* or in Christ, he does not mean, as many

understand, on the ground of satisfaction made by Christ — for we plainly enough can not make satisfaction for the sin of our enemy — but he means that we are to forgive, as volunteering in the cost of sacrifice, after Christ's example. Indeed there could be no forgiveness in God on the ground of satisfaction; it would only be his admission that nothing is any longer due.

Let it not be suspected that we fall into a case of inversion here, that implies mistake in the argument; viz., that we conceive Christ in his forgivenesses, or his propitiation, to be following the type of ours. Causations and examples imply a state of priority or precedence, but a mere analogy does not. It only signifies that the two sides of it are in correspondence, no matter how. Christ, in all that pertains to his propitiation and his forgiveness to enemies, furnishes the ideas and helps we work by in ours, and we are even to allow that we have no complete adequacy without them; but our propitiations and forgivenesses, when these are wrought, suppose analogical properties in our very nature, by which Christ may set us on working correspondently with himself, and forgiving our enemies even as he does his.

Supposing now the fact of such constituent analogies existing both in us and him, certain questions will arise in pursuing the exposition proposed, that require to be answered.

1. Is it to be understood that Christ goes to the cross just to get the reaction of so great suffering on himself, and so to mitigate or propitiate his own feeling in the way of preparing to forgive? That would be a very constrained, self-attentive attitude, and we could not think of it with respect. No such thing is implied or supposed in the human examples referred to. We do not ourselves go into sacrifice for our enemy to gain or soften ourselves, but only to help him in his trouble, and minister to his bad mind in ways that may gain him to repentance; every thing we do and suffer is for his benefit, or for effect on him, only it results that our sacrifice affects our mind or disposition also towards him. We are in a way of being completely reconciled to him, as we hope he sometime will be to us. The stress of all we do or suffer is for him, and in that consciousness it is that we are atoned, having all our aversions, disgusts, and condemnations liquefied, or dissolved away. In this there is nothing artificial or constrained; we are simply acting ourselves into forgiveness towards him in our endeavor to bless him and bring him into a better mind towards us.

2. Is it objected that God loves his adversary already, and needs not

love him more to forgive? Of course he needs not love him more, and it is no office of the propitiation to produce in him a greater love for that purpose. The propitiation itself proceeds from his love, and is only designed to work on other unreducible sentiments that hinder his love, in forgiveness it might otherwise bestow. Our own love, as we saw, might be sufficient if it were not hindered by certain collateral, obstructive sentiments, and God is in this moral analogy with us. He is put in arms against wrongdoers, just as we are, by his moral disgusts, displeasures, abhorrences, indignations, revulsions, and what is more than all, by his offended holiness, and by force of these partly recalcitrant sentiments he is so far shut back, in the sympathies of his love, that he can nerve himself to the severities of government so long as such severities are wanted. He is not less perfect because these antagonistic sentiments are in him, but even more perfect than he would be without them; and a propitiation is required, not because they are bad, but only to move them aside when they are not wanted. They are never to be extirpated from the mind of God, but are always to be in him even as parts of his perfection; only they do not act uniformly into his character, but casually, when, all things considered, they should; just as we have casual factors letting in their action here and there among the constant factors. God has it for a part of his liberty to be held by these casual factors when he should be, and not held when he can do better works for his repentant children by letting forgiveness take their place. Propitiation then, as the necessary pre-condition of forgiveness, supposes no necessity that God should be made better. And he will forgive without damage to his character, just when his love, in making cost for his enemy, gains that enemy to himself. The beauty of the true conception is that God is not obliged, by his side factors or subordinate sentiments, to be everlastingly disgusted, revolted, heated with condemnation, but that he has self-government, and world government, and full liberty left him. His severities of sentiment remain, just as the Red Sea remained after the children of Israel passed through. And yet they had passed through.

3. It will be imagined, perhaps, by objectors of a different class, that God's holiness, or spiritual chastity, puts him in a condition where all the analogies of human forgiveness fail. It is enough for us to be a little gentled in feeling, to make our forgivenesses flow. Whereas he must even morally wrong his own pure nature, to forgive any transgression without being satisfied for it — as he can be only when some other bears the offense and by adequate suffering atones it. That is, he can forgive sin

only on receiving adequate pay! But we never propose that way of forgiveness for our human enemy, restricted as we are in our holiness. It would even subject a man to ignominy to do it — all the more certainly if he is counted a specially holy man. It is very true that God's offense toward sin is deepest because of his holiness. But the depth of his holiness will match itself also in the depth of his forgiveness. And what do we see but that the holiest men, who are the men most deeply wounded by wrong, forgive most easily. God too holy to forgive an enemy! Rather judge that forgiveness is itself the supreme joy of holiness, whether in God or man.

4. It will be imagined that God is in a different case from us, in the fact that he maintains a government as we do not, and that he is therefore restricted in the matter of forgiveness by considerations of order and public authority, when we are not so restricted. Hence that we may be softened or propitiated towards our enemy by what we do to gain him, when God can not be without exacting somehow what the penal institute of the law requires. I shall have more to say of this when I come to speak in the next chapter of the necessities of Law. For the present I have these two points to put forward as being in themselves sufficient. First that no forgiveness, whether by man or God, obliterates the fact of a wrong, or at all salves the wounds of violated obligations. It operates only on, or between, the two parties personally. The bad act stands forever, plainly enough, for nothing can efface or any way alter what is done. The law and its sanctions also stand as immovable as the eternal morality. And the penal sanctions work on still in the man by natural causation after he is forgiven, till they are worn out or winnowed away by the supernatural causations of grace in his life. Add to this, secondly, that we as mortals do in fact govern with God, and are held to the maintenance of good government with him. Every law of his kingdom is ours. His governing interest is ours. We have the same reason to be jealous of wrong and shocked by disorder. We reign with him in fact in what is his Great Monarchy and our Republic, and we are just as free to forgive and be reconciled as he.

5. It may be objected that when we are propitiated towards our enemy, by the cost we make for him, the whole process takes place within ourselves, and the forgiving grace is not obtained of us by the intercession or mediation of another; whereas Christ obtains the forgiveness of sins for us by what he does before God, acting in our behalf. Even so, by acting before God; and yet not by acting before God and obtaining from God, as being strictly *other*. That would be tritheism and not trin-

ity. Trinity makes him "same in substance," not other. We entirely mis-conceive this acting before God, when we make God one and Christ an-other acting in real otherhood before him. The three are still the one, and the threefolding is but a plural in so many finite forms, used representa-tively as personations of the infinite One. Their very plurality implies their acting towards and before each other, in which they all become in-strumentations for the one, but never, in any sense, other. . . . It is no fault therefore in this behalf that the analogy we draw from ourselves only shows us working out a propitiation in ourselves. Christ is not other than God in any such way that his propitiation is any the less truly a self-propitiation of God.

6. But it may be urged with emphasis and high confidence by some, as being a great derogation from God's honor, to suppose that he is held in detention, as respects forgiveness, till he has first mitigated his opposing sentiments, or let Christ do it by suffering and sacrifice in his behalf. That there is nothing to support this objection was just now sufficiently shown; for that which obstructs forgiveness in him is not something wherein he is less good than he should be, or something wherein he re-quires to be made better. The propitiation only takes away out of range certain subordinate and partly casual sentiments that wait on God's abso-lute principles and purposes, to act as displeasures and revulsions may in the toning of his legal discipline, and act no longer when their dominating force may properly cease.

However, I perceive that speculation will easily twist this answer out of its proprieties, by questioning as to that little word *when:* Is it true that God must be gained or tempered transactionally, that is by acts in time, in order to the letting forth of grace upon his enemies? Certainly not; there is no such thing as date in God's dispositions. They are not dead fact, but living factors in his living nature. They condition each other, as the brain conditions breathing and breathing the brain, being such as he generates everlastingly between what he feels and what he wills. Without such consideration, we seem to be imagining often that Christ has come into the world to make God better, and we very nearly say or sing it in a supposed key of orthodoxy; but if we understand him rather as having come to show us how God is acting himself always into the great time-currents of our story, we shall think him far more worth-ily. For his dispositions towards sin are shaped and colored everlastingly by what he thinks of it, and inwardly contrives and does and suffers for it. And his blessed forgivenesses were all in him, and ready grown, before

Christ arrived, and before the world was made; and what he does among us by his sacrifice is to have its value in revealing, under time, how by sacrifice and much cost above time, the divine charities were always mitigating his dispositions and flowing out, as it were, by anticipation subduingly on his enemies. The transactional matter of Christ's life and death is a specimen chapter, so to speak, of the infinite book that records the eternal going on of God's blessed nature within. Being made in his image, we are able to see his moral dispositions, always forging their forgivenesses, under the reactions of endurance and sacrifice, as we do ours. And this is the eternal story of which Christ shows us but a single leaf.

Beheld in its outward human incidents, it is the tragedy of the love of God. And the dispositions of God are so wrought up in it that he is seen embracing, not the lovely only, as we are wont to speak, when we imagine or teach that love is begotten by loveliness, but embracing the bad or unlovely in proffers beforehand of forgiveness. Most human love is unsacrificial love, thinking only to make fit answer to the lovable. We never go beyond this till we make loss, and sacrifice, and cost, for some adversary of ours, or of goodness. By these propitiated, we forgive. All God's forgiving dispositions are dateless, and are cast in this mold. The Lambhood nature is in him, and the cross set up, before the incarnate Son arrives. His own love bows itself to endurance, by the prescriptive habit of his eternity, and the forgivenesses shown us in their formative era, so to speak, under the great transaction of Calvary, are in fact the everlasting predispositions of his nature. The cross, *ab aeterno*, is in them — "the Lamb that was slain from the foundation of the world."

We can not have a God in fit sensibility unless the ante-mundane touch of it is in him. He can not be a forgiving God, if he is yet to begin the making cost for an enemy. A God therefore whose eternity has been impassible, untouched by suffering experience, will never be at all relational to my experience. He is wood, he is granite, or no better. What can he do for me, when he can not feel me? and what can I offer him, when he can not feel what I offer? If he is pleased with my good, he must have some feeling of my not good, and that is dis-pleasure, which is so far suffering. Just consider at this gate, as it opens, what a living God must suffer and be suffering always in his good sensibility. He pities, and pity going through a bad soul or body, by inward inspection, has how much to look upon that is painful. He abhors a wicked and cruel soul, and what is abhorrence but a recoil that is, at least etymologically, related to horror. In a vile and filthy mind he encounters disgust, and what is that but to suffer? All the persecutions of his friends, all the rage and scoffing of his enemies, all the hate and hatefulness of natures made for love, all desecrations of his honor, all perversions of his truth, impurity, lust, diseased inheritance — what are all these things to God's pure sensibility, since he has it, but evils to bear, offenses to suffer, such as can be forgiven only by a nature whose dispositions have been configured to sacrifice and cost, before the worlds were made? It is in God's character everlastingly, if we should not rather say his nature, to be always enduring the bad in their badness, and so melting his way lovingly through into forgiveness. Benefactor thus to all, and king of joy as of sorrow to himself. If his streams ran all one way, he would be too simply placid to be great, but he lives in everlasting countertides of struggle and victory — victory both over enemies without and violated good in himself. What is to come of all moral natures created, he well understood before their creation, and he peopled the world with them as one girding himself for war; that is, to live and reign by the mastery of their evil, including all the disasters to feeling in which evil comes. Thus he began early, as it were, in affliction for the bad, or only partly good; for "in their affliction he was afflicted, and he bare and carried them all the days of old." And so along down through the smoke of the ages — why not say of the eternities? — he has been joyously "enduring the contradiction of sinners against himself," propitiated by his endurances, and so at all times ready to forgive their sin. And this exactly is the truth that Christ impresses by the affectingly beautiful short chapter of his story — it is the inward going on of God's nature in the sacrifices of love. He hates and abhors as we do, only never with a trace of malignity. His indignations burn hot against the outrages of wrong; just as in what we call our remorse, it is the terrible *orgē* of our own bosom that scorches and scathes our sin, doing it, as it were, benignantly and without injustice. So in respect of all God's sensibilities, forgivenesses, and sacrifices.

III

Having made our statement thus of the Christian forgiveness and propitiation, interpreted and represented by analogies in our own human sentiment and practice, it now remains, going into the Scripture, to find how far we are borne out by it in the doctrine proposed. Everything turns here, it will be discovered, on the meaning of sacrifice. And we have three sets of words in our three Scripture languages, the Hebrew, the Greek, and the English, in and by which the meaning is to be determined.

In the Hebrew Scriptures the word is uniformly *kaphar*. This is translated in the Septuagint and the New Testament by *hilaskomai*. And this again is translated in the English by *reconciliation, atonement,* and *propitiation;* by the first in a very few cases only; by the second almost uniformly in the English Old Testament; by the third as uniformly in the English New Testament. Only the New Testament has the word *reconciliation,* several times over; translating, however, another and wholly different word, that has no altar significance at all, and is therefore to be wholly disregarded in the inquest we are making.

We begin then at the Hebrew word *kaphar,* which is in fact the English word *cover,* the idea being that the sin is covered, hid, taken away by the sacrifice. And this idea it will be seen is not far from the idea of a smoothing away of the offense, a mitigation, a placation, a propitiation of the mind offended, which appears to be an element of meaning always present in the uses of the word. Thus if we step aside in the Old Testament from the altar uses of this word, we fall on examples in common life, where the real *usus loquendi* is plainly discovered; as when Jacob says, sending on his drove to meet Esau, his righteously offended brother: "I will *appease* him with the present that goeth before me" (Gen. 32:20). The word of appeasement or propitiation here is *kaphar,* the altar word, showing beyond a question what ideas or impressions it has there carried. We have another example of the same word exactly correspondent: "The wrath of a king is as messengers of death, but a wise man will *pacify* it" (Prov. 16:14). Here the smoothing, mitigating, mollifying, placating element is conspicuous as before.

Passing next to the Greek word of the New Testament, by which the Hebrew *kaphar* is translated, we look again for the true *usus loquendi,* to examples not occurring at the altar and under the altar forms, because collateral examples are a great deal more significant and decisive as to the true genius of the word. Thus we fall on the prayer of the publican — "God be *merciful* to me a sinner" (Lk. 18:13). Here the "be merciful" is the old altar word of sacrifice *hilaskomai* used in the passive imperative, saying literally, "Be thou propitiated, or propitiate thyself, bend thyself on me in forgiveness" — showing very clearly how the element of placation, or propitiation, has been connected always with the word in the uses of the altar. We also discover a little way off two cousins in the family of *hilaskomai, hileōs* and *anileōs,* which may be taken as witnesses to the dispositions of the family. Thus we read, "I will be *merciful* (propitiated in feeling) to their unrighteousness." And again "he shall have judgment

without mercy" (unmitigated, *unappeased* judgment) "that showed no
mercy" (Jas. 2:13).

As regards the English words that are used to represent the two Hebrew and Greek words, the remarkable thing is that they so nearly agree.
Thus the word *reconciliation* employed in translation, to carry a meaning
that belongs to the altar, has the element of conciliation visible on its face.
As when we read, "to make an end of sins, and to make reconciliation for
iniquity, and to bring in everlasting righteousness," the meaning would not
be essentially different if it were written "to make propitiation for iniquity" (Dan. 9:24). The word *atonement*, more frequently used, carries the
same element of conciliation or propitiation in a different manner by just
naming the results; that is to *at-one;* for this is the old English word in the
old English way of printing, and the word in that original use never
meant, as now, "to make amends," which is a perfectly unchristian use,
but to gather into accord as by love and cost and heavy expense of feeling. The New Testament English word *propitiation* coincides with these
other two, without more than a shade of difference.

We are ready therefore now, after sifting all these words with as much
of accuracy as we are able, to go back first upon the Old Testament sacrifice and settle the significance of it, showing also how, or by what means,
it obtained that significance. And here the first thing to be noted is that it
makes nothing of the pain of the victim. Nothing is ever done to increase
the pain of the animal when slain, and there is never any thing said which
indicates the least mental attention to it. The pain is plainly a matter of
supreme indifference. The next thing is that there is no vestige of retributive quality in the sacrifice. The smoke is to be rolled up as a sweet-
smelling savor, and not as a smoke of retribution. The associations never
once suggest retribution. Thirdly, there is no compensation in the sacrifices. They are never proposed in a way of payment, or of obligation
compounded. They are not satisfactions, nor any way linked with ideas
of satisfaction — no man's lamb pays for his sin. Fourthly, they are never
offered as a legal substitution. There is a certain mystic and ritual way of
substitution practiced indeed, as when the worshiper puts his hands on
the head of the sacrifice, or on the head of the goat, driven out to signify
the deportation of his sin, but nobody ever imagines, unless it be to make
out some point of theology, that the animal is held in legal substitution.
To have the sins legally on him, the goat must be a legal subject, else they
are as little on him as they would be on a barrow or a cart. Doubtless they
are on him in a figure, and then of course their deportation is signified in

a figure — the reality of which will be that the faith of the transgressor makes what he is thereby helped to believe, an actual and free deliverance.

But what of the blood? for the sacrifice is a rite of blood; as if it were not in God's nature, some shallow casuist will often object, to be any more pacified towards sin, or at all mitigated in his wrath, except by the sight of blood! Somebody, that is, must bleed for it, else there is no forgiveness. In which way of speaking, the impression is that blood comes into the sacrifice invested with all our freezing conceptions of guilt, because no otherwise but by its horror-dripping stains could God find fit expression made in the sacrifice, of our detestation of the sin we come to have forgiven. But we greatly mistake if we suppose that any so delicate impression of blood was ever felt among those old pasture-men of the East, with whom sacrifice began; accustomed as they were to the killing of some animal from their herds, at their tent door, three or four times a day, and trained to use the knife even from childhood. But there was a more genuine, really delicate impression of blood prepared in their minds, by artificial, institutional causes, which having been prepared for that purpose, *were* the reason why so much is made of bleeding and blood in the sacrifices. The problem was to make the sacrifice a power, by collecting about the victim intensely sacred impressions. And to this end a statute was passed concerning blood, at a very early period, which was in fact the fountain of all meaning in sacrifice, even down to the sacrifice of Christ himself. "For the life of the flesh is in the blood, and I have given it to you upon the altar to make an atonement (or propitiation) for your souls; for it is the blood that maketh an atonement for the soul. Therefore I said unto the children of Israel, No soul of you shall eat blood. Whosoever eateth it shall be cut off" (Lev. 17:11, 12, and 14). These worshipers of the old time took nothing in their religious experience by definition or analysis, they experienced only what they saw or acted. And God gave them a symbol of something sacred by which to come before him, viz., blood made sacred by being separated from every other use; the idea being that, in having offered their holiest and best thing to God, they have made an expression that carries the strongest sense of their sin, and will most certainly conciliate the offended purity of God. . . . What if there chance to be something here, in this humble offering of lambs, that will sometime be made to represent the sacred and dear life of Christ, offered up at greater cost to God's feeling than any thing ever was or could be to ours. And what if that simple designation "Lamb of God that taketh away the sin of the world" — defining nothing, spinning no analogies — were just wept into the world's heart and left to quicken the feeling of a new life, how certainly would the sinning myriads of the world begin to confess, This surely is the body that was prepared, this must be the atonement indeed.

Even so! this is the Sacrifice that all sacrifices were looking after and climbing up to behold. They were the literal base-level sacrifices, offered by priests and by fire upon an altar, atoning the man by what he offered, and also God by implication — engaged to be atoned on his part by these hallowed symbols of cost, in the blood and the life. Whereas in that other better Lamb of Sacrifice, that really true sacrifice that was fore-shadowed, there is neither any lamb at all nor any sacrifice, and it is only meant to be a sacrifice a great way out of correspondence, that we may not class it, too closely, with the very dull and prosy rites which have had their uses now fulfilled, in preparing a language for something more sig-nificant and in a higher key. The real truth, if we tell it as it is, makes the sacrifice a murder, and the blood on Calvary the blood of murder: there is no altar, no fire, no priest; it is simply the act of a mob outside of the temple and the city gibbeting the Sacred Life yielded up to their fury. And what they have done is called the sacrifice, in a word that would even be irony if it did not cover the awfully transcendent, interior fact of a cost so terrible, endured by the feeling of God. This is the blood, and this the life, expected of old, when the blood and the life were conse-crated by the statute of the altar. Looking on here with our eyes, we see nothing religious, even the offering is wholly blank to us, only that the world itself, shuddering and darkening into night, tries visibly to be tell-ing us something of it, if it could! There is at any rate no atonement in the form. The blood of the murder buys nothing as in pay, wins nothing as by suit or compensation, mitigates no feeling of God that we can see, as by intercession before him; and yet there is to God, in his own deep nature, a propitiation accomplished for sin, because of the divine Lamb-hood that has been lovingly offered in the smoke of so fierce transgres-sion.

Our Scripture excursion comes round finally, after the wide range taken, to be concluded by the famous full-period text of Paul in his epis-tle to the Romans, "Whom God hath set forth to be a propitiation, through faith in his blood," etc. (Rom. 3:25). I do not cite the whole pas-sage, but only the first two clauses, reserving the part that is left to be used hereafter, when the matter of justification is to be discussed. Three points noted, in the briefest manner possible, will sufficiently indicate the import of the words. (1) There is a propitiation accomplished in Christ's life, and especially in his very tragic death, which prepares a way of forgiveness for the sins of the world. The forgiveness now will be more than verbal, it will be real, clean, complete. (2) It is God himself who is forward in this transaction — "whom God hath set forth." It is not Pilate who has done it, not Caiaphas, nor the soldiers, but it is that God has suffered them so far to make irruption upon his throne, and pluck down him, who by the determinate counsel and foreknowledge was delivered into their hands; for how can it be imagined what the propitiation can do, save as it is set forth by the worst that sin can do, worsted itself in turn by the blood of its crime? And (3) this propitiation is to be received only by faith — a "propitiation through faith in his blood." For it is this faith in fact which makes the murder a sacrifice; which it does by accepting it as the sacred altar-blood and life, and beholding in it that sublime act of cost, in which God has bent himself downward, in loss and sorrow, over the hard face of sin, to say, and saying to make good, "Thy sins are forgiven thee."

IV

The propitiation that was necessary to forgiveness we have now discovered and constructively verified, under its human analogies; but there is a very important objection to propitiation itself that requires to be removed — an objection that is incurred by every scheme which assumes the word propitiation, as truly as by that which I have here proposed. The need of any such mitigation or amendment in God's dispositions supposes, it is often maintained, to just the same extent, his spiritual defectiveness; and the fact of his being thus amended by a transaction in time, supposes an improvement, to the same degree, and a correspondent derogation from the stability or immutability of his character. I have been discussing, before, an objection closely related to this, and yet very different. There the question was how God can have his dignity, when he is supposed to be transactionally mitigated by what is done or suffered in time? Here the question is how he can have his dignity, when his eternal mind itself requires to be propitiated, in order to the supreme act of goodness to an enemy. The argument of the two questions, wide apart as they are in their nature, runs more nearly in the same vein than might be wished. But the objections themselves are so very important, that small varieties of treatment may have their use. I have said already that the propitiation, so called, is not a fact accomplished in time, but an historic matter represented in that way, to exhibit the interior, ante-mundane, eternally proceeding sacrifice of the Lamb that was slain before the foundation of the world. In saying this I am not striking the predestination string of Calvinism, but am simply finding how the everlasting God, in a particular year of the calendar, viz., the year of Christ's death, was gained *representatively* to new dispositions, and became, in some new sense, a Saviour — incredible, impossible as it may seem — and how, in fact, he proved himself the more grandly, in that he here sets forth in time and story, what occupies, and fills, and glorifies, the whole interior working of his own eternity, and could by no other method be fitly revealed to mortal apprehension. The great salvation was not, in this view, wrought by the new composure of God in that particular year, but it was set forth as an everlasting new composure, so to speak, made evident in that year's doings — "whom God hath set forth to be a propitiation, through faith in his blood, to declare his righteousness in the remission of sins that are past, through the forbearance of God." Faith only sees, in the outward blessing of today, what covers matter going on before, in the eternal, inward proceeding of his mind towards human creatures and affairs.

Now if it shall seem to some that, in thus removing our objection, we very nearly make a nullity of the gospel itself, reducing it to a fact significant in what it shows only, and not in what it is or does, I will not stop to inquire how far the same kind of doubt hangs over every thing, but will hasten to concede that a great part of mankind, trained to no such modes of thought, will undoubtedly best appropriate the gospel, by keeping down as closely as possible on the level of a transaction in time. Indeed, there is some doubt how far it may be needed for us all to stay by the historic forms, and see the gospel done transactionally in time — to hear the word of Jesus, watch his healings, read his face, study his masterhood, bow down with him in Gethsemane, die with him on the cross — only we may have it as our privilege, I think, when our mind recoils from the tremendous difficulty of propitiation itself, to carry the whole matter up above the ranges of time, and look on him who stands there "in the midst of the throne, as it had been a Lamb slain from the foundation of the world."

But there is yet another way, if really it be another, as I think it is, of removing this to some, it may be, rather intractable objection. We do not properly conceive God's attributes when we pack them as so many solid blocks of perfection in his perfect nature. Least of all do we fitly conceive his sentiments and dispositions in that manner. If we take his wrath-principle as one block, calling it his justice; his omnipotence as another, able to do any thing which can be thought; his will-principle as another, essentially autocratic and absolute; his hatred-of-wrong-principle, in deifically fixed animosity, as another; and then if we bring in the patiences and tender charities, and the vicariously suffering grace, it will be very difficult to make blocks of them any way, and when they flow in through the interstices, they will have power to move, configure, combine, compelling all the others to offer them a yielding side, and to come into a newly constructed whole. Indeed, it will begin to be as if they were all being propitiated. They are no more blocks, in fact, but elements of life rather, flowing pervasively into, and among, and over, and under, and through one another — liquids all, flowing in to liquefy, and temper, and color, and sweeten each other, in such way as to compose a perfect rule, and a grand harmonic character. And this harmonic character will so be cast as to keep all purpose, sentiment, and disposition chiming with the wants, conditions, wrongs, relentings, personal affections, providential changes, and prayers of the world. And what have we thus, in the eternal going on of God's interior nature, but an eternal going on of propitiations, ready for every human creature in his time?

It may occur to some as a very strange thing, amounting in fact to another objection, that God should be any way restricted in his forgivenesses, when the mere instinct of kind or natural paternity is so free, and drops out all displeasures with such prompt facility. Why is God to be gained as one who forgives reluctantly? Should not such a being have his pardons ready beforehand? Why, a human mother in her simple, motherhood nature — is she not good enough to forgive an erring son, without parley, or without a question? She may do it, I answer, simply because she is not good enough to raise the parley, or to make it a moral affair at all, when of course it is not forgiveness. In every true moral transaction the thing done is made ready by moral dispositions prepared for it. Let us not be in haste to measure God's forgivenesses by the mother-pardon spilled on a reprobate son. Expecting in God what we boast in her, we should certainly do him great irreverence. As if the mere maternity of natural instinct, having no moral ingredient whatever, could be cited as a match and parallel for the clean, everlastingly sealed acceptance and moral embrace of God. Just contrary to this, the wrath or offended holiness, the pure sensibilities shocked by disgust, the moral repugnances and displeasures, the immovable indignations, must not hurry to clasp a wild and filthy reprobate. Probably God has nature-sentiment enough in him to do even that, but so far and in that point of view, he would really need to be made better; to go up out of his nature-plane into the moral, and prepare a moral settlement based in a moral forgiveness. And yet, as we have said many times over, he has done it — did it eternal ages ago — moving so promptly and with such spontaneous facility that the grace is ready long before the man arrives to receive it. If there is any look of reluctance in the matter, it is that the propitiation requires to be revealed by a transactional process, and that the subjects to be forgiven are so very slow in coming to the point of faith that makes forgiveness possible. And yet, though done as in the general and before time, it is a grace so personally gauged and tempered when it is inwardly pronounced that each may say, along down the ages, with even a better right than if the Master had kissed a farewell on his cheek, ". . . who loved me and gave himself for me."

Closing here my argument for the propitiation, I think I shall be permitted to speak of the religious benefits to be expected from the worthier and better ideal conceptions of God, that will of course go with it and keep it company. Every strongly variant or peculiar type of thought concerning God carries with it an ideal of God proper only to itself. Thus from his Creatorship, and especially from the great and scientific, world-massing facts of astronomy, we are set upon the idealizing of God as being omnipotent. And so strong is the impression we receive, that it not unlikely gulfs every other, even the impression of his responsibility to right. He becomes in chief significance the Almighty, and what after that, many are not much concerned to know. All theological questions involved in human liberty, are brought to an end by the fact that God can do any thing which either he or we can think. In the same way, it is often declared to be the praise of Calvinism that it makes God "big" by the autocratic rule of his decrees and predestinations. So that holding us fast in the vise of the sovereignty, and bending us down always under the overhang of his will the awful discipline makes imprints of authority and law that fasten immovably both society and religion. Again there is a certain ideal of God which is raised by our orthodox modes of legal atonement, such as deal in substituted punishment, satisfactions of justice, compensations, governmental equivalents, remissions bought and paid for — where nothing turns upon a sympathy or feeling, but every thing on a computative calculation, sharpened to the point of a jot or tittle of the law. Here the ideal raised is that of an exact or stringently exacting God, and the impression is not altogether ill, if it were not so far mixed with offense as to cause revulsion only, in all the broadly generous, thoughtfully circumspect natures. Another ideal of God, much valued by many, does not come in as a resultant, but is directly chosen for its own sake, and is called the Fatherhood of God. It has the merit of raising no offense, but there is such a certainty of diminution for God in any merely human type of paternity, that he is too inefficiently conceived in it for any strain of high-going rule or endeavor. What I am here proposing in the way of propitiation begins at the summit of God's eternity, where he lets in sorrow in the right of his supremacy, bathing his will in it when he reigns, recognizing always, and expecting always to recognize, the fact that it belongs to every moral nature, as truly to atone its adversaries, as to observe equity with its friends. He is brought down thus, or, shall we rather say? brought up, before the worlds are made, into the Passive Virtues. For he it is that accepts them by spontaneous choice, in advance of all creatures, and counts all other good too dry for joy without them. They are with him in the beginning of his way, and before his works of old. He creates the world thus in their counsel, consenting to have it on hand as a bad world, because in them he has found a ransom. The dread possibility of sin, incidental to the existence of moral natures, does not prevent his act of creation; for his great love wants them nigh, and the Patience of Sins is in him, able to bear the cost of their undoing and deliverance; so that when the outbreak comes, he is able to let it be, able to suffer it and for it, able to rule it, in the Kingly Majesty of his Patience.

v

To avoid the confusion that might be created by bringing into my argument another and very different matter, and having on hand for discussion two important issues at once, I have carried along the great subject of propitiation to its final conclusion by itself. Still my argument is not finished when I thus ignore the other issue referred to, and pass it wholly by without notice or attention. I go back, therefore, now to the point where that other question might have come forward also to claim its part in the discussion, and resume the investigation at that point. Having found that the two words of sacrifice in the Hebrew and Greek Scriptures, *kaphar* and *hilaskomai*, bear a sense of mitigation, and in that manner of propitiation, I considered the latter to be sufficiently established as the meaning also of the Christian sacrifice. But it happens that the Greek word is used also in the classics, where I am not able to deny that it is largely or quite commonly used to signify expiation. And so the question is raised whether, after all, expiation is not a meaning in these words, compatible with the Scripture uses. In this manner we have the question, Propitiation or Expiation? back upon us in the alternative, and the whole budget of doubt is loose again.

We are also the more heavily pressed by the question in this form, that our orthodox theologians and confessions are all the while saying *expiation* for the Christian sacrifice, without any apparent suspicion of impropriety. They even go to the classic historians and poets, to cite instances of expiation as proofs of the necessity of sacrifice, and do it without any misgiving or scruple. Happily our English Scriptures are clear of this impeachment, for the word *expiation* is not once found in them.[3] Indeed, I think our English translators are shy of so heathenish a word, as they very well might be.

In the facts that are classed as expiations there is of course a very great diversity, but they are discovered, when closely examined, to be all alike defective in principle. We may take as a worst and most shocking example the spectacle of human fathers and mothers whipping their children through beds of fire, to please some god who is turning plague, or battle, or weather against them. Or if we prefer to look on a best example rather, I remember no instance at all comparable, in dignity or benignity, with the legend of the Roman Curtius, plunging headlong man and horse into the gulf which had opened in the ground of the forum, and which it was declared, by some oracle, should never be closed till the glory of Rome was thrown into it. A truly grand patriot we have in the man; who would yet have been as much more ennobled if he could have seen how mean the oracle, and contemptible the god, and stood back from the sacrifice. Clearly enough there is nothing to be carried back into Christianity from such examples. A suffusion of the mere idea breeds inevitable confusion in the doctrine, and a great part of the trouble we have in our efforts to settle the Christian truth, is caused by the admission of this false element.

The divergence it creates begins to be evident when it is observed that we propitiate only a person, and expiate only a fact, or act, or thing; winning, it may be, any sort of favor, good or bad, by the pains undergone. Propitiation seeks the preparing always of a disposition morally right and good. Expiation is indifferent, caring never for the morality or justice of

3. It is supposed to have come into English from the Vulgate, and not till shortly after the translation. However, the translators, who learned half their theology from the Latin, must have been familiar with it.

what is gained, but only for the agreeableness of it. No righteous being or god is propitiated by any contribution of pains, as being pains, or by any kind of naked suffering; but such pains are good in expiation according to the temper of the god, no matter what the motive, or the meaning, in which they are offered. The Christian sacrifice of propitiation, we are told, is offered, or set forth, "to declare the righteousness of God," and to gain all such as will believe in it to a new life quickened in righteousness. In the expiations of the heathen peoples the main thing is to have enough suffered, for the apprehended wrath will be stayed when the rages of the gods are glutted. No new relationship in character is expected, no ingenerated righteousness in the life, the distinctive idea being that the god offended is to have an evil given him by consent, for an evil due by retribution, or feared from his tokens of exasperation. It throws in before God, or the gods, some deprecating evil, in the expectation that the wrath may be satisfied by its compensation. The power of the expiation depends not on the sentiments, or repentances, or pious intentions connected with it, but entirely on the voluntary damage incurred in it. According to the Latin idea, *Diis violatis expiatio debetur* — "When the gods are wronged, expiation is their due" — and the understanding is that, when the wrong-doers punish themselves in great losses, it buys off the wrath of the gods and turns them to the side of favor.

The pagan religions were corruptions, plainly enough in this view, of the original, ante-Mosaic *cultus* — superstitions of degenerate brood, such as guilt, and fear, and the spurious motherhood of ignorance, have it for their law to propagate. As repentance settles into penance under this regimen of superstition, so the sacrifices settled into expiations under the same. And the process only went a little farther when they fell, as they did the pagan world over, into the practice of human sacrifices; for since the gods were to be gained by expiatory evils, the greater the evil the more sure the favor; and therefore they sometimes offered their captives, sometimes their sons and daughters, counting it possible in no other manner to sufficiently placate their envious and bloody deities. Expiation figured in this manner not as a merely casual and occasional part of religion, but as being very nearly the same thing as religion itself. For as Tacitus could say that "the gods interfere in human concerns but to punish," what could men think of doing, in religion, but to expiate?

How low the pitch given to religion must be under such rites, maintained for such purposes, may be seen from the fact that almost never, in the expiations offered as in deprecation of hostility and wrath on the part of the gods appealed to, is any least consideration had of their character. They are even thought to be unsaintly and base, actuated by jealousy of other gods, working in revenge, and lust, and deceit. As to their justice, nobody thinks of it, and the question never is how to make good before them any fault of crime or personal misconduct. The expiation has commonly no fairer chance because it makes suit to the virtue of the god; on the contrary, any most politic scheme to get the advance of an adversary, in coming at the cunning deity's favor, promises not only as well as a more timidly conscientious appeal, but even better. Every one at all versed in the classics perfectly well knows that getting beforehand with the gods is the main thing in expiations. Their very smoke is the smoke of stratagem. The devotees and the gods are for the most part liars and cheats together. Nobody has any doubt of it, or conscience concerning it, and the integrity of the heathen world in general is just so far labefact, prostitute, and morally rotted away, as it has religiously abounded in expiations. And yet how many Christian teachers and disciples imagine that our gospel is to have its gain by following the classic expiations, and that the law and justice of God are to be rightly seconded by their example! Are not classic authorities good? And is not our religion finely complimented by them?

At the same time it is not to be denied that, drawing back from the field of the classics into the field of Scripture, it is possible there to hold a severer and more nearly moral view of sacrifices, which still classes them as expiations. Sin, being a violation of the law of God, incurs in that manner a dread liability of pain or punishment, and sacrifices, it is conceived, make satisfaction to God for the offense and consequent bad liability, obtaining in that manner a just release. Thus a third party, Christ himself, comes in to offer the suffering of pain as an evil, which is accepted as being a good enough match for the evil that is due. In this manner he makes amends for the sin by evil paid for evil due, and that is expiation. But the scheme, if not immoral, is fairly unmoral, as it ought to be under that word; showing that God accepts the pains of the good in payment for the pains of the bad, and is more intent on getting his modicum of pains than he is on having proper justice done — taking clean away the word and fact of forgiveness; for if the debt of sin is paid, there is no longer any thing to forgive; substituting government also by a kind of proceeding that has no relation whatever to conscience and right. Happily there is not a single case of expiation in the whole Christian Scriptures, or any thing in the Scripture sacrifices which bears a look that way, significant enough to support an argument. . . .

Nothing is ever made in the sacrifices, as I have already observed, of the pains of the animal. The occasion itself is very generally regarded as a festive occasion, and the sacrifices are called "sacrifices of joy." And it is a very singular fact to be historically accounted for, that two of our most merrily jocund words in English are lineal descendants of the same stock with the altar word *hilaskomai*, and related of course in meaning. I speak of the words *hilarity* and *exhilaration;* which if they somewhat overdo the gladness and emancipative grace of propitiation, very plainly never felt the touch of pains and penalties, so greatly magnified in expiation. Abraham was put through a trial of sacrifice; or rather was not put through, but stopped short in the midst of it, to learn that a sheep is better than a man for the offering; with a deliberate view, no doubt, to his being set up in his family, for all future time, as a bulwark against the unnatural and monstrous practice of human sacrifice, which was getting to be the distinctive practice of his time. There is no trace of expiation in the passover-rite; which, considering that it is the original of the Lord's Supper, makes it the more remarkable; since plainly there is some reference in the supper to pains endured, though endured, as the apostle teaches, not for pay but for propitiation.

Expiations never occur on occasions where we most naturally look for them; as in the judgment of Korah where there is an outbreak of mutiny and riotous tumult, and where, as we half naturally judge, a considerable smart of expiation might cool the rage of their fever. By and by, in the progress of the story, it begins to look as if the sacrifices were outgrown, and the human sacrifices of the heathen are sharply rebuked: "To what purpose is the multitude of your sacrifices? Bring no more vain oblations. Wash you, make you clean." So speaks the great preacher Isaiah, and Micah follows in a strain equally pungent: "Will the Lord be pleased with thousands of rams, or with tens of thousands of rivers of oil? Shall I give my first-born for my transgression, the fruit of my body for the sin of my soul? What doth the Lord require of thee, O man, but to do justly, and to love mercy, and to walk humbly with thy God?" Once more, we discover that a certain day is appointed to be observed, every year, by the people, which is to be the specially serious day of their calendar. It is to be a day of abstinence and deep thoughtfulness, in which the whole nation, considered as being unclean in every faculty and sense — in their

houses, their worship, their priesthood, and their very altars — is to undergo a complete lustration and come forth clean. "On that day shall the
priest make atonement for you, to cleanse you, that ye may be clean from
all your sins before the Lord" (Lev. 16:30). The atonement, it will be
observed, is lustral and not expiatory — "an atonement for you to
cleanse you." This religious day is generally called, especially by the
Jews, their great day of expiation, though never as holding the term in
any closely defined meaning. The day is deeply serious and very impressive, but there is really nothing in it that has any least appearance of pen-
ality, or of evil suffered to make amends for evil done.

In this sketch I think it will sufficiently appear that expiatory suffering
is not a Scripture idea. To further extend the argument is unnecessary. It
was clear enough in the beginning that one or the other, propitiation or
expiation, must go down; the two being morally incompatible. Which of
the two it must be, I think we now have no room left for doubt. If the
moral pitch of our gospel is low enough to be satisfied with a bought salvation, quantitatively suffered for, and paid up as in expiation, it certainly
can not rise high enough to even think a salvation unbought, yet distilled
in that great alembic of cost-making love wherein God prepares the
reconciliation of his enemies. If, on the contrary, it is in a pitch of character high enough to conceive the transcendent movements of propitiation,
it most assuredly can never sink low enough to count it a salvation that
pains are simply bought off by pains, in the close exchange of expiation.

I make this explicit renouncement of expiation with less satisfaction,
that so many disciples appear to be under a partly superstitious impression
of its immense practical value. They look upon it as the central truth
about which genuinely Christian experience must revolve. They conceive
a certain mysterious fitness in it to the needs of the conscience, alleging
that the conscience is no casuist, deals in no refinements, questions never
about the delicate distinctions, never waits to have the gospel smooth itself out in the psychologic proprieties; wanting, therefore, never any
thing so much as a good square paying in of pains for pains, penalties
suffered for penalties deserved. Let there be no winnowing out of substance and power by our explanations. Let the emancipation be as under
the Roman law, when a slave is made free by a blow on his head. No matter if questions rise and doubts remain, they come from the head; let the
head take care of them, and let the conscience be going its way sheltered

by God's peace. Many teachers magnify expiation thus under an appeal of ignorance. They acknowledge that it does not stand well in speculation, and that many reasons are lifted up in mutiny against it. Still it is the simple gospel, they think, because it makes good the conscience; for the conscience, having no philosophy, can be pacified only by a way of settlement that transcends philosophy, and ignores all casuistries. It has, at any rate, they say, the necessary ring; for which reason the strongest, most pronounced ideas of expiation are necessary to the best effects in Christian living. For self is thus cut off, and self-endeavor and all the legalities of duty. Speculation is given up; for when expiation is taken for the religion, there is no room for speculation left. And what shall we look for but to see the simple man be simply good and righteous? — for the reason that he is taken away from all doubting and even opinion.

Now that such impressions are groundless I most confidently believe, and also think observation will show. Indeed, I will venture the assertion that the most intensely expiational form of Christianity, instead of being most robust and steadfast, is poorest in the general, most unreliable, most frequently immoral. And that for the almost necessary reason that it expects to have salvation by a coarse commercial transaction in the exchange of pains. Are not the punishments all made up? is not the law quite satisfied? What shall we do then but let go concern, and plunge ourselves in the unanalyzed, unfiltered waters of salvation? Why so delicate in making critically nice distinctions of things in our approach to God, when he expiates our sins by the death of his Son, without caring to do it in a way that meets our dainty feelings and convictions. No! it is an awful mistake to speak in this coarse way of clearing the conscience. Such kind of uncaring peace will be only a dry-rot in the conscience, absolving it from duty instead of sin, and preparing the man to be religiously and, as it were, devoutly irresponsible. Looseness and unthinkingness are themselves disorder begun, and will run to worse and worse disorder as they proceed. Let us know in whom we believe, what he has done, what his atoning is, how he could and did, and how he could not and did not, become our sacrifice. Let us count our salvation a matter high enough and rich enough to be studied, searched out, nicely discriminated. No faith in the cross, that makes a fetish of the cross, is going to stand proof. The disciple will become distinctly, nobly Christian only when he takes the propitiation as it is offered, and lives by faith in it, as the tide-flow of God's free forgiveness.

Chapter II

Law and Commandment

The forgiveness of sins, already considered in the chapter on Forgiveness and Propitiation, is a purely personal matter, in which the Fatherhood love and feeling and the offended holiness of God are concerned. The proceeding here is intelligible and simple, because the forgiveness in question is to be a strictly personal settlement, that and that only. Then comes the farther question of the impersonal wrongs of law, and their legal settlement. All wrongs, taken as personal offenses, are yet violations also of law, and forgiveness being personal has no power, of course, to right the injuries of broken law. The law, too, being impersonal can not of course forgive any thing itself; or any way compound its own wrong; neither is it conceivable that God, as the administrator of law, has any power to annul the fact of such wrong, or the fact of a damage done by it to the law. Forgiveness, we thus find, puts a man personally right with God, but it does not put him right with law, and it is not easy to see that any thing can. The retributive consequences of violated law are running still in his nature; only so far reduced as the moral disorders of his nature are rectified, and the blight of his transgressions removed by the health-restoring efficacy of the regeneration. Made partly or completely whole, he will be partly or completely clear of the penal effects of the law, never till then. At this single point and so far, forgiveness has to do with law, and law with forgiveness, and I really do not see that they have a single point of contact any where else; except as the law continues to press the enforcement of a life that can fitly be forgiven.

And yet we appear to be assuming always, in this matter of atonement, that a principal concern of the salvation is to mend up, or somehow rehabilitate the law, when the indulgences of forgiveness are allowed; and especially to find how the standing offer of forgiveness can be proclaimed without consequent damage to its integrity. We assume, as if any thing could satisfy a law but simply and eternally to keep it, that the law broken by transgression must be satisfied. Not satisfied by obedience, it must be by punishment; not satisfied by the punishment of the wrongdoer, it must be by the punishment of a substitute; not by the punishment of a substitute in legal measure, it must be by some governmental equivalent in the expression of suffering, that will mend the public honor of the law and keep it good. Meantime, as regards this matter of satisfying law, it is a very great question whether enduring the penalty of transgression in full measure satisfies it; for the felon who has served the time of his sentence completely out, is really no more approved by the law than he was before. He is not, in fact, approved at all, and never can be till he makes a new character, and conquers to himself a new approbation. Still we go on contriving theologic ways of satisfying God's law, till, by one or another mode of getting its penalties made up, we think it is done. We propose substitutions for penalty, and compensations for penalty, and transferable merits provided, and righteousnesses made up to even accounts, and sins carried over by transfer to another, and sins accepted for the sinner in the liabilities of his guilt, with justice executed upon the guilt thus responsibly taken. Using these for theologic counters, we go on working out computations of atonement, and showing how it is that Christ is able to unlock the gates of law and bring transgressors through, without damage to its integrity. To any Christian believer the story ought to be a very sad one; for the schemes built on these vocables are, of course, not more genuine than they. I will not charge that they are an altogether spurious brood, but the artificial look they carry is conspicuous. . . .

I can not undertake, at this point, to state in a formal way the doctrine I am going to advance, for that is not yet possible. I shall be obliged, instead, to throw myself on the patience of my readers, and ask them to go along with me, stage by stage, till I have opened the subject far enough to make it possible. I will then set forth a general proposition that will cover the whole ground of the chapter.

I

I know not any better point where to open the proposed discussion than where, at a certain favoring hour, it seemed to be first opened to me. Were it not a fact so thoroughly sealed by our dull repetitions, I think it would certainly be most remarkable that the man Jesus — call him divine, or simply human, for outwardly, at least, he is but a man — should so often and boldly insist on "the keeping of his commandments," as the standard test of his disciples. The wonder is, too, that he does it so much as a matter of course! . . .

Our attention then is here called to the commandments Christ will have us keep as our standard, and to the law of God before enacted to be our standard; especially to what they are in their mutual relations to each other. And it may serve to make our way more intelligible, if we set up beforehand the point on which we shall be moving; viz., that what is called the law is to be consummated, brought to pass, fulfilled, in Christ's commandments. The law by itself makes nothing in us answer to its own high intentions, and is never expected, simply as law, to become a footing of salvation. But it is to make a beginning of moral impression, or enforced obligation, afterwards to be consummated in the state of allegiance to Christ, and the keeping of his commandments; where the old enforcements are substituted largely by a service in liberty; where, in fact, a new character is born, answering both to the law and the commandments by which the law was to be fulfilled. It is not to be said that the law is satisfied as being accurately kept — the satisfaction idea has no place here, unless it be understood as being satisfied in that it comes at last to be fulfilled. This brief statement will suffice to indicate beforehand the doctrine I am going to undertake, and it will be more fully and explicitly discovered in the future progress of my argument.

The two words *law* and *commandment* — *nomos* and *entolē* — will settle into place most easily in our exposition, if we consider them I, separately, in what they signify apart from each other; II, in their offices and uses; and then III, in their mutual relations to each other. Only I desire at this early stage of the inquiry to place it as distinctly as possible before the observation of my reader that I do not represent, and do not in fact believe that the two words *nomos* and *entolē* uniformly hold in the Scripture the precise relative significance given them in the exposition that follows. They vary, sometimes one falling very nearly into the sense of the other, so that discrimination is lost. And sometimes they even seem to cross over and make an exchange of meaning. Still a very close insertion of the critical knife will generally uncover some aspect of reason for the fluctuations discovered. But it must be enough for my present purpose, as I think it will be allowed, that the two words commonly, and almost always in the New Testament, stand in the relative significance I have given them. And this will be the more readily conceded, that I do not use them so much for authority as for convenience; though I most certainly discover in them just the complexions of meaning that make them convenient for my uses. I think also it will be agreed that I subject them to no violence. We proceed then to inquire —

I. What the two terms signify taken separately. In what is called the law we have, at the foundation, that great distinction of our moral nature, which makes us moral beings by a property inherent; viz., the eternal, absolute, self-asserting idea of right; that which is the law before government, and a law to God in composing his government, as truly as to us after it is composed; that in which we become a law to ourselves, showing the work of the law written on our hearts. And then we have superadded to this, for its more specific application, or carrying out into practice, statutes instituted by God in a way of positive enactment, appointing what we are to do, or not to do, for the due fulfillment of the aforesaid absolute, all-inclusive law. These positive word-statutes are also themselves enlarged and farther expounded, in turn, by the moral legislations of the Scripture, and by the common law of society; that is by custom, by legal definition, by refinements of esthetic perception, as well as by the drill-practice of all the functional experiences. By these two concurrent methods, divine legislation and the custom of society, we obtain a moral code more or less complete; that, for example, of the ten commandments, and that which is ethically developed about them and separately from them. . . .

In this description then we have the law (the *nomos*); a rigidly unpersonal, abstract, statutory code of conduct, based in the everlasting, inherent, moral imperative that underlies it, and gives authority both to the Supreme Legislator and his legislations. It is the law before government, and then by government; enforced by sanctions self-pronounced, and then by sanctions also that are legally prescribed. On the whole we shall probably understand what the law is, most comprehensively and most exactly, if we take the Saviour's own summation of it; for this, it will be seen, covers in fact all we have said both of its absolute right and its practical necessity. "Thou shalt love the Lord thy God with all thy heart, and with all thy soul, and with all thy strength, and with all thy mind; and thy neighbor as thyself." For if we call this God's consummate act of legislation, it still was law, absolute, in a sense, before all legislation.

Let us next consider what is meant by the commandment (*entolē*), that which Christ understands when he enjoins the keeping of his commandments, and gives to be the test henceforth of true discipleship. Any one can see that the word *commandment* is generally a less statutory, less tabulated, and more flexibly personal word than the word *law*. As used by Christ, it commands in the sense of enjoining, and enjoins in the sense of a personal authority, and assumes to be a personal authority, by reason of the qualities embodied, and offices performed, in his ministry. It covers just all that is commended to man's feeling and conscience by his life and death. . . .

II. The offices and uses of the law and the commandment. And here we shall see at a glance that the law, by itself, is not expected or intended to result in any complete form of personal virtue or character. It is to make a beginning in the level of constrained motive, using intimidations for the enforcement of principles, hammering in thus, or grinding in as it were, certain first impressions and first obligations necessary to character, as being its previous conditions. More exactly still it has for its office, to unfold the moral sense, and break the confidence of guilt, by revealing the dangers of disobedience. It ordains no fruitional, but a frictional experience rather, such as puts the subject writhing in condemnations, and conscious bondages, and apprehensions of evil to come. Accepted for its excellence, it would be life, and this it was designed to be, if only it could; but though it is ordained for life, it is found to be unto death. But the death is to be, in fact, a main element of its value. For the subject, slain by the law, is yet in a training under it that is a highway opening into life. . . .

So far the law has no value save as a first stage of discipline, to be followed by another that will bring on the discipline to a result that is complete. It is, and is declared to be, "the ministration of death," "the letter that killeth," and it is only "the ministration of righteousness," "the spirit that giveth life," that can make it better than a simply disastrous appointment. . . .

Passing onward now to this second stage, we have it as our next point to consider the offices and uses of the commandment Christ is giving us to keep as our new standard. And here we are to notice, first, the enlarged spread of the standard. Under the terms *love* and *righteousness* Christ goes a full day's journey, so to speak, beyond the law as held in men's thoughts, opening a vast province of culture, where the evangelic riches and liberties are gloriously enlarged and widened in their flow. According to the merely human or legally humanized notions, love means only love to our neighbor, on the footing of our fellow nature. The word of Christ goes farther — "But I say unto you love your enemies, bless them that curse you, do good to them that hate you, and pray for them that despitefully use you and persecute you." The law of natural society is, love the lovely, and the law of God conceived under that restriction amounts to scarcely more than a law of good society. But Christ proposes a nobler and more sovereign love — love the unlovely, the base, the wicked, the hateful, the disgustful — instituting thus a new divine order of love in sacrifice, and cost, and patience. This is the love that goes under, and up through evil, and regenerates all it touches; heaving, as it were, every mountain of encumbrance that sin has piled on the world. So again there is a righteousness in Christ's view that the scribes and Pharisees had not, under the law in their most superstitious observance of it; and scarcely better, I fear, is our half-commercial righteousness, where we assume that right means only what is fair, equitable, or just. To Christ there is no right or righteousness that does not go a long way farther. No man is in the right, or up to the right, who is not ready for sacrifice and the enduring of cost for the ill-deserving. And hence it is that our Great Master is pronounced, as it were, on discovery to the world, "Jesus Christ the righteous" — and the definite article is prefixed, to challenge for him his pre-eminent distinction. Hence, also, that other pronouncement not less remarkable, "faithful and righteous" — (not just, but righteous) "to forgive us our sins"; as if God would not think himself completely righteous in his Son, were there any utmost sacrifice and cost he could not undergo for the forgiveness of sins.

And what a chapter is opened for us here, in these words *love* and *right*, as they will henceforth be represented in the life of Christ by commandment. How far on do they reach beyond the measures of the merely legal code! In this legal code we live, as it were, outside of God, under the statute, shrunken up, and shriveled by the stringency of mere penal enforcement. Here, in the commandment, we live inside, where we range in glorious enlargement by God's measures, and are no more scanted in love and right by the meager notions, whether of Pharisees or ethical professors.

Secondly, there is, I think, sufficient distinctness in the fact to require some distinct notice of it, that we not only come abroad here into wider and more enriched ways of excellence, but that we have our discipline by a different and more genial method. We leave the mere tabulated, impersonal, statutory way of rule, and pass out into a way of commandment that is personal, and is in fact the rounded, all-containing sway of personality itself. In simply being what it is, it is commandment, and word, and way, and yoke, made easy; for it is the living and dying Christ in whom all the authorities and captivating majesties of good are contained. The intimidations are gone by, at least for the time. The word is a word of Christly inspiration — Take my yoke, take up my cross, walk in my way, as I live, live with me, as I die, be joined to me in death. Our life code is given in the person of Jesus, and in that *living book* gets authority to be our commandment. And it is a way of commandment that leaves us free, nay that makes us free. Legal obedience is gone by forever. Impulse, inspiration, duties that are meat and drink — these are the tide-sweep of the new life quickened in us. The Son makes us free, and therefore we are free indeed. The Spirit goes with the word and commandment, as it does not with the law, wafting us onward, and where the Spirit of the Lord is there is liberty. Nay the law itself, if we use that word, being in us no more by enforcement, is become the perfect law of liberty. And so the result is that when we are engagd to keep the commandment of Jesus, we have it keeping us, floating us on, tiding us in upon the divine fullness where we rest.

There is yet a third consideration that must not be omitted; viz., that the commandment differs from the law as being offered to faith. The law is apprehended, or expected to be, only as all statutes are; that is, by ocular inspection, audible pronouncement, and other like natural ways of cognition. But the Christ-law, or commandment, is given to faith, even as Christ himself is, for in fact it is himself in the scope of its ideas and resulting obligations. It has no penal sanctions whatever, but speaking directly to faith it offers promise, always promise, working thus by comforts, inspirations, openings upwards into God. . . .

III. We come now to the third and last point in our proposed explication; viz., the relation of the law and the commandment to each other. They have a common object, there is to be no doubt of that; viz., to establish right and finish up a truly ennobled character of deific righteousness in mankind. But they never did it, or proposed to do it, by either, in its own separate agency. In the first place, the law, it is agreed, makes no righteousness of its own. Indeed, it is even declared to be the letter that killeth — ordained unto life, but found to be unto death. I think too we can see beforehand that any table of statute working by itself, and forcing on virtues by motives in the nature of retribution, must bring failure and precipitation; though even that may become the necessary footing of a new second-stage movement forward. Be it so, still they are both in line together, moving, each in its way, on the common interest of character. By one is the knowledge of sin, by the other the deliverance from it; and the knowledge being necessary to the deliverance, has a certain common value with it. We shall discover thus, as regards the relative action of the two great factors, law and commandment, that the law is just as necessary to the result as the commandment, and that the latter, taken by itself, can do as little as the law by itself. The expectation was, and is, that a beginning made under the latter and the legal intimidations, will stamp in such imprints of authority and obligation, and raise such storms of disorder and wild remorse within, when they are violated, that the subject, driven out of all confidence in himself, will be casting about for almost any deliverance from the dreadful precipitation that is thrusting him down. Whereupon it is the plan to bring him out and up by his faith in the commandment, or second stage of discipline, into a state of new-born life. So that, between the two, and by one as truly as the other, the great final end of liberty and holy character will be consummated. If we say fulfilled, we mean the same thing; for the law, when even already broken, is to be fulfilled in the commandment as truly and totally as if it had never been broken; perhaps the more completely fulfilled that, after the breach, exasperated longings, and heart-sinking bondages, and writhings of remorse, will have created a hell in the mind, that is to be the eternal possibility of juster apprehensions and vaster yearnings; such as will be spanning forever the chasm that the breach has made.

It needs also to be noted, as regards the two great factors, law and commandment, that one is a factor in nature and among natural causes, and the other supernatural. The apostle shows them working both together — the weakness of one and the relative might of the other. "For what the law could not do, in that it was weak through the flesh" — that is, through the mere constitution-life in which both law and penalty are to get their pronouncement — "God sending his own Son in the likeness of sinful flesh, condemned sin in the flesh, that the righteousness of the law might be fulfilled in us, who walk not after the flesh but after the Spirit." Every thing is weak on the footing of law, but every thing begun there triumphs in the supernatural vigor of the Spirit; for the commandment, as being spirit and truth, is supernatural vigor itself. Penal causations are the power in the one, and it is a dreadful power; supernatural ministrations, separating the guilty from their hidden poisons and their low-bred disabilities, are the power in the other. Natural causes, appointed to avenge the law, suffer no violence or displacement by the supernatural grace, but this latter visitation, quickening good in the man and the man to good, in a manner of silent sovereignty, makes the natural causes slacken their hold on him and let him forth made whole and free.

The law, it is important to add, is in this view never abolished or annulled by the commandment, though it is a common way of the evangelic teaching to very nearly say it. . . .

A thousand crosses, ransoms, atonements, would leave it exactly where it was. The taking away of sin was possible, but no taking away of the law. The sacrifice of Calvary itself, set against the law, would have had as little effect on it as upon the principles of Euclid. Therefore we must never allow to be slid into our secret apprehension, back of thought, any most latent feeling that God is at work in his Son to mend, or mitigate, or get us by, the law. It is whole as it ever was. Broken oft, as in figure, it is yet not flawed; condemning still and always every thing in principle it has condemned; certain to outlast the world, even as it lived before the world in the eternal bosom of God.

II

This very specific and scriptural exposition of the two great factors, the commandment and the law, and their relative work and office, is a gathering up of material, it will be understood, for the great Legal Settlement or Consummation which is the proposed subject of our inquiry. But we are not yet ready to use this material to the best advantage, and can not be till we have gone over another field not scriptural, and brought in the rich fund of matters there supplied for our help. Knowing, as we all do, that God's way, in casting the molds of things, is to show us first what is natural, and afterwards what is spiritual, as it may be signified thereby; to show us things in human life and society set to represent, by analogic correspondences, things of the Spirit and things Celestial, making always the lower to be interpreters of the higher — men's forgivenesses, of God's forgivenesses — the family, of God's great Fatherhood — the state, of God's infinite kingdom — knowing this, I say, it is the more remarkable that we miss observing the numerous analogies of law and gospel continually crowded upon us in our natural and earthly state. It can not be that these low-ranging, sub-atoning ways of discipline, all beginning with law and meant to be issued in liberty, have no important lessons to give us in the field of religion. Let me call attention to a few of the numerous examples.[4] . . .

III

We pass over now to the main subject for which this excursion has been made; viz., God's twofold way of training under his law, and the redemptive grace in his Son. The matter of this training, as we now perceive, is not so peculiar as to make it a case wholly by itself, but it holds a place, instead, at the head of a vast, widespread system of analogies that,

4. [ED.] In this section Bushnell undertook "to show how the grand analogy of letter and spirit, law and liberty, or law and free commandment, runs through all the organific discipline of life and society." He drew illustrations from the family, the school, the army, and the civil state.

in their lower grade, look up to be its interpreters. It is grounded partly, at least, in the same necessities and reasons, though moving in a scale so transcendent as to scarcely allow the relationship of its humbler kinsmen to be observed. Here, in this higher discipline, we are asking always, What of the law? — in particular, What is to be apprehended for it in redemption? what losses will occur to its authority? what compensations will be needed? what satisfactions must be provided? Where one thing, at least, is quite certain beforehand, which we may have our comfort in, carrying it on with us; viz., that it is the law of God, and is not likely to go down, whatever we may say, or omit to say, or think, or omit to think, concerning it.

That we may have our mark before us, and steady our thought by it, in the inquiries that remain, I now set forth in formal statement the following conclusion, which has been looming up more and more distinctly upon us in all the previous approaches.

That our present state of life, or probation, is a state of penally coercive discipline, in which the law, broken by sin, is sufficiently consecrated by Christ, incarnated into and co-operating with it, in his life and cross.

Three points in this proposed summation require to be distinctly stated.

I. The penally coercive discipline. It is not penal, of course, or penalty, in any such sense that it must be destruction, and can not be discipline. In calling it discipline, I call it schooling; for schooling is what we mean by discipline. Calling it our schoolmaster to bring us to Christ, we mean the same thing; viz., that it is promotive, corrective, coercive, no matter what our deserts may be, or what penalties in the principle of desert they would bring us. I use the terms "penally coercive discipline," in the understanding that our training toward God is carried on under a motivity thus named, which is not judicially penal, and is not meant to be; for it is not graded by the desert of actions, but by what is wanted for the future benefit and due correction of the actors. . . .

II. It is another point to be considered, as regards our supposed scheme of discipline, that while it includes the law of God as a necessary factor in its operation, it must not here be the law as backed by judicial sanctions, but only by such casual, ungraduated sanctions as will duly enforce the discipline. There is accordingly no justice work done here, as we perfectly know. We do not live in a scheme of awards, but in a scheme of probatory discipline. Persons are not treated alike, nor wrongs alike, neither is any thing kept in the scale of desert. God reserves the liberty in his own hands, to turn our experience here in what way of stress or modified comfort will best advance his good purpose in us. At the same time, while nothing is being done with us here in the terms of justice, we are duly notified and certified of a time future, when our present mixed way of discipline will be over, and we shall be carried on with our bad ways uncorrected, if so it must be, to be settled on the hard-pan basis of justice pure and simple, receiving every man according to his work. . . .

III. It now remains to speak of the last and most distinctively Christian of the three points named in my general statement, or deduction; viz., that the coercive discipline we are under — including the law element and what elements of Providential enforcement are added — waiting for no pains of justice to re-establish it and re-cement its broken order, is consecrated anew forever, and more than consecrated, endued with transcendent efficacy, by Christ incarnated into it, and dying in it and for it. The coercive discipline was organically framed and set in order for the world, even from the first, and long ages before the appearing of Christ. It included, of course, the law, and beside that, all the vast material of outward expression such as might second or assist the general endeavor of the discipline — the health or disease of the body, the seasons, the bounties of nature, the oppressions and liberties, the wars, the captivities and migrations, all the private and personal benefits too secret to be named, all the ministries of human love and friendship. These all together are not Christ, but taken as additions to the naked authority of law, they go a certain way to help its otherwise barely coercive efficacy. But a great and supereminently glorious addition now arrives — Christ is born into the discipline as before in operation, and becomes the quickening life and central factor of it. And this is the change that we celebrate as Christianity; a change that is just as great as must needs take place when the impersonal and dry machine composed of law and world — absolute law and scarcely responsive world — has God's full sensibility and sanctifying life poured in, to moisten the dryness of the discipline and make it a complete gospel. So that now it goes no more by thrustings on of enforcement only, but by such powers of unenforcement as may be looked for, in the suffering love and gentle endurance of the Lamb. The commandment is here come, and the discipline that was like to be too nearly penal, working too much in the way of fear and mere self-interest, and too little in the way of inspiration, is now to be consummated as a way of complete and perfect liberty.

Christ then is here, we now proceed to say, incarnated into the discipline we are under, and membership with us in its adversities and trials; in the enduring of which he is brought into conditions of unspeakable suffering. When we say that Christ is incarnate thus in our humanity, we commonly appear to mean very little by it, more than that he takes on the look and speaks with the voice of a man. We seem to think of him more as a passenger than as a born resident, and we only see him on his way through, doing many beautiful things, and suffering specially nothing except in a sharp theologic crisis at the close. What it means for him to be incarnate, we do not consider deliberately enough to grasp the idea and measure the consequences; and above all the consequences of personal suffering to himself. True, it is understood that he is here as one of us for a time, but what special cause of tragedy there may be in that, more than belongs to the average experience of men themselves, we do not perceive. Besides it is the cross, we think, that brought upon him all that was to be accounted specially severe in his experience. His incarnation was no part of his suffering, being only a matter of less cost to him probably than our incarnate state is to us. In this manner we fall out of key as regards any proper estimate of his life; for the particular crisis of his death, short and sharp as it was, comprised but a very small part of the suffering and sacrifice his mission cost him. . . .

Let us glance now at three or four of the scenes where Christ's great suffering is most remarkably displayed, and also the fact that he has it upon him, consciously, as the curse or penal shame and disaster of our transgression. First, I name the temptation, at which his public life began. Incarnated into the curse of the world, he is now to have his part in a state demonized by evil; and it will be the point of his first great trial to master all the physical taint of his birth, and so far humanly corrupted participation. Another storm let loose upon him by the new-born consciousness of his Messiahship is the felt solidarity of the sin-wrath, rolled in now so tempestuously, that it takes a whole forty days to get that full possession of himself and his plans, that will enable him to go out upon his work. Meantime he is closeted in the grim wilderness, wrestling with the troubles that crowd upon his mind and disturb his counsel, and even forgetting that he is hungry. Angels come about to minister, and it appears to be intimated that the wild beasts are drawn together round him, by strange sympathy with some awful sorrow perceptible even to them. It is not common to class this scene with other scenes of suffering in Christ's life, but it has an aspect dreadfully forlorn, and a sin-stamp quite unmatched unless by the crucifixion.

The weeping of Christ over the city is told in fewer words, but it is the more important because it is so casual in the occurrence as to show what feeling he is in habitually — what mountain loads of sorrow from the blasted, guilt-stricken world are always upon him — "If thou hadst known in this thy day the things that belong to thy peace, but now they are hid from thine eyes!"

But we pass, at this point, to the agonies so called of the garden and the cross, both of which are often conceived to borrow their intensity of suffering from the wrath or justice of God, let fall upon the sufferer that he may take the brunt of our penalty, and compensate or satisfy the law in our behalf. "The cup," it is imagined, can mean nothing less than this. It can not be the "cup of *trembling*," or "the cup of *astonishment*," but must be "the cup of justice," because nothing less than the justice-power of God's hand upon the sufferer could produce such demonstrations. It may be so, but I see not how any one can be sure that he might not suffer as severely under the solidarity principle or the world's penal-sanction causes, as he would under justice. Be that as it may, we have a most improbable, perfectly incredible mixture, when he is set before us under such a conception, calling on his poor disciples, in his awful prostrations, to stay by him and help him — yes, help him to bear God's justice! To his groaning on the ground, and his body dripping blood from the pores, they might possibly give the comfort of a little sympathy, but if he is being wrenched in this manner by the justice of God, what right have they to help him against that? True, the suffering is strangely severe, and yet indications of the same kind are reported as having sometimes been observed in the case of men suffering under great mental distress. Moreover demonstrations of this nature appear to be quite sufficiently accounted for, when three facts are brought together; (1) the structural frailty of the physically human person, too little able to support the reactions of a superhuman sensibility; (2) the extraordinary movement on that sensibility, by the madness and wild exasperation of so great multitudes hasting to precipitate themselves unwittingly on him in a deed that comprehends both sacrilege and murder; (3) the mortal exhaustion that has now come upon him by his brotherhood relation, so long continued, with humanity; where he has nothing to receive, only wrongs and disgusts to bear, and sympathy and suffering patience to give.

As regards the cross, taken often for a scene of divine justice, the argument would be much easier and better supported if the problem were to show that the justice displayed is a visitation of God upon the people. They really seem to do all in a way of judicial blindness, and take on the lunatic airs of their dispossession, in ways of cunning and prejudice and passion that completely represent the penal madness of sin — Pilate, Herod, Caiaphas, the soldiers, the multitude, all in character under the curse together. And when that awful word is spoken — "This is your hour, the power of darkness," we even shudder at the suggestion. And yet it is not these, we hear, but Christ himself who is under the ban of justice! Innocence gibbeted and dying by what every body pronounces the most horrible murder on record, he is having laid upon him, we are told, the justice of God, and these monsters in their murder are God's ministers, doing the justice upon him! The mixture of idea, character, and fact — the Good Being using wickedness, and wickedness doing the honors of justice — make up a compound so incongruously bad that we are cruelly revolted by it. Yes, but the Saviour cries out himself — "My God, my God, why hast thou forsaken me?" And this, we are taught, is a plain declaration of the judicial withdrawment of the Father. Does any human creature then believe that Christ is actually complaining here, in his last breath, of being left to die deserted of God, or under the ban of his justice? Interjections are never to be taken pathologically in this manner; for what is this outcry but an interjection of distress vented in Scripture words crowding at the moment on his brain? And he as little means that God has deserted him as the Psalmist himself who was coming out shortly in praise — "For he hath not despised nor abhorred the affliction of the afflicted, neither hath he hid his face from him, but when he cried unto him he heard" (Ps. 22:1 and 24). God had forsaken him, yet now he finds that he had not hid his face! Furthermore what does Christ promise the poor malefactor dying at his side, but that he shall be with him this very day in paradise? He seems to have forgotten that he is under the justice of God! Was he not also saying a little while ago in glorious confidence, "Therefore doth my Father love me because I lay down my life for the sheep"? And again — "I have glorified thee on the earth, and now I come to thee." And again, about the same time, in the same confidence — "Thinkest thou that I can not now pray to my Father, and he shall presently give me more than twelve legions of angels?" It could not on the whole be more clear that Christ came to his cross in the full consciousness of the Father's loving accord and sympathy, and that on the cross itself, he was hovering in thought round the gates of paradise just waiting to be opened, and beholding, close at hand, "the glory that he had with the Father before the world was."

IV

. . . It only remains now to sum up the results arrived at, as regards the subject matter of the chapter. The law part of our coercive discipline was never expected to establish obedience and righteousness by itself;

neither was it expected to be a complete government by itself, letting no
other means or method intervene to bring away from its condemnation,
without first paying up its dues of penalty. On the contrary it was designed, from the first, to be joined with other means, working by other
methods, and both together to make up the complete order of discipline
for men; which discipline is to be kept on foot with every man even to
the last, no part of it being displaced by substitutional or compensatory
agencies. One part never brings away from the other, and has of course
no price to pay for release by the other, the common concern of both
being how to fashion a character of perfect obedience and righteous liberty. At first the law and its enforcing agency has greater prominence in
the discipline, and appears to be less conspicuously helped by the attractive and gracious powers that are to operate conjunctively with it. These
are the good inspirations of public history, the great acts and characters
of righteous men, the bounties and beautiful things of the world, the
blessings of health and family and property, great escapes and deliverances from peril, the festivals and rites of religion, the hymns of the temple worship and the word of the prophets, all working with the law as
gracious and softening influences, to raise up fear into love, and obedience
into liberty. These and such as these were the powers that went before, to
represent Christ in the discipline, down to the time of his full appearing;
and then from that time on, the discipline begins to seem rooted almost
wholly in him and his glorious overshadowing personality. The legal aspect is now no longer prominent, and the law appears to be fulfilling itself
in the commandment. The discipline we called coercive, takes on the look
of a saving power, and we call it a gospel of salvation. We find a full competence in it now to the mastery of sin. The motivities of the law, acting
always by appeals to self-regard, operate strongly by the vice of their
very nature, to fasten the bad state of sin, and make it a state of thrall.
That death-fall, that collapse of possibility, by which man is so fatally
broken, as regards any gathering up of himself into good, is even made
more hopeless, or at least scarcely more hopeful, by the pressure of mere
legal enforcement, for the fault of it is that the motivities and the man are
on the death-side of sin together. It can press the subject on, but it can
not draw him off. What is wanted here is a new motivity, inspirational in
its nature, spontaneous, and free. And therefore it is that Christ comes
over into our discipline from his own divine side, and brings his everlasting liberties with him. So that being incarnated into and dying into our
world-discipline with us, his glorious and sublime personality overtops
every thing in it and us beside. He can show us, and does, how liberty can

even die, and he gives it as our tender call of brotherhood to die with him, into his liberty. For now, and by our faith in his person or transcendent personality, we both die and live, and the mastery of our sin is complete. The abstract, tabulated law is fulfilled and crowned in the personal commandment.

Equally true it would be, at the same time, if we should invert all this, and say that the law itself is made personal by the insertion of the Christly love and feeling into it. We are wont to imagine, and are all the while saying, that it is the sin of sin to be taking down the authority of law; and we sometimes think of it as a hard, non-elastic and frangible pillar, flawed and broken, which can no way be repaired, and can only be replaced, on payment, by something different; whereas all the grand authority it had, and more, is made good by the tonic life and sovereign vigor of the cross. It is as if the tables of the ten commandments themselves, after Moses threw them down, were mended by passover blood sprinkled on them. So when Christ dies into the law, it becomes itself commandment written out in blood and sacrifice; as much more sovereign over human hearts and consciences as it is more thoroughly personal, and having an authority from the cross which no thunder of Sinai could impress.

It is not our conclusion, then, that the commandment takes away from the law, or the law from the commandment, but that they mutually endow and uphold each other; locked together in a complete whole that is one and indivisible. God, we say, never made any so great misfit in a plan as to organize a great first half of it that he must somehow, any how, at any cost, get rid of, before he could bring it on to success. That is not his way. On the contrary his beginning will reach through to his end, and the law and law-sanctions, never abated or bought off, will be working faithfully on, with all the gracious powers and tender motivities in Christ — part and parcel with them, in the one comprehensive purpose; even as the lightnings and the dews take part together in the growth of the world.

3. Justification by Faith [1]

EDITOR'S INTRODUCTION

From the outset of the Bushnell controversy, the ministers of Fairfield West Association argued that Bushnell denied the doctrine of justification

1. *Forgiveness and Law, Grounded in Principles Interpreted by Human Analogies* (New York, 1874), Chap. III (177–79, 189–91, 197–217).

by faith as commonly understood.[2] He replied: "I hold most emphatically, the doctrine of justification by faith, and that any and every form of religion which proposes to save mankind on terms of merit or desert, is not Christianity."[3] It is true, however, that Bushnell and the Edwardeans of Fairfield West disagreed over the question of what was the antecedent condition of being forgiven. According to the Edwardeans, that condition consisted in holding that Christ's suffering was necessary to compensate God's honor and rectoral justice, or that it was necessary to express God's abhorrence of sin. Bushnell repudiated this idea.[4]

Nevertheless, Bushnell held a profound view of Christian justification. It is sufficient here merely to offer a threefold hint, since his own text is reproduced below. First, he insisted that salvation was by grace, and he rejected every theory which predicated salvation upon personal merit or human effort. Second, he opposed all schemes of legal justification in favor of a moral and dynamic theory. He insisted that God's fundamental attribute as related to justification was "righteousness," not "justice." Thus Christian justification involves the process of being actually made righteous. "Any proper and true justification," said Bushnell, "is a state renewed in righteousness — that and nothing else." Third, justifying faith is not a belief in any fact or proposition; it is trusting one's self over to Christ to be "new charactered" by him.

The following text is drawn from *Forgiveness and Law*, but it is largely a verbatim repetition of the material printed earlier in *The Vicarious Sacrifice*, Part III, Chapter 7.

❖   ❖   ❖   ❖

We most properly begin our discussion of this great subject at the text of Scripture whence, in a sense, it has its own beginning — "whom God hath set forth to be a propitiation, through faith in his blood, to declare his righteousness, for the remission of sins that are past, through the forbearance of God; to declare, I say, at this time his righteousness, that he might be just, and the justifier of him which believeth in Jesus" (Rom. 3:25–26).

The first clause of the passage respecting propitiation has been ex-

2. *Remonstrance and Complaint of Fairfield West to the Hartford Central Association, Together with the Reply of the Hartford Central Association* (New York, 1850), 19–23, 29–31.

3. Manuscript "Records of the Hartford Central Association [1843–1901]," 39 (MS. in Congregational House, Hartford, Connecticut).

4. *God in Christ* (Hartford, 1849), 217–18.

pounded already in the chapter given on that subject.[1] Our present concern is with the latter clause, relating to the alleged declaring of God's
righteousness and the purpose or intent of it.

The "declaring" here intended is not so much a declaring in words, but
more in a way of manifestation; as by the facts and acts of Christ's incarnate ministry, considered as the revelation made of his divinely great
character, which is itself the righteousness of God. The original word for
the declaring is *in-showing, endeixis,* that which, being displayed inwardly, begets an inward impression. It is more important, however,
rightly to conceive what the declaring, or in-showing, is for; viz., that
when God's excellence is declared, it will both show us how, and why, he
was able to overlook, or pass by, the sins of past ages which he suffered in
so great forbearance; and how, as respects the sins of this present time, he
is able to be "just" enough, that is great enough, in the power of his
"righteousness" to make righteous him that believeth — every one, that
is, whose heart is opened by faith to the possible reception of his character. For this, if we rightly understand our word, is what justification signifies. It is that which takes away our condemnation; setting us in confidence with God, by setting God in upon us, in such transforming power
that we become new-charactered from his righteousness.

If now it should seem that I put a strain of hard practice on these words
"just" and "justify," when I convert them in this manner to "righteous"
and "make righteous," it must be enough to answer that the hard strain
came long time ago, when the "righteous" and "make righteous" were
displaced by "just" and "justify," and torn away from their natural kins-
man "righteousness," in the beginning of the sentence. By a most singular
fatality it has come to pass, in this manner, in our English version, that
where the Greek Testament gives us three words, noun, adjective, and
verb, *dikaisosunē, dikaios,* and *dikaiounta* — all of one root — we have
two sets of words in the English to represent them; one from the Saxon,
righteousness, and two from the Latin, *just* and *justify.* Whence it results
that as the Latin words *justitia, justus, &c.,* have two sets of meanings; a
legal or judicial, as pertaining to the penal redress of crimes, and a moral,
as relating wholly to character; the two nationalities of tongue in our
English version throw us into a jumble of ambiguities, where we have as
good chance of mental confusion as the worst enemy of truth could
desire.

I really wish it were possible to be rid of these Latin-born terms; for

1. [ED.] *Forgiveness and Law,* Chap. 1; see *supra,* 312–43.

that syllable *jus* puts us thinking inevitably of something done for law and justice, and gravitating always downward on ideas simply political; when we perfectly know, or may, that the Greek words translated by them have never any but some far-off reference to law and justice, even when applied to men, and much less can be expected to have when used as staple words, to signify the moral excellence, or holiness, or righteousness of God, set forth to quicken righteousness in us, and beget in us a character graciously derivative from his. Plainly enough there is no such quickening, reproductive power in justice. . . .

I

Thus far I have been occupied mainly with matters negative. I now pass on to verify the doctrine already vindicated, and very plainly asserted in the passage from the epistle to the Romans, at which this discussion began; viz., *that the true Christian justification is that which makes righteous.*

If Christianity, or the Christian Scripture, has any thing to boast, it is that it proves its grand superiority, and shows the manifest seal of God's inspirations, in having given to the world far back, in advance of all other literature, this most noble, stately, intellectually massive name for character; viz., RIGHTEOUSNESS. We have other words in the Scripture and out of the Scripture, built on different symbols, that answer well many of the requisite uses of morality or moral obligation, and sometimes of religion, but none that carry the distinctions of character with equal force and sharpness. *Law* is a word more nearly political and parliamentary, and better for a legal virtue than a free. *Obedience* supposes some other nature in a superior relation of authority, which leaves no room, save by a large accommodation, for its application to God. *Justice* (*justitia*) was even a more favorite moral word than *rectitudo* among the Romans because of their intensely legal character, but the forensic and judicial habit of the word associates always a false element when it is applied to moral uses. *Goodness* is a word truly divine, when used by one who is in a spiritual habit, but it will be observed that unreligious minds are always sinking it to things done with generosity only, or out of a merely kind disposition. *Love* is the popular word of Scripture obligation, partly because it has the disadvantage of being only a word of the affections, demanding always some intellectual word to sharpen its applications, and be a regulative standard of its measures, times, and occasions. Higher than all these, and least ambiguous, and sharpest in the moral ring of it, is *right* or *right-eousness*. The other flags require holding, all of them, but this can hold itself. A right line is the most inflexible of all symbols, and having this central image of necessary meaning in it, corrupt uses can not warp it; still it stands to its integrity as the plainly divine, visibly eternal word for character; declaring with Solomon, "Let thine eyes look right on, and thine eyelids look straight before thee" (Prov. 4:25); where — it may not be amiss to mention the fact — this word *straight* is represented in the Septuagint by the Greek word *dikaia*. . . .

Descending to the New Testament, we have the Saviour himself testi-fying in his very first sermon, "Blessed are they that hunger and thirst after righteousness, for they shall be filled"(Mt. 5:6). He does not say, observe, they that hunger and thirst after *a* righteousness, but after right-eousness. And again he declares at this earliest moment of his ministry, "Seek ye first the kingdom of God and his righteousness"(Mt. 6:33). A most bold thought to put in any mortal mind that it is to seek the righteousness itself of God! Accordingly his new dispensation is called the ministration of righteousness (2 Cor. 3:9), and that, too, plainly in the sense of justification, because it antagonizes and quells, when embraced, the ministration of condemnation. To the same point comes another dec-laration: that "now the righteousness of God without the law is mani-fested, being witnessed by the law and the prophets, even the righteous-ness of God which is by faith in Jesus Christ unto all and upon all them that believe"(Rom. 3:21–22). It is not, observe, a grace of penal suffering for, but a grace of righteousness *unto* and *upon* all them that believe. Hence the call of our salvation is "to yield our members instruments of righteousness unto God" (Rom. 6:13), as if nothing now were necessary to put us fully in God's character but to yield our whole nature believ-ingly up to his all transforming righteousness. Thus when God has all our faculties offered up together to the harmonizing power of his righteous-ness, and to inspired co-working with it, they will be instruments dis-coursing only music from that time forth.

What I am here advancing then under this head is the fact of a grand, stock character in God, that has been and is to be forevermore the spring of all character in his believing people. Thus it was long before any one ever had a thought of the possible satisfying of God's law and justice by a contribution of pains to fill the legal quota of transgression, that Abra-ham, believing God in the promise of an heir, had the faith counted unto him for righteousness. Simply because every one brought home to God in such a way of faith, passes into God, so to speak, and is hid and covered and charactered in all action by his righteousness.

But a higher, finer point is finally reached, or finally will be, in the Scripture development of this ideal standard. We are not only to have our righteousness derivatively from God, but God himself, as being its eternal source, will be in it, after a standard more perfect than we, to this hour, have commonly been able to imagine. How seldom do we think it requires any thing above justice and equity and fair consideration! Whereas God would not be right or righteous to himself, if he could think it less than wrong to not make cost, or endure even a cross for his enemy. Hence the representation that his Son is set forth to be a propitiation, because righteousness or right conviction — the eternal law before government — required it of him. Whence it follows, in a reverse order, that the blood and sacrifice of his Son declare "the righteousness of God in the forgiveness of sins." All this "that he may be righteous," not *just* in the retributive sense as our version is supposed to represent, but "righteous" — and have it seen that for righteousness' sake he will forgive at bloody cost; so to new-character in righteousness him that believeth in Jesus. And how beautifully is the conception borne out, in the words of apostolic epithet under which he is presented — *"Jesus Christ the righteous"* (1 Jn. 2:1). He is called *the* righteous, observe, as if this were somehow the most emphatic and principally distinctive designation of his person. And that the epithet is used with a deliberate reference to the cross and the sacrifice for sin, is plainly seen from the words preceding: "We have an advocate with the Father"; as if he were *"the* righteous" in that very grace itself. The same thing also we have once more in the same epistle — "He is faithful and just" (that is, righteous), "to forgive us our sins." There the unhappy translation, *just*, really mocks the significance of the words; for who will imagine that God is faithful to forgive sins because he is forensically just? What, in fact, are we shown all the while with so great stress of misbegotten argument, as that God can not forgive sins without something done to satisfy his justice and take it out of the way? Here then it is that we behold the sublime peak of obligation where true righteousness culminates; viz., that it is to be fulfilled, and can be, only by sacrifice. Righteousness and sacrifice are even relative ideas. That Christ himself had this impression is sufficiently clear from his promise of the Spirit coming to reprove the world of righteousness, because his death will have taken him home now to the Father to be seen no more. The pure great image of the righteousness of God, will now be discovered in his re-ascension to the Father, showing plainly that he is not a being of this world.

How different a matter now is the justification that comes of justice satisfied, from this over-spreading, all-assuring character in the righteousness of God. One believes in the cold-iron click of the turnkey opening his door; the other in the sunrise and the soft-glowing, free-breathing radiance of the morning — always to rise and glow and breathe and be fresh morning for the soul's high liberty. And how strongly cast the contrast is we all discover, in the shock of incongruity it gives us to simply substitute justice for righteousness in the Scripture uses. We can not read "sacrifices of justice" — "justice from the God of his salvation" — "the Lord our justice" — "Blessed are they that hunger and thirst after justice for they shall be filled" — "So by the justice of one the free gift came on all" — "the justice of God which is by faith of Jesus Christ unto all and upon all them that believe" — "Much more doth the ministration of justice exceed in glory" — "new heavens and new earth wherein dwelleth justice"; indeed there is scarcely a passage, I know not one, in the Old and New Testament, that will not groan almost audibly when the word justice is stuck upon it as the synonym of righteousness. So clear it is that any proper and true justification is a state renewed in righteousness — that and nothing else.

Two other points concerning justification still remain, the presentation of which could not well be intermixed with the largely scriptural and verbal discussion of its nature just now closed. And first of all it needs to be observed, in order to a full understanding of justification, that it comes in the divine idea not after sin as a fact or condition previous, but was to be unconditionally every where and forever. For according to the original normal state of being, God was to be a power all-diffusive, a central, self-radiating orb — Sun itself of Righteousness, shining abroad on all created minds and over-spreading them with the sovereign day of its own excellence. The plan never was that created beings should be righteous, in such a sense, by their own works, or their own inherent force, as not to be derivatively righteous and by faith. They had and were eternally to have their righteousness in God. Remaining upright, they would consciously have had their righteousness in God's inspirations, and would have been disturbed by a contrary suggestion.

Hence the dismal incapacity of sin: because it separates the soul from God's life-giving character and inspirations. Having him no more, as the fontal source of righteousness, it falls off into an abnormal, self-centered state, where it comes under mere self-interest, and struggles vainly, if at all, in the tangle of that kind of endeavor to recover itself to its own ideals. Works of the law, dead works carefully piled, will-works, works of supererogation, penances, alms, austerities of self-mortification — none of these, nor all of them, make out the needed righteousness. Still there is a felt deficiency, which the apostle calls "a coming short of the glory of God." Nothing will suffice for this but to come back, finite to infinite, creature to Creator, and take derivatively what, in its nature, must be derivative; viz., the righteousness that was normally and forever to be unto, and upon, all them that believe.

Here then is the grand renewing office and aim of the gospel of Christ. He comes to men groping in a state of separation from God, consciously not even with their own standards of good, and, what is more, consciously not able to be — self-condemned when they are trying most to justify themselves, and despairing the more, the more they endeavor to make themselves righteous by their own works — to such Christ comes forth, out of the righteousness of God, and also in the righteousness of God, that he may be the righteousness of God upon all them that believe, and are so brought close enough to him in their faith, to receive his inspirations. And this is the state of justification, not because some debt is made even, by the penal suffering of Christ, but because that normal connection with God is restored by his sacrifice, which permits the righteousness of God to renew its everlasting flow.

When I speak thus of the connection with God as being restored by the sacrifice of Christ, let me not be understood as meaning by the sacrifice only what is tenderly sympathetic and submissive in Christ's death. I include all that is energetic, strong, and piercing; his warnings, the pressure of his discipline, all that is done, by his powerful ministry and doctrine, to save us from the wrath to come. His sacrifice is no mere suit or plaint of weakness, for the righteousness of God is in it. When the metallic ring of principle, or everlasting right, is heard in the distress and wail of the cross, the sacrifice becomes itself a sword of conviction, piercing irresistibly through the sinner, and causing him to quiver on the point by which he is fastened. Mere sympathy, as we commonly speak, is no great power; it must be somehow a tremendous sympathy, to have the true divine efficacy. Hence the glorious justifying efficacy of Christ; because the righteousness of God is declared in his sacrifice.

Again, secondly, a more deliberate statement of the relations of faith to justification appears to be demanded. Though the righteousness of God is declared and made to shine with its true divine luster and glory by Christ, still the justification is not conceived to be an accomplished fact, as indeed it never can be, prior to faith in the subject. It is justification by faith and not without — "and the justifier of him that believeth in Jesus." What is this faith, and why is it necessary?

It is not the belief that Christ has come to even our account with justice; neither is it the belief that he has obtained a surplus merit, which is offered, over and above, as a positive righteousness, and set to our credit, if we will have it. Neither of the two is a fact, or at all credible any way. Nor would both, if believed as mere facts, do any thing more for us than a belief in any other facts. Our sins do not fly away because we believe in a fact of any kind. We can even believe in all the historic facts of Christianity, as thousands do, without being any the more truly justified.

No, the real faith is this, and very little intelligence is required to see the necessity of it; viz., the trusting of one's self over, sinner to Saviour, to be in him, and of him, and new-charactered by him; because it is only in that way that the power of Christ gets opportunity to work. So the sinner is justified, and the justification is a most vital affair: "the justification of life." The true account of it is that Jesus, coming into the world with all God's righteousness upon him, declaring it to guilty souls in all the manifold evidences of his life and passion, wins their faith, and by that faith they are connected again with the life of God, and filled and overspread with his righteousness. And there springs up, in this reconnection of the soul with God's righteousness, a perfect liberty and confidence; for it is no more trying to climb up into a righteous consciousness and confidence by itself, but it has the righteousness by derivation; flowing down upon it, into it, and through it, by the eternal permeation of God's Spirit. And just here it is that Christianity wins its triumph. It shows man how to be free in good, and makes it possible. The best that all other religions and moralities can do is to institute a practice of works, and a climbing up into perfection by our own righteous deeds; but the gospel of Jesus comes to our relief, in showing us how to find righteousness, and have it as an eternal inspiration; "even the righteousness of God that is by the faith of Jesus Christ unto all and upon all them that believe"

(Rom. 3:22.) In it we do not climb, but rest; we goad ourselves into no impossibilities, groan under no bondage that we can not lift; sink into no deep mires because we try to struggle out. We have a possible righteousness, because it is not ours but God's; Christ received by our faith, to be upon us and for us, all that we could wish to be for ourselves. This is the transcendent distinction, the practically sublime glory of our gospel, our great all-truth — Justification by Faith. Here is conquered the grandest of all problems, how to put confidence in the bosom of guilt, and settle a platform of virtue that shall make duty free and joyful under all conscious disabilities.

Here it was that Luther broke into ecstasy, and a great bewilderment of change that he could not, for the time, understand. He had been trying to be justified by works; that is, by fastings, penances, alms, vigils, wearing down the body under the load of his sins, and crying to God in his cell, day and night, for some deliverance that should ease the torment of his still and always self-condemning soul. A right word from Staupitz let him see the fool that he was — that Christ would take him because he was guilty, having died for him because he was guilty, and not because he was righteous. At that point broke in, what light and confidence! His emancipated soul burst off all its chains in a moment, and took, as it were, the range of heaven in its liberty. He was new himself, the world was new, the gospel was new. It had not entered into his heart to conceive the things that were freely given him of God, but now he has them all at once. Justification by faith, justification by faith — his great soul is full of it; he must preach it, he must fight for it, die for it, know nothing else.

In the inspiration of this truth it was, that his great career as a reformer and spiritual hero began. If any thing will make a man a hero, it will be the righteousness of God upon him, and the confidence he gets in the sense of it. If he can be eloquent for any thing, it will be in the testimony of what Christ is to him, in the now glorified consciousness of his inward life. But we must not fall into a very great mistake here. Luther is, in fact, two, not one; viz., a Christian, and a theologian; and his Christian justification by faith, that which puts such a grand impulsion into his feeling, and raises the tone of his manhood to such a pitch of vigor, is a very different, altogether separate matter, from that theologic contriving of his head, which he took so confidently for the certain equivalent. Taking this latter, it would be difficult to find how any one should become much of a hero, or be lifted to the pitch of any great sentiment, in it. Indeed, the very great wonder is, that a man so intelligent should imagine for a moment that he was fired with a passion so mighty, and a joy so transcendent, by the fact that an innocent being had taken his sins, and evened the account of Justice by suffering their punishment! This he thought he believed; but we are not obliged to believe that he did. Really believing it, and conceiving what it means, the fact would have set his stout frame shuddering, and turned his life to gall. The truth indeed appears to be, that his heart sailed over his theology, and did not come down to see it. We find him contriving, in his "Epistle to the Galatians," how Christ, having all the sins of mankind imputed to him, "becomes the greatest transgressor, murderer, adulterer, thief, rebel, and blasphemer, that ever was, or could be in all the world"; [2] and his doctrine is, that suffering the just wrath of God, for the sin that is upon him, Christ makes out a right of justification for us before God, which is complete, because it completely satisfies the law. And then to be just cleared of punishment, and believe that he is, he conceives to be the very thing that makes his glorious liberty and raises the tempest of his joy! The manner appears to be hideous, the deliverance to be negative and legal only; but his heart is ranging high enough, in its better element — the righteousness of God — not to be offended by the crudities he is taking for a gospel.

But this is not the first time that the head of a great man has not been equal to the understanding, or true interpretation, of his heart. Indeed, nothing is more common, as a matter of fact, than for men of real or even the highest intelligence, to so far misinterpret their own experience in matters of religion, as to ascribe to it, and find it springing radically out of, that which has no sound verity, and could never have produced such an experience. Let no one be surprised, then, that Luther's justification by faith, that which puts his soul ringing with such an exultant and really sublime liberty, makes a plunge so bewildering into bathos and general unreason, when it comes to be affirmed theologically in his doctrine. As he had it in his Christian consciousness, the soul of his joy, the rest of his confidence, the enlargement of his gracious liberty, nothing could be more evidently real and related to the deepest realities of feeling; but as he gave it in his dogmatic record, I confess that calling it justification by faith — *articulus stantis, vel cadentis ecclesiae* — I could more easily see the church fall than believe it. Happily our very great reverence and admiration for the man may be accommodated in the confidence that any one may reject it utterly, and yet receive all that his faith received in his justification; and may also be with him in profoundest sympathy, in the

2. [ED.] Cf. *Luther's Works*, XXVI: *Lectures on Galatians* (1535), Jaroslav Pelikan, ed. (St. Louis, 1963), 277.

magnificat he chants, and, with such exhaustless eloquence of boasting, reiterates, in his preaching of the cross and the glorious liberty it brings. Certain it is that no man is a proper Christian who is not practically, at least, in the power of this great truth. If any thing defines a Christian, it is that he is one who seeks and also finds his righteousness in God.

II

I am well aware how insufficient this exposition of the great Christian truth, justification by faith, will be to many — to some, because it is a truth that can be sufficiently expounded by nothing but a living experience of its power; to others, because they have already learned to find their experience in words and forms of doctrine, by which it is poorly, or even falsely represented. What questions the view presented will encounter, especially from this latter class, I very well know, and will therefore bring the subject to a conclusion by answering a few of them.

Do we not then, by holding a view of justification so essentially subjective, virtually annihilate the distinction between justification and sanctification? This is one of the questions, and I answer it by saying that if the two experiences were more closely related than they are commonly supposed to be, I do not see that we need be greatly disturbed on that account. Still they are sufficiently distinct. According to the Catholic doctrine they are virtually identical; because the "making just," or "making righteous," which is conceived to be the sense of justification, is understood to be a complete subjective change, one that goes below consciousness and makes the soul inherently right — which is the very significance also of sanctification. But if we only conceive the soul to be so joined, by its faith, to the righteousness of God, as to be rather invested by it, or enveloped in it, than to be transformed all through in its own inherent quality; if the righteousness goes on, even as the sun goes on shining when it makes the day, and stops of necessity when the faith withdrawn permits it to go on no longer; then we have a very wide and palpable distinction. The consciousness of the subject, in justification, is raised in its order, filled with the confidence of right, set free from the bondage of all fears and scruples of legality; but there is a vast realm back of the consciousness, or below it, which remains to be changed or sanctified, and never will be, except as a new habit is generated by time, and the better consciousness descending into the secret roots below, gets a healing into them more and more perfect. In this manner, one who is justified at once can be sanctified only in time; and one who is completely justified is only incipiently sanctified; and one who has consciously "yielded his members as instruments of righteousness unto God," may discover even more and more distinctly, and by manifold tokens, a law in his members not yet sanctified away. There is also a certain reference in justification to one's standing in everlasting principle; whereas sanctification refers more especially to the conscious purity of the soul's aims, and the separation of its moral habit from evil. By another distinction, justification is the purgation of the conscience, and sanctification a cleansing of the soul's affections and passions. Both of course are operated by God's inspirations, and are operated only in and through the faith of the subject.

There is indeed no objection to saying that, in a certain general way, they are one — just as faith is one with love, and love with regeneration, and this with genuine repentance, and all good states with all others. The same divine life or quickening in God is supposed in every sort of holy exercise, and the different names we give it represent real and important differences of meaning, accordingly as we consider the new life quickened in relation to our own agency, or to God's, or to means accepted, or trusts reposed, or effects wrought. In the same way, justification is sanctification, and both are faith; and yet their difference is by no means annihilated.

Another question likely to be raised in the way of objection is whether, in the kind of justification stated, I do not give in to the rather antiquated notion of imputed righteousness? To this I answer that if the notion supposed to be thus antiquated, is the theologic fiction of a surplus obedience, over and above what was due from Christ as a man — contributed by him in pains and acts of duty from the obedience of his higher nature — which surplus is imputed to us and reckoned to our account, such imputation is plainly enough rejected; still there will be left the grand, experimental, Scripture truth of imputed righteousness, a truth never more to be antiquated than holiness itself.

The theologic fiction more fully stated appears to have been something like this: that Christ, taken simply as a man, was under all the obligations that belong to a man; therefore that he was only righteous as he should be in fulfilling those obligations, and had no righteousness to spare; but that, as being the God-man, he was under no such obligations; whence it resulted that, by his twofold obedience, passive and active, he gained two kinds of surplus righteousness: a passive to stand in the place of our punishment and be a complete satisfaction for it, and an active to be set to our account as being our positive obedience — both received by imputation. And so we are justified and saved by a double imputed righteousness, one to be our suffered penalty, the other to be such an obedience for us as will put us even with the precept of the law. It is even a sad office to recite the scholastic jingle of such a scheme, made up and received for a gospel. Plainly it is all a fiction. The distinction of a passive and active obedience is a fiction; the passive obedience being just as voluntary as the active, and therefore just as active. The assumption that Christ, to put righteousness upon us, must provide a spare righteousness not wanted for himself, is a fiction that excludes even the possible *koinonia* of the righteousness of God. And a still greater fiction is the totally impossible conception of a surplus righteousness. Christ was just as righteous as he should be, neither more nor less, and the beauty of his sacrifice lay in the fact, not that it overlapped the eternal law, but that it so exactly fulfilled that law. His merit therefore was not that he was better than he should be, but all that he should be; for if he was perfect without the surplus, then he was more than perfect with it, and we are left holding the opinion, that there is a righteousness above and outside of perfection! Still again the imputation of such a perfection to us, so that we shall have the credit of it, is a fiction also of the coldest, most unfructifying kind, and impossible even at that. What has any such pile of merit in Christ, be it suffering, or sacrifice, or punishment, or active righteousness, to do with my personal deserts? If a thousand worlds-full of the surplus had been provided for me, I should be none the less ill deserving if I had the total reckoning in possession.

The experimental, never-to-be antiquated, Scripture truth of imputed righteousness, on the other hand, is this: that the soul, when it is gained to faith, is brought back, according to the degree of faith, into its original, normal relation to God; to be invested in God's light, feeling, character — in one word, righteousness — and live derivatively from him. It is not made righteous, in the sense of being set in a state of self-centered righteousness, to be maintained by an ability complete in the person, but it is made righteous in the sense of being always to be made righteous; just as the day is made luminous, not by the light of sunrise staying in it, or held fast by it, but by the ceaseless outflow of the solar effulgence. Considered in this view, the sinning man justified is never thought of as being, or to be, just in himself; but he is to be counted so, be so by imputation, because his faith holds him to a relation to God where the sun of his righteousness will be forever gilding him with its fresh radiations. Thus Abraham believed God enough to become the friend of God — saying nothing of justice satisfied, nothing of surplus merit, nothing of Christ whatever

— and it was imputed to him for righteousness. No soul comes into such a relation of trust, without having God's investment upon it; and whatever there may be in God's righteousness — love, truth, sacrifice — will be rightfully imputed, or counted to be in it, because, being united to him, it will have them coming over derivatively from him. Precisely here therefore, in this most sublimely practical of all truths, imputed righteousness, Christianity culminates. Here we have coming upon us, or upon our faith, all that we most want, whether for our confidence, or the complete deliverance and upraising of our guilty and dreadfully enthralled nature. Here we triumph. There is therefore now no condemnation, the law of the spirit of life in Christ Jesus hath made us free. If we had a righteousness of the law to work out, we should feel a dreadful captivity upon us. If we were put into the key of righteous living, and then, being so started, were left to keep the key ourselves, by manipulating our own thoughts, affections, actions, in a way of self-superintendence, the practice would be so artificial, so inherently weak, as to pitch us into utter despair in a single day. Nothing meets our want but to have our life and righteousness in God, thus to be kept in liberty and victory always by our trust in him. Calling this imputed righteousness, it is no conceit of theology, no fiction, but the grandest and most life-giving of all the Christian truths.

We have this imputation also in another form that is equally natural and practical. Thus, instead of having our faith imputed unto us for righteousness, we ourselves teach our faith to locate all our righteousness putatively in God; saying "the Lord our righteousness," "Christ who is our life," "made unto us righteousness"; as if the stock of our virtue, or holiness, were laid up for us in God. All the hope of our character that is to be, we place, not in the inherent good we are to work out, or become in ourselves, but in the capital stock that is funded for us in him. And then the character, the righteousness, is the more dear to us, because it is to have so high a spring; and God is the more dear to us, that he will have us hang upon him by our faith, for a matter so divine. And the joy also, the confidence, the assurance and rest — all that we include in our justification — is the more sublimely dear, that we have it on a footing of permitted unity with God, so transforming and glorious. There is, in short, no truth that is richer, and fuller of meaning and power, than this same figure of mental imputation, in which we behold our character laid up and funded for us in the righteousness of God. In one view it is not true; there is no such quantity, or substance, separate from him, and laid up in store for us; but there is a power in him everlastingly able to beget in us, or keep flowing over upon us, every gift our sin most needs; and this we represent to our hearts by conceiving, in a figure, that we have a stock, just what we call "our righteousness," laid up for us beforehand, in the richly funded stores of his eternity.

It is no fault then of our doctrine of justification by faith, that it favors a notion of imputed righteousness; for in just this fact it is that the gospel takes us out of the bondage of works into a really new divine liberty. Here, in fact, is the grand triumph of Christianity; viz., in the new stage of righteousness inaugurated, which makes the footing of a sinner good, and helps the striving bondman of duty to be free; even the righteousness of God that is by faith of Jesus Christ, unto all, and upon all them that believe. When this is antiquated, just then also will salvation be.

```
    ❖  ❖  ❖  ❖  ❖  ❖  ❖  ❖
    ❖                    ❖
    ❖      V             ❖
    ❖                    ❖
    ❖  ❖  ❖  ❖  ❖  ❖  ❖  ❖
```

CHRISTIAN NURTURE [1]

EDITOR'S INTRODUCTION

In the year 1844 Bushnell put forth a theory which was destined to involve him in his first major controversy.

> We hold that children are, in a sense, included in the faith of their parents, partakers with them in their covenant, and brought into a peculiar relation to God, in virtue of it. On this ground they receive a common seal of faith with them, in their baptism, and God on his part, contemplates, in the rite, the fact that they are to grow up as Christians, or spiritually renewed persons. As to the precise time or manner in which they are to receive the germ of holy principle, nothing is affirmed. Only it is understood, that God includes their infant age in the womb of parental culture, and pledges himself to them and their parents, in such a way, as to offer the presumption, that they may grow up in love with all goodness, and remember no definite time when they became subjects of Christian principle. Christian education is then to conform to this view, and nothing is to be called Christian education which does not.[2]

In that concise statement Bushnell was, in principle — though not necessarily on the same theological presuppositions — reviving the almost forgotten convenant doctrine of early New England Congregationalism. According to that doctrine, the children of church members were presumed to be "federally holy," and were to be baptized at birth.[3] From the beginning such children were, in a sense, members of the visible church, although full membership awaited the time when they could "own the

---

1. *Discourses on Christian Nurture* (Boston, 1847), 5-33.
2. "The Kingdom of God as a Grain of Mustard Seed," *New Englander*, II (1844), 610.
3. H. Shelton Smith, Robert T. Handy, and Lefferts A. Loetscher, "The Cambridge Platform," *American Christianity: An Historical Interpretation with Representative Documents* (2 vols., New York, 1960-63), I, 131.

covenant" in their own right. It was presumed that they would grow up spiritually from within the community of the faithful.

Under the impact of the Great Awakening, with its emphasis upon individual decision and sudden conversion, the unique spiritual status of the child of the covenant was ignored. Like the child born outside of the covenant, he was told that he must undergo a conversion experience known as the "new birth," or be damned. This was still the prevailing notion in New England Congregationalism when Bushnell's essay of 1844 appeared.

Evidently the essay aroused concern, for on June 2, 1846, the Hartford Central Association requested Bushnell to present a paper on the question, "Do the rite of infant baptism and the household covenant contemplate the fact that a child should grow up a Christian or a converted person?" [4] On the following August 4, he read to the Association the substance of two sermons on Christian nurture which he had previously preached to his congregation. In the discussion that followed no one objected seriously to the paper, although some wanted to add a few minor qualifications at certain points. After minutely scrutinizing the discourses, the Massachusetts Sabbath School Society published them in 1847 in a slender volume entitled *Discourses on Christian Nurture*.

The public response was mixed; a few orthodox reviewers cautiously endorsed Bushnell's central thesis, but most of them were decidedly hostile. Bennet Tyler issued a vigorous open letter to the author, accusing him of propagating "error of a very dangerous tendency," notably with respect to native depravity and regeneration.[5] Within a few days, the *New England Puritan* — published at Boston — warmly applauded Tyler's criticisms and added strictures of its own. "We cannot but regard its [the book's] extensive circulation and use as a great calamity," said the reviewer, "and we greatly marvel that the publishing Committee of that Society have put their *imprimatur* on such a work." [6] The *Christian Observatory* — another Boston publication — hastened into print with a caustic piece, containing a personal insult.[7] Accusing Bushnell of having "a vicious thirst for originality," the reviewer added: "He can scarce

---

4. Manuscript "Records of the Hartford Central Association [1843–1901]," 17. (MS. in Congregational House, Hartford, Connecticut).

5. *Dr. Tyler's Letter to Dr. Bushnell, on Christian Nurture* (East Windsor Hill, Connecticut, June 7, 1847).

6. "Dr. Tyler's Letter to Dr. Bushnell on Christian Nurture," *New England Puritan*, June 24, 1847, 99.

7. "Discourses on Christian Nurture," *Christian Observatory*, I (1847), 323–30.

drink from a chalice without seeking to kiss the brim on some part which human lip had never touched before." [8]

Panic-stricken, the Sabbath School Society quickly suspended publication of the book, without giving any reason for its action. Understandably aggrieved, Bushnell published a forty-eight-page pamphlet, assembling considerable historical data in support of his doctrine.[9] In addition to quoting from the writings of earlier Christian ages, he appealed especially to the *System of Doctrines* of Samuel Hopkins, citing several passages which certainly did lend substantial support to the doctrine of the *Discourses*.[10] In the same year he published *Views of Christian Nurture, and of Subjects Adjacent Thereto*, in which he brought together the *Discourses*, the *Argument*, the article of 1844 on "The Kingdom of God as a Grain of Mustard Seed," and three other related pieces.[11]

The *Views* also drew fire from Tyler, who predicted that if Bushnell's doctrine should finally prevail, "multitudes will grow up in a fatal delusion." [12] By October of 1847 the *New Englander* had good reason to say, "The theological world of New England is again threatened with storm." [13] The fact that the Unitarians commended Bushnell's doctrine served to increase the furor in orthodox quarters.[14] Noah Porter of Yale became a strong factor in quelling the storm, for at a strategic moment he published a formidable article reviewing *Views of Christian Nurture* and endorsing its central thesis.[15] On top of that he added, "The writer of these remarks has always believed and preached the doctrine advanced by Dr. Bushnell." [16]

After an interval of some twelve years, Bushnell returned to this question and produced a work of enduring value. It contained not only the productions already printed in *Views of Christian Nurture*, but many

8. *Ibid.*, 324.

9. *An Argument for "Discourses on Christian Nurture," Addressed to the Publishing Committee of the Massachusetts Sabbath School Society* (Hartford, 1847).

10. *Ibid.*, 16–18. See Hopkins, "The Nature and Design of Infant Baptism," *Works of Samuel Hopkins, D.D.* (3 vols., Boston, 1854), II, 116–66.

11. Hartford, 1847.

12. *Letters to the Rev. Horace Bushnell, D.D., Containing Strictures on His Book entitled "Views of Christian Nurture, and of Subjects Adjacent Thereto"* (Hartford, 1848).

13. [Noah Porter,] "The New Theological Controversy," *New Englander*, V (1847), 613.

14. G. W. Burnap, "Bushnell on Christian Nurture," *Christian Examiner*, 4th series, VIII (1847), 435–51.

15. "Bushnell on Christian Nurture," *New Englander*, VI (1848), 120–47.

16. *Ibid.*, 123.

freshly prepared essays. The volume appeared under the short title of *Christian Nurture* (1861), a name it has borne ever since. This is the best known of Bushnell's books, and it has exerted more influence on the modern theory of Christian education than any other single work.

The first of the two discourses, as published in 1847, is here reproduced in full. Except for the addition of a clarifying clause — which is indicated in a footnote at the proper place in the text — this discourse has remained unchanged in all subsequently published editions.

❖   ❖   ❖   ❖

Discourse I

Bring them up in the nurture and admonition of the Lord (Eph. 6:4).

There is then some kind of nurture which is of the Lord, deriving a quality and a power from him, and communicating the same. Being instituted by him it will of necessity have a method and a character peculiar to itself, or rather to him, and if realized in its full intent, terminating in results impossible to be reached by any merely human method.

What then is the true idea of Christian, or divine nurture, as distinguished from that which is not Christian? What is its purposed aim? what its method of working? what its powers and instruments? what its contemplated results? Few questions have greater moment, and it is one of the pleasant signs of the times, that the subject involved is beginning to attract new interest, and excite a spirit of inquiry which heretofore has not prevailed in our churches.

In ordinary cases, the better and more instructive way of handling this subject would be to go directly into the practical methods of parental discipline, and show by what modes of government and instruction we may hope to realize the best results. But unhappily the public mind is preoccupied extensively by a view of the whole subject which I must regard as a theoretical mistake, and one which must involve, as long as it continues, practical results, systematically injurious. This mistaken view it is necessary, if possible, to remove. And accordingly what I have to say will take the form of an argument on the question thus put in issue; though I design to gather round the subject, as I proceed, as much of practical instruction as the mode of the argument will suffer. Assuming then the question above stated, What is the true idea of Christian education? I answer in the following proposition, which it will be the aim of my argument to establish, viz.:

THAT THE CHILD IS TO GROW UP A CHRISTIAN.[1] In other words, the aim, effort, and expectation should be, not, as is commonly assumed, that the child is to grow up in sin, to be converted after he comes to a mature age, but that he is to open on the world as one that is spiritually renewed, not remembering the time when he went through a technical experience, but seeming rather to have loved what is good from his earliest years. I do not affirm that every child may, in fact and without exception, be so trained that he certainly will grow up a Christian. The qualifications it may be necessary to add, will be given in another place, where they can be stated more intelligibly.

This doctrine is not a novelty, now rashly and for the first time propounded, as some of you may be tempted to suppose. I shall show you, before I have done with the argument, that it is as old as the Christian church, and prevails extensively at the present day, in other parts of the world. Neither let your own experience raise a prejudice against it. If you have endeavored to realize the very truth I here affirm, but find that your children do not exhibit the character you have looked for; if they seem to be intractable to religious influences, and sometimes to display an apparent aversion to the very subject of religion itself, you are not, of course, to conclude that the doctrine I here maintain is untrue or impracticable. You may be unreasonable in your expectations of your children. Possibly, there may be seeds of holy principle in them, which you do not discover. A child acts out his present feelings, the feelings of the moment, without qualification or disguise. And how, many times, would all you appear, if you were to do the same? Will you expect of them to be better and more constant and consistent than yourselves; or will you rather expect them to be children, human children still, living a mixed life, trying out the good and evil of the world, and preparing, as older Christians do, when they have taken a lesson of sorrow and emptiness, to turn again to the true good? Perhaps they will go through a rough mental struggle, at some future day, and seem to others and to themselves there to have entered on a Christian life. And yet it may be true that there was still some root of right principle established in their childhood, which is here only quickened and developed, as when Christians of a mature age are revived in their piety, after a period of spiritual lethargy; for it is conceivable that regenerate character may exist, long before it is fully and formally devel-

1. [ED.] In subsequent editions of this discourse, beginning with the *Views of Christian Nurture* (1847), Bushnell here added the words, "and never know himself as being otherwise."

oped. But suppose there is really no trace or seed of holy principle in your children, has there been no fault of piety and constancy in your church, no want of Christian sensibility and love to God, no carnal spirit visible to them and to all, and imparting its noxious and poisonous quality to the Christian atmosphere in which they have had their nurture? For it is not for you alone to realize all that is included in the idea of Christian education. It belongs to the church of God, according to the degree of its social power over you and in you and around your children, to bear a part of the responsibility with you. Then, again, have you nothing to blame in yourselves, no lack of faithfulness, no indiscretion of manner or of temper, no mistake of duty, which, with a better and more cultivated piety, you would have been able to avoid? Have you been so nearly even with your privilege and duty, that you can find no relief but to lay some charge upon God, or comfort yourselves in the conviction that he has appointed the failure you deplore? When God marks out a plan of education, or sets up an aim to direct its efforts, you will see at once that he could not base it on a want of piety in you, or on any imperfections that flow from a want of piety. It must be a plan measured by himself and the fullness of his own gracious intentions. Besides, you must not assume that we, in this age, are the best Christians that have ever lived, or most likely to produce all the fruits of piety. An assumption so pleasing to our vanity is more easily made than verified, but vanity is the weakest as it is the cheapest of all arguments. We have some good points, in which we compare favorably with other Christians, and Christians of other times, but our style of piety is sadly deficient, in many respects, and that to such a degree that we have little cause for self-congratulation. With all our activity and boldness of movement, there is a certain hardness and rudeness, a want of sensibility to things that do not lie in action, which cannot be too much deplored, or too soon rectified. We hold a piety of conquest rather than of love. A kind of public piety that is strenuous and fiery on great occasions, but wants the beauty of holiness, wants constancy, singleness of aim, loveliness, purity, richness, blamelessness, and — if I may add another term not so immediately religious, but one that carries, by association, a thousand religious qualities — wants domesticity of character; wants them, I mean, not as compared with the perfect standard of Christ, but as compared with other examples of piety that have been given in former times, and others that are given now.

For some reason, we do not make a Christian atmosphere about us — do not produce the conviction that we are living unto God. There is a marvelous want of savor in our piety. It is a flower of autumn, colored as highly as it need be to the eye, but destitute of fragrance. It is too much to hope that, with such an instrument, we can fulfill the true idea of Christian education. Any such hope were even presumptuous. At the same time, there is no so ready way of removing the deficiences just described, as to recall our churches to their duties in domestic life; those humble, daily, hourly duties, where the spirit we breathe shall be a perpetual element of power and love bathing the life of childhood.

Thus much it was necessary to say, for the removal of prejudices, that are likely to rise up in your minds, and make you inaccessible to the arguments I may offer. Let all such prejudices be removed, or, if this be too much, let them, at least, be suspended till you have heard what I have to advance; for it cannot be desired of you to believe any thing more than what is shown you by adequate proofs. Which also it is right to ask, that you will hear, if offered, in a spirit of mind such as becomes our wretched and low attainments, and with a willingness to let God be exalted, though at the expense of some abasement in yourselves. In pursuing the argument, I shall —

I. Collect some considerations which occur to us, viewing the subject on the human side, and then —

II. Show how far and by what methods God has justified, on his part, the doctrine we maintain.[2]

There is then, as the subject appears to us —

I. No absurdity in supposing that children are to grow up in Christ. On the other hand, if there is no absurdity, there is a very clear, moral incongruity in setting up a contrary supposition, to be the aim of a system of Christian education. There could not be a worse or more baleful implication given to a child, than that he is to reject God and all holy principle, till he has come to a mature age. What authority have you from the Scriptures to tell your child, or, by any sign, to show him that you do not expect him truly to love and obey God, till after he has spent whole years in hatred and wrong? What authority to make him feel that he is the most unprivileged of all human beings, capable of sin, but incapable of repentance; old enough to resist all good, but too young to receive any good whatever? It is reasonable to suppose that you have some express authority for a lesson so manifestly cruel and hurtful, else you would shudder to give it. I ask you for the chapter and verse out of which it is

2. [ED.] This section is explicated in Discourse II and therefore is not included in the present selection.

derived. Meantime, wherein would it be less incongruous for you to teach your child that he is to lie and steal, and go the whole round of the vices, and then, after he comes to mature age, reform his conduct by the rules of virtue? Perhaps you do not give your child to expect that he is to grow up in sin, you only expect that he will yourself. That is scarcely better, for that which is your expectation will assuredly be his; and, what is more, any attempt to maintain a discipline at war with your own secret expectations will only make a hollow and worthless figment of that which should be an open earnest reality. You will never practically aim at what you practically despair of, and if you do not practically aim to unite your child to God, you will aim at something less, that is, something unchristian, wrong, sinful.

But my child is a sinner, you will say, and how can I expect him to begin a right life, until God gives him a new heart? This is the common way of speaking, and I state the objection in its own phraseology, that it may recognize itself. Who then has told you that a child cannot have the new heart of which you speak? Whence do you learn that if you live the life of Christ, before him and with him, the law of the Spirit of Life may not be such as to include and quicken him also? And why should it be thought incredible that there should be some really good principle awakened in the mind of a child? For this is all that is implied in a Christian state. The Christian is one who has simply begun to love what is good for its own sake, and why should it be thought impossible for a child to have this love begotten in him? Take any scheme of depravity you please, there is yet nothing in it to forbid the possibility that a child should be led, in his first moral act, to cleave unto what is good and right, any more than in the first of his twentieth year. He is, in that case, only a child converted to good, leading a mixed life as all Christians do. The good in him goes into combat with the evil, and holds a qualified sovereignty. And why may not this internal conflict of goodness cover the whole life from its dawn, as well as any part of it? And what more appropriate to the doctrine of spiritual influence itself, than to believe that as the Spirit of Jehovah fills all the worlds of matter, and holds a presence of power and government in all objects, so all souls of all ages and capacities have a moral presence of the Divine Love in them, and a nurture of the Spirit appropriate to their wants?

2. It is to be expected that Christian education will radically differ from that which is not Christian. Now it is the very character and mark of all unchristian education, that it brings up the child for future conversion.

No effort is made save to form a habit of outward virtue; and if God please to convert the family to something higher and better, after they come to the age of maturity — it is well. Is then Christian education or the nurture of the Lord no way different from this? Or is it rather to be supposed that it will have a higher aim and a more sacred character?

And, since it is the distinction of Christian parents that they are themselves in the nurture of the Lord, since Christ and the Divine Love, communicated through him, are become the food of their life, what will they so naturally seek as to have their children partakers with them, heirs together with them in the grace of life? I am well aware of the common impression that Christian education is sufficiently distinguished by the endeavor of Christian parents to teach their children the lessons of Scripture history and the doctrines or dogmas of Scripture theology. But if they are given to understand, at the same time, that these lessons can be expected to produce no fruit till they are come to a mature age, that they are to grow up still in the same character as other children do, who have no such instruction, what is this but to enforce the practical rejection of all the lessons taught them? And which in truth is better for them, to grow up in sin under Scripture light, with a heart hardened by so many religious lessons, or to grow up in sin unvexed and unannoyed by the wearisome drill of lectures that only discourage all practical benefit? Which is better, to be piously brought up to sin, or to be allowed quietly to vegetate in it? These are questions that I know not how to decide, but the doubt in which they leave us will at least suffice to show that Christian education has, in this view, no such eminent advantages over that which is unchristian, as to raise any broad and dignified distinction between them. We certainly know that much of what is called Christian nurture only serves to make the subject of religion odious, and that, as nearly as we can discover, in exact proportion to the amount of religious teaching received. And no small share of the difficulty to be overcome afterwards, in the struggle of conversion, is created in just this way. On the other hand, you will hear, for example, of cases like the following. A young man correctly but not religiously brought up, light and gay in his manners and thoughtless hitherto in regard to any thing of a serious nature, happens accidentally one Sunday, while his friends are gone to ride, to take down a book on the evidences of Christianity. His eye, floating over one of the pages, becomes fixed, and he is surprised to find his feelings flowing out strangely into its holy truths. He is conscious of no struggle of hostility, but a new joy dawns in his being. Henceforth to the end of a long and useful life he is a Christian man. The love into which he was surprised continues to flow, and he is remarkable, in the churches, all his life long, as one of the most beautiful, healthful, and dignified examples of Christian piety. Now a very little mis-education called Christian, discouraging the piety it teaches and making enmity itself a necessary ingredient in the struggle of conversion, conversion no reality without a struggle, might have sufficed to close the mind of this man against every thought of religion to the end of life. Such facts compel us to suspect the value of much that is called Christian education. They suggest the possibility also that Christian piety should begin in other and milder forms of exercise than those which commonly distinguish the conversion of adults — that Christ himself, by that renewing Spirit who can sanctify from the womb, should be practically infused into the childish mind; in other words, that the house, having a domestic Spirit of grace dwelling in it, should become the church of childhood, the table and hearth a holy rite, and life an element of saving power. Something is wanted that is better than teaching, something that transcends mere effort and will work — the loveliness of a good life, the repose of faith, the confidence of righteous expectation, the sacred and cheerful liberty of the Spirit — all glowing about the young soul as a warm and genial nurture, and forming in it, by methods that are silent and imperceptible, a spirit of duty and religious obedience to God. This only is Christian nurture, the nurture of the Lord.

3. It is a fact that all Christian parents would like to see their children grow up in piety; and, the better Christians they are, the more earnestly they desire it; and, the more lovely and constant the Christian spirit they manifest, the more likely is it, in general, that their children will early display the Christian character. This is current opinion. But why should a Christian parent, the deeper his piety and the more closely he is drawn to God, be led to desire the more earnestly what, in God's view, is even absurd or impossible? And, if it be generally seen that the children of such are the more likely to become Christians early, what forbids the hope that, if they were better Christians still, living a more single and Christlike life and more cultivated in their views of family nurture, they might not see their children grow up in piety towards God? Or if they may not always see it as clearly as they desire, might they not still be able to implant some holy principle which shall be the seed of a Christian character in their children, though not developed fully and visibly till a later period in life?

4. Assuming the corruption of human nature, when should we think it wisest to undertake or expect a remedy? When evil is young and pliant to good, or when it is confirmed by years of sinful habit? And when, in fact, is the human heart found to be so ductile to the motives of religion, as in the simple, ingenuous age of childhood? How easy it is then, as compared with the stubbornness of adult years, to make all wrong seem odious, all good lovely and desirable! If not discouraged by some ill temper, which bruises all the gentle sensibilities, or repelled by some technical view of religious character, which puts it beyond his age, how ready is he to be taken by good, as it were, beforehand, and yield his ductile nature to the truth and Spirit of God, and to a fixed prejudice against all that God forbids! He cannot understand, of course, in the earliest stage of childhood, the philosophy of religion as a renovated experience, and that is not the form of the first lessons he is to receive. He is not to be told that he must have a new heart and exercise faith in Christ's atonement. We are to understand that a right spirit may be virtually exercised in children when, as yet, it is not intellectually received, or as a form of doctrine. Thus if they are put upon an effort to be good, connecting the fact that God desires it and will help them in the endeavor, that is all which, in a very early age, they can receive, and that includes every thing — repentance, love, duty, dependence, faith. Nay, the operative truth necessary to a new life may possibly be communicated through and from the parent, being revealed in his looks, manners, and ways of life, before they are of an age to understand the teaching of words; for the Christian scheme, the gospel, is really wrapped up in the life of every Christian parent, and beams out from him as a living epistle, before it escapes from the lips, or is taught in words. And the Spirit of truth may as well make this living truth effectual, as the preaching of the gospel itself. Never is it too early for good to be communicated. Infancy and childhood are the ages most pliant to good. And who can think it necessary that the plastic nature of childhood must first be hardened into stone and stiffened into enmity towards God and all duty, before it can become a candidate for Christian character! There could not be a more unnecessary mistake, and it is as unnatural and pernicious, I fear, as it is unnecessary.

There are many who assume the radical goodness of human nature, and the work of Christian education is, in their view, only to educate, or educe the good that is in us. Let no one be disturbed by the suspicion of a coincidence between what I have here said and such a theory. The natural pravity of man is plainly asserted in the Scriptures, and if it were not, the familiar laws of physiology would require us to believe what amounts to the same thing. And if neither Scripture nor physiology taught us the doctrine, if the child was born as clear of natural prejudice or damage as Adam before his sin, spiritual education, that which trains a being for a stable, intelligent virtue hereafter, would still involve an experiment of evil,[3] therefore a fall and bondage under the laws of evil; so that, view the matter as we will, there is no so unreasonable assumption, none so wide of all just philosophy, as that which proposes to form a child to virtue, by simply educing or drawing out what is in him. The growth of Christian virtue is no vegetable process, no mere onward development. It involves a struggle with evil, a fall and rescue. The soul becomes established in holy virtue, as a free exercise, only as it is passed round the corner of fall and redemption, ascending thus unto God through a double experience, in which it learns the bitterness of evil and the worth of good, fighting its way out of one and achieving the other as a victory. The child, therefore, may as well begin life under a law of hereditary damage, as to plunge himself into evil by his own experiment, which he will as naturally do from the simple impulse of curiosity, or the instinct of knowledge, as from any noxious quality in his mold derived by descent. For it is not sin which he derives from his parents; at least not sin in any sense which imports blame, but only some prejudice to the perfect harmony of his mold, some kind of pravity or obliquity which inclines him to evil. These suggestions are offered, not as necessary to be received in every particular, but simply to show that the scheme of education proposed is not to be identified with another, which assumes the radical goodness of human nature, and according to which, if it be true, Christian education is insignificant.

5. It is implied in all our religious philosophy that, if a child ever does any thing in a right spirit, ever loves any thing because it is good and right, it involves the dawn of a new life. This we cannot deny or doubt, without bringing in question our whole scheme of doctrine. Is it then incredible that some really good feeling should be called into exercise in a child? In all the discipline of the house, quickened as it should be by the Spirit of God, is it true that he can never once be brought to submit to parental authority lovingly and because it is right? Must we even hold the absurdity of the Scripture counsel — "Children, obey your parents in the Lord, for this is right"? When we speak thus of a love to what is right and good, we must of course discriminate between the mere exitement of

3. [ED.] This thesis is fully developed in Bushnell, *Nature and the Supernatural* (New York, 1858), Chap. 4; for the substance of that chapter, see *supra*, 221-40.

a natural sensibility to pleasure in the contemplation of what is good (of which the worst minds are more or less capable) and a practical subordination of the soul to its power, a practical embrace of its law. The child must not only be touched with some gentle emotions towards what is right, but he must love it with a fixed love, love it for the sake of its principle, receive it as a vital and formative power. Nor is there any age which offers itself to God's truth and love, and to that quickening Spirit whence all good proceeds, with so much of ductile feeling and susceptibilities so tender. The child is under power and authority too for the very purpose, it would seem, of having the otherwise abstract principle of all duty impersonated and made visible and thus brought home to his practical embrace; so that, learning to obey his parents in the Lord because it is right, he may thus receive, before he can receive it intellectually, the principle of all piety and holy obedience. And when he is brought to exercise a spirit of true and loving submission to the good law of his parents, what will you see, many times, but a look of childish joy and a happy sweetness of manner and a ready delight in authority, as like to all the demonstrations of Christian experience, as any thing childish can be to what is mature?

6. Children have been so trained as never to remember the time when they began to be religious. Baxter [4] was, at one time, greatly troubled concerning himself, because he could recollect no time when there was a gracious change in his character. But he discovered, at length, that "education is as properly a means of grace as preaching," and thus found a sweeter comfort in his love to God, that he learned to love him so early. The European churches, generally, regard Christian piety more as a habit of life, formed under the training of childhood, and less as a marked spiritual change in experience. In Germany, for example, the church includes all the people, and it is remarkable that, under a scheme so loose and with so much of pernicious error taught in the pulpit, there is yet so much of deep religious feeling, so much of lovely and simple character and a savor of Christian piety so generally prevalent in the community. So true is this that the German people are every day spoken of as a people religious by nature; no other way being observed of accounting for the strong religious bent they manifest. Whereas it is due, beyond any reasonable question, to the fact that children are placed under a form of treatment which expects them to be religious, and are not discouraged by

4. [ED.] Richard Baxter (1615–91), English Puritan divine, who is perhaps best known as the author of *The Saints Everlasting Rest* (1650).

the demand of an experience above their years. Again, the Moravian
Brethren, it is agreed by all, give as ripe and graceful an exhibition of piety
as any body of Christians living on the earth, and it is the radical distinction of their system that it rests its power on Christian education. They
make their churches schools of holy nurture to childhood, and expect their
children to grow up there, as plants in the house of the Lord. Accordingly it is affirmed that not one in ten of the members of that church
recollects any time when he began to be religious. Is it then incredible
that what has been can be? Would it not be wiser and more modest, when
facts are against us, to admit that there is certainly some bad error, either
in our life, or in our doctrine, or in both, which it becomes us to
amend?

Once more, if we narrowly examine the relation of parent and child,
we shall not fail to discover something like a law of organic connection,
as regards character, subsisting between them: such a connection as
makes it easy to believe, and natural to expect, that the faith of one will
be propagated in the other. Perhaps I should rather say, such a connection
as induces the conviction that the character of one is actually included in
that of the other, as a seed is formed in the capsule; and being there matured, by a nutriment derived from the stem, is gradually separated from
it. It is a singular fact that many believe substantially the same thing, in
regard to evil character, but have no thought of any such possibility in
regard to good. There has been much speculation, of late, as to whether a
child is born in depravity, or whether the depraved character is superin-
duced afterwards. But, like many other great questions, it determines
much less than is commonly supposed; for, according to the most proper
view of the subject, a child is really not born till he emerges from the
infantile state, and never before that time can be said to receive a separate
and properly individual nature. The declarations of Scripture, and the
laws of physiology, I have already intimated, compel the belief that a
child's nature is somehow depravated by descent from parents, who are
under the corrupting effects of sin. But this, taken as a question relating
to the mere *punctum temporis*, or precise point of birth, is not a question
of any so grave import as is generally supposed; for the child, after birth,
is still within the matrix of the parental life, and will be more or less, for
many years. And the parental life will be flowing into him all that time,
just as naturally, and by a law as truly organic, as when the sap of a trunk
flows into a limb. We must not govern our thoughts in such a matter by
our eyes, and, because the physical separation has taken place, conclude

that no organic relation remains. Even the physical being of the child is dependent still for nutrition on organic processes not in itself. Meantime, the mental being and character have scarcely begun to have a proper individual life. Will, in connection with conscience, is the basis of personality, or individuality, and these exist as yet only in their rudimental type, as when the form of a seed is beginning to be unfolded at the root of the flower. At first, the child is held as a mere passive lump in the arms, and he opens into conscious life under the soul of the parent streaming into his eyes and ears, through the manners and tones of the nursery. The kind and degree of passivity are gradually changed as life advances. A little farther on it is observed that a smile wakens a smile — any kind of sentiment or passion, playing in the face of the parent, wakens a responsive sentiment or passion. Irritation irritates, a frown withers, love expands a look congenial to itself, and why not holy love? Next the ear is opened to the understanding of words, but what words the child shall hear, he cannot choose, and has as little capacity to select the sentiments that are poured into his soul. Farther on, the parents begin to govern him by appeals to will, expressed in commands, and whatever their requirement may be, he can as little withstand it as the violet can cool the scorching sun, or the tattered leaf can tame the hurricane. Next they appoint his school, choose his books, regulate his company, decide what form of religion and what religious opinions he shall be taught, by taking him to a church of their own selection. In all this, they infringe upon no right of the child, they only fulfill an office which belongs to them. Their will and character are designed to be the matrix of the child's will and character. Meantime he approaches more and more closely, and by a gradual process, to the proper rank and responsibility of an individual creature, during all which process of separation, he is having their exercises and ways translated into him. Then, at last, he comes forth to act his part in such color of evil — and why not of good? — as he has derived from them. The tendency of all our modern speculations is to an extreme individualism, and we carry our doctrines of free will so far as to make little or nothing of organic laws; not observing that character may be, to a great extent, only the free development of exercises previously wrought in us, or extended to us, when other wills had us within their sphere. All the Baptist theories of religion are based in this error. They assume as a first truth that no such thing is possible as an organic connection of character, an assumption which is plainly refuted by what we see with our eyes, and, as I shall by and by show, by the declarations of Scripture. We have much to say also, in common with the Baptists, about the beginning of moral agency, and we seem to fancy that there is some definite moment when a child becomes a moral agent, passing out of a condition where he is a moral nullity, and where no moral agency touches his being. Whereas he is rather to be regarded, at the first, as lying within the moral agency of the parent and passing out by degrees through a course of mixed agency, to a proper independency and self-possession. The supposition that he becomes, at some certain moment, a complete moral agent, which a moment before he was not, is clumsy and has no agreement with observation. The separation is gradual. He is never, at any moment after birth, to be regarded as perfectly beyond the sphere of good and bad exercises; for the parent exercises himself in the child, playing his emotions and sentiments, and working a character in him, by virtue of an organic power. And this is the very idea of Christian education, that it begins with nurture or cultivation. And the intention is that the Christian life and spirit of the parents shall flow into the mind of the child, to blend with his incipient and half-formed exercises; that they shall thus beget their own good within him, their thoughts, opinions, faith and love, which are to become a little more, and yet a little more his own separate exercise, but still the same in character. The contrary assumption, that virtue must be the product of separate and absolutely independent choice, is pure assumption. As regards the measure of personal merit and demerit, it is doutless true that every subject of God is to be responsible only for what is his own. But virtue still is rather a *state* of being than an act or series of acts; and if we look at the causes which induce or prepare such a state, the will of the person himself may have a part among those causes more or less important, and it works no absurdity to suppose that one may be even prepared to such a state, by causes prior to his own will; so that, when he sets off to act for himself, his struggle and duty may be rather to sustain and perfect the state begun, than to produce a new one. Certain it is that we are never, at any age, so independent as to be wholly out of the reach of organic laws which affect our character. All society is organic — the church, the state, the school, the family — and there is a spirit in each of these organisms, peculiar to itself, and more or less hostile, more or less favorable to religious character, and to some extent, at least, sovereign over the individual man. A very great share of the power in what is called a revival of religion, is organic power; nor is it any the less divine on that account. The child is only more within the power of organic laws than we all are. We possess only a mixed individuality all our life long. A pure, separate, individual man, living *wholly* within and from himself is a mere fiction. No such person ever existed, or ever can. I need not say that this view of an organic connection of character subsisting between parent and child, lays a basis for notions of Christian education, far different from those which now prevail, under the cover of a merely fictitious and michievous individualism.

Perhaps it may be necessary to add that, in the strong language I have used concerning the organic connection of character between the parent and the child, it is not designed to assert a power in the parent to renew the child, or that the child can be renewed by any agency of the Spirit less immediate, than that which renews the parent himself. When a germ is formed on the stem of any plant, the formative instinct of the plant may be said in one view to produce it; but the same solar heat which quickens the plant, must quicken also the germ and sustain the internal action of growth, by a common presence in both. So if there be an organic power of character in the parent, such as that of which I have spoken, it is not a complete power in itself, but only such a power as demands the realizing presence of the Spirit of God, both in the parent and the child, to give it effect. As Paul said, "I have begotten you through the gospel," so may we say of the parent who, having a living gospel enveloped in his life, brings it into organic connection with the soul of childhood. But the declaration excludes the necessity of a divine influence, not more in one case than in the other.

Such are some of the considerations that offer themselves, viewing our subject on the human side, or as it appears in the light of human evidence — all concurring to produce the conviction that it is the only true idea of Christian education, that the child is to grow up in the life of the parent, and be a Christian, in principle, from his earliest years.

Selected Bibliography

I. THE WRITINGS OF HORACE BUSHNELL

1. MANUSCRIPTS

["Natural Science and Moral Philosophy."] A paper written in May 1832 (MS. in Yale Divinity School Library).

"There is a Moral Governor." A paper written in July 1832 (MS. in Yale Divinity School Library).

"Revelation." An address delivered before the Porter Rhetorical Society of Andover Theological Seminary, September 3, 1839. The closing paragraphs of this address are published in Bushnell, *The Spirit in Man*, centenary ed. (New York, 1910), 357–59 (MS. in Yale Divinity School Library).

"Dudleian Lecture." Delivered at Harvard College, May 12, 1852. The substance of this lecture is reproduced in Bushnell, *Nature and the Supernatural* (New York, 1858), Chap. 6 (MS. in Harvard University Library).

2. BOOKS

Only a few of the editions of Bushnell's works are here indicated; many others have appeared.

Discourses on Christian Nurture (Boston, 1847).

An Argument for "Discourses on Christian Nurture" (Hartford, 1847).

Views of Christian Nurture, and of Subjects Adjacent Thereto (Hartford, 1847).

God in Christ (Hartford, 1849; centenary ed., New York, 1910; London, 1850).

Christ in Theology (Hartford, 1851).

Sermons for the New Life (New York, 1858; London, 1860).

Nature and the Supernatural, as Together Constituting the One System of God (New York, 1858; London, 1860; Edinburgh, 1861).

The Character of Jesus: Forbidding His Possible Classification with Men (New York, 1860; London, 1861; Edinburgh, 1861). A reprint of Chap. 10 of *Nature and the Supernatural* (1858).

Christian Nurture (New York, 1861; London, 1861; Edinburgh, 1861).

Work and Play (New York, 1864, 1881; London, 1888).

Christ and His Salvation: In Sermons Variously Related Thereto (New York, 1864; London, 1880).

The Vicarious Sacrifice, Grounded in Principles of Universal Obligation (New York, 1866; London, 1866).

Moral Uses of Dark Things (New York, 1868, 1881; London, 1881).

Women's Suffrage: The Reform Against Nature (New York, 1869).

Sermons on Living Subjects (New York, 1872; centenary ed., 1910; London, 1872).

Forgiveness and Law, Grounded in Principles Interpreted by Human Analogies (New York, 1874; London, 1874).

Building Eras in Religion (New York, 1881; centenary ed., 1910; London, 1882).

The Spirit in Man: Sermons and Selections, centenary ed. (New York, 1910).

3. ARTICLES, ADDRESSES, AND SERMONS

For additional articles and addresses, see Bibliography in Bushnell, *The Spirit in Man*, centenary ed. (New York, 1910), 445–63.

Crisis of the Church (Hartford, 1835).

"Spiritual Economy of Revivals of Religion," *Quarterly Christian Spectator*, X (1838), 131–48. Republished in *Building Eras in Religion* (1881).

A Discourse on the Moral Tendencies and Results of Human History (New Haven, 1843). Republished as "Growth of Law" in *Building Eras in Religion* (1881).

Politics Under the Law of God (Hartford, 1844).

"The Kingdom of Heaven as a Grain of Mustard Seed," *New Englander*, II (1844), 600–19. Republished as "Growth, Not Conquest, the True Method of Christian Progress" in *Views of Christian Nurture* (1847).

A Letter to His Holiness, Pope Gregory XVI (London, 1846).

"The Evangelical Alliance," *New Englander*, V (1847), 102–25.

Barbarism the First Danger (New York, 1847). Republished in *Work and Play* (1881).

"Christian Comprehensiveness," *New Englander*, VI (1848), 81–111. Republished in *Building Eras in Religion* (1881).

The Fathers of New England (New York, 1850). Republished as "The Founders Great in Their Unconsciousness" in *Work and Play* (1864).

The Age of Homespun (Hartford, 1851). Republished in *Work and Play* (1864).

Religious Music (Hartford, 1852).

Twentieth Anniversary: A Commemorative Discourse (Hartford, 1853).

"The Christian Trinity a Practical Truth," *New Englander*, XII (1854), 485–509. Republished in *Building Eras in Religion* (1881).

The Census and Slavery (Hartford, 1860).

"The Doctrine of Loyalty," *New Englander*, XXII (1863), 560–81. Republished in *Work and Play* (1881).

Popular Government by Divine Right (Hartford, 1864). Republished in *Building Eras in Religion* (1881).

Our Obligations to the Dead (New Haven, 1866). Republished in *Building Eras in Religion* (1881).

Training for the Pulpit Manward. An address delivered before the Rhetorical Society of Chicago Theological Seminary, April 29, 1868. Published in *Hours at Home*, VII (July 1868), 193–203; republished in *Building Eras in Religion* (1881).

"Of the Condition of Solidarity," *Hours at Home*, V (June 1867), 97–102. Republished in *Moral Uses of Dark Things* (1867).

"Science and Religion," *Putnam's Magazine*, I (March 1868), 265–75.

"Progress," *Hours at Home*, VIII (January 1869), 197–210.

"Our Gospel a Gift to the Imagination," *Hours at Home*, X (December 1869), 159–72.

II. WRITINGS CONCERNING HORACE BUSHNELL

1. BOOKS AND PAMPHLETS

ANDREWS, W. W., *Remarks on Dr. Bushnell's "Vicarious Sacrifice"* (Hartford, 1866).

Appeal of the Association of Fairfield West to the Associated Ministers Connected with the General Association of Connecticut (New York, 1852).

ARCHIBALD, WARREN S., *Horace Bushnell* (Hartford, 1930).

Bushnell Centenary. Minutes of the General Association of Connecticut at the One Hundred and Ninety-Third Annual Meeting Held in Hartford, June 17, 18, 1902 (Hartford, 1902).

CHENEY, MARY BUSHNELL, *Life and Letters of Horace Bushnell* (New York, 1880).

[CHESEBROUGH, AMOS S.,] *Contributions of CC., Now Declared in Full as Criticus Criticorum* (Hartford, 1849).

CROSS, BARBARA M., *Horace Bushnell: Minister to a Changing America* (Chicago, 1958).

[GOODRICH, CHAUNCEY A.,] *What Does Dr. Bushnell Mean?* (Hartford, 1849). Reprinted from the *New York Evangelist*.

JOHNSON, WILLIAM A., *Nature and the Supernatural in the Theology of Horace Bushnell* (Lund, 1963).

MUNGER, THEODORE THORNTON, *Horace Bushnell: Preacher and Theologian* (Boston, 1899).

MYERS, A. J. W., *Horace Bushnell and Religious Education* (Boston, 1937).

PARKER, EDWIN POND, *The Hartford Central Association and the Bushnell Controversy* (Hartford, 1896).

Remonstrance and Complaint of the Association of Fairfield West, to the Hartford Central Association: Together with the Reply of the Hartford Central Association (New York, 1850).

Dr. Tyler's Letter to Dr. Bushnell, on Christian Nurture (East Windsor Hill, Conn., June 7, 1847).

TYLER, BENNET, *Letters to the Rev. Horace Bushnell, D.D., Containing Strictures on His Book, entitled "Views of Christian Nurture, and of Subjects Adjacent Thereto"* (Hartford, 1848).

2. ARTICLES AND CRITICAL REVIEWS

ATWATER, LYMAN H., "Horace Bushnell," *Presbyterian Review*, II (1881), 114–44.

BACON, LEONARD, "[A Letter] Concerning a Recent Chapter of Ecclesiastical History," *New Englander*, XXXVIII (1879), 701–12.

BARTLETT, IRVING H., "Bushnell, Cousin, and Comprehensive Christianity," *Journal of Religion*, XXXVII (1957), 99–104.

CHESEBROUGH, AMOS S., "The Theological Opinions of Horace Bushnell as Related to His Character and Christian Experience," *Andover Review*, VI (1886), 113–30.

CLARKE, JAMES FREEMAN, "Bushnell on Vicarious Sacrifice," *Christian Examiner*, LXXX (May 1866), 360–77.

COLE, CHARLES G., "Horace Bushnell and the Slavery Question," *New England Quarterly*, XXIII (1950), 19–30.

FISHER, GEORGE P., "Horace Bushnell," *International Review*, X (January 1881), 13–25.

FOSTER, FRANK H., "Horace Bushnell as a Theologian," *Bibliotheca Sacra*, LIX (1902), 601–22.

GARDNER, E. CLINTON, "Horace Bushnell's Doctrine of Depravity," *Theology Today*, XII (1955), 10–26.

GOODWIN, HENRY M., "Dr. Bushnell's 'Christian Nurture,'" *New Englander*, XIX (1861), 474–95.

HODGE, CHARLES, "Bushnell's Discourses" [review of *God in Christ*], *Biblical Repertory and Princeton Review*, XXI (1849), 259–98.

———, "Bushnell on Christian Nurture," *Biblical Repertory and Princeton Review*, XIX (1847), 502–39.

———, "Doctrinal and Ecclesiastical Conflicts in Connecticut," *Biblical Repertory and Princeton Review*, XXV (1853), 598–637.

KIRSCHENMANN, FRED, "Horace Bushnell: Orthodox or Sabellian?" *Church History*, XXXIII (March 1964), 49–59.

LORD, DAVID N., "Dr. Bushnell's Dissertation on Language," *Theological and Literary Journal*, II (July 1849), 61–131.

——, "Dr. Bushnell's Discourses [*God in Christ*]," *Theological and Literary Journal*, II (October 1849), 173–222.

——, "Dr. Bushnell's Nature and the Supernatural," *Theological and Literary Journal*, XI (January 1859), 529–76.

MUNGER, THEODORE T., "The Secret of Horace Bushnell," *The Outlook*, LXXI (August 1902), 1063–68.

POND, ENOCH, *Review of Dr. Bushnell's "God in Christ"* (Bangor, 1849).

PORTER, NOAH, "Bushnell on Christian Nurture," *New Englander*, VI (1848), 121–47.

——, "Nature and the Supernatural," *New Englander*, XVII (1859), 224–58.

——, "Review of Dr. Bushnell on 'The Vicarious Sacrifice,'" *New Englander*, XXV (1866), 228–82.

——, "Horace Bushnell. A Memorial Sermon Preached in the Chapel of Yale College, Sunday, March 26th, 1876," *New Englander*, XXXVI (1877), 152–69.

SALMOND, S. D. F., "The Theology of Horace Bushnell," *London Quarterly Review*, XCV (January–April 1901), 133–58.

STEVENS, GEORGE B., "The Theology of Horace Bushnell," *Methodist Review*, LXXXIV (1902), 692–707.

——, "Horace Bushnell and Albrecht Ritschl. A Comparison," *American Journal of Theology*, VI (1902), 35–56.

III. THE NEW ENGLAND THEOLOGICAL BACKGROUND OF HORACE BUSHNELL

For a more comprehensive bibliography of relevant writings, see Nelson R. Burr, ed., *A Critical Bibliography of Religion in America* (Princeton, 1961), Part V.

AHLSTROM, SYDNEY E., "The Scottish Philosophy and American Theology," *Church History*, XXIV (1955), 257–72.

——, "Theology in America: A Historical Survey," *The Shaping of American Religion*, James Ward Smith and A. Leland Jamison, eds. (Princeton, 1961), 232–321.

BAINTON, ROLAND H., *Yale and the Ministry: a History of Education for the Christian Ministry at Yale from the Founding in 1701* (New York, 1957).

BUCKHAM, JOHN W., "James Marsh and Coleridge," *Bibliotheca Sacra*, LXI (1904), 305–17.

——, *Progressive Religious Thought in America* (Boston, 1919).

CHANNING, W. H., *Memoir of William Ellery Channing; with Extracts from His Correspondence and Manuscripts* (3 vols., Boston, 1848).

Cousin, Victor, *Introduction to the History of Philosophy*, trans. by Henning G. Linberg (Boston, 1832).

———, *Elements of Psychology*, trans. by Caleb Sprague Henry (Hartford, 1834).

Davis, Merrell R., "Emerson's 'Reason' and the Scottish Philosophers," *New England Quarterly*, XVII (1944), 209–28.

DeJong, Peter Ymen, *The Covenant Idea in New England Theology, 1620–1847* (Grand Rapids, Mich., 1945).

Dillenberger, John, *Protestant Thought and Natural Science* (New York, 1960).

Dirks, J. Edward, *The Critical Theology of Theodore Parker* (New York, 1948).

Ellis, George E., *A Half-Century of the Unitarian Controversy* (Boston, 1857).

Elwood, Douglas J., *The Philosophical Theology of Jonathan Edwards* (New York, 1960).

Fisher, George P., "The System of Dr. N. W. Taylor in its Connection with Prior New England Theology," *Discussions in History and Theology* (New York, 1880), 285–354.

———, "Channing as a Philosopher and Theologian," *Discussions in History and Theology* (New York, 1880), 253–84.

Foster, Frank H., *A Genetic History of the New England Theology* (Chicago, 1907).

———, *The Modern Movement in American Theology* (New York, 1939).

Gaustad, Edwin S., "The Theological Effects of the Great Awakening in New England," *Mississippi Valley Historical Review*, XL (1954), 681–706.

Gohdes, Clarence L. F., *The Periodicals of American Transcendentalism* (Durham, N.C., 1931).

Goodwin, Henry M., "Thoughts, Words, and Things," *Bibliotheca Sacra*, VI (1849), 271–300.

Haller, William, *The Rise of Puritanism* (New York, 1938; Harper Torchbook, 1957).

Haroutunian, Joseph, *Piety Versus Moralism: The Passing of the New England Theology* (New York, 1932).

Hutchison, William R., *The Transcendentalist Ministers: Church Reform in the New England Renaissance* (New Haven, 1959).

Kern, Alexander, "The Rise of Transcendentalism, 1815–1860," in Harry Hayden Clark, ed., *Transitions in American Literary History* (Durham, N.C., 1931).

McGiffert, Arthur C., *The Rise of Modern Religious Ideas* (New York, 1915).

McGiffert, Arthur C., Jr., ed., *Young Emerson Speaks* (Boston, 1938).

McLoughlin, William G., *Modern Revivalism: Charles Grandison Finney to Billy Graham* (New York, 1959).

Mead, Sidney E., *Nathaniel William Taylor, 1786–1858: A Connecticut Liberal* (Chicago, 1942).

Miller, Perry, *Errand Into the Wilderness* (Cambridge, Mass., 1956).

———, "From the Covenant to the Revival," *The Shaping of American Religion*, James Ward Smith and A. Leland Jamison, eds. (Princeton, 1961), 322–68.

———, ed., *Images or Shadows of Divine Things by Jonathan Edwards* (New Haven, 1948).

———, *Jonathan Edwards* (New York, 1949).

———, "Johnathan Edwards on the Sense of the Heart," *Harvard Theological Review*, XLI (1948), 123–45.

———, *The New England Mind: The Seventeenth Century* (New York, 1939).

———, *The New England Mind: From Colony to Province* (Cambridge, Mass., 1953).

———, *The Trancendentalists: An Anthology* (Cambridge, Mass., 1950).

Nichols, James H., *Romanticism in American Theology: Nevin and Schaff at Mercersburg* (Chicago, 1961).

Nicholson, Marjorie H., "James Marsh and the Vermont Transcendentalists," *Philosophical Review*, XXXIV (1925), 28–50.

Niebuhr, Richard, *The Kingdom of God in America* (Chicago, 1937).

Nuttall, Geoffrey F., *The Holy Spirit in Puritan Faith and Experience* (Oxford, 1946).

Park, Edwards A., ed., *The Atonement. Discourses and Treatises by Edwards, Smalley, Maxcy, Emmons, Griffin, Burge, and Weeks* (Boston, 1859).

Patterson, Robert L., *The Philosophy of William Ellery Channing* (New York, 1952).

Pochmann, Henry A., *German Culture in America: Philosophical and Literary Influences, 1600–1900* (Madison, Wis., 1957).

Porter, Noah, "Coleridge and His American Disciples," *Bibliotheca Sacra*, IV (1847), 117–71.

Schafer, Thomas A., "Jonathan Edwards and Justification by Faith," *Church History*, XX (1951), 55–67.

Schleiermacher, Friedrich, "On the Discrepancy between the Sabellian and Athanasian Method of Representing the Doctrine of the Trinity," trans. by Moses Stuart, *Biblical Repository*, V (April 1835), 265–353; VI (July 1835), 1–116.

Schneider, Herbert W., "The Intellectual Background of William Ellery Channing," *Church History*, VII (1938), 3–23.

Smith, Henry B., "The Theological System of [Nathanael] Emmons," in Smith, *Faith and Philosophy*, George L. Prentiss, ed. (Edinburgh, 1878), 215–63.

SMITH, H. SHELTON, *Changing Conceptions of Original Sin: A Study in American Theology Since 1750* (New York, 1955).

SMITH, H. SHELTON; HANDY, ROBERT T.; and LOETSCHER, LEFFERTS A., *Amercan Christianity: An Historical Interpretation with Representative Documents* (2 vols., New York, 1960–63).

THOMPSON, ERNEST TRICE, *Changng Emphases in American Preaching* (Philadelphia, 1943).

TODD, EDGELEY W., "Philosophical Ideas at Harvard College, 1817–37," *New England Quarterly*, XVI (1943), 63–90.

TOWNSEND, HARVEY G., ed., *The Philosophy of Jonathan Edwards from His Private Notebooks* (Eugene, Ore., 1955).

TRINTERUD, LEONARD J., "The Origins of Puritanism," *Church History*, XX (1951), 37–57.

WALKER, WILLISTON, *Creeds and Platforms of Congregationalism* (New York, 1893).

WELLS, RONALD V., *Three Christian Transcendentalists* (New York, 1943).

WILBUR, EARL MORSE, *A History of Unitarianism in Transylvania, England and America* (Cambridge, Mass., 1952).

WILLIAMS, DANIEL D., "Tradition and Experience in American Theology," *The Shaping of American Religion*, James Ward Smith and A. Leland Jamison, eds. (Princeton, 1961), 443–95.

WILLIAMS, GEORGE H., ed., *The Harvard Divinity School: Its Place in Harvard University and in American Culture* (Boston, 1954).

WRIGHT, CONRAD, *The Beginnings of Unitarianism in America* (Boston, 1955).

———, "The Rediscovery of Channing," *Proceedings of the Unitarian Historical Society*, XII (1959), 8–25.

Index

401